Religion and Human Rights

Volume 4

Series editors
Hans-Georg Ziebertz, University of Würzburg, Germany
Carl Sterkens, Radboud University, Nijmegen, The Netherlands
Roger Finke, Penn State University, USA

This series investigates how religion can both challenge and contribute to a vibrant human rights culture in different national contexts, as well as in cross-national contexts. It offers empirical and theoretical perspectives on the different generations of human rights, and generates new knowledge on the connection between religion and human rights.

All religions claim that their ethical aspirations and moral duties contribute to the well-being and welfare of individual human beings, groups, and communities. This applies particularly to the golden rule which plays an important role in the ethical groundwork of all religious traditions, and which is also foundational for human rights. However, to what extent is this universal principle actually observed within and between different religions, within and between nations, and within the secular world? To what extent (if at all) do religions contribute to the realisation of human rights or to the prevention of violations of human rights? This series addresses these questions by means of an empirical and comparative approach. Each volume focuses on specific human rights, and this volume addresses political rights such as active and passive right to vote, the right to protest and the political rights of refugees; and judicial rights such as equality before the law, the right to independent and imparital judgement, and the presumption of innocence.

More information about this series at http://www.springer.com/series/15597

Hans-Georg Ziebertz • Francesco Zaccaria
Editors

Euthanasia, Abortion, Death Penalty and Religion – The Right to Life and its Limitations

International Empirical Research

Springer

Editors
Hans-Georg Ziebertz
Faculty of Theology
University of Würzburg
Würzburg, Germany

Francesco Zaccaria
Department of Practical Theology
Apulian Theological Faculty
Bari, Italy

ISSN 2510-4306 ISSN 2510-4314 (electronic)
Religion and Human Rights
ISBN 978-3-319-98772-9 ISBN 978-3-319-98773-6 (eBook)
https://doi.org/10.1007/978-3-319-98773-6

Library of Congress Control Number: 2018957828

This Springer imprint is published by the registered company Springer Nature Switzerland AG
The registered company address is: Gewerbestrasse 11, 6330 Cham, Switzerland

The editors and authors involved in this project wish to dedicate this book to Professor Johannes A. van der Ven, Professor Emeritus at Radboud University of Nijmegen in the Netherlands, for whose support and academic input in this project we are extremely grateful. Professor van der Ven was the leading force in our previous research project, 'Religion and Human Rights', and participated extensively in this project until his health circumstances no longer made this possible. With his brilliant academic input he has contributed so much to this project.

Contents

Chapter 1
The Right to Life Questioned. Introductory Remarks

Hans-Georg Ziebertz and Francesco Zaccaria

The right to life is understood as being a fundamental right. It is the purpose and the inner nature of all human rights to protect the individual against physical and mental treatment that violates the personal integrity. This concern converges with the anthropology of religions such Christianity and Islam, who grant the human dignity a high status. As an image of God, every person has a dignity which must not be subordinated to any other purpose and which must be protected. Therefore, these religions are sensitive to violations of human dignity. That does not take away from the fact that the practice of a religion or members of a religion can miss this goal. How the relationship between religious beliefs and the protection of life is empirically designed is the theme of this book. The right to life is becoming virulent in many areas of human rights. In order to make the studies in this book comparable, this volume presents a selection of topics in which the right to live is particularly under discussion. It is not primarily the question of what a good life should be, which must be discussed in the context of human rights, but rather the question of whether the right to life could be restricted or withheld.

The Right to Life and Its Limitations

In the modern understanding of human rights, the individual human being is put in the centre as the goal and the end. The concept of human dignity is closely connected with this respect for the life of every person. Many declarations of human rights refer to the inherent dignity of every person which is regarded as the foundation of human rights. The right to life is an expression of the dignity that humans

H.-G. Ziebertz (✉)
Faculty of Theology, University of Würzburg, Würzburg, Germany
e-mail: hg.ziebertz@uni-wuerzburg.de

F. Zaccaria
Department of Practical Theology, Apulian Theological Faculty, Bari, Italy

H.-G. Ziebertz, F. Zaccaria (eds.), *Euthanasia, Abortion, Death Penalty and Religion – The Right to Life and its Limitations*, Religion and Human Rights 4, https://doi.org/10.1007/978-3-319-98773-6_1

have because of being humans. That makes both concepts, the right to life and inherent human dignity, as being essentially two sides of the same coin.

In a religious perspective life is a gift from God. God is the Lord of life, and therefore no one is to rise above the ruler of life and death. As a gift of God, life is sacred, and therefore human beings cannot autonomously dispose of it. From a religious point of view, the dignity of every human life derives from this belief that it is given by God, and therefore it has to be accepted, cherished and protected, and not violated or terminated (Van der Ven 2010, 173–182). That is why, generally speaking, religious world views are very sensitive when it comes to the protection of the right to life, and they are not easily inclined to consider any mitigating circumstances which might justify its limitations. Because of this transcendent sacred value of life, religious institutions are generally critical when its dignity is questioned, for example in the first or last stages of life, or when its non-disposability is violated, i.e. by biomedical experiments or procedures, or when its value becomes dependent on moral, psychological or economic circumstances.

Although the right to life is a fundamental right, it is also very controversial. Smith (2013, 217) argues that one of the problems is that there exists no agreement on the definition when life begins and when it ends. This agreement is lacking within and between many countries, when values and worldviews collide. There are also cases of disagreement between certain religious convictions and the legislation in a country. For example, whether medical technology is allowed to do what it is capable of and whether humans may autonomously decide on the beginning and the end of life. In most cases religions have a stricter view on the protection of life. It is important to remember that in the legal and political sphere the right to life is not understood as an absolute right, as is the case in military conflicts, when it comes to genocide or war or in cases of the most heinous of crimes, when some legal systems allow the state to execute criminals. The problem of the right to life is the stretchable interpretation of this right and the difficulty of clearly defining what the negative and positive responsibility and obligation of the state is.

Many issues are related to the right to life. This book focuses on three exceptions of the obligation to protect life. The first of these exceptions is abortion, when pregnancy is terminated, the second is euthanasia, when action is taken to bring about death more quickly, and the third is when the law allows the sentence of death as a valid penalty to end human life. All three cases are extremely complex. In the case of abortion, it is necessary to define exactly when life begins, the well-being of the child and the mother also need to be taken into account in addition to the desire of the mother to have the child, the vicarious exercise of the child's right to live but also the psychosocial circumstances into which new life grows. Whether these complexes should be ethically and legally relevant at all and how they should be weighted is highly controversial. In the case of euthanasia, a distinction is made as to whether the assistance is active or passive. Active help is highly controversial and generally prohibited, but even when considering passive help a number of criteria are discussed as to when and under what circumstances such help should be allowed, for example when the possibilities of palliative medicine are exhausted. An alternative perspective stresses the question of whether there should also be a right to die in certain circumstances. In the case of the death penalty, supporters and opponents are not clearly assigned to a camp. Among the supporters of the death penalty are both modern Western-oriented countries such as the United States of America, but also totalitarian states such as North Korea. Although the international discussion is more in favour of a ban on the death penalty, populist politicians are not afraid to express sympathy for the re-introduction of the death penalty (as in Turkey, for example).

These examples show that the right to life is not an absolute right. Therefore, the term "fundamental right" must not hide the fact that it is a very fragile right and very vulnerable to interest-based interpretations. However, there is no doubt that the right to life is an obligation of the state. The state should not only fend off attacks on life, but it is also obliged to take positive action so that life can be lived. To achieve greater clarity on this issue, a look into some central documents is helpful. The right to life is enshrined on a huge number of Human Rights declarations.

Human Rights Declarations

In 1948 the UN stated in article 3 of its *Universal Declaration of Human Rights* (UDHR) that "everyone has the right to life, liberty and security of person." This article is very short, following article 1 which concerns freedom and equal dignity and equal rights for everyone and article 2 which states that everyone is entitled to all rights in the declaration without any restriction. Possible attacks on the right to life are considered in subsequent articles, e.g. by slavery, torture or inhuman treatment. A reference to the death penalty cannot however be found in the UDHR. Later human rights declarations build upon and nuance it further.

The *International Covenant on Civil and Political Rights* (ICCPR), adopted by the General Assembly of the UN in 1966, refers to the right to life in article 6: "Every human being has the inherent right to life. This right shall be protected by law. No one shall be arbitrarily deprived of his life." This covenant makes a critical comment on the death penalty, but it avoids banning the death penalty outright. Instead it is noted that death penalty "can only be carried out pursuant to a final judgement rendered by a competent court" and that it "shall not be imposed for crimes committed by persons below eighteen years of age and shall not be carried out on pregnant women" (art. 6). In the general comment no. 6, with regard to article 6 (The Right to Life), the 16th session of the Human Rights Committee (1982) reflects on the reception history of the covenant. The committee states "that quite often the information given concerning article 6 was limited to only one or other aspect of this right. It is a right which should not be interpreted narrowly" (1). "The deprivation of life by the authorities of the State is a matter of the utmost gravity. Therefore, the law must strictly control and limit the circumstances in which a person may be deprived of his life by such authorities" (3). "Moreover, the Committee has noted that the right to life has been too often narrowly interpreted. The expression 'inherent right to life' cannot properly be understood in a restrictive manner, and the protection of this right requires that States adopt positive measures" (5). Regarding the death penalty the committee gives the assurance that "States parties are not obliged to abolish the death penalty totally, they are obliged to limit its use and, in particular, to abolish it for other than the 'most serious crimes'" (6); and "The expression 'most serious crimes' must be read restrictively to mean that the death penalty should be a quite exceptional measure" (7). Even if strong criteria are formulated, the text does not contain a condemnation of the death penalty.

The *American Convention on Human Rights* (1969) refers to the right to life in article 4: "Every person has the right to have his life respected. This right shall be protected by law and, in general, from the moment of conception. No one shall be arbitrarily deprived of his life." An added aspect of this convention is that it refers to the 'moment of conception' with regard to the validity of the right to life. Even though the statements about the death penalty are rather critical, (art. 4,3: "shall not be re-established in states that have abolished it") there is no clear ban. Instead, it is recommended that this penalty should only be imposed for the most serious crimes and that the judgment must be rendered by a competent court. A sentence of death may not be inflicted for political offenses or related common crimes (art. 4,4) and it may not apply to people under 18 or above 70 years of age or pregnant women.

The attitude of the Arab countries is of great interest given that most of them are Islamic. The *Arab Charter on Human Rights* (2004) says in article 5 that "Every human being has the inherent right to life" and that "this right shall be protected by law. No one shall be arbitrarily deprived of his life." The document allows exceptions in situations of emergency, although the rights mentioned in the charter may not be suspended. Another differentiation is made regarding gender. Article 3 points out: "Men and women are equal in respect of human dignity, rights and obligations within the framework of the positive discrimination established in favour of women by the Islamic Shariah, other divine laws and by applicable laws and legal instruments. Accordingly, each State party pledges to take all the requisite measures to guarantee equal opportunities and effective equality between men and women in the enjoyment of all the rights set out in this Charter." Article 6 allows the death penalty "only for the most serious crimes in accordance with the laws in force at the time of the commission of the crime and pursuant to a final judgment rendered by a competent court." The sentence of death "shall not be imposed on persons under 18 years of age" (art. 7) or "on a pregnant woman prior to her delivery or on a nursing mother within two years from the date of her delivery; in all cases, the best interests of the infant shall be the primary consideration (art. 7)." This document remains vague. It can be questioned if the term "positive discrimination" is adequate at all within the framework of human rights and how the hierarchy is regarded between human rights declarations and the Islamic Shariah, divine laws, applicable laws and legal instruments. These formulations open many doors for interpretations and exceptions.

The *African Charter on Human and Peoples' Rights* (Banjul Charter) (1987) intended to promote and protect human rights and basic freedoms in the African continent. Article 4 says: "Human beings are inviolable. Every human being shall be entitled to respect for his life and the integrity of his person. No one may be arbitrarily deprived of this right", followed by article 5 "Every individual shall have the right to the respect of the dignity inherent in a human being and to the recognition of his legal status. All forms of exploitation and degradation of man, particularly slavery, slave trade, torture, cruel, inhuman or degrading punishment and treatment shall be prohibited." The charter is reluctant to condemn violations of personal integrity, in particular regarding the death penalty. In 2011 the African Commission on Human and Peoples' Rights admitted in a paper on the *Death Penalty in Africa* that "the *African Charter on Human and Peoples' Rights* does not speak unequivocally to this nagging question." The adopted paper summarises the pros and cons regarding the death penalty and concludes by posing the question of "whether a system based on the rule of law can continue to run the risk of depriving persons of the right to life; whether it is acceptable to apply the death penalty where there are appropriate alternative punishments; whether it is really humane to keep a person on the death row for years, [or] with him/her not knowing if the next day will be his/her last." This might be understood as an attempt to continue to advocate the condemnation of the death penalty on the African continent.

Article 2 of the *European Convention for the Protection of Human Rights and Fundamental Freedoms* (1950) says: "Everyone's right to life shall be protected by law. No-one shall be deprived of his life intentionally save in the execution of a sentence of a court following his conviction of a crime for which this penalty is provided by law." The state has negative and positive obligations regarding the right to life.[1] On the one hand the state has to protect every person from violent acts by others. A condition is that the state knows about it and fails to avoid it. The state must act effectively, it is not enough just to express the intention. The state must also protect people from self-harm, for example where detainees are known to be a suicide risk. The state must also protect those living near hazardous industrial sites, and the state has to safeguard everyone confronted by a foreseeable natural disaster. On the other hand, the state may use lethal force under very specific situations. These situations are given if someone has to be defended from unlawful violence, to effect a lawful arrest or to prevent the escape of someone lawfully detained and in lawful action to quell a riot or insurrection. The Council of Europe refers to such situations as 'exhaustive exceptions' and makes the following provision: "The State has to satisfy a very high test before resorting to lethal force: it must be no more than absolutely necessary to achieve one or more of the authorised purposes and strictly proportionate to that purpose. It is not enough to balance the individual right against the public interest."[2] In this regard, the right to life is currently under discussion when it has to be decided whether people who have fled to Europe can be deported to their unsafe countries of origin. A noteworthy change has been made by the European countries with regard to the death penalty. While protocol No. 6 (1983) abolishes the death penalty in peacetime but allows states to provide for its imposition in times of war or when there is a threat of war, protocol No. 13 (2002) abolishes the death penalty in all circumstances. Belarus is the only European country that has a law on the use of the death penalty.[3]

[1] See: https://www.coe.int/en/web/echr-toolkit/droit-a-la-vie

[2] Ibid.

[3] See: https://www.coe.int/en/web/echr-toolkit/droit-a-la-vie?inheritRedirect=true

The documents we refer to do not reflect specifically on the questions of abortion and euthanasia – as they don't with many other issues that affect the right to life. According to Smith (2013, 220) human rights bodies were reserved to applicate the right to life to abortion and euthanasia. However, the life of the unborn child is indirectly taken into account when it is stated that the death sentence should not be carried out on pregnant women. But on the level of the nation-state both, abortion and euthanasia, are prominent problems when the right to life is up for discussion. There are considerable differences of opinion in a number of countries over whether and under which conditions abortion and euthanasia should be prohibited. While some insist on the self-determination of the person affected, others believe that no one should be allowed to decide on his/her own life or the life of another human being. The question of who has the right to dispose of life is particularly an important topic in religions.

The Interest of Religious Traditions in the Protection of Life

All religions have an understanding of the value of life and humanity that is not simply a matter of majority opinion, but refers to a religious authority and finally to the divine will. In a religious view, life is sacred because it is a gift from God and human beings cannot dispose of it in an autonomous way. Nevertheless, different religious traditions have different views on the protection of life, and they might differ not only in the theological foundations of this protection but also on the possibilities of its limitations, such as in the three cases analysed in this volume: abortion, euthanasia and the death penalty. These different religious views on the protection of life will be addressed more specifically and thoroughly in the different chapters of this book, now we only sketch them in a synthetic way to show that, in spite of different theological perspectives and different nuances in their teachings about life issues, these religions all tend to protect the sacredness of life in the debates on abortion, euthanasia and the death penalty.

Official teachings of the Catholic Church strongly affirm the protection of life from its conception to its natural end, and are therefore against abortion and euthanasia, which are considered "intrinsic evils" and as such should be avoided in all circumstances. This position is rooted in the belief that life stems from God, the creator, and human beings should respect God's will and gift: human beings are custodians of this gift and not owners of it. Therefore, they should protect it, not only to be faithful to the divine commandment not to kill but also as followers of Jesus Christ who commanded to love one's neighbour, to being kind and doing good. According to Catholic moral doctrine on abortion, only a serious risk for the life of the mother would justify medical procedures which can lead to the termination of a pregnancy. Euthanasia is never permitted, even though palliative care is encouraged, and the Church advocates refraining from burdensome medical treatments which are disproportionate to the expected outcome. In August 2018 Pope Francis approved a new revision of paragraph 2267 of the Catechism of the Catholic Church, which allowed death penalty as a remote possibility; after this decision the Catholic Church teaches that "death penalty is inadmissible because it is an attack on the inviolability and dignity of the person", and that the Church "works with determination for its abolition worldwide".

Protestant Churches, or more specifically for the religious context of the countries examined in this book, Lutheran Churches, emphasize the religious principle that life should be protected and based this on biblical traditions. Nevertheless, apparently they allow more circumstances in which abortion and euthanasia are acceptable. A woman can decide to terminate her pregnancy not only because of health issues but also for psychological, social and financial reasons: the protection of unborn life cannot be imposed over the will of the mother. Nevertheless, within the same Protestant Churches, there are stricter views about this issue stressing that abortion is always unacceptable from an ethical point of view. Regarding euthanasia, Protestant Churches reject active euthanasia or assisted suicide while allowing passive euthanasia, i.e. refraining from medical treatments when terminally ill patients specifically request this. Especially the Lutheran Churches in Europe, are active in the campaign for the abolition of the death penalty, which they consider to be unjustifiable from a Christian point of view.

Islamic theology on life issues is differentiated in many legal opinions which refer to different theological schools and streams. There are scholars who prohibit abortion in all circumstances while others teach that a pregnancy can be terminated under certain circumstances only before the 120th day of pregnancy, while others also allow abortion after this threshold, but only for health issues. Regarding euthanasia, Islamic theological opinions appear to be less differentiated and more inclined towards forbidding it on the basis that only God, the Creator, determines human life. Nevertheless, more liberal circles within Islamic schools seem to accept passive euthanasia as allowing God's plan to occur. The death penalty is prescribed by *Sharia* (Islamic law) and is therefore accepted in principle to punish grievous criminal acts, even though Muslim jurists make its implementation very difficult since the higher moral and religious standards in Islam pursue forgiveness and compassion rather than vengeance and retaliation.

Hinduism, which is also addressed in one chapter of this book, differs from the previous religious traditions insofar it allows considerable pluralism in beliefs and ethical norms, the latter being presented in this religious tradition more as a set of guiding principles for the believer's conscience than divine commandments. A central aspect of Hinduism is preserving and promoting life, therefore abortion is regarded as an atrocious act, but nevertheless, it can be acceptable when the mother's life is in danger. By the same token, euthanasia is not considered as a righteous way to face a terminal illness, although suicide can be morally acceptable as a form of grief or penance in some circumstances. Pluralism and flexibility also occur in discussions on the death penalty; for example, in some cases of murder it may be permitted while in others it may not, depending on the intention of the act, or on the social or moral status of the victim or the perpetrator.

Empirical Research on the Limitations of the Right to Life

The empirical research presented in this book is essentially research about young people's perceptions and assessments of the right to life. This research shows how the limitations of the right to life are legitimised from the "bottom up". In this respect, the following research papers do not contribute directly to discussions concerning the legal status of the right to life or to its philosophical and ethical substantiation. Rather, such empirical research shows whether and to what extent respondents agree or disagree with different existing opinions. This is not only a question of "Yes" and "No", but a complex issue because the valuation of rights is an individual process that occurs within a certain cultural and religious context. The studies in this book pay particular attention to the impact of religious convictions and practices on the evaluation of the right to life. The general assumption is that life-issues are strongly connected to religious world views. The more respondents describe themselves as religious, the stronger they will defend the obligation to protect life and the lesser they will accept any limitation of the right to life. This book contains studies in 14 countries in Europe, Asia, Africa and Latin America. The main religions in these countries are Catholicism, Protestantism and Orthodox Christianity, but also Islam and Hinduism. In the first chapters of the book we present seven national studies and in the later ones three comparative studies. The considerable differences between the countries do not allow a comparative analysis with all countries together.

In the first research paper *Francis-Vincent Anthony and Carl Sterkens* present a study of the attitude of Christian, Muslim and Hindu students in India concerning the limitation of the right to life concerning the death penalty, euthanasia and abortion. India is an interesting case because it is one of the oldest democracies in the world and it has a long-established experience with religious diversity. With this study among the youth in India the perspective of the Hindu religion is also added. The paper offers a detailed description how the three religions, Christianity, Islam and Hinduism, interpret the right to life and how they evaluate the permissibility of abortion, euthanasia and the death penalty. The paper also elaborates the legal context in India regarding these issues. The authors ask which role these religions play in soliciting and legitimising the (non-)disposability of life. The empirical research was carried out among 1215 Christian, Muslim and Hindu college students in Tamil Nadu. Attitudes towards the death penalty, euthanasia and abortion are related to the possible impact of personal and contextual religious attitudes and the value of human dignity. The paper shows that the three religious groups manifest opposition to the capital punishment and some ambivalence to the termination of life by euthanasia and abortion for the victim's sake. Regarding euthanasia, Christians and Hindus show some openness to the ending of life, while Muslims tend to be uncertain. The overall interpretation of the findings is that religions provide a meta-ethical basis for both, the 'sacredness' and the 'quality' of human life.

The second paper concerns Chile. The authors of this paper, *Jorge Manzi and Joaquin Silva*, also take the three limitations of the right to life by the death penalty, euthanasia and abortion into account. Chile, as many countries in Latin-America, is traditionally Catholic, although the Roman-Catholic Church is experiencing a crisis. There are clear tendencies towards a secularisation process, but at the same time there is a rise of Evangelical Free Churches. This paper analyses first the legal context of the right to life in Chile and also refers to the position of the Catholic Church. In the empirical section of their paper the authors present findings from a survey among 1300 secondary students. They show that the death penalty, euthanasia and abortion are only weakly correlated. In the respondents' perception of the three issues the impact of religion and religiosity differs. Only regarding abortion can a significant role of religious affiliation be discerned. Compared to other religious groups and non-religious students Catholics and Evangelicals show a higher support for the protection of the right to life. Generally speaking, the higher the degree of religiosity, the more the opposition to abortion, euthanasia and the death penalty increases.

The next paper presents research among the youth in Germany. The data *Hans-Georg Ziebertz* analyses focused on abortion and euthanasia. Both topics are of undiminished importance in the German society. The question of this paper is how young people in Germany evaluate the contradicting arguments surrounding the termination of life (i.e. whether the termination of life should be prohibited or permitted) and what motives determine their attitudes towards these topics. The assumption is that the attitudes of young people towards the limitations of the right to life are only moderately biased by their religious commitment, because the religious commitment is low. Instead it is assumed that values are more important, particularly those that refer to individual needs. As a result, hedonistic values have been taken into account. The sample consists of 1862 German students of secondary schools with a sufficient proportion of Catholics, Protestants, Muslims and non-religious respondents. The general finding is that young Germans show some openness to permit euthanasia, but abortion only to a lesser extent. A connection between the permission of euthanasia and abortion and religion could be found. Non-religious students show the strongest support to permit abortion and euthanasia, followed by Protestants and to a lower extent Catholics. Muslims do not express positive attitudes, in both cases their answers are ambivalent. An important finding is that a hedonistic orientation is the strongest predictor for a permissive attitude towards euthanasia and abortion.

Francesco Zaccaria, Francis-Vincent Anthony and *Carl Sterkens* offer an analysis of a survey of 1076 Italian students with regard to abortion and euthanasia. Bioethical issues, especially those surrounding the beginning and the end of life, were notably discussed in the Italian public debate of the past years. This study presents these issues in the Italian context and the position of the Catholic Church in these debates. Empirical results show how young Italians differentiate clearly between the legitimacy of abortion in cases of violence or health issues and of abortion for psychological and economic reasons; in general, they favour the possibility to terminate a pregnancy in the first case but not in the latter, they also support the option for suffering terminally ill patients to ask for euthanasia. Regarding the role of religion in shaping these bioethical attitudes of young Italians, this study shows how religious variables, such as beliefs and practices, have a statistically significant impact on students' attitudes towards abortion and euthanasia: the more religious the students are, the less they support a termination of life in these cases.

The next paper explores the association between the attitudes towards euthanasia and abortion and both religious practices and self-assigned religious affiliation. The study, which is presented by *Leslie J. Francis, Ursula McKenna* and *Abdullah Sahin*, contains data from 966 Protestant, Catholic, Muslim and non-religious students in England and Wales. The authors take personal factors (age and sex) and psychological factors (extraversion, neuroticism, and psychoticism) into account and they show that respondents with a higher degree of religiosity are more critical of the permission of euthanasia and abortion. An important result is a significant negative correlation between prayer frequency and acceptance of euthanasia and abortion which demonstrates that religious practice is a key indicator. This indicator is followed by religious affiliation of the students. Similar to the findings in Germany, Muslim and Catholic students accept euthanasia and abortion less than Protestant and non-religious students.

Raymond J. Webb and *Fatma Jamal Asa'd* have done empirical research among 905 young Palestinian Muslims in the Bethlehem area. Palestine is confronted with many problems which are essential for survival in a politically unstable environment. Nevertheless, topics like abortion, euthanasia and the death penalty are important within Islamic thinking. As other research among Muslims in this book shows, this religious group is more temperate when the limitation of the right to life is on the agenda. The result is similar in the Palestine-study. The Muslim youth shows support for the position that abortion should be forbidden because it terminates human life. The exception Muslim students make is if the life of the mother is at risk. Regarding euthanasia, the attitude is negative, even in the case of unbearable suffering. Young Muslims in Palestine do not oppose the death penalty, which mirrors the position that capital punishment can serve justice. The authors conclude that the findings, prohibition of abortion and euthanasia as well as acceptance of the death penalty, are corresponding to Islamic teaching.

What young Lithuanians think about the right to life is researched by *Milda Ališauskienė* and *Aušra Maslauskaitė*. The paper focuses on the issues of abortion and euthanasia which the authors connect with women's rights. Although Lithuania is culturally influenced by the Roman Catholic Church, abortion and euthanasia are rarely discussed in the public sphere. The sample of this study contains 427 respondents. Those young people who live their faith in a traditional context, agree more with the prohibition of euthanasia and abortion, while religiously individualised students show more liberal attitudes. The expectation that respondents who are rather opposed to abortion also reject women's rights could not be confirmed.

The next three studies in this book offer comparative analyses. The paper presented by *Clement Fumbo*, *Modestus Adimekwe* and *Hans-Georg Ziebertz* takes note of the attitudes of young people towards the death penalty in Tanzania and Nigeria. In both countries the death penalty is not explicitly prohibited, but not all death sentences are carried out. This context gives the question a special meaning when young people evaluate the death penalty as a crime against humanity. Before the empirical analysis is presented, the paper offers a differentiating analysis of the legal and political context in Tanzania and Nigeria. The samples in both countries each include around 1200 respondents. The authors expect correspondences between young people in both countries because they share a similar human rights culture. The assumption is that the right to life is highly supported because the development of a culture of human rights across the African continent is a vivid topic on the public agenda. Further it is expected that in both countries religion functions as a predictor for positive attitudes towards the right to life. Although religion could be identified as an important indicator for critical attitudes towards the practice of the death penalty, the findings do not confirm that high support for human rights, which can be explained by the cultural ambivalence with regard to punishments in the cases of the most serious crimes.

The next comparative research study measures attitudes towards abortion and euthanasia among young people in Poland and Norway. With this study, *Pål Ketil Botvar, Claudia Sarti, Katarzyna Zielińska* and *Marcin K. Zwierżdżyński* compare countries with different Christian impregnations, namely Catholic and Protestant. While religion is still a strong factor in Poland, Norway is known as widely secular. Therefore, the assumption is evident that young people in both countries should show different attitudes towards the limitation of the right to life by abortion and euthanasia. In the first part of the paper the authors refer to the different legal frameworks regarding abortion and euthanasia. In the empirical analysis it is surprising that despite their cultural differences there are many similarities in the attitudes of young people in those two countries. For the Norwegian and Polish youth the influence of religiosity on attitudes towards the right to life point in the same direction. The higher the degree of religiosity among young people, the more negative the attitudes towards abortion and euthanasia. A similar result is that a more desired publicly active role of the churches correlates to stronger negative attitudes towards abortion and euthanasia. These findings demonstrate that religious commitment expresses a certain degree of identification with the churches and their positions on the ethics of life. In contrast, students who support the idea that churches should assimilate with current trends in society have the most positive attitudes towards the permission of abortion and euthanasia.

The last comparative study in this book differentiates between Lutheran (Norway and Sweden) and Christian Orthodox countries (Belarus and Romania) with regard to abortion. *Olga Breskaya, Pål Ketil Botvar, Anders Sjöborg* and *Silviu Rogobete* reflect first on contextual issues, given that, apart from the religious traditions, history in those countries ran quite differently during the times of Communism. This also had an impact on human rights issues in general and on abortion laws in particular. The authors connect the question of the right to life with issues of reproductive health and women's rights. The data analysis shows that respondents in these countries strongly differ when the prohibition of abortion is questioned. The first important result is that young people in Belarus and Romania the support prohibition much more than young people in Norway and Sweden. The second important finding is that the religiosity of the respondents is the strongest predictor that explains a critical attitude towards the permission of abortion. It is interesting that religiosity has nearly the same weight as a predictor in all countries included in this study, independent from the religious and political culture. The strongest counter-indicator is the students' support for a separation of state and church. Students who support the separation are more open to the permission of abortion, and at the same time they are strong supporters of women's rights.

The contributions in this volume show the complexity of the relationship between religion and the right to life. The theoretical parts of these studies, which sometimes inevitably overlap, help to understand the various tenets of the main world religions in regard to these issues from different disciplinary perspectives, shedding light on the patrimony of religious teachings as being in favour of life and its protection and on the relationship between religion and public debate on human rights in many national contexts. The empirical findings show that young people's ideas on life issues also differ because of the diverse cultural and social context of their countries, rather than merely because of their personal convictions and attitudes. Nevertheless, an important common finding in all the studies of this volume is that, in spite of these contextual and personal differences, religious affiliations, beliefs and practices appear to relate with more protective attitudes towards life so far as abortion, euthanasia and the death penalty are concerned. A further gain of this volume is that these attitudes could be measured using the same questionnaire in all countries, testing the instrument in different contexts and facilitating comparisons between national data. We hope that this volume contributes to the interest in continuing the study of the impact of religion on issues regarding the right of life and its protection in today's public discourse, following a transdisciplinary approach and comparing different national contexts.

References

Smith, R. K. M. (2013). *Textbook on International Human Rights* (6th ed.). Oxford: Oxford University Press.

Van der Ven, J. A. (2010). *Human rights or religious rules?* Leiden/Boston: Brill.

Documents

African Charter on Human and Peoples' Rights (Banjul Charter), 1987.

American Convention on Human Rights, 1969.

Arab Charter on Human Rights, 2004.

European Convention for the Protection of Human Rights and fundamental Freedoms, 1950.

International Covenant on Civil and Political Rights (ICCPR), UN 1966.

Universal Declaration of Human Rights (UDHR), UN 1948.

Chapter 2
Religion and the Right to (Dispose of) Life: A Study of the Attitude of Christian, Muslim and Hindu Students in India Concerning Death Penalty, Euthanasia and Abortion

Francis-Vincent Anthony and Carl Sterkens

The debate over death penalty, euthanasia and abortion reached a climax during the second half of the twentieth century. It brings into focus the underlying contrasting currents of right to life and right to dispose of life. The pluralistic Indian context in its turn can add to the ambivalent relationship between religion and the (non-)disposability of life. Hence, the question that we address in this paper concerns the role religions play in soliciting and legitimizing the (non-)disposability of life. Our empirical research, among 1215 Christian, Muslim and Hindu college students in Tamil Nadu, focuses on the possible impact of personal religious attitude, contextual religious attitude, and the value of human dignity, on the perception of right to life in the face of death penalty, euthanasia, and abortion. Overall, we find that the three religious groups manifest opposition to disposal of life by death penalty, and an uncertain openness to disposal of life by euthanasia and abortion for victim's sake. However, as regards euthanasia, while Christians and Hindus tend to be open to disposal of life, Muslims tend to be uncertain. As regards abortion for psycho-economic reasons, the tendency among Christians is non-disposal of life and the tendency among Hindus and Muslims is an uncertain openness to disposal of life. In dealing with the complex issue of (non-)disposal of life, our findings related to personal and contextual religious attitude suggest that religions can provide a meta-ethical basis for both 'sacredness' and 'quality' of human life.

F.-V. Anthony (✉)
Department of Practical Theology, Salesian Pontifical University, Rome, Italy
e-mail: vincent@unisal.it

C. Sterkens
Faculty of Philosophy, Theology and Religious Studies, Radboud University Nijmegen, Nijmegen, The Netherlands
e-mail: c.sterkens@rs.ru.nl

H.-G. Ziebertz, F. Zaccaria (eds.), *Euthanasia, Abortion, Death Penalty and Religion – The Right to Life and its Limitations*, Religion and Human Rights 4, https://doi.org/10.1007/978-3-319-98773-6_2

Introduction

Notwithstanding the plea for mercy from the governments of Australia, France and the European Union, on 29 April 2015 the two convicted drug traffickers, Andrew Chan (31 years) and Myuran Sukumaran (34 years), were executed along with six others by a firing squad on the Indonesian prison island of Nusakambangan. Indonesia is among the four most populous countries – the others being China, India, and the USA – that on 19 December 2016 voted against the sixth resolution (A/RES/71/187) of the 71st General Assembly of the United Nations seeking to ban death penalty.

While death penalty is a stark affront on the right to life, other issues like euthanasia[1] and abortion[2] add intricate features to the debate. The significance of considering the three issues together lies in that they bring to the fore an underlying paradox: that right to life may imply right to dispose of human life, depending on whether we are dealing with innocent or criminal life, conscious or unconscious life, flourishing or deteriorating life, one's own or other's life. While religious traditions have been rather supportive of death penalty for social security reasons, they tend to oppose abortion and euthanasia in compelling terms. Instead, the secular society, that is ever more opposed to death penalty for pro-life motives, is rather tolerant of abortion and euthanasia for pro-choice reasons.

Taking stock of these contrasting trends, we focus on the underlying dilemma of the (non-)disposability of life and explore how religious traditions may contribute to the normative level of ethical questions (Fuchs 1985). In specific terms, the present study seeks to explore the association between the (non-)disposability of life – implied in the issues of death penalty, euthanasia and abortion – and the religious attitudes of

---

[1] In defining the term 'euthanasia' a number of facets need to be taken into account: the motive and the method of treatment, the will of the patient, and the role of the physician. (a) In the first place, considering the motive and the method of treatment, distinction is generally made between *active, direct,* or *positive* euthanasia and *passive, indirect,* or *negative* euthanasia. In the former case, the treatment of the physician, which aims at eliminating unbearable suffering, causes the death of the patient, and in the latter, the medical professional deliberately withholds or withdraws the medical treatment, thus indirectly causing death. The latter, namely, the passive euthanasia, has to be distinguished from 'refusal of therapeutic obstinacy', i.e., not insisting on useless and ineffective therapy in the absence of alternatives, with the mere possibility of prolonging the end of life. (b) Secondly, taking into account the will of the patient, distinction has to be made between *voluntary* euthanasia and *non-voluntary* euthanasia. The former occurs when the patient consciously chooses to end his/her life; the latter when the patient cannot yet or cannot anymore consciously choose to end his/her life – although anticipating it in a 'biological testament'. When the patient is capable of making a choice but is not consulted or has expressed himself/herself contrary to euthanasia, if it is practiced in the interest of the patient, to terminate unbearable suffering, this would be termed *involuntary* euthanasia. (c) Considering the role of the physician, euthanasia has to be distinguished from *physician-assisted suicide* (PAS): in the case of euthanasia, it is physician who administers the means of death, and in the case of assisted suicide it is the patient's self-administration of drugs supplied by a physician that brings about death (Magni 2011, 83; Kelly 1994, 348; Merlo 2009, 339–348).

[2] *Natural* abortion (miscarriage) is distinguished from *procured* abortion; it is the latter, namely, intentional interruption of pregnancy with drugs or some mechanical device, which raises ethical questions (Magni 2011, 47; Hostetler and Coulter 2007, 1).

Christian, Muslim and Hindu students in Tamil Nadu, India. Given the diverse anthropological visions that underlie their religious beliefs and practices, we can expect differences between Christians (2.3% in India, 6.1% in Tamil Nadu), Muslims (14.2% in India, 5.9% in Tamil Nadu) and Hindus (79.8% in India, 87.6% in Tamil Nadu).[3]

Ethical concern for life, namely, bioethics, *per se* would embrace all forms of life, including animal life and plant life. However, in this study we focus on human life – an area of concern also of social ethics – and explore the attitude of young persons with regard to (non-)disposability of life in the concrete cases of death penalty, euthanasia and abortion. Biosocial ethical debate over these thorny questions can arise at meta-ethical, normative ethical and applied ethical levels. While meta-ethical discourse deals with religious or transcendent foundations, and applied ethical discourse with social and legal practices, normative ethical discourse seeks to clarify the criteria for evaluating human action. As there are different normative ethical currents, the criteria for evaluating human action may differ according to currents such as ethics of consequences, deontological ethics, and ethics of virtues (Magni 2011, 43–46).

The right to life being basic to all other rights, the ethical discourse being at three different levels, and the context of our research being multi-religious, our approach in this study is necessarily complex. That is, we address the three crucial instances of death penalty, euthanasia and abortion from the perspective of Christian, Muslim and Hindu traditions, on the one hand, and from the secular perspective, on the other. Meta-ethical and normative discourses related to these perspectives are then complemented by the applied level of social and legal practices. Thus, to clarify the biosocial ethical debate over the (non-)disposability of human life, we first examine death penalty, euthanasia and abortion from the perspective of the three religious traditions (Section "(Non-)disposability of human life: religious perspective") and the secular tradition (Section "(Non-)disposability of human life: secular perspective"), before offering an overview of the social and legal practice related to the three issues (Section "(Non-)disposability of human life: social and legal practice"). We then clarify the conceptual model that links personal and contextual religious attitudes with the three instances of the right to life, and specify the research questions (Section "Conceptual model and research questions"). This is followed by a brief mention of the method (Section "Method"), the presentation of the results (Section "Results of empirical analysis"), and finally a discussion on the salient findings (Section "Discussion and conclusion").

(Non-)Disposability of Human Life: Religious Perspective

The non-disposability stance sustains that no one can terminate human life because of its sacredness or sanctity. Although 'sacredness of life' is generally associated with religious traditions, it seems to have been introduced and upheld by secular

[3] See http://www.censusindia.gov.in/2011census/C-01.html

currents, where 'sacredness' stands for the intrinsic value of human life (Drutchas 1998; Magni 2011, 39f). Leaving the secular perspective to the next section, here we examine the meta-ethical visions of human life in the Christian, Islamic and Hindu religious traditions, together with the normative-ethical implications that follow for death penalty, euthanasia and abortion. Obviously, the stand with regard to (non-) disposal of life is diversified not only between religious traditions, but also within each of them, with or without an official position. Among the Christian traditions, we refer particularly to the Catholic official directives and norms.

Christian Tradition

According to the Christian tradition, human beings created in God's image (Gen 1:27; 5:1–2), reflecting God's own spirit, have an intrinsic value (McCartney 1994, 8). "Human life is sacred because from its beginning it involves the creative action of God and it remains for ever in a special relationship with the Creator, who is its sole end. God alone is the Lord of life from its beginning until its end: no one can under any circumstance claim for himself the right directly to destroy an innocent human being" (Congregation for the Doctrine of the Faith [CDF] 1988, n. 5). "It is God who remains the sovereign Master of life. [...] We are stewards, not owners, of the life God has entrusted to us. It is not ours to dispose of" (Catechism of the Catholic Church [CCC] 2003, n. 2281).

The sacredness of human life is confirmed by the Son of God assuming it and making it an instrument of human salvation; "a manifestation of God in the world, a sign of his presence, a trace of his glory" (John Paul II 1995, n. 34; cf. n. 33, 35). As the pope reiterates time and again in *Evangelium Vitae* (EV n. 5, 20, 40, 53, 81, 87), the sacredness associated with human life gives rise to its inviolability and integrity at every stage and every situation. Earlier the CDF (1974, n. 11) had underscored: "The first right of the human person is his life. He has other goods and some are more precious, but this one is fundamental – the condition of all the others. Hence it must be protected above all others".

The underlying neo-Thomistic Catholic tradition by viewing human nature as oriented towards an end determined by divine plan, clarifies that human action, to be moral, has to follow the natural law based on natural order. The sacrality of life and its non-disposability ensue from the respect for the natural order (Magni 2011, 40f; Brugger 2014, 27; Drutchas 1998, 116–119).

(a) *Death penalty*: In the book of Exodus (20:13), the commandment 'not to kill' is viewed as part of the Covenant with God on Mount Sinai. At the same time, the biblical tradition prescribed death penalty for serious crimes against religion (blasphemy, idolatry, etc.), family (incest, adultery, etc.,), community (kidnapping, afflicting orphans and widows, etc.,) and above all against innocent human life. Oddly, it imposed death penalty for the very reason of defending life: "If anyone sheds the blood of man, by man shall his blood be shed; for in the image of God has man been made" (Gen 9:6). Although the Law of Moses foresaw death penalty in such cases, the rabbinic traditions have generally tended to restrain its use. As for the New Testament, the Letter to the Romans (13:1–7) is interpreted as upholding State's authority to inflict death penalty when common good and innocent lives are at stake (Brugger 2014, 59–73; McCarthy 1994, 109f; Berkowitz 2006).

An analysis of the Church's teaching through the centuries (Brugger 2014, 59–139; Tamanti 2004, 21–197) reveals that death penalty was justified from a social perspective for the reason of common good, societal protection, and preventive deterrent; and from a personal perspective for the sake of retribution, expiation and even repentance. The moral right to kill was justified in the case of capital punishment and just war by way of State's authority, which derives from that of God. Hence, when the Waldensians challenged public authority's power to take life, Pope Innocent III (1198–1216) clarified that capital punishment could serve as a deterrent, corrective and means for preserving public order, when implemented for serious motives, without hatred (Denzinger 1995, n. 795; Brugger 2014, 103–107).

According to Thomas Aquinas (1485, *Summa Theologiae* II-II, q 64, a 2), because common good is more than the particular good of an individual, for safeguarding the former a dangerous individual may be put to death. Besides, a grave sinner who has lost his human dignity could be treated as a beast (Brugger 2014, 108–111). In other words, a criminal "has already disposed himself of his right to live" (Pius XII 1952, 787). Thus, "The traditional teaching of the Church does not exclude, […] recourse to the death penalty, when this is the only practicable way to defend the lives of human beings effectively against the aggressor" (CCC 2003, n. 2267).

Even so, from the second half of the twentieth century – particularly during the 1960s and 1970s – there has been a growing opposition to death penalty in the Catholic Church (Brugger 2014, 132–138). John Paul II (1995) in *Evangelium Vitae* voices a strong opposition to the infliction of death penalty and sets in motion a wide-ranging reevaluation of the morality of capital punishment (Brugger 2007, 381). Such a stand was later integrated in the CCC, since the *editio tipica* (1997).[4] The CCC (2003, n. 2267) states: "If, instead, bloodless means are sufficient to defend against the aggressor and to protect the safety of persons, public authority should limit itself to such means, because they better correspond to the concrete conditions of the common good and are more in conformity to the dignity of the human person. Today, in fact, given the means at the State's disposal to effectively repress crime by rendering inoffensive the one who has committed it, without depriving him definitively of the possibility of redeeming himself, cases of absolute necessity for suppression of the offender 'today ... are very rare, if not practically

[4]The 1992 edition of the CCC does not contain this view. According to Cardinal Christoph Schönborn, chairman of the commission that wrote and revised the CCC, there are substantial changes in the section on punishment, particularly in n. 2265–2267. The expression "not excluding, in cases of extreme gravity, the death penalty" is omitted in 1997 *editio tipica* (Brugger 2014, xiii, 22).

non-existent' (EV n. 56)". In fact, the Pope viewed the growing opposition to death penalty in the modern society as a sign of hope (EV n. 27). The Youth Catechism of the Catholic Church, borrowing an expression of John Paul II, qualifies death penalty as "cruel and unnecessary" (n. 381); for, even a murderer does not lose his human dignity (EV n. 9). Such a stand is also summed up in the Compendium of the Social Doctrine of the Church (Pontifical Council for Justice and Peace 2004, n. 405). Reinforcing it in his recent address on the 25th anniversary of the promulgation of the CCC, Pope Francis adds: "It must be clearly stated that the death penalty is an inhumane measure that, regardless of how it is carried out, abases human dignity. It is per se contrary to the Gospel, because it entails the willful suppression of a human life that never ceases to be sacred in the eyes of its Creator [...]. It is necessary, therefore, to reaffirm that no matter how serious the crime that has been committed, the death penalty is inadmissible because it is an attack on the inviolability and the dignity of the person."[5]

In this vein, it is believed that continuance of death penalty would only further dehumanize society, lowering it to the level of the criminal. Moreover, it does not seem to be in line with the biblical trajectory of forgiveness, hope and redemption. Worst of all, it leaves no room for rectification in cases of judicial error, which are not so uncommon. For the foregoing reasons, the contemporary Catholic theology opposes death penalty and views its abolition as in tune with Church's stand on abortion and euthanasia in defence of human life (McCarthy 1994, 110f; Brown 2007, 256).

(b) *Euthanasia*: In the biblical tradition, there is no explicit condemnation of suicide; instead, enduring martyrdom to resist grave sins is even encouraged (Drutchas 1998, 16). Nevertheless, early Christians following Augustin (354–430 CE) considered taking one's life a self-murder, also when with the intension of martyrdom one sought to be killed or took up severe ascetic practices. The general spirit of the Christian communities through the centuries is represented by the medieval devotional literature *ars moriendi* (art of good death) which, recognizing the significance of suffering made sure that the physician did not interfere with the spiritual journey of the patient by hastening the dying process. In the shrouded history of euthanasia, Thomas More (1474–1535) is remembered for an ironic reference to it – in his *Utopia* (1515) – as a pious and holy action by which one loses nothing but suffering, even though he rejected suicide as a temptation of the devil (Dowbiggin 2005, 12–47; Drutchas 1998, 47).

In recent times, appealing to the Second Vatican Council's *Gaudium et Spes* (1966, n. 27), John Paul II (1993) in *Veritatis Splendor* (VS n. 80) condemned euthanasia as an "intrinsic evil" and later reiterated it as "a grave violation of the law

[5]Address of Pope Francis to participants in the meeting promoted by the Pontifical Council for promoting the New Evangelization, 11 October 2017, http://w2.vatican.va/content/francesco/it/speeches/2017/october.index.html (accessed on 27 October 2017). See also the updated version of CCC n. 2267.

of God" (EV n. 65) that goes against the natural law and the written word of God. In this vein, he makes an outright defence of life (EV n. 57), quoting *Declaration on euthanasia* (CDF 1980): "Nothing and no one can in any way permit the killing of an innocent human being, whether a foetus or an embryo, an infant or an adult, an old person, or one suffering from an incurable disease, or a person who is dying. Furthermore, no one is permitted to ask for this act of killing, either for himself or herself or for another person entrusted to his or her care, nor can he or she consent to it, either explicitly or implicitly. Nor can any authority legitimately recommend or permit such an action".

Since life is God's gift, euthanasia undermines the respect due to the Creator (CCC n. 2277) and in a way gives God's prerogatives to the human person (Brown 2007, 252). Likewise, it ignores the redemptive value of suffering testified by the passion and death of Jesus. These two theological principles, namely, God's sovereignty over human life and the redemptive value of human suffering, cannot directly solve ethical questions as these are more hermeneutic themes (Kelly 1979) or maieutic hints (Fuchs 1985) expressing man's relation to the Creator. As such, they are bivalent: human beings are both creatures and co-agents, called to find meaning in suffering but also alleviate it. On the one hand, in the face of suffering some treatment must be offered, but not necessarily every possible treatment; on the other hand, man has to find meaning in suffering, but this does not imply deifying it or succumbing to it. Catholic tradition, as voiced by Pius XII (1957), upholds the sanctity of life but also the ethical import of quality of life, which implies that life need not be prolonged by all means (Kelly 1994, 348–350; Dowbiggin 2005, 115f).

Therefore, the traditional distinction between ordinary and extraordinary means of preserving life, between allowing a person to die and active euthanasia should be considered (Drutchas 1998, 50–50). In such situations, the principle of double effect – developed by moralists of the mid-twentieth century – can shed some light. Withdrawing extraordinary medical treatment, i.e., allowing a person die, can be morally right; as also when wanting to relieve pain, death may result as an indirect effect. In these cases, the patient's wish, desire for consciousness and readiness for death must be taken into account (Kelly 1994, 349f). On the contrary, assisted suicide, i.e., assistance offered to a patient by health-care practitioners or someone else, to put an end to his/her life, would be morally wrong as killing an innocent person (Kelly 1994, 350).

While the Church documents represent the official stand of the Catholic Church, in the ongoing debate, some Catholic moral theologians express the opinion that the distinction between killing and allowing a person to die "is not sufficient by itself to make all acts of euthanasia morally wrong. This revisionist position is basically consistent with the normative method known as proportionalism, which rejects the notion that actions in and of themselves can be judged immoral (intrinsically immoral acts). Thus, some Catholic moral theologians now argue that once the dying process is irreversibly begun the proscription of killing loses some of its moral weight. It may be more loving, and thus more consistent with the Christian moral demand, to actively and mercifully abet the process of dying than to permit continued pain and suffering" (Kelly 1994, 350f).

(c) *Abortion*: Although there is no explicit mention or condemnation of abortion, the biblical tradition views the unborn child as a gift from God: "For you created my innermost being: you knit me together in my mother's womb" (Psalm 139: 13). Early Christianity condemned the then prevalent practice of abortion and infanticide. Abortion was viewed as killing of an innocent person, although there was no consensus about when the foetus becomes a person. According to Aquinas, it would be murder to abort after the ensoulment, which occurred 40 days after conception in the case of a male and 90 days after conception in the case of a female. The movement of the foetus within the womb was also regarded as a sign of this crucial moment. However, Protestant reformers like Luther and Calvin held that body and soul existed from the moment of conception. For the same reason, Pope Pius IX, in 1869, imposed the penalty of excommunication for abortions at any stage of pregnancy (Brown 2007, 249). Such a firm stand was taken up in the *Code of Cannon Law* of 1917 and the excommunication *latae sententiae* (can. 1398) was reaffirmed in the *Code* of 1983. Pius XI (1930) in *Casti connubii* (n. 28–29) referred to abortion as going against the *sacredness* of an innocent life, the first time human life being qualified explicitly as sacred by the Catholic magisterium.

The Declaration on Procured Abortion of the Congregation for the Doctrine of the Faith (1974, n. 12) considers it a terrible crime: "From the time that the ovum is fertilized, a new life is begun which is neither that of the father nor of the mother, it is rather the life of a new human being with its own growth. It would never be made human if it were not human already". The non-disposability of human life follows from considering embryo and subsequently foetus as a human person (n. 2270–2274), based on the principles of continuity and potentiality. Church leaders therefore tend to "emphasize what is called a 'seamless garment' approach to life issues, which holds that an emphasis on human dignity demands that human life at all its stages and in every context be protected and that its quality be enhanced and improved" (McCartney 1994, 8; cf. Drutchas 1998, 127–130). 'Seamless garment' approach implies not only the right to life of the unborn, but also outlaws capital punishment and euthanasia (McCartney 1994, 9; Dowbiggin 2005, 133). Nevertheless, when there is danger to the mother and child, the principle of double effect may result in saving one or the other. In such circumstances, the Anglican Church, soliciting compassion for the mother and responsibility for the unborn child, would leave the decision to individual cases (Brown 2007, 250). Also within the Catholic tradition the possibility of unintentional abortion is recognized through the principle of double effect (CCC 1752), which together with the principle of causality or the ends-mean discussion (CCC 1759) and the principle of proportional gravity (CCC 1754) are important criteria to morally evaluate actions that are in themselves, nevertheless, evil.

The Church's option for the poor and the marginalized reveals another side of the problem. "Not only are unborn persons vulnerable, but many people of colour are convinced that abortion is being promoted in order to bring about genocide for reasons of race and ethnicity under the guise of concern about population control. [...]

Sometimes even well-intentioned ecclesial sanctions (e.g., excommunication) have had the unintended side effect of alienating and spiritually dispossessing the very people the church should be most concerned about helping. These penalties should be reconsidered in the light of the church's fundamental commitment to the marginalized" (McCartney 1994, 9). Pope Francis has addressed this concern in his recent Apostolic letter *Misericordia et Misera* (2016) by permitting all priests to absolve those who implore God's mercy after having resorted to abortion. Recognizing the fact that poor women more easily become victims of mistreatment and violence, earlier in his apostolic exhortation *Evangelii Gaudium* (2013, n. 212–214), Pope Francis pleaded that care be taken to accompany women who may be considering abortion caught up in profound anguish. At the same time, the pope underscored that the defence of unborn life is closely linked to the defence of other human rights, even as Church's stand in these matters is often dubbed as ideological, obscurantist and conservative.

John Paul II (1995) in *Evangelium Vitae* sums up the current official stand of the Catholic Church on inviolability of human life. In dealing with the three questions concerning right to life, the pope warns about the paradox that acts which were once considered as crimes now seem to assume the nature of 'rights' (EV n. 11). He solemnly condemns intentional killing of the innocent persons in general (EV n. 57), procured abortion (EV n. 62) and euthanasia (EV n. 65). These are crimes which no human law can legitimize (EV n. 70–73) and represent the absolute limits below which free individuals cannot lower themselves (EV n. 75). He also backs the move towards the abolition of death penalty (EV n. 56), and points to the emerging clash between life-affirming and life-denying cultures, between "culture of life" (Brennan 2007b) and "culture of death" (Brennan 2007a).[6]

Islamic Tradition

Muslims consider their religion as last in the line of revealed traditions, which "links the world of transcendence with human affairs, highlighting the sovereignty of God, the reality of the non-material world and the idea of the accountability of human actions. There is thus a dynamic interaction between what can be conceived as the realm of faith (*din*) and the realm of human affairs (*dunya*), which underlines the general Muslim understanding of an encompassing relationship between spiritual and material aspect of life" (Nanji 2007, 284).

According to the Islamic tradition, Qur'an (2:77; 33:35; 25:63–75) not only propounds the content of faith but also the fundamental principles of just actions. Yet, diverse ethical currents do exit: "with the 'rationalists' insisting that we can know much of what is right and obligatory by independent reasoning, while the 'traditionalists' acknowledged only revelation as an appropriate source for such knowledge"

[6] When dealing with "culture of death", while abortion and euthanasia are mentioned by the pope, death penalty is bracketed out.

(Leaman 2002, 147). A milder 'rationalist' version claims that "independent reason is required in some cases, scripture in others, and so there is no incompatibility between them" (Ibid. 147f).

For Islam, human beings, with their liberty, have a special place and dignity in God's creation as vicegerent (Sammak 2017), and hence "no matter what the material conditions of life, their ethical life is to be governed by moral reasoning, choice and accountability" (Nanji 2007, 287). On the other hand, as God has sanctified human life (*harrama Allah*), it is to be honoured and revered (Qur'an 17:70). It is inviolable (Qur'an 6:151; 17:33; 25:68), for to deal with life is to step into the territory of God's moral jurisdiction (*hudud Allah*) (Abou Ed Fadl 2004, 87f).

(a) *Death penalty*: The punishment prescribed by *Sharia* (Islamic law) for wrongs such as murder, adultery, fraud and theft, can range from lashes, imprisonment, amputation of limbs to death penalty (Nanji 2007, 320). The underlying reason being: "If anyone kills a person – unless it is for murder or for spreading mischief in the land – it would be as if he killed all people. And if anyone saves a life, it would be as if he saved the life of all people" (Qur'an 5:32).

If human life is sacred, then it cannot be disposed of without explicit, unwavering authorization from God; any doubt or ambiguity with regard to it would make termination of life immoral and illegal. Killing would be a crime, "except by way of justice and law" (Qur'an 6:151); therefore, death penalty may be implemented only by a court. When a State metes out death penalty, it is acting in the name of God and not of the citizens or the majority. Nevertheless, viewing the State, as God's faithful executioner is rather problematic as procedural guarantees are not enough to terminate life (Abou Ed Fadl 2004, 73–79). "While it is possible that a non-despotic State would feel empowered to execute individuals, it cannot derive such empowerment from the Qur'an itself. If anything, the Qur'an seems to empower private individuals with the decision to demand a life for a life or any other paradigm of exaction. However, several factors militate against the exaction of talion by private individuals" (Ibid. 97). Generally, victim's family is encouraged to practice forgiveness and compassion; they can demand death penalty or pardon the perpetrator accepting monetary compensation for their loss (2:178). If a Muslim seeks to follow the high moral vision of Islam, then vengeance and retaliation cannot be the option.

Fasad fil-ardh (spreading mischief in the land), punishable by death, is rather open to interpretation. It generally includes crimes that affect the community and destabilize the society, such as treason/apostasy, terrorism, rape and adultery. Even in such cases, harsh punishments are served more as deterrent; for, the Islamic penal code aims at saving life, promoting justice and preventing corruption and tyranny. Even when Muslim jurists accept death penalty in principle, they make its implementation very arduous. The primitive measures of punishments are now rarely implemented in most modern societies, as these have set up correctional institutions and prisons that apply modern principles of punishment. According to the religious vision of Islam, it is mercy, not retribution or retaliation that can restore the balance of justice, ethics and existence (Nanji 2007, 320; Abou Ed Fadl 2004, 104f).

(b) *Euthanasia*: In general, a Muslim has the duty to take care of his/her own health and seek medical intervention when ill, since with every ailment God has also given the capacity to find cure. Hence, suicide or deliberate ending of life would be considered "a violation of divine trust and an act of rebellion against God's merciful and compassionate nature" (Nanji 2007, 315).

Although Islam condemns all forms of suicide, martyrs who lay down their lives in defence of their faith are commended. Some of the modern-day suicide bombers are considered martyrs for their faith. While martyrs would be rewarded in paradise, others who commit self-murder would be punished in hell. In this vein, euthanasia would be viewed as interfering with the expiation for sin, therefore with the plan of God (Dowbiggin 2005, 15). Yet, according to some Muslim scholars, in the technologically advanced societies, life-sustaining mechanisms of terminally ill patients – when futile – may be withdrawn to allow for natural death, taking into account community values and family considerations (Nanji 2007, 315f).

(c) *Abortion*: The pre-Islamic practice of female infanticide by some tribes in Arabia was condemned in the Qur'an (17:31): "Do not kill your children because you are afraid of poverty and hunger, for We shall provide for them and for you".

Qur'an (23:12–15; 22:5) views the formation of foetus as a series of transformations or 'creations' leading up to 'ensoulment'. Scholars of the past affirmed the personhood of the foetus, viewing it as a body endowed with a soul, possessing both material and spiritual life. Male and female contribute to the formation of the organism of the child, even as the entire process is governed by God. The foetus at the ensoulment has the right of survival, and hence is a legal entity. However, there is no consensus about the moment of ensoulment. According to some, the ensoulment takes place after 120 days of pregnancy. At this stage, abortion would be considered a homicide, not before it is 'infused with life'; others instead object to it on the ground that it was 'going to be ensouled'. When the life of the mother is in danger, according to some Muslim scholars, abortion may be permitted after due consultation with family members and medical personnel. Instead, the *Ẓāhirī* (literalist) school of law forbids absolutely both contraception and abortion (Rahman 1996, 202–209; Nanji 2007, 314f; Engineer 2012, 10).

Having briefly considered the value of life from the perspective of Islamic tradition and its ethical consequences for the issue of death penalty, euthanasia and abortion, we move on to an overview of the meta-ethical and normative orientation in Hinduism.

Hindu Tradition

On pluralistic ethical grounds, Hinduism offers considerable flexibility in beliefs, values and practices. Flexibility and plurality in ethical matters derive from the fact that Hindus follow more an inductive procedure than a deductive one. In other words, to regulate their action in real-life situations, Hindus would have recourse first to their own conscience, and then to the lives of models, leaders and elders, and subsequently consult books (*smṛiti* literature) or experts on *dharma*; and only as a last resort would they turn to divine revelation, the *Vedas* (*śruti*) (Menski 2007, 5).

Amidst flexibility and ethical pluralism, *dharmic* and *cosmotheandric* vision (Panikkar 1993) provide guiding principles. The concept of *dharma*, underscores that every individual should act in every life-situation with the intent of establishing righteousness. As this would depend to a great extent on the four *varṇa* (social castes), each individual is said to have a *svadharma*, i.e., specific *dharma*. The Hindu *dharma* lays emphasis on duties rather than on rights; in a way, duties of one person become the rights of another. While *dharma* obliges the individual to act as a social being, the complementary concept of *karma* points to the repercussions of individual's action on oneself and the rest of reality. This follows from the *cosmotheandric* vision that refers to the Cosmos-God-Man interconnectedness. The principle of interdependence lays emphasis not so much on being autonomous individuals as on being part of a cosmic whole (Menski 2007, 3–6; Sontheimer 1993). In this anthropological scheme, human dignity is closely bound to the consciousness one has and the responsibility one feels as the bridge between the transcendent and the cosmic reality (Anthony 2017).

(a) *Death penalty*: Hinduism does not have a central commandment that forbids killing. Instead, sometimes killing may be inevitable and even necessary as dramatically narrated in *Bhagavadgītā.* When all is set for the battle, seeing the reluctance of the warrior-hero Arjuna, Lord Krishna who serves as his charioteer, instructs him about his duty to kill even close relatives in order to protect *dharma* (Menski 2007, 4f).

When it comes to death penalty, Hindu teachings are ambivalent: they may permit it for some reasons and forbid it for others. On the one hand, Hinduism preaches *ahimsa* (non-violence), and on the other, it teaches that the soul cannot be killed as death touches only the physical body. According to the theory of *karma*, the soul would be reborn into another body until its final dissolution in *mokṣa.*

The religious, civil and criminal law of Hindus is encoded in the *Dharmaśāstras* and the *Arthasastra*. These provide the rules and describe punishments to be meted out for different types of crimes, and specify death penalty in instances such as murder and righteous warfare. In this vein, *Vishnusmriti* (5:1) states that "great criminals should all be put to death"; and *Manusmriti* (8:352–86) in dealing with adultery advocates cruel death sentence in some cases (Menski 2007, 41).

Although murder is the worst of crimes, death penalty for it would depend on the intention behind the act. According to *Manusmriti* (8:349–51) there are instances when killing is lawful, for example, "by killing an assassin the slayer incurs no guilt" (8:351) (Menski 2007, 41). As *dharma* is closely bound to *varṇa*, the seriousness of a crime is assessed on the basis of the *varṇa* status of the perpetrator and the victim. For example, *Brahmahatya* (killing a Brahmin), according to sacred texts, is the most serious offence, the greatest of mortal sins (*Manusmriti* 9:235), and yet in the case of a Brahmin who murders another Brahmin the criminal is not subject to death penalty. "*Vishnusmriti* 5:2, otherwise strict on death sentences, adds that 'in the case of a Brahmin no corporal punishment must be inflicted' and advises that a Brahmin murderer must be banished from the country with a mark of his offence branded on his body (5:3)" (Menski 2007, 41f).

(b) *Euthanasia*: The respect for all forms of life and unfavourableness to unnecessary killing do not offer justification for euthanasia in Hinduism. "A prominent Hindu attitude is to say that the terminally ill individual has to wait till the right time (*kāla*) has come for him or her to die. Those that care for the terminally ill may well seek to lessen pain and suffering, but in principle they have no right to end the other person's life" (Ibid. 37). Generally, mental and physical suffering is associated with the theories of *karma* and *saṃsāra* (cycle of rebirth), and as such, suffering is viewed as a just consequence of negative behaviour. In the face of suffering, then, an attitude of equanimity is called for, as it does not affect the inner self, moving towards the ultimate goal of liberation (*mokṣa*). Moreover, suicide or assisted suicide would be contrary to the ethical norm of nonviolence (*ahiṃsā*) (Wujastyk 2012, 635).

Although Hinduism lays emphasis on defending life and on the ideal of nonviolence, suicide may be morally and ethically acceptable in some situations. "In a 'willed death' people who are old and weak, but not terminally ill, may virtually wait till death arrives, refusing to take any food or drink" (Ibid. 37); an old man becoming a *samnyāsi* may perform his own funeral rites and then leave this world (cf. *Manusmriti* 6:31); an ideal wife may take up to *satī* and burn herself to death with her husband's body on the funeral pyre, gaining the status of goddess (*devī*) and ideal female. Suicide may result from grief over the loss of a loved one; it may be chosen as a penance, to make up for the crime committed; it may even be taken up as a moral duty to spare the ruler from enforcing the death penalty (Menski 2007, 38).

(c) *Abortion*: The first term *āyur* of classical Indian science of life *Āyurveda* signifies the prolongation and preservation life; the second term *veda* implies its close link with the Hindu religious tradition. According to Hinduism, one of the major aims of life is to procreate; a central aspect of *dharma* is to preserve and promote life. Hence, medical manuals since the ancient times attach high value to the life in the womb, and consider feticide as killing. In a way, the womb is the creative centre of the universe where divine-human activities intersect, where creatures meet the 'Lord of life'. It is the *Prajāpati*, the 'Lord of creation', who brings forth the child in the union of man and woman (Crawford 1996, 226–229).

As per *Manusmriti*, in the act of conception there is already a man in the making. Likewise, *Caraka Saṁhitā* affirms that spirit is present in matter from the time of conception. The new life is an inseparable blending of human and psychobiological existence; hence at no stage of its development is it just matter or tissue that can be eliminated. Abortion would then be termination of a person-in-being. In other words, foetal existence is an elementarily human existence; hence, killing of an embryo is one of the five most atrocious acts. It is judged as a heinous crime in the

Brāhmanas as well as in the *Upaniṣads*. Such a crime would have karmic effect both in this life and in the next, and for such reasons women who resort to abortion are considered impure and inauspicious (Crawford 1996, 230–237; Menski 2007, 36).

According to *Bhagavatgītā* (16:2), the most vulnerable form life, namely, the child in the womb, deserves *ahiṃsā* (non-violence). At the same time, the right to life of the foetus is not to be absolutized. When there is a situation of competing rights and values, mother's life may be favoured on the basis of the greater karmic obligation she has than the foetus. *Suśruta Saṁhitā* would allow for the removal of gravely damaged or defective foetus on the basis of *dayā* or compassion (Crawford 1996, 234–237; Menski 2007, 36; Wujastyk 2012, 636f).

In this section we have synthetically exposed the Christian, Muslim and Hindu meta-ethical and normative basis for the (non-)disposal of human life by death penalty, euthanasia and abortion. Obviously, our short overview cannot represent the full variety of reflections by influential thinkers belonging to the respective religious traditions. While we have focused on the official stand of the Catholic Church and of some other denominations in the case of Christianity, this is more difficult when it comes to Islam and Hinduism. We therefore consider the above sections only as a synopsis of the variety of religiously inspired views on (end-of-) life issues. In the following section we shall briefly explore the (non-)disposability of life from the secular perspective.

(Non-)Disposability of Human Life: Secular Perspective

From the secular perspective, 'sacrality' or intrinsic value of human life is the meta-ethical ground for the (non-)disposal of life. Drutchas (1998, 56–74), with a meticulous analysis, elucidates that 'sacredness of life' is not explicitly articulated in the biblical tradition nor in the extensive Church traditions up to the seventeenth century. Instead, the roots of 'sacredness of life' are to be sought rather in Stoicism antecedent to Christianity and revived during the European Renaissance and Enlightenment. With its 'monistic materialism', Stoicism highlighted the 'divine spark' in every human being, which led ultimately to the acknowledgement of human sacredness or dignity. This was viewed as the source of human equality and autonomy. With the Renaissance, Stoics' notion of sanctity or sacredness of life was taken up as the basis of secular currents. In the Enlightenment period, 'sacred' referred to human dignity and subsequently led to the human rights discourse. Immanuel Kant's 'categorical imperative' of universalizing principle and 'practical imperative' of retaining the human person never only as a means, but always at the same time as an end, underscored the Enlightenment's notion of ultimate worth and sacredness of human life. In Kant's view, autonomy of man was bound by the categorical and practical imperatives, which imply that man has the moral duty to preserve his life. In this vein, at the turn of the nineteenth century, Albert Schweitzer's 'reverence for life' philosophy added a new impetus to the sanctity of all life, not just human.

An analysis of the changes in the penal system, particularly death penalty, brings Joas (2013, 49) to the following conclusion: "In the history of criminal law, the worst crime has generally been that which violates the sacred core of the community. So it seems reasonable to trace changes in the penal system back to changes in the understanding of the sacred". In his view, "the reforms of penal law and penal practice, and the rise of human rights in the late eighteenth century, are expressions of a profound cultural shift in which the human person became a sacred object" (Ibid. 49). Thus Joas, in line with Émile Durkheim underscores the "sacralisation or sacredness of the person" as the basis for human rights discourse. The author elucidates how the experience of violence is interrelated to the history of human rights even in its very formulation (Ibid. 58, 60, 70). Referring to the Nazi crimes, Joas affirms: "The emphasis on the unity of the human race in Article 1 is consciously intended to counter the destruction of universalism in racial theories. The emphasis on the 'right to life' in Article 3 was just as consciously inspired by the Nazi 'euthanasia' of the disabled" (Ibid. 73).

As regards (non-)disposal of life by death penalty, euthanasia and abortion, the normative-ethical discourse based on the secular perspective of sacrality of life give rise to contrasting trends centred on individual autonomy and common good, on the one hand, and on modern technological potential and professional responsibility, on the other. In the cases of euthanasia and abortion, the debate tends to be quite complex as we shall discuss in the following subsections.

Instead, with regard to death penalty, the discussion may be succinctly rendered in two annotations. In the first place – as referred to by Karl Barth – the initiative to restrict and ultimately abolish death penalty arose from the secular sphere than from the Christian sphere. The other worldly orientation of saving the souls perhaps contributed to Christians' hesitancy in opposing death penalty outright. Secondly, death penalty was invoked for eliminating dangerous criminals for the reason of justice, public safety and common good. Most people today believe that the modern prison facilities that allow for life imprisonment make death penalty unwarranted. Nevertheless, some raise the question, if limited resources should be spent on catering to the needs of criminals (Drutchas 1998, 46).

Individual Autonomy and Common Good

(a) The term *euthanasia* (good death) was revived by Francis Bacon (1561–1626) after its initial use by the Roman historian Suetonius (c 70–140 BCE). Amidst religious and secular response to what is or is not a good death, a turning point was struck with an article published 1870 by Samuel D. Williams, which appealed to Seneca, and the Enlightenment's argument of freedom to take one's life, and introduced the concept of 'worthwhile' life as equivalent to 'sacredness' of life. Already, Charles Darwin's *Origin of Species* (1859) in a way subverted the moral principles based on human nature, central to Christianity and other religions. In his view, the value of human life was no more than any other form of natural life. From Darwin's pessimistic view of heredity development, it was only a small step to Francis Galton's concept of 'eugenics' (1883) and to its identification as Nazi science following the Nazi law of 1933. Nevertheless, the emerging secularism that brought into question religious beliefs and moral standards, gave rise to pro-choice movement in the twentieth century, viewing 'death control' and 'birth control' as a matter of human dignity. In contrast, the right-to-life movement that arose to oppose abortion issues in the mid-1970s soon included opposition to mercy killing in their advocacy, insofar as both issues dealt with innocent life. These currents are reflected in the present conflict between radical pro-life religious groups and rationalist pro-choice activists (Dowbiggin 2005, 23, 49–68, 106–126, 131–135).

From the individual's point of view, euthanasia paradoxically implies the right to die, namely, dispose of one's life or assist others in doing so, when life is not worthwhile anymore, due to terminal sickness or degenerating conditions. In this sense, euthanasia comes close to the understanding of suicide or assisted suicide. Those who favour such choices do so for reasons of individual autonomy and self-determination. "According to this view of life, human dignity is rooted in a person's capacity to freely shape his own life according to his own beliefs and desires. Therefore, the argument goes, every person also has a 'right to die', the right to determine the time and circumstances of his death especially in the face of suffering, apparent indignity, or hardship. [...] Moreover, they claim that assisted suicide is not unjust, because it does not deprive the individual of something that he values or desires. [...] Finally, proponents claim that assisted suicide or euthanasia is often the most compassionate response to unbearable suffering. It is an act of mercy" (Austriaco 2007, 58).

Those who take a pro-life stand fear that euthanasia by choice can gradually end up in euthanasia by stealth, in the direction of eugenics, and could lead to easy medical experimentation and manipulation (Mauceri 2007). It would be a small step moving from voluntary euthanasia to non-voluntary and involuntary one (see footnote 1). In their opinion, suicide or assisted suicide would mean not absolving one's duty towards oneself and others; in the Kantian terms, it would be treating oneself as a means rather than an end, and would not be a moral act as it cannot be the basis for a universal law (Magni 2011, 81, 88f; Dowbiggin 2005, 37).

From the perspective of common good, some hold that euthanasia, as well as assisted suicide, could be beneficial to the terminally ill patient and to others, namely, to family members, society and the State (Magni 2011, 82). As care giving of terminally ill persons generally touches women, they view euthanasia as favourable to women's welfare. In their view, prolonging at all cost a life not worth living entails waste of limited resources. The danger in such a line of reasoning is that active euthanasia could gradually become a socially acceptable form of cost containment, and give way to eliminating poverty by eliminating the poor (Kelly 1994, 252).

(b) In the case of *abortion*, as highlighted by Van der Ven et al. (2004, 85f), the heated debate between pro-life and pro-choice groups lays bare two sides of the same coin. On the one side, the proponents of pro-life demand that human embryo and foetus be protected on account of the right to life, and on the other, the pro-choice group appeal to mother's dignity as a human person underlining the need for her liberty, security, privacy and productive autonomy.

Insofar as mother's right may conflict with that of the growing child, abortion presents a peculiar case of disposing of a distinct life entirely dependent on another life. The concern seems to be for the quality of life of the mother on the one hand, and that of the foetus on the other. Upholding woman's dignity, some feminist currents favour abortion in cases such as incest, rape or unwanted pregnancy. Besides the safety and honour of the mother, the good of the present and future family members also enter the debate (Brown 2007, 250).

The web of relationship in which a pregnant woman is involved means that terminating pregnancy is not a private matter, but inherently a social decision. The modern emphasis on individualism and privacy tends to ignore mutual relatedness and responsibility among persons, diminishing the sense of 'common good' (McCartney 1994, 6). For this reason, there is strong opposition to abortions resulting from an extreme form of individualism: for career enhancement, convenience or sex selection – rather prevalent in the Indian context. Likewise, some disapprove the public funding of abortion or the use of public medical facilities, as the State should have legitimate interest in protecting the foetus (McCartney 1994, 6f).

Eugenic or other nontherapeutic abortions are sought because the life of the child is valued as not worth living or that society would be excessively burdened by it. It must be remembered that interest in such social beneficence was the underlying justification of Nazi doctors' genetic and hypothermic experiments. Such trends would undermine the true nature of medical profession and health care institutions (McCartney 1994, 7), as we shall see below.

Modern Technological Potential and Professional Responsibility

In the highly scientific and technological world, some professions directly get involved in the debate on (non-)disposability of life: judicial profession in the case of death penalty and medical profession in the case of euthanasia and abortion.

(a) With reference to *euthanasia*, modern medical facilities capable of prolonging life blur the border between necessary care and therapeutic intransigence (Magni 2011, 81). Even if distinction can be made between action and omission, the diving line between the two may not be easy to draw, when, for example, disconnecting an artificial respirator and causing the death of a terminally ill person. Ethics of consequentialism would judge both on the basis of the consequence of action and omission, whereas deontological ethic would not view omission as unjust. Evaluation of the action or omission becomes further complicated when we consider the intention with which one acts (Magni 2011, 84–86).

As to the potential of modern medical facilities, the Catholic Church affirms: “Discontinuing medical procedures that are burdensome, dangerous, extraordinary, or disproportionate to the expected outcome can be legitimate; it is the refusal of ‘over-zealous’ treatment. Here one does not will to cause death; one’s inability to impede it is merely accepted” (CCC n. 2278). While ordinary care should not be denied to the sick, provision could be made for palliative care. “The use of painkillers to alleviate the sufferings of the dying, even at the risk of shortening their days, can be morally in conformity with human dignity if death is not willed as either an end or a means, but only foreseen and tolerated as inevitable. Palliative care is a special form of disinterested charity. As such it should be encouraged” (CCC n. 2279). Reaffirming this stand, Pope Francis, in his recent message to the participants in the European Regional Meeting of the World Medical Association (16–17 November 2017) warns: “Greater wisdom is called for today, because of the temptation to insist on treatments that have powerful effects on the body, yet at times do not serve the integral good of the person”.[7]

From a professional perspective, some are of the opinion that legalising active euthanasia and assisted suicide would go against common good, as it would gradually “undermine the medical profession by eroding the trust of patients in their physicians and caregivers” (Austriaco 2007, 58; cf. Kelly 1994, 252). In fact, the Hippocratic Oath (fifth-third Century BCE), a milestone in the history of medicine, forbade the intervention of physicians to shorten the life of the patient (EV n. 89; CDF 2009). For this reason, some would call for a compassionate and effective end-of-life care rather than resort to euthanasia (Dowbiggin 2005, 5–10).

(b) As for *abortion*, it may be remembered that during the nineteenth century, it was the medical profession that gave expression to the Enlightenment ideal of sacredness of life by opposing the public tolerance of abortion and standing for the outlawing of abortion except for therapeutic purpose. It is true that Christian Churches were generally opposed to abortion, but only at the close of the century did they firmly condemn abortion (Drutchas 1998, 69–72).

Presently, modern medical facilities make possible safe abortion at the early stage of pregnancy, particularly in the case of defective foetus that could endanger the life of the mother. At the same time, with the technological progress, its potential for treating the foetus has also increased. “One can hope that such progress will continue, in accordance with the vocation of doctors, which is not to suppress life but to care for it and favour it as much as possible” (CDF 1974, n. 26).

Overall, those who favour the disposal of human life by euthanasia and abortion hold that what really counts is not mere biological life, but the quality of life. Therefore, when life is not worthwhile, because it lacks consciousness, autonomy, self-determination, etc., it may well be disposed of. Yet, how the quality of life can

[7] http://w2.vatican.va/content/francesco/en/messages/pont-messages/2017/documents/papa-francesco_20171107_ messaggio-monspaglia.html (accessed on 19 November 2017).

be understood and gauged, without absolute respect for life, remains debatable (Magni 2011, 41f).

(Non-)Disposability of Human Life: Social and Legal Practice

Having dealt with the meta-ethical and normative aspects of religious and secular perspectives, we now turn to the social and legal practice. Article 3 of the Universal Declaration of Human Rights (1948) – "Everyone has the right to life, liberty and security of person" – may be considered as the basis of all other rights. Article 21 of the Indian Constitution (1949), in its turn endorses the right to life and personal liberty in these terms: "No person shall be deprived of his life or personal liberty except according to procedure established by law".

The three problem areas that we address in our research bring into focus the rapport between the value of 'life' and the other two values of 'liberty' and 'security' of the person. The debate over death penalty brings up the conflict between the values of 'life' and 'security' of persons in society. Instead, the debate over euthanasia and abortion bring into contrast the values of 'life' and 'liberty' of individuals: liberty to end one's life when not worthwhile in the case of euthanasia; and liberty to terminate an incipient new life to safeguard mother's life when at risk biologically, or socially in case of rape and incest. The contrasting trends concerning these three issues arise from the priority given to 'life' over 'liberty and security', or vice-versa.

Death Penalty

Of the three issues concerning right to life, namely, death penalty, euthanasia and abortion, it is the first that has been further specified in the Human Rights tradition. Recalling Article 3 of the Universal Declaration of Human Rights, Article 6 of the International Covenant on Civil and Political Rights of 1966 solemnly states: "Every human being has the inherent right to life. This right shall be protected by law. No one shall be arbitrarily deprived of his life. […] Anyone sentenced to death shall have the right to seek pardon or commutation of the sentence. Amnesty, pardon or commutation of the sentence of death may be granted in all cases. […] Sentence of death shall not be imposed for crimes committed by persons below eighteen years of age and shall not be carried out on pregnant women".

The Indian Penal Code (IPC)[8] – originating as British colonial legislation in 1860 – foresees death sentence, but it also allows for its commutation into life

[8] http://www.advocatekhoj.com/library/bareacts/indianpenalcode/index.php?Title=Indian%20Penal%20Code,%201860 (accessed on 14 September 2017).

sentence (Art. 54–55). In 1983, the Supreme Court of India ruled that death penalty should be imposed only in "the rarest of rare cases". Nevertheless, the Supreme Court has sanctioned death penalty to be carried out in four instances since 1995.[9]

In December 2007, India voted against a United Nations General Assembly resolution calling for a moratorium on death penalty. In November 2012, India again upheld its stance on capital punishment by voting against the UN General Assembly draft resolution seeking to ban death penalty. Recently, on 19 December 2016, with 117 out of 193 States voting in favour of the sixth resolution (A/RES/71/187), the UN member states reasserted their support for a universal moratorium on death penalty. While 31 countries abstained, five were absent. Then again, India was one of the 40 countries voting against it.[10] India is of the opinion that its penal code guarantees sufficiently against indiscreet use of death penalty.

Euthanasia

Euthanasia was viewed by Seneca – who committed suicide in 65 CE – as valuable and handy means of exiting the world. Closer to our own times, namely, during the 1980s and the 1990s, when AIDS began to spread among homosexual communities, these communities became a fertile ground for the right-to-die movement (Dowbiggin 2005, 2–6). In the contemporary society, those who follow liberalism and liberal constitution of the State claim that individuals should be able decide about it according to their faith, conscience and conviction. Currently euthanasia and assisted suicide are generally prohibited; yet three types of juridical recognition are in place: renouncing the juridical action, depenalization, and legalization of active and passive euthanasia. As of September 2017, active euthanasia is legal, under specific but differing conditions in the Netherlands, Belgium, Colombia, Luxembourg and Canada; and some form of assisted suicide in Switzerland, Germany, Japan, Albania, Canada and a few US States (Magni 2011, 92f; Austriaco 2007, 58).

In the Indian context, IPC 299 on culpable homicide states: "Whoever causes death by doing an act with the intention of causing death, or with the intention of causing such bodily injury as is likely to cause death, or with the knowledge that he

---

[9] The last execution to take place in India was the July 30, 2015 hanging of Yakub Memon, convicted of financing the 1993 Mumbai bombings. The three executions prior this were: the February 8, 2013 hanging of Muhammad Afzal, convicted of plotting the 2001 attack on India's Parliament; the hanging of 2008 Mumbai attack gunman Mohammad Ajmal Amir Qasab on November 21, 2012; and the hanging of Dhananjoy Chatterjee in 2004 for the murder and rape of a 14-year old girl: https://www.deathpenaltyworldwide.org/country-search-post.cfm?country=India (accessed on 14 September 2017). According to Amnesty International, in 2017 Indian courts gave 109 death sentences, but none were executed.

[10] http://www.worldcoalition.org/The-UN-General-Assembly-voted-overwhelmingly-for-a-6th-resolution-calling-for-a-universal-moratorium-on-executions.html (accessed on 14 September 2017).

is likely by such act to cause death, commits the offence of culpable homicide". With reference to this norm, it is clarified that accelerating the death of another labouring under disease or bodily infirmity can amount to causing death. Although euthanasia is not mentioned explicitly, this norm may be considered to include it. Concerning suicide and assisted suicide, IPC 305 states: "If any person under eighteen years of age, any insane person, any idiot, or any person in a state of intoxication, commits suicide, whoever abets the commission of such suicide" is guilty. Similarly, IPC 309 regards attempted suicide as a punishable offence.

In the Indian social context, religious traditions such as Jainism, Hinduism, and Buddhism consider it a religious act to choose to die by refusing/withholding all types of nutrition. Some human rights advocates, calling for proper legislation, challenge such practices today. When, for example, a devout Jain resorted to *Santhara/Sallekhana* (ritual of fasting unto death), an act of supreme renunciation undertaken only by the most spiritually pure, the Rajasthan High Court order made it an offence punishable under the IPC. Human rights activists compared it to involuntary euthanasia, whereas the High Court petition compared to *Satī* (a practice outlawed by the British in 1829). The Jain community responded to this with protests, and the Indian Supreme Court ended up reversing the order until further deliberations (*Indian Express*, September 2, 2015). Priyamvadha Mohansingh, Assistant Professor in the Department of Criminology of Madras University, brought to light that *Thalaikoothal,* a form of intentionally killing elderly or 'geronticide' was practiced in Madurai, Virudhunagar and Theni districts of Tamil Nadu (*The Hindu*, February 18, 2016). These social and legal practices point to an emerging debate over euthanasia in the Indian context.

Abortion

The opening statement of Article 6 (§1) of the International Covenant on Civil and Political Rights of 1966, solemnly declares: "Every human being has the inherent right to life". The question that arises in the face of abortion is if 'every human being' includes the foetus. In other words, does foetus have legal rights?

After abortion was legalized under Soviet norms in the 1950s, permissive abortion laws were passed in the Soviet bloc countries. With the Abortion Act of 1967, Britain became first Western country to allow it with other countries following suit. In Britain, it is illegal to abort foetuses after 24 weeks of pregnancy, unless there is risk to the life of the pregnant woman, injury to her physical or mental health or her existing children, or serious health or mental abnormalities to the child in the womb. After this period, namely, 24 weeks of pregnancy, the foetus is viable to live outside the womb, and destroying such a foetus would be equivalent to murder (Brown 2007, 249; Brugger 2014, 135). During the second half of the twentieth century, after Britain and the USA, abortion was legalized in several European countries and Asian communist countries, with an estimated 50 million abortions worldwide each year (Hostetler and Coulter 2007, 1).

Abortion was legalised in India by the Medical Termination of the Pregnancy Act of 1971.[11] It permits the termination of pregnancy by registered medical practitioners up to the 20th week of gestation, for specific reasons such as danger to the mother or to her mental health, mother being minor or lunatic, risk to the child, and pregnancy resulting from rape. The definition of the grounds for termination of the pregnancy after amendments is so wide, that the World Health Organization (WHO 2011, 4) considers India as one of the six countries that permits abortion on all grounds, though not on request, meaning that endorsement of a doctor is necessary. The magnitude of the abortion phenomenon may be grasped from statistics of the World Health Organization (Sedgh et al. 2016): it is estimated that about 35 abortions occurred annually per 1000 women aged 15–44 years worldwide in 2010–14, which in absolute numbers is about 56,3 million induced abortions per year. In India, official figures of abortion ratios are relatively low. It sets the abortion ratio at 6.1 abortions per 1000 women aged 15–44 (Indian Council of Medical Research statistics), but it is estimated that in addition to this figure about two thirds of abortions take place outside the authorized health services (WHO 2011, 22; George et al. 2017, 532). In the male-dominated Indian society, where girl child is sometimes seen as an unwanted extra burden, particularly in view of dowry, the possibility of determining the sex of the unborn child have led to the widespread practice of aborting female foetuses. For this reason, several Indian states have prohibited sex testing the unborn child. Even so, faced with the problem of population explosion, the Indian State appears to connive in unauthorized abortion, consequently in the abortion of female foetuses (Menski 2007, 36f; Wujastyk 2012, 637). Sex-selective abortion is clearly reflected in the birth figures. India has shocking statistics on sex ratios with a disproportionately higher number of births of boys since the early 1980s. Although some excessive birth of boys is the biological norm, for sure not to the extent as seen in some places in India. Preponderant male birth rates are as high as 136 boys to 100 girls in certain districts, particularly in the west of the country from Punjab to Maharashtra. According to the 2011 census, the birth sex ratio in India was 109.1 boys to 100 girls (i.e. 917 girls for 1000 boys). Surprisingly, sex ratio imbalance of births also correlates with religious groups, the biggest excess of male birth being among Sikhs (129.8 boys against 100 girls) and Jains (118.0), followed by Hindus (110.9), Muslims (107.4) and Christians (103.8) in 2001 (Guilmoto 2007, 8; Hvistendahl 2011, 5ff). Such differences make a cross-religious study on the influence of religious beliefs and practices on attitudes towards abortion highly relevant.

In connection with IPC 299 on culpable homicide, it is clarified that "causing of the death of child in the mother's womb is not homicide. But it may amount to culpable homicide to cause the death of a living child, if any part of that child has been brought forth, though the child may not have breathed or been completely born".

[11] Further amendments were made: The Medical Termination of Pregnancy Act, No. 34 of 1971, as amended by the Medical Termination of Pregnancy Act, No. 64 of 2002. The Pre-natal Diagnostic Techniques (Regulation and Prevention of Misuse) Act, No. 57 of 1994, and the Pre-natal Diagnostic Technologies (Regulation and Prevention of Misuse) Amendment Act, 2002, No. 14 of 2003 (see discussion in Crawford 1996, 234–237).

Similarly, causing death of unborn quick child would amount to culpable homicide (IPC 316).

There is a justifiable fear that permitting legal exceptions to the law forbidding killing – as in the cases of euthanasia and abortion – is a slippery slope. "When a society decides that certain kinds of killing are moral, there is an ever-increased chance that the society will extend such permission even further" (Kelly 1994, 351).

Having considered the (non-)disposability of life with reference to death penalty, euthanasia and abortion, from the perspective of the three religions – Christianity, Islam and Hinduism – and that of secular trends, and having highlighted briefly the current social and legal practice with regard to these issues, we proceed to the conceptual model that introduces the empirical phase of our research.

Conceptual Model and Research Questions

The range of our empirical study covers besides right to life, civil rights (Anthony and Sterkens 2016), political rights (Anthony and Sterkens 2018), juridical rights, socioeconomic rights and the underlying principle of separation between religion and State. However, in the present chapter we focus on (non-)disposability of life in association with religious attitudes, insofar as the latter can have an impact on the ethical practice of individuals and communities.

Based on the theoretical framework – described above – a conceptual model (see Fig. 2.1) was designed with (non-)disposability of life as dependent variable, focused specifically on the attitude concerning death penalty, euthanasia and abortion.

As for religious attitudes – the independent variables – we distinguish between personal and contextual aspects. The personal aspects include religious beliefs, experiences and practices. The contextual aspects comprise the function of religion in society, the approach to religious plurality, and the trust in one's own and others' religions. Besides, from a secular perspective the value of human dignity being central to right to life, it also forms part of the independent variables.

The background features taken into account refer to personal characteristics, religious characteristics, psychological traits and socio-political traits.

The conceptualization and operationalization of these variables form part of the International Empirical Research Project 'Religion and Human Rights 2.0'.[12] Hence, we limit ourselves to a synthetic presentation of the operationalization of the three sets of variables in the following section.

[12] For further documentation, see http://www.rp.theologie.uni-wuerzburg.de/research/religion_and_human_rights_2012_2019/ (accessed 14 September 2017). This research project builds on the previous one: Religion and Human Rights (1997–2011). For findings referring to Tamil Nadu, see Van der Ven and Anthony (2008) and Anthony (2013).

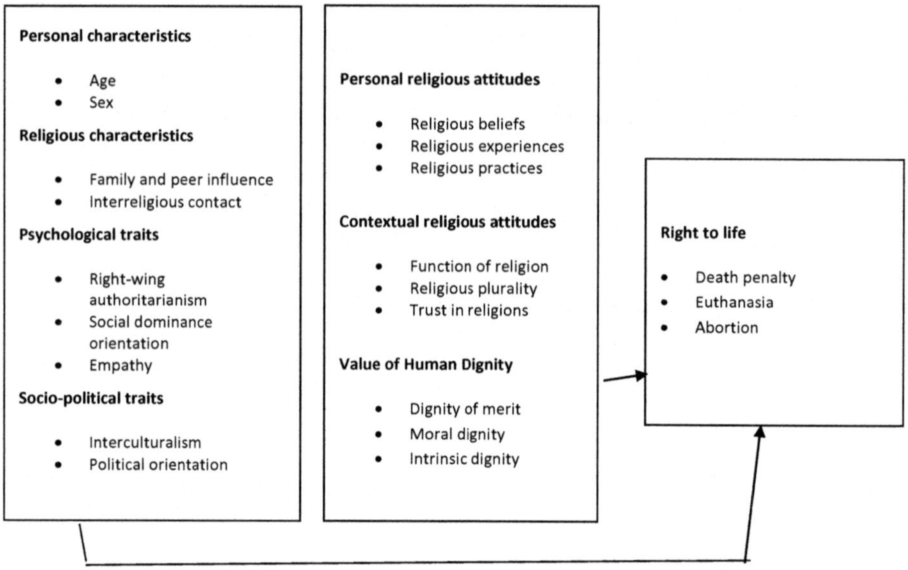

Fig. 2.1 Conceptual model: effects of independent variables (personal and contextual religious attitudes and value of human dignity) and background variables (personal and religious characteristics, psychological and socio-political traits) on the dependent variable (Right to life related to death penalty, euthanasia, and abortion)

The research questions that we seek to address are:

1. What tendency emerges among the college students regarding non-disposal of life by death penalty and disposal of life by euthanasia and abortion?
2. Are there significant differences between Christian, Muslim and Hindu students regarding non-disposal of life by death penalty and disposal of life by euthanasia and abortion?
3. Which personal and contextual religious attitudes and valuing of human dignity relate to non-disposal of life by death penalty and disposal of life by euthanasia and abortion?
4. Which personal and religious characteristics and psychological and socio-political traits relate to non-disposal of life by death penalty and disposal of life by euthanasia and abortion?
5. Which independent variables (personal and contextual religious attitudes and valuing of human dignity) and background variables (personal and religious characteristics, and psychological and socio-political traits) emerge as predictors of non-disposal of life by death penalty and disposal of life by euthanasia and abortion?

Method

Sample and Data Collection

With the view to examining the students' agreement with (non-)disposability of life and its rapport with their religious attitudes, we draw on the data collected in September–October 2014 in Tamil Nadu, India. We decided to collect data from around 1200 respondents, among whom men and women, and religious traditions were equally represented; and hence we used a stratified quota sampling with random selection of respondents in each stratum.

The respondents of the study primarily included undergraduate students of seven Arts and Science colleges. Two colleges were chosen from each of the three regions and one from the State capital, resulting in the following number of respondents for the different regions: northern region (308), western region (304), southern region (303) and Chennai (300). The total sample arrived at comprised 1215 respondents with 400 Hindus, 408 Muslims and 407 Christians. There were 614 male and 601 female respondents, and they mostly belonged to the age group 17–20 years. We consider this age group suitable for studying the sensitivity concerning right to life, as at this stage they begin to make initial decisions with regard to their future family and social life.

Measuring Instrument

The students who formed our sample were asked to fill in a questionnaire in the framework of the International Religion and Human Rights research project mentioned above. The items related to the dependent variable (right to life), independent variables (personal and contextual religious attitudes and valuing of human dignity) and background variables (personal and religious characteristics, and psychological and socio-political traits) were part of this wider research project.

The dependent variable (see Table 2.1) consists of a measurement of agreement with twelve items representing the three issues of right to life: death penalty (items 1a and 1b); euthanasia (items 2a, 2b, and 2c); and abortion (items 3a, 3b, 3c, 3d, 3e, 3f and 3g).

The independent variables comprise personal religious attitudes and contextual religious attitudes. *Personal religious attitudes* are specified in terms of religious beliefs, experiences and practices. Religious beliefs include: (a) belief in the existence of God, (b) belief in a personal God (theism, pan-en-theism, and natural pan-en-theism) and in a non-personal God (deism, pantheism), and (c) critical approach to one's religious beliefs. Religious experience is represented as (a) faith

Table 2.1 Levels of agreement (mean and standard deviation) with items concerning right to life, namely, death penalty, euthanasia and abortion for all respondents in descending order of average agreement

	N	Mean	S.d.
Death penalty:			
1b. A death sentence should always be commuted to life sentence	1211	3.45	1.31
1a. The death penalty should strictly be prohibited because of the right to life	1211	3.33	1.39
Euthanasia:			
2b. Euthanasia should be permitted in case of unbearable and irreversible suffering	1201	3.28	1.27
2c. Euthanasia should be permitted in the case of unbearable and irreversible suffering, if palliative care is exhausted	1199	3.23	1.28
2a. Euthanasia should be prohibited in all circumstances	1202	3.09	1.37
Abortion:			
3e. Abortion should be permitted when the woman's own health is seriously endangered by the pregnancy	1205	3.59	1.32
3d. Abortion should be permitted when there is a strong chance of serious defect in the baby	1212	3.54	1.35
3a. Abortion should be prohibited in all circumstances because it terminates beginning human life	1211	3.36	1.54
3b. Abortion should be permitted in case of rape	1213	3.32	1.44
3c. Abortion should be permitted in case of incest	1209	3.17	1.38
3g. Abortion should be permitted when the woman cannot afford any more children psychologically	1213	3.12	1.36
3f. Abortion should be permitted when the woman cannot afford any more children economically	1212	2.87	1.42

Scale: 1 = strong disagreement; 2 = disagreement; 3 = uncertain; 4 = agreement; 5 = strong agreement

experience and spiritual experience, and (b) experience of the divine intervention. Religious practices refer to (a) frequency of prayer, (b) participation in religious services, and (c) influence of religion on daily life. The *contextual religious attitudes* focus on: (a) functions of religion related to public opinion, national culture, prophetic voice, spiritual service, and cultural conformity, (b) exclusivist and pluralist approach to other religions, and (c) trust in one's own religion and in others' religions.

The independent variable *value of human dignity* is operationalized in terms of dignity based on merit, moral behaviour, and intrinsic worth. All these independent variables – except for those consisting of single items – are results of rigorous procedure of factor analyses. However, we do not report on the factor analyses of the independent variables, except for two cases where new configurations emerge (see footnote 11 and 12).

Four sets of background variables have been taken into account. *Personal profile* focuses on sex and age. Variables related to *religious socialization* include: (a) belief of parents and of the best friend, (b) expectation of parents that their children adopt their faith, and (c) interaction with adherents of other religious traditions. The *psychological traits* that could be significant to the religion and human rights rapport are: (a) right-wing authoritarianism, (b) social dominance orientation, and (c) empathy. The *socio-political* traits that could be significant are: (a) intercultural openness, and (b) political orientation (measured on a 1–10 scale from left to right). Generally, the students' responses have been measured on a Likert scale 1–5, from disagreement to agreement with 'uncertain' as the middle point.

Methods of Analysis

With the view to understanding the general tendency of the respondents to (non-) disposability of life, descriptive analysis, namely, the calculation of mean and standard deviation for each of the twelve items, was done. In the factor analysis undertaken subsequently, the factors representing death penalty, euthanasia and abortion were found to be rather reliable.

To test for significant differences between Christian, Muslim and Hindu students in their agreement with (non-)disposal of life by death penalty, euthanasia and abortion, Scheffé's test was employed.

Simple correlation analysis evinced some moderately strong correlations (Pearson's *r*) between independent variables (personal and contextual religious attitudes, and value of human dignity) and agreement with (non-)disposability of life. Similarly, correlation analysis was done between personal and religious characteristics, and psychological and socio-political traits on the one hand and agreement with (non-)disposability of life on the other.

Finally, with the view to identifying the predictors of agreement with (non-)disposal of life by death penalty, euthanasia and abortion, regression analysis was undertaken with independent and background variables. We included those independent variables which showed at least moderate correlation ($r \geq 15$) with the specific variant of (non-)disposal of life in at least one of the three religious groups.

Results of Empirical Analysis

Taking up the five research questions in order, we shall analyse the respondents' understanding of the (non-)disposability of life by examining the data at item level and at scale level, followed by correlation and regression analyses of emerging factors with independent and background variables.

Research Question 1 What tendency emerges among the college students regarding non-disposal of life by death penalty and disposal of life by euthanasia and abortion?

Descriptive statistics (mean and standard deviation) on item level brings to light the general tendency among our respondents. Concerning death penalty (Table 2.1), our respondents tend to agree with the view that death sentence should always be commuted to life sentence (item 1b: mean 3.45), and that death penalty should be strictly prohibited because of the right to life (item 1a: mean 3.33). Overall, our respondents tend to be opposed to death penalty; that is, they tend to be unfavourable to the disposal of life by death penalty. Although these two items have limited correlation, we decided to keep them together in one scale for theoretical reasons. We may term this scale as 'non-disposal of life by death penalty' (α .29; number of cases 1207).

As for euthanasia (Table 2.1), our respondents manifest positive uncertainty (in descending order) with regard to two items: that it should be permitted in case of unbearable and irreversible suffering (item 2b: mean 3.28), and particularly if palliative care is exhausted (item 2c: 3.23). Concerning the third item, that euthanasia should be prohibited in all circumstances, they tend to be rather uncertain (item 2a: 3.09). It may be noted that item 2a is formulated as resisting euthanasia, while items 2b and 2c are formulated as supporting euthanasia. Overall, our students show some positive uncertainty concerning disposal of life by euthanasia. Factor analysis (PAF, oblimin rotation) with the three items results in the removal of item 2a because of low factor loading and low communality. Evidently, item 2a was reverse coded before factor analysis. It results in a two item scale (2b and 2c) labelled 'disposal of life by euthanasia' (α .51; number of cases 1215).

The final section of Table 2.1 presents the mean scores (in the descending order) of the seven items representing the question of abortion. The respondents manifest clear agreement to abortion when the woman's health is seriously endangered (item 3e: mean 3.59) and when there is strong chance of serious defect in the baby (item 3d: mean 3.54). With regard to three other items, they manifest tendencies toward agreement: abortion should be permitted in the case of rape (item 3b: mean 3.32), incest (item 3c: mean 3.17), and when the woman cannot afford any more children psychologically (item 3g: mean 3.12). Only in the case of abortion when the woman cannot afford any more children economically, the respondents show some tendency toward disagreement (item 3f: mean 2.87). Considering the (weak) agreement with disposal of life in the other items, we note a certain anomaly in the agreement with item 3a which is formulated as an appeal against abortion (mean 3.36): "Abortion should be prohibited in all circumstances because it terminates beginning human life". In the factor analysis, the score of this item was obviously inverted; however, it had to be eliminated because of very low commonality.

As shown in Table 2.2, factor analysis of items referring to abortion (PAF, oblimin rotation) reveals two rather reliable factors explaining a total variance of 33.40%. Factor 1 representing 'disposal of life by abortion for victim's sake' includes pregnancy resulting from rape or incest and the woman's or child's health hazard. The reliability is rather high (Cronbach's alpha .63). Factor 2 representing psycho-economic reasons for abortion is also reliable with high Cronbach's alpha (α .57), and it may be termed as 'disposal of life by abortion for psycho-economic reasons'.

Table 2.2 Factor analysis (PAF) of right to life: abortion

	F1	F2	h^2
3c. Abortion should be permitted in case of incest	**.61**	.10	.33
3b. Abortion should be permitted in case of rape	**.59**	−.00	.35
3d. Abortion should be permitted when there is a strong chance of serious defect in the baby	**.51**	−.09	.32
3e. Abortion should be permitted when the woman's own health is seriously endangered by the pregnancy	**.34**	−.18	.21
3g. Abortion should be permitted when the woman cannot afford any more children psychologically	.00	**−.71**	.51
3f. Abortion should be permitted when the woman cannot afford any more children economically	.02	**−.54**	.30
Cronbach's Alpha	.63	.57	
Number of valid cases	1196	1210	

Eigenvalue = 1; Oblimin rotation with Kaiser Normalization; extraction: PAF; Total explained variance 33.40%; N = 1215
F1 = Disposal of life by abortion for victim's sake; F2 = Disposal of life by abortion for psycho-economic reasons

Research Question 2 Are there significant differences between Christian, Muslim and Hindu students regarding non-disposal of life by death penalty and disposal of life by euthanasia and abortion?

As shown in Table 2.3, Scheffé's test reveals that there are few significant differences between the three religious groups concerning their attitude towards (non-) disposal of life.

As regards non-disposal of life by death penalty, the mean scores show that Christian (3.40), Muslim (3.39) and Hindu students (3.37) tend to reject death penalty. Such a stand probably results from the global movement for abolition of death penalty, sustained also by the United Nations. It could also be the effect of the debate provoked by the execution of three criminals between 2012 and 2015 in India (see footnote 7).

With regard to disposal of life by euthanasia, Muslims students differ significantly from the other two groups, with Muslims (mean 3.09) showing the least agreement compared to Christian (3.36) and Hindu (3.30) respondents. Students' positive uncertainty is understandable, since euthanasia here stands for active euthanasia at an extreme stage when suffering is unbearable and irreversible with palliative care exhausted. It appears that students are caught between non-disposability of life, which has deep roots in the religious traditions, and patient's extreme state of agony. As we mentioned above, euthanasia seems to be an emerging area of ethical debate in India, where 'voluntary suicide' by renouncing nutrition is deemed a religious act particularly among Jains. Besides, there are indications that intentional and involuntary euthanasia of elderly (geronticide) is also quietly being practiced in Tamil Nadu. Currently, human rights activists are beginning to challenge such practices. In our previous research among Higher Secondary Schools in Tamil Nadu (Van der Ven and Anthony 2008), the Christian, Muslim and Hindu students tended

Table 2.3 Levels of agreement (mean and standard deviation) with regard to death penalty, euthanasia, and abortion for Christian, Muslim and Hindu students and comparison of means between religious groups of respondents (Scheffé's test for Euthanasia: F-value 7.24; p < .001; and for Abortion psycho-economic: F-value: 16.69; p < .000)

	Groups	N	mean	S.d.	Muslim	Hindu
Non-disposal of life by **Death penalty**	Christian	407	3.40	1.11		
	Muslim	408	3.39	0.93		
	Hindu	400	3.37	1.06		
Disposal of life by **Euthanasia**	Christian	404	3.36	1.16	*	
	Muslim	402	3.09	0.91		
	Hindu	397	3.30	1.03	*	
Disposal of life by **Abortion: Victim's sake**	Christian	407	3.30	1.01		
	Muslim	408	3.45	0.87		
	Hindu	400	3.46	0.90		
Disposal of life by **Abortion: psycho-economic reasons**	Christian	407	2.73	1.22	*	*
	Muslim	408	3.09	1.09		
	Hindu	400	3.17	1.13		

Scale: 1 = strong disagreement; 2 = disagreement; 3 = uncertain; 4 = agreement; 5 = strong agreement
Intergroup difference are significant at p < .05 (*)

to accept that politicians should decide about euthanasia irrespective of religious leaders' affirmations. Probably, they view euthanasia as a social issue, which concerns the political sphere rather than the religious. Still, we find in our dataset that Muslims (3.29) show the lowest agreement compared to Christians (3.34) and Hindus (3.37) with the following item: "Politicians may consult religious leaders about any ethical problem in the country, but should decide independently by themselves".

As for abortion when the mother is a victim of sexual abuse or her health and/or that of the foetus is in danger, the three religious groups manifest agreement tendency with regard to the disposal of life. Scheffé's analysis reveals that the differences in mean scores between Christian (3.30), Muslim (3.45) and Hindu students (3.46) in levels of acceptance are not statistically significant. Incest, rape and health hazards of the mother and foetus are held as sufficient reasons for abortion. This observation obviously does not dispense with the necessity of ethical reflection on these cases.

As regards abortion for psycho-economic reasons, we find that Christian students (mean 2.73) show some tendency toward disagreement and differ significantly from Muslims (mean 3.09) and Hindus (mean 3.17) who manifest positive uncertainty. While Christians tend to disagree, Muslims and Hindus tend to doubt whether the psychological and economic situation of the mother can justify the disposal of life. It is quite possible that the pregnant women in Muslim and Hindu families are more conditioned by psychological and economic pressures.

Research Question 3 Which personal and contextual religious attitudes and valuing of human dignity relate to non-disposal of life by death penalty and disposal of life by euthanasia and abortion?

What then is the social location of (non-)disposability of life? Examining the (non-)disposal of life by death penalty, euthanasia and abortion, for each of the three religious groups, we find a number of significant correlations with independent variables (Table 2.4). We shall comment on the moderately strong correlations for each religious group starting with death penalty and euthanasia, followed by abortion for victim's sake and abortion for psycho-economic reasons.

Non-disposal of Life by Death Penalty

Considering the *personal religious attitudes* (Table 2.4), in the case of Christians we find that opposition to death penalty is moderately associated with belief in both personal God (r .15) and non-personal God (r .15), whereas in the case of Muslims there is moderately strong association with belief in non-personal God (r .15). It is interesting to note that non-disposal of life by death penalty manifests moderately strong association with religious experience[13] in the case of all the three groups: Christians (r .17), Muslims (r .15) and Hindus (r .22). Among Muslims, religion's influence on daily life (r .16) also has moderately strong association with opposition to death penalty. Overall, belief in God and religious experience imply greater opposition to death penalty.

When analysing the *contextual religious attitudes* we note an interesting pattern of correlations particularly among Muslims and Hindus. In the first place, the integral transformative function of religion[14] has moderately strong association with non-disposal of life by death penalty in the case of Christians (r .18) and Muslims (r .22); instead, the cultural conformity function has moderately strong association in the case of Muslims (r .15) and Hindus (r .14). It is significant that the transforma-

[13] Factor analysis brought the two items representing spiritual experience (i.e., people say that they have had an experience of profound inner peace; that they have had an experience of oneness with all things) and the two representing faith experience (i.e., people say that their faith has often helped them not to lose courage in particular situations; that their religion gives them a certainty in life that they otherwise would not have) into one meaningful and reliable factor 'religious experience' (Cronbach's alpha .72).

[14] In the factor analysis of eight items, factors representing two meaningful functions of religion emerged: integral transformative function (Cronbach's alpha .69) and cultural conformity function (Cronbach's alpha .39). The integral transformative function included six items: religions should try to influence public opinion on social problems; should publicly stand up for the underclass; should take a joint responsibility with the State for the national culture; should take public responsibility for the societal development; should take responsibility for their members' spiritual growth; and should create places for deep spiritual experiences. The cultural conformity function instead included two items: religions should always keep up with current social trends; and should go along with changing ideas in society.

Table 2.4 Correlations (Pearson's r, 2-tailed) between dependent variables of death penalty, euthanasia and abortion and independent variables

	Non-disposal of life by **Death Penalty**			Disposal of life by **Euthanasia**			Disposal of life by **Abortion: Victim's sake**			Disposal of life by **Abortion: psycho-economic reasons**		
	Chris	Mus	Hind	Chris	Mus	Hind	Chris	Mus	Hind	Chris	Mus	Hind
Personal religious attitudes												
Belief in personal god	**.15****	.08	.08	.06	.11*	.11*	–.09	**.19****	.05	–.08	–.02	–.03
Belief in non-personal god	**.15****	**.15****	.10	.07	.12*	.11*	–.05	**.34****	.09	–.10*	–.02	–.02
Belief in the existence of god	.11*	.02	.07	.01	.12*	.09	.02	**.25****	.07	.05	.10	.01
Critical approach to religious belief	.04	.08	.04	.09	.11*	.06	.08	.00	–.07	.08	.13*	–.06
Religious experiences	**.17****	**.15****	**.22****	.02	**.20****	.00	.06	**.33****	.10	–.07	**.15****	.01
Experience of divine intervention	.08	.09	.02	.07	.13**	.07	–.02	**.21****	–.03	–.03	.01	.00
Frequency of prayer	–.03	–.02	–.06	–.03	.09	.02	–.01	.14**	–.02	.00	–.04	–.08
Participation in religious service	–.04	.01	.00	.00	.01	–.05	–.11*	.07	–.09	–.04	.14**	–.07
Influence on daily life	–.02	**.16****	.05	.02	.09	**.15****	.07	**.17****	–.09	.05	.01	.11*
Contextual religious attitudes												
Integral transformative function	**.18****	**.22****	.12*	.11*	.11*	.00	.12*	**.17****	**.26****	–.07	–.05	.02
Cultural conformity function	.08	**.15****	**.14****	.01	.11*	.05	.03	–.05	**.16****	.07	.02	.01
Exclusivist approach to religions	.02	.14**	.12*	.14*	.09	–.07	.14**	**.28****	.03	.02	.04	–.05
Pluralist approach to religions	.11*	**.15****	.11*	**.18****	.08	–.02	**.22****	.12*	**.16****	.02	.08	.00
Trust in one's religion	.07	.03	**.16****	.03	.02	.11*	–.00	**.15****	.07	–.10	.06	–.10*
Trust in others' religion	.04	–.00	**.16****	.00	–.05	.03	.00	–.13*	.02	–.03	.05	–.05
Value of human dignity												
Dignity of merit	.06	**.18****	**.15****	**.21****	.14**	**.19****	.03	**.15****	.09	–.00	**.15****	.02
Moral dignity	**.16****	**.19****	.03	.13*	.11**	.12*	.01	**.22****	**.16****	–.00	.07	–.03
Intrinsic human dignity	.10*	**.16****	.12*	.04	**.17****	–.07	.01	**.20****	.06	–.01	.04	.02

Correlations are significant at $p < .00$ (**) or $p < .05$ (*) level (2-tailed)
Interpretation of correlations: weak ($r < .15$), moderately strong ($.15 \le r < .30$) and strong ($r \ge .30$) associations

tive function of religion supports the non-disposal of life by death penalty among Christians and Muslims, and the need to keep abreast of cultural development makes Muslims and Hindus open to the abolition of death penalty.

Among Muslims, both exclusive (r. 14) and pluralist approaches (r. 15) to religion have moderately strong association with non-disposal of life by death penalty, whereas among Hindus, trust in one's religion (r .16) and in others' religion (r. 16) has moderately strong correlation. In the case of Muslims and Hindus, esteem for one's religion and openness to other's religion support the non-disposal life by death penalty.

As for *value of human dignity*, viewing it on the basis of merit has moderately strong association with opposition to death penalty in the case of Muslims (r .18) and Hindus (r .15). Whereas in the case of Christians (r .16) and Muslims (r .19), human dignity as based on the moral dignity of persons has moderately strong correlations with resistance to death penalty. Furthermore, among Muslims considering human dignity as intrinsic to human beings has moderately strong association (r .16) with the non-disposal of life by death penalty. We find that the value of human dignity has a particular significance for Muslims in their opposition to death penalty.

Disposal of Life by Euthanasia

As shown in Table 2.4, *personal religious attitudes* seem relevant particularly for Muslims, although most correlation are weak (i.e. $r < .15$). Religious experiences (r .20) have moderately strong association with disposal of life by euthanasia. In the case of Hindus, religion's influence on daily life (.15) seems to be supportive of euthanasia. The favourableness of Muslims to euthanasia on the basis of their personal religious attitudes seems rather puzzling, as we expected religious beliefs to be opposed to euthanasia.

Among the *contextual religious attitudes*, pluralist approach to religion (.18) manifests a moderately strong association with openness to euthanasia in the case of Christians

As for the *value of human dignity*, viewing it as depending on merit has moderately strong association with openness to euthanasia in the case of all the three religious groups: Christians (r .21), Muslims (r .14) and Hindus (r .19). Among Muslims, intrinsic human dignity (r .17) also manifests moderately strong association with disposal of life by euthanasia. The positive relation between human dignity and openness to euthanasia is probably mediated by compassion felt for the extreme suffering of fellow human beings.

Disposal of Life by Abortion for Victim's Sake

As shown in Table 2.4, only in the case of Muslims, *personal religious attitudes* have strong or moderately strong association with abortion for victim's sake: belief in personal God (r .19), belief in non-personal God (r .34), belief in the existence of God (r .25), religious experience (r .33), experience of divine intervention (r .21), frequency of prayer (r .14), and religion's influence on daily life (r .17). Personal religious attitude seem particularly relevant to Muslims' favourableness to disposal of life by abortion for the sake of the affected mother and/or foetus.

Among the *contextual religious attitudes*, the integral transformative function of religion in the case of Muslims (r .17) and Hindus (r .26), and the cultural transformative function in the case of Hindus (r .16) manifest moderately strong association with disposal of life by abortion for victim's sake.

As regards approaches to religions, the exclusivist approach manifests moderately strong correlation with abortion for the sake of the victim in the case of Christians (r .14) and Muslims (r .28), so also the pluralist approach among Christians (r .22) and Hindus (r .16). Besides, for Muslims, trust in one's own religion (r .15) has moderately strong association with disposal of life by abortion for victim's sake.

As for the *value of human dignity*, among Muslims viewing it as based on merit (r .15), on moral conduct (r. 22) and as intrinsic to the person (r. 20) manifest moderately strong association with disposal of life by abortion for the sake of the victim. In the case of Hindus, we find that moral dignity (r. 16) has moderately strong correlation with abortion for victim's sake. Again, the understanding of human dignity emerges as particularly significant to Muslims in their openness to abortion for the sake of the affected mother and/or the unborn child.

Disposal of Life by Abortion for Psycho-Economic Reasons

Only in the case of Muslims we find three variables, namely, religious experience (r .15), participation in religious service (r .14), and the value of human dignity as based on merit (r .15), have moderately strong association with disposal of life by abortion for psycho-economic reasons. Overall, personal and contextual attitudes and the value of human dignity do not seem to be much relevant to the question of abortion for psycho-economic reasons.

Research Question 4 Which personal and religious characteristics and psychological and socio-political traits relate to non-disposal of life by death penalty and disposal of life by euthanasia and abortion?

Examining the (non-)disposal of life by death penalty, euthanasia and abortion, for each of the three religious groups, we find some significant correlations with background variables (Table 2.5). We shall comment on the moderately strong

Table 2.5 Correlations (Pearson's r, 2-tailed) between dependent variables of death penalty, euthanasia and abortion and background variables

	Non-disposal of life by			Disposal of life by			Disposal of life by			Disposal of life by		
	Death Penalty			**Euthanasia**			**Abortion: Victim's sake**			**Abortion: psycho-economic reasons**		
	Chris	Mus	Hind	Chris	Mus	Hind	Chris	Mus	Hind	Chris	Mus	Hind
Personal characteristics												
Age	–.02	–.10*	–.04	.00	–.02	.07	–.03	**–.20****	–.12*	.01	–.10*	.02
Sex (female 1; male 2)	–.09	**–.16****	**–.14****	.02	–.02	–.03	.07	**–.18****	–.02	–.10	.02	.06
Father's education	**–.15****	–.05	.02	.00	–.08	.02	–.06	–.03	.14**	–.13*	–.04	.05
Mother's education	–.14**	–.03	–.10*	–.02	–.04	.00	–.01	–.01	.05	–.09	–.03	–.01
Religious characteristics												
Father's belief and faith	–.02	.12*	.02	.00	–.02	.01	–.03	.13**	.09	–.06	.04	.06
Mother's belief and faith	.05	.07	.05	.04	–.08	–.05	–.04	**.15****	.10	–.10	–.00	–.00
Best friend's belief and faith	.02	.09	.04	.05	–.10	.03	–.03	.13*	.00	–.12*	–.09	.03
Father's expectation to adopt his faith	–.01	.05	.02	.00	–.07	.02	–.01	.13*	.08	.00	–.00	–.03
Mother's expectation to adopt her faith	–.05	.07	.02	–.02	–.08	–.02	–.06	.13*	.04	–.05	.01	.01
Interreligious contact	.03	**.19****	–.04	.08	.12*	.01	.05	.10*	.08	–.11*	.12*	–.03
Psychological traits												
Right-wing authoritarianism	.01	.09	.14**	.02	.09	.03	–.05	**.16****	.11*	.02	–.03	–.02
Social dominance orientation	–.01	.07	**.16****	.11*	.03	.04	–.07	.01	.02	**.16****	**.25****	.08
Empathy	.12*	.12*	.12*	–.04	.01	.01	–.05	**.19****	.12*	–.01	.02	.02
Socio-political traits												
Interculturalism	.04	.12*	.05	.05	.13*	–.10*	.00	.07	.01	**–.20****	–.02	–.05
Political orientation	–.07	.06	.03	.04	–.07	–.01	**.17****	.06	.13*	–.04	.12*	–.01

Correlations are significant at $p < .00$ (**) or $p < .05$ (*) level (2-tailed)

Interpretation of correlations: weak ($r < .15$), moderately strong ($.15 \le r < .30$) and strong ($r \ge .30$) associations correlations for each religious group, starting with death penalty and euthanasia, followed by abortion for victim's sake and abortion for psycho-economic reasons.

Non-disposal of Life by Death Penalty

Examining the *personal characteristics*, we find that women among Muslims (r – .16) and Hindus (r – .14), and Christians whose father (r – .15) and mother (r – .14) have had lower level of education are more opposed to death penalty. It is significant that Muslim and Hindu women and Christians with less educated parents disagree more with death penalty.

As shown in Table 2.5, among *religious characteristics,* only interreligious contact (r .19) has moderately strong association with non-disposal of life by death penalty in the case of Muslims. It is significant that interreligious contact favours opposition to death penalty among Muslims.

When it comes to *psychological traits*, we find that Hindus approving right-wing authoritarianism (r .14) and social dominance orientation (r .16) have moderately strong association with non-disposal of life by death penalty. It appears that Hindus' opposition to death penalty is enforced from above by elite.

Disposal of Life by Euthanasia

In the case of euthanasia, personal characteristics seem to be rather irrelevant. However, examining the *religious characteristics* and *socio-political traits*, we find that Muslims open to interreligious contact (r .12) and to interculturalism (r .13) are moderately open to disposal of life by euthanasia. In their case, interaction with other religions and cultures seems to make them favourable to euthanasia.

When it comes to *psychological traits*, Christians approving social dominance orientation (r .11) manifest weak favourableness to permitting euthanasia.

Disposal of Life by Abortion for Victim's Sake

Examining the *personal characteristics* (Table 2.5), we find that among Muslims, younger respondents (r – .20) and women (r – .18), and among Hindus those whose father has had higher levels of education (r .14), are moderately open to abortion for victim's sake. In a traditional Islamic context, it is understandable that women and younger persons should be favourable to abortion.

Among the *religious characteristics*, in the case of Muslims, father's (r .13) and mother's (r .15) belief and faith, and to some extent their expectation that their faith be adopted by their children (r .13), have moderate association with disposal of life by abortion for victim's sake. This is true also in the case of best friend's belief and faith (r .13). Religious socialization seems to favour openness to abortion for the sake of the affected mother and/or the unborn child.

Among the *psychological traits*, in the case of Muslims, right-wing authoritarianism (r .16) and empathy (r .19) have moderately strong association with disposal of life by abortion for the sake of the victim. It is understandable that empathy should favour abortion on account of the condition of the mother and/or of the unborn child.

Among the *socio-political traits*, in the case of Christians, right-wing political orientation (r .17) has moderately strong association with disposal of life by abortion for victim's sake. This may result from the fact that the victim's honour may be a vital aspect for the right-wing currents.

Disposal of Life by Abortion for Psycho-Economic Reasons

Examining the background variables, we find that social dominance orientation in the case of Christians (r .16) and Muslims (r .25) has moderately strong influence on permitting abortion for psycho-economic reasons. Social dominance is a psychological attitude that prevalently has an economic basis, and so it is understandable that it should be favourable to abortion for psycho-economic reasons. Instead, in the case of Christians, interculturalism (r − .20) has moderately strong negative influence on allowing abortion for psycho-economic reasons. In other words, openness to diverse cultural values makes Christians unfavourable to the disposal of life by abortion for psycho-economic reasons.

Research Question 5 Which independent variables (personal and contextual religious attitudes and valuing of human dignity) and background variables (personal and religious characteristics, and psychological and socio-political traits) emerge as predictors of non-disposal of life by death penalty and disposal of life by euthanasia and abortion?

Table 2.6 presents the regression analyses of right to (dispose of) life among Christian, Muslim and Hindu respondents separately. We shall first present the impact of the variables on non-disposal of life by death penalty and then on the disposal of life by euthanasia and by abortion for victim's sake and for psycho-economic reasons.

Table 2.6 Regression analyses of death penalty, euthanasia and abortion for Christian, Muslim and Hindu students separately

	Non-disposal of life by			Disposal of life by			Disposal of life by			Disposal of life by		
	Death Penalty			**Euthanasia**			**Abortion: Victim's sake**			**Abortion: psycho-economic reasons**		
	Chris	Mus	Hind	Chris	Mus	Hind	Chris	Mus	Hind	Chris	Mus	Hind
Personal religious attitudes												
Belief in personal god	–	–	–	–	–	–	–.22**	–.22**	–.06	–	–	–
Belief in non-personal god	–	–	–	–	–	–	.05	.37**	.06	–	–	–
Religious experiences	–	–	–	.00	.12*	–.02	.05	.24**	.02			
Experience of divine intervention	–	–	–	–	–	–	–	–	–	–	–	–
Influence on daily life	–.07	.11*	.05	–	–	–	–	–	–	–	–	–
Contextual religious attitudes												
Integral transformative function	.22**	.17*	.12*	–	–	–	.04	–.12*	.23**	–	–	–
Exclusivist approach to religions	–	–	–	–	–	–	.06	.22*	–.09	–	–	–
Pluralist approach to religions				.15**	.03	.00	.22**	–.01	.13*	–	–	–
Value of human dignity												
Dignity of merit	–	–	–	.20*	.07	.19**	–	–	–	–	–	–
Moral dignity	–	–	–	–	–	–	–.00	.17**	.13*	–	–	–
Intrinsic human dignity	–	–	–	.00	.13*	–.04	–	–	–	–	–	–
Personal characteristics												
Age	–	–	–	–	–	–	–.04	–.09	–.13*	–	–	–
Sex (female 1; male 2)	–.11*	–.11*	–.12*	–	–	–	–	–	–	–	–	–
Father's education	–.14*	–.05	.02	–	–	–	–	–	–	–	–	–
Religious characteristics												
Interreligious contact	.00	.16**	–.03	–	–	–	–	–	–	–	–	–

Psychological traits												
Social dominance orientation	–.02	.11*	.15**	–	–	–	–	–	–	.14*	.25**	.07
Socio-political traits												
Interculturalism	–	–	–	–	–	–	–	–	–	–.18**	–.02	–.04
Political orientation	–	–	–	–	–	–	.14*	.00	.12*	–	–	–
R^2	6%	12%	6%	7%	6%	4%	11%	27%	14%	6%	6%	1%
Adj R^2	6%	10%	4%	6%	5%	3%	8%	25%	12%	5%	5%	0%

Standardised regression coefficients (β) are significant at $p < .00$ (**) or $p < .05$ (*) level

Non-disposal of Life by Death Penalty

For Christian respondents, the regression analysis of death penalty explains only a small amount of the variance (R^2 6%; Adj. R^2 6%). Among the independent variables, only the integral transformative function of religion (β .22) is a rather strong predictor of opposition to death penalty. It is significant that for Christian students, religion with its transformative function in the society can promote the non-disposability of life. Interestingly, while examining the background variables, we find that women (β − .11) and those whose fathers have had lower level of education (β − .14) tend to oppose death penalty.

For Muslim respondents, the regression analysis of death penalty explains about one tenth of the variance (R^2 12%; Adj. R^2 10%). Among the religious attitudes, we find that influence of religion on daily life (β .11) and the integral transformative function of religion (β .17) are rather moderate predictors of opposition to death penalty. The influence of religion on the society and on the day-to-day life of Muslims seem to reduce support for capital punishment. Among the background variables, women (β − .11) manifest surprisingly more opposition to death penalty than men and we observe that interreligious contact (β .16) and social dominance orientation (β .11) induce opposition to death penalty.

For Hindu respondents, only a small amount of variance of opposition to death penalty is explained (R^2 6%; Adj. R^2 4%). Among religious attitudes, the transformative function of religion (β .12) emerges as a moderate predictor of opposition to death penalty. As for Christians and Muslims, so too for Hindus the transformative function of religion can promote the non-disposability of life. Among the background variables, as in the case of Christians and Muslims, Hindu women (β − .12) are more opposed to death penalty, while social dominance orientation (β .15) emerges as rather moderate predictor of opposition to death penalty.

Overall, among religious factors the transformative function of religion seems to have some impact on the non-disposal of life in the case of all the three religious groups. We also find that women among the three religious groups are more opposed to death penalty. The impact of social dominance orientation in the case of Muslims and Hindus may refer to higher sensitivity of dominant elite groups with regard to death penalty. The explained variance suggest that the impact of these and other variables are stronger in the case of Muslims than that of Christians and Hindus.

Disposal of Life by Euthanasia

As can be seen in Table 2.6, in the case of Christian respondents, the variance of relative support of euthanasia is only explained for a small part by the four predictors we included (R^2 7%; Adj. R^2 6%). A pluralist approach to religion (β .15) and dignity of merit (β .20) induce support for euthanasia in case of unbearable and irreversible suffering.

For Muslim respondents, variance in support for euthanasia is somewhat explained by religious experiences (β .12) and intrinsic human dignity (β .13). Here too, the explanatory model is weak (R^2 6%; Adj. R^2 5%). It is surprising and rather puzzling that religious experience and the recognition of the intrinsic human dignity can favour the disposal of life by euthanasia. But as we mentioned earlier, among religious groups such as Jains, 'euthanasia' may even mark a profound religious experience.

For Hindu respondents, regression analysis of euthanasia explains only a small amount of the variance (R^2 4%; Adj. R^2 3%). Only the variable of human dignity as acknowledged by others (β .19) has some predictive value for permitting euthanasia.

As may be noted in the case of the religious groups, the recognition of patient's dignity by others (for Christians and Hindus) and moral dignity (for Muslims) can favour disposal of life by euthanasia, most likely based on compassionate grounds. However, the explained variance suggest that religious and human dignity variables – mentioned above – have only little impact.

Disposal of Life by Abortion for Victim's Sake

As shown in Table 2.6, for Christian respondents, the regression analysis of abortion for victim's sake explains about one-tenth of the variance (R^2 11%; Adj. R^2 8%). Among the personal religious attitudes, belief in personal God (β − .22) has a rather strong negative impact. It means that belief in personal God reduces support for abortion even when the mother is a victim of rape or incest, and there is serious health problems to her and/or to the unborn child. Among the contextual religious attitudes, the pluralist approach to religions (β .22) positively contributes to greater openness to abortion for victim's sake. Among socio-political traits, the right-wing political orientation (β .14) moderately predicts favourableness to abortion for the sake of the victim.

For Muslims, the regression analysis of abortion for victim's sake explains about one-fourth of the variance (R^2 27%; Adj. R^2 25%). Among personal religious attitudes, belief in personal God (β − .22) has a rather strong negative impact on abortion for the sake of the victim, whereas belief in non-personal God (β .37) and religious experience (β .24) strongly predict favourableness to abortion. It is noteworthy that belief in God as personal or as non-personal has respectively unfavourable or favourable impact on the disposal of life by abortion. Among the contextual religious attitudes, the integral transformative function of religion has a negative moderate impact (β − .12), whereas the exclusivist approach to religion (β .22) moderately predicts allowing abortion for victim's sake. It means that among Muslims, the transformative function of religion can challenge abortion for the sake of the victim, instead affirming the exclusive truth of their religion can favour disposal of life. Considering human dignity as depending on the moral behaviour of persons (β .17) also predicts more favourableness to abortion for the sake of victim.

For Hindu respondents, the regression analysis of abortion for victim's sake explains about one-eighth of the variance (R^2 14%; Adj. R^2 12%). Among contextual religious attitudes, the integral transformative function of religion (β .23) has moderately strong impact on permitting abortion for victim's sake. Besides, the pluralist approach to religion (β .13) and viewing human dignity as moral dignity (β .13) emerge as weak predictors of abortion for the sake of victim. Unlike the case of Muslims, for Hindus the transformative function of religion and the pluralist approach to religion can favour the disposal of life by abortion, particularly when the moral dignity of the victim is involved.

Overall, we find that quite a number of religious factors induce or reduce agreement with abortion for victim's sake. There are more relevant religious variables in the case of Muslims than that of Christians and Hindus. We shall discuss the significance of some of these variables in the next section.

Disposal of Life by Abortion for Psycho-Economic Reasons

As shown in Table 2.6, for Christian respondents, the regression analysis of abortion for psycho-economic reasons explains only a small amount of the variance (R^2 6%; Adj. R^2 5%). We find that only two background variables have some impact. The psychological trait of social dominance orientation (β .14) supports more abortion for psycho-economic reasons. Instead, interculturalism (β − .18) reduces agreement with abortion for psycho-economic reasons. The acceptance that there is status difference between people in society seems to favour disposal of life for psycho-economic reasons, while interaction with other cultures, perhaps of Western Christianity – since Indian Muslims and Hindus show significantly more support for abortion for psycho-economic reasons – makes Christian students less favourable to disposal of life for psycho-economic reasons.

For Muslim respondents, the regression analysis of abortion for psycho-economic reasons explains only a small amount of the variance (R^2 6%; Adj. R^2 5%). Only the psychological trait of social dominance orientation (β .25) rather strongly predicts openness to abortion for psycho-economic reasons. In this regard, none of the variables seem to have any impact on the Hindu students' stand.

It is significant that for all the three religious groups none of the variables of religious attitudes and value of human dignity have impact on the disposal of life by abortion for psycho-economic reasons. It appears that among minority Islamic and Christian communities, openness to social dominance, namely, the acceptance of status difference between people in society, seems to favour abortion for psycho-economic reasons.

Discussion and Conclusion

In this final section, we make a summary of the findings and comment on the salient ones, keeping in focus the objective of our research, namely, to verify the impact of religion on the (non-)disposability of life. We shall do so by dealing with the opposing trends of (non-)disposal of life by death penalty, euthanasia and abortion, and the impact of religious attitudes and understanding of human dignity on them.

Tendency with Regard to (Non-)Disposal of Life

Our intention was to probe the attitudes of students with regard to the (non-)disposal of life in the cases of death penalty, euthanasia and abortion. Factor analyses brought to light four rather reliable factors: non-disposal of life by death penalty and disposal of life by euthanasia, abortion for victim's sake, and abortion for psycho-economic reasons.

Non-disposal of life by death penalty refers to the case of a convicted criminal. The dispute is whether sentence should reach the level capital punishment. The statements to which our respondents indicated their level of agreement were the following: death penalty should strictly be prohibited; and life sentence should always be commuted to life imprisonment. The scores therefore express the extent of opposition to capital punishment. We found that students are opposed to death penalty and that there is no significant differences between Christian, Muslim and Hindu respondents. It is noteworthy that the students tend to affirm the non-disposability of life even though death penalty continues to be practiced – although very rarely – in India. Such pro-life stand of the students may be attributed to the current international debate on abolishing death penalty.

Disposal of life by euthanasia refers to the termination of life in a situation of severe illness and suffering. The question posed to the students was whether a person could be permitted to end his/her life when suffering becomes unbearable and irreversible, and when palliative care is exhausted. In their response, the students show positive uncertainty to disposal of life in such instances, with Muslims showing significantly less agreement than Christians and Hindus. The question of (active) euthanasia seems to raise a tension between the value of life in itself and the quality of life amidst agonizing suffering. The students' doubtful stand with slight agreement to voluntary euthanasia seems to indicate that pro-choice trend is gaining ground in a context where actively ending one's life is not so rare.

Disposal of life by abortion refers to the elimination of new life in the mother's womb. Factor analysis revealed that students distinguish between abortion for victim's sake and abortion for psycho-economic reasons. The results indicate that the students tend to approve abortion for victim's sake without significant differences between Christians, Muslims and Hindus. It means that students tend to be pro-choice in circumstances of rape and incest, when the mother's life is at risk, or when the foetus is affected by a serious defect. Instead, in the case of abortion for psycho-economic reasons, we find that Christian students tend to disagree, whereas Muslim and Hindu students show positive uncertainty. In the opinion of the students, particularly of Christians, abortion for psycho-economic reasons does not seem justifiable.

Overall, the three religious groups manifest opposition to disposal of life by death penalty, and an uncertain openness to disposal of life by euthanasia and abortion for victim's sake. The high standard distributions (i.e. around a full point on a five point Likert scale) indicate that there are quite differing opinions among the members of each religious group. Nevertheless, there are also some significant differences between the religious groups. As regards euthanasia, the tendency among Christians and Hindus is openness to disposal of life, while Muslims tend to be uncertain. As regards abortion for psycho-economic reasons, the tendency among Christians is non-disposal of life and the tendency among Hindus and Muslims is an uncertain openness to disposal of life. However, as a whole the intergroup differences are rather small against the range of 5-point Likert scales.

A normative appraisal of these findings implies an assessment of the right to (dispose of) life in the extreme circumstances we operationalized. The right to (dispose of) life, brings up, among others, the following fundamental questions regarding the quality of life and its ownership: When is life truly human? Who owns human life? Concerning the first question, some would hold that human life is not a question of degree. There is life or there isn't; and if there is life, it deserves absolute respect and protection independently of any further qualification. Among religious traditions, the Catholic Church – as expounded earlier – affirms that absolute respect for human life from conception to its natural end is the condition for the exercise of all other human rights (Pontifical Council for Justice and Peace 2004, n. 155). Deliberate acts that do not have absolute respect for life are simply wrong, as respect for human life is founded on the dignity proper to the person embedded in the natural law (VS n. 50). That there are no degrees in life, and that quality levels are irrelevant to absolute respect for it, also mean that life begins from the moment the ovum is fertilized (CDF 1974, n. 12) and only ends when the spiritual soul separates from the body at the moment of death (CCC n. 366). Such a vision implies that persistent vegetative state and even 'cerebral death' do not represent absence of life. For, "body and soul are inseparable: in the person, in the willing agent and in the deliberate act, they stand or fall together" (VS n. 40). Nevertheless, there are other currents, which hold that human life may be so compromised by the privation of dignity that it may not be considered human anymore. In other words, unbearable suffering with no prospect of improvement may lead a patient or the onlookers to judge such a life as not worth living. Something similar is at stake when a woman's pregnancy results from rape or incest, or when medical professionals anticipate serious danger to the mother and/or serious defect in the foetus. Such considerations have led several countries (see above) to vote abortion and euthanasia laws, and to maintain or resume death penalty.

This brings up the related question: Who owns life as to be able to dispose of it? Is human life owned by the individual? Does society at large have a say on the ownership of life? Does the ownership of life go beyond human beings' capacities as to make people ultimately unqualified judge over life, even one's own? Again, answers to these may take opposing directions. Appealing to the categorical principles of Immanuel Kant (1785) some affirm the absolute non-disposability of life, while others highlighting the principle of John Stuart Mill (1859; 1998) that each person is autonomous or free to pursue his or her own good without depriving or impeding others to do the same, express the concern for quality of life.

In an attempt to reconcile absolute respect for life[15] on the one hand, and concern for the quality of life on the other, as well as to reconcile heteronomy on the one hand, and autonomy concerning life-ownership on the other, Schotsmans speaks of double decentring. The first decentring refers to the fundamental inaccessibility of the human self to itself, and the second concerns the intersubjectivity of the human person. According to Schotsmans (2008, 278f), "they give emphasis to the importance of an axiological interpretation of the notions 'sanctity' and 'quality' of life. The first mode of *decentrement* can bring us toward a more moderate view of autonomy and self-determination; a view that makes clear the ontological fact that the human self is not as transparent and controllable, as advocates of autonomy suggest. [...] Another ground to reject the overpowering role some want autonomy to have, has its origin in Judeo-Christianity. From this perspective, autonomy is a necessary condition for the fulfilment of creatural solidarity. [...] The human autonomy we are required to respect, therefore, cannot result in an absolute dominion over one's own life but has to be understood in a broader framework that acknowledges both the intrapersonal limits and interpersonal boundaries to the sanctity of autonomy". In this vein, Joas (2013, 91) underscores that a certain 'moral decentring' is inherent to the Christian faith that calls us to view the world from the perspective of others, particularly the "least of my brothers" (Mt 25:40). It means that 'transcendent' and 'relational' anthropology (Joas 2013, 154), namely, person as constituted by relation (Bordignon 2013), can help overcome the contrast between 'absolute respect for life itself' and 'quality of life', between 'heteronomy' and 'autonomy', between pro-life and pro-choice concerns.

Impact of Religious Variables on (Non-)Disposal of Life

The primary aim of this study is to examine the role that religions play in this all-important area of right to life. As shown in the conceptual model, personal religious attitudes (comprising beliefs, experiences and practices) and contextual religious

[15] Drutchas (1998) is of the opinion that for a fruitful dialogue in a pluralistic world the notion of 'respect for human life' is more useful than the principle of 'sanctity or sacredness of life'.

attitudes (such as functions of religion, approach to religions, and trust in religion) were hypothesized to induce or reduce the (non-)disposal of life.

Examining the religious variables that could contribute to the *non-disposal of life by death penalty*, we find that a number of them have moderately strong association in one or more of the religious traditions: belief in (non-)personal God, religious experience, religion's influence on daily life, integral transformative and cultural conformity functions, pluralist approach to religion, and trust in one's own and others' religion. However, it is the integral transformative function of religion that moderately predicts objection to death penalty in the case of all the three religions. This is significant, given that religious traditions in the past have supported death penalty for various reasons. Among Muslims, we find that religion's influence on daily life and interreligious contact have some predictive value in opposing death penalty.

A number of religious variables have moderately strong association with *disposal of life by euthanasia* particularly among Muslims. Belief in a (non-)personal God, religious experience, experience of divine intervention, frequency of prayer, integrative transformative function of religion and exclusivist approach to religion, are positively related with Muslims' openness to euthanasia. However, only religious experience induces to some extent Muslim students' approval of euthanasia in the regression analysis. Among Christian students, pluralist approach to religions has some influence on their openness to euthanasia.

When it comes to the *disposal of life by abortion for victim's sake*, we find rather strong influence of religious attitudes among Muslims: belief in a personal God and integral transformative function of religion reduce agreement with abortion for victim's sake; while belief in a non-personal God, religious experiences and exclusivist approach to religions induce agreement with abortion for victim's sake. It is interesting to note the bivalent roles, namely pro-choice and pro-life, that religious attitudes play concerning abortion. While belief in a personal God reduces agreement with abortion even in extreme conditions of the mother, the exclusivist approach to religion favours agreement with abortion; the latter may have some affinity to honour killing practiced in some Islamic contexts. Among Christian students, we find a similar pattern of influence. Belief in a personal God reduces agreement with abortion for the sake of the affected mother and/or unborn child, while the pluralist approach to religion predicts approval of abortion for victim's sake. In the case of Hindus, the integral transformative function and pluralist approach to religion have some influence in the direction of more favourableness to disposal of life by abortion for victim's sake.

When it comes to *disposal of life by abortion for psycho-economic reasons*, the results show that none of the religious attitudes has predictable value in the case of the three religious groups.

Overall, we find that diverse elements of the religious attitudes contribute to the (non-)disposability of life. Belief in a personal God is a predictor that reduces agreement with abortion for the victim's sake among Christians and Muslims. Belief in a non-personal God induces agreement with abortion for the victim's sake only among Muslims. Integral transformative function predicts disapproval of death penalty in the case of all the three religious groups but also predicts Hindus' approval of abortion for victim's sake. Pluralist approach to religion induces agreement with euthanasia and abortion for victim's sake particularly in the case of Christians. Overall, the total explained variance is not very high (with exception for abortion for victim's sake among Muslims and, to a lesser degree, among Hindus). This means that religion does not play a pivotal role in the ethical judgements concerning the right to life among our respondents. However, when religion plays a role, its influence depends on the specific issues at stake, and on the specific religious traditions. Religion therefore can offer some basis for both 'sacrality' and 'quality' of life discourse supporting pro-life and pro-choice currents respectively. The influences of religious factors need to be further explored with regard to specific bioethical cases, against the background of the specific teaching of the religions involved, but also against the background of the social and economic circumstances in which the adherents of these religious traditions live.

Impact of the Value of Human Dignity on (Non-)Disposal of Life

From a secular perspective, the value of human dignity is considered in three different ways, namely, as value acknowledged by others (dignity of merit), as depending on the moral behaviour of the person (moral dignity), and as proper to the person (intrinsic human dignity).

These three understanding of human dignity seem to favour the *non-disposal of life by death penalty* among Muslims. It means that in their case, overall value of human dignity has some influence on the opposition to death penalty. In the case of Christian students, acknowledging the moral dignity of the person favours non-disposability of life by death penalty. It means that Christians particularly oppose death penalty for reasons of moral behaviour. Among Hindus, the dignity of merit acknowledged by others tends to disapprove death penalty. However, in none of the cases value of human dignity has predictive value.

With regard to *disposal of life by euthanasia*, the three notions of human dignity have some association in the case of one or the other group. For our respondents, human dignity seems to be associated with dignity of the dying person rather than with safeguarding life in contexts of unbearable suffering. The regression analyses show that more agreement with euthanasia is explained by dignity of merit among Christians and Hindus, and intrinsic human dignity among Muslims.

Concerning *abortion for victim's sake*, more agreement can be found among Muslims who score higher on our human dignity items, and this is true for moral dignity in the case of Hindus. The respect for human dignity takes here the form of compassion for the mother who is a victim of rape or incest, or whose life is threatened because of pregnancy or whose unborn child is marked by serious defect. In the regression analysis, moral dignity induces support for abortion for victim's sake among Muslims and Hindus.

As for *disposal of life by abortion for psycho-economic reasons*, we find that only the dignity of merit has some association with Muslims' approval of abortion for such reasons, but it does not emerge as a predictor.

Overall, we find relatively strong associations between the three understanding of human dignity and the right (to dispose) of life. However, they do not emerge as strong predictors. Only the support for euthanasia and abortion for victim's sake is somewhat explained by dignity of merit and moral dignity respectively. In these cases, the results are also somewhat surprising: if the value of human dignity plays a role, it contributes to more agreement with euthanasia and abortion for victim's sake. For our respondents, dignity is associated with the dignity of dying person who suffers and asks to end his or her life, or with the dignity of the woman who is pregnant because of rape or incest, whose health may be endangered or the foetus she carries may present a serious defect. Only in the case of Muslims, intrinsic human dignity has some impact on the disposal of life by euthanasia. Surprisingly, the notion of intrinsic human dignity, clearly affirmed in the Catholic tradition (VS n. 50; Brugger 2014, 28), does not seem to influence Christians' stand on life issues.

In conclusion, based on the findings and the foregoing discussion we may underscore the following. Firstly, it is seemingly difficult to overcome the differences between approaches that stress 'autonomy in life-ownership' and 'quality of life' on the one hand, and on the other, those that stress the limits of autonomous decisions and 'absolute respect for life'. This suggests the need for integrating the 'sanctity' and 'quality' of life discourses by recognizing the fundamental inaccessibility of human self to itself and the constitutive intersubjectivity of the human person (Schotsmans 2008). Secondly, from a Christian perspective, by rearticulating the understanding of human being as created in the image of God and as children of God, we may rediscover the significance of the human soul and the gift of life. "The notion that we are made in the image of God becomes the idea of a divine essence in every human being: his immortal soul. The notion that we are the children of God becomes the idea that our life is a gift, which like every gift incurs certain obligation that limit our disposal over ourselves" (Joas 2013, 143; cf. 140–172). Thirdly, in a multicultural and multi-religious world marked also by secularization, intercultural and interreligious interaction can give rise to the value generation and generalization that the right to life represents. And lastly, we may conclude with Joas (2013, 190f) that a combination three things are necessary to fully realize the sacralisation of the person with respect to human rights in general and right to life in particular: sensitivity to experiences of injustice and violence, rational justification of the claim of universality of crucial values, and codifications of rights through national and international institutions. Our findings suggest that religions – together with secular currents – can play an important role in promoting values and practices by providing the meta-ethical basis for 'sacredness of/respect for' and 'quality of' human life.

References

Abou Ed Fadl, K. (2004). The death penalty, mercy, and Islam: A call for retrospection. In E. C. Owens, J. D. Carlson, & E. P. Elshtain (Eds.), *Religion and the death penalty. A call for reckoning* (pp. 73–105). Grand Rapids/Cambridge: William B. Eerdmans Publishing Company.

Anthony, F.-V. (2013). Public significance of religion with regard to socioeconomic rights in the multireligious context of Tamil Nadu, India. In J. A. Van der Ven & H.-G. Ziebertz (Eds.), *Human rights and the impact of religion* (pp. 205–244). Leiden/Boston: Brill.

Anthony, F.-V. (2017). Anthropological annotations on human dignity from an Asian perspective. In K. Krämer & K. Vellguth (Eds.), *Human dignity. Discourses on universality and inalienability* (One World Theology, Vol. 8, pp. 27–35). Quezon City: Claretian Communications Foundations Inc.

Anthony, F.-V., & Sterkens, C. (2016). The impact of religion on civil human rights: An empirical-theological study. In C. F. Wolfteich & E. Dillen (Eds.), *Catholic approaches in practical theology. International and interdisciplinary perspectives* (Bibliotheca Ephemeridum Theologicarum Lovaniensium 286, pp. 225–252). Leuven: Peeters Publishers.

Anthony F.-V. & Sterkens C. (2018). Extending political rights to immigrants and refugees. Empirical study among Christian, Muslim and Hindu students in the context of Indian secularism and the politics of inclusion. In C. Sterkens & H.-G. Ziebertz (Eds.), *Political and judicial rights through the prism of religious belief* (Religion and Human Rights 3, pp. 145–183) Berlin: Springer.

Aquinas, T. (1485). *Summa Theologiae.* (trans. by Fathers of the English Dominican Province, 1947–48). New York: Benzinger Bros.

Austriaco, N. P. G. (2007). Assisted suicide. In M. L. Coulter, S. M. Krason, et al. (Eds.), *Encyclopedia of Catholic social thought, social science, and social policy* (pp. 58–59). Lanham/Toronto/Plymouth: The Scarecrow Press.

Berkowitz, B. A. (2006). *Execution and invention. Death penalty discourse in early rabbinic and Christian cultures*. New York/Oxford: Oxford University Press.

Bordignon, B. (2013). *Persona è relazione*. Soveria Mannelli: Rubbettino.

Brennan, W. C. (2007a). Culture of death. In M. L. Coulter, S. M. Krason, et al. (Eds.), *Encyclopedia of Catholic social thought, social science, and social policy* (pp. 268–269). Lanham/Toronto/Plymouth: The Scarecrow Press.

Brennan, W. C. (2007b). Culture of life. In M. L. Coulter, S. M. Krason, et al. (Eds.), *Encyclopedia of Catholic social thought, social science, and social policy* (p. 269). Lanham/Toronto/Plymouth: The Scarecrow Press.

Brown, A. (2007). Christianity. In P. Morgan & C. A. Lawton (Eds.), *Ethical issues in six religious traditions* (2nd ed., pp. 216–282). Edinburgh: Edinburgh University Press.

Brugger, E. C. (2007). Evangelium Vitae. In M. L. Coulter, S. M. Krason, et al. (Eds.), *Encyclopedia of Catholic social thought, social science, and social policy* (pp. 380–381). Lanham/Toronto/Plymouth: The Scarecrow Press.

Brugger, E. C. (2014). *Capital punishment and Roman Catholic moral tradition* (2nd ed.). Notre Dame/Indiana: University of Notre Dame Press.

Catechism of the Catholic Church. (2003). Città del Vaticano: Libreria Editrice Vaticana.

Congregation for the Doctrine of the Faith. (1974). Declaration on procured abortion *Quaestio de abortu procurato. Acta Apostolicae Sedis, 66*(1974–12), 730–747.

Congregation for the Doctrine of the Faith. (1980). Declaration on Euthanasia *Iura et Bona. Acta Apostolicae Sedis, 72*(1980–4), 542–552.

Congregation for the Doctrine of the Faith. (1988). Instruction on respect for human life in its origin and on the dignity of procreation *Donum Vitae. Acta Apostolicae Sedis, 80*(1988–1), 70–102.

Congregation for the Doctrine of the Faith. (2009). Clarification on procured abortion. *L'Osservatore Romano,* 149(11 July 2009–157), 7.

Crawford, S. C. (1996). The Hindu perspective. In L. Steffen (Ed.), *Abortion. A reader* (pp. 226–242). Cleveland: The Pilgrim Press.
Denzinger, H. (1995). *Enchiridion Symbolorum, definitionum et declarationum de rebus fidei et morum.* (Edizione bilingue a cura di Hünermann P.) Bologna: Edizioni Dehoniane.
Dowbiggin, I. (2005). *A concise history of euthanasia. Life, death, God and medicine*. Lanham/Oxford: Rowman & Littlefield Publishers.
Drutchas, G. (1998). *Is life sacred?* Cleveland: The Pilgrim Press.
Engineer, A. A. (2012). *Islam. Restructuring theology*. New Delhi: Vitasta.
Francis. (2013). *Evangelii Gaudium.* Apostolic exhortation. *Acta Apostolicae Sedis, 105*(2013–12), 1019–1137.
Francis. (2016). *Misericordia et misera.* Apostolic letter. Città del Vaticano: Libreria Editrice Vaticana.
Fuchs, J. (1985). Christian faith and the disposing of human life. *Theological Studies, 46*(1985), 664–684.
George, R. R., Devendraakhilesh, P., Iahmo, T. T., Varun, R. P., Moray, K. V., Cherian, A. G., & Prasad, J. H. (2017). Why are abortions the answer? Prevalence, knowledge and attitude towards induced abortions among women attending a secondary level health care facility in Tamil Nadu, Southern India. *International Journal of Community Medicine and Public Health, 4*(2), 532–536. https://doi.org/10.18203/2394-6040.ijcmph20170286.
Guilmoto, C. Z. (2007). Characteristics of sex-ratio imbalance in India, and future scenarios. *Fourth Asia Pacific Conference on reproductive and sexual health and rights.* Paris: LPDED/IRD.
Hostetler, J., & Coulter, M. L. (2007). Abortion. In M. L. Coulter, S. M. Krason, et al. (Eds.), *Encyclopedia of Catholic social thought, social science, and social policy* (pp. 1–2). Lanham/Toronto/Plymouth: The Scarecrow Press.
Hvistendahl, M. (2011). *Unnatural selection. Choosing boys over girls, and the consequences of a world full of men*. New York: Public Affairs.
Joas, H. (2013). *The sacredness of the person. A new genealogy of human rights*. Washington: Georgetown University Press.
John Paul, II. (1993). *Veritatis Splendor*. Encyclical letter. *Acta Apostolicae Sedis, 85*(1993–12), 1133–1228.
John Paul, II. (1995). *Evangelium Vitae*. Encyclical letter. *Acta Apostolicae Sedis, 87*(1995–5), 401–522.
Kelly, D. F. (1979). *The emergence of Roman Catholic medical ethics in North America: An historical, methodological, bibliographical study*. New York: Mellen.
Kelly, D. F. (1994). Social implications of euthanasia. In J. A. Dwyer (Ed.), *The new dictionary of Catholic social thought* (pp. 348–353). Collegeville: Liturgical Press.
Leaman, O. (2002). *An introduction to classical Islamic philosophy* (2nd ed.). Cambridge: Cambridge University Press.
Magni, S. F. (2011). *Bioetica*. Roma: Carocci editore.
Mauceri, J. M. (2007). Euthanasia. In M. L. Coulter, S. M. Krason, et al. (Eds.), *Encyclopedia of Catholic social thought, social science, and social policy* (pp. 377–378). Lanham/Toronto/Plymouth: The Scarecrow Press.
McCarthy, J. J. (1994). Capital punishment. In J. A. Dwyer (Ed.), *The new dictionary of Catholic social thought* (pp. 109–111). Collegeville: Liturgical Press.
McCartney, J. J. (1994). Social implications of abortion. In J. A. Dwyer (Ed.), *The new dictionary of Catholic social thought* (pp. 5–9). Collegeville: Liturgical Press.
Menski, W. (2007). Hinduism. In P. Morgan & C. A. Lawton (Eds.), *Ethical issues in six religious traditions* (2nd ed., pp. 1–60). Edinburgh: Edinburgh University Press.
Merlo, P. (2009). *Fondamenti & temi di bioetica*. Roma: LAS.
Mill, J. S. (1859;1998). *On liberty and other essays*. Oxford: Oxford University Press.
Nanji, A. (2007). Islam. In P. Morgan & C. A. Lawton (Eds.), *Ethical issues in six religious traditions* (2nd ed., pp. 283–342). Edinburgh: Edinburgh University Press.

Panikkar, R. (1993). *The cosmotheandric experience. Emerging religious consciousness*. Maryknoll: Orbis Books.
Pius, XI. (1930). *Casti connubii*. Encyclical letter. *Acta Apostolicae Sedis, 22*(1930–13), 539–595.
Pius, XII. (1952). Discours aux participants au Congrès International d'Histopathologie du Système Nerveux. *Acta Apostolicae Sedis, 44*(1952–15), 779–789.
Pius, XII. (1957). Address to anaesthesiologists and intensive care specialists. *Acta Apostolicae Sedis, 49*(1957–16), 1027–1033.
Pontifical Council for Justice and Peace. (2004). *Compendium of the social doctrine of the church*. Città del Vaticano: Libreria Editrice Vaticana.
Rahman, F. (1996). Birth and abortion in Islam. In L. Steffen (Ed.), *Abortion. A reader* (pp. 202–209). Cleveland: The Pilgrim Press.
Sammak, M. (2017). Human dignity – An Islamic perspective. In K. Krämer & K. Vellguth (Eds.), *Human dignity. Discourses on universality and inalienability* (One World Theology, Vol. 8, pp. 233–247). Quezon City: Claretian Communications Foundations Inc.
Schotsmans, P. (2008). Sanctity of autonomy in contemporary bioethics: A matter of concern for theological bioethics. In P. Gnanapragasam & S. Fiorenza (Eds.), *Negotiating borders. Theological explorations in the global era*. Essays in honour of Prof. Felix Wilfred. Delhi: ISPCK. pp. 259–280.
Second Vatican Council. (1966). *Gaudium et Spes*. Pastoral constitution on the Church in the modern world. *Acta Apostolicae Sedis, 58*(1966–15), 1025–1120.
Sedgh, G., [World Health Organization], et al. (2016). Abortion incidence between 1990 and 2014: Global, regional, and subregional levels and trends. *Lancet, 388*, 258–267. https://doi.org/10.1016/S0140-6736(16)30380-4.
Sontheimer, G. (1993). Etica: Induismo. In H. Waldenfels (Ed.), *Nuovo Dizionario delle Religioni* (pp. 326–328). Cinisello Balsamo: Edizioni San Paolo.
Tamanti, R. (2004). *La pena di morte. Tra etica della vita e autorità dello stato*. Assisi: Cittadella Editrice.
Van der Ven, J., & Anthony, F.-V. (2008). Impact of religion on social integration from an empirical civil rights perspective. *Salesianum, 70*(2008–2, 3), 317–338, 463–489.
Van der Ven, J., Dreyer, J. S., & Pieterse, H. J. C. (2004). *Is there a God of human rights? The complex relationship between human rights and religion: A South African case*. Brill: Leiden/Boston.
World Health Organization [WHO]. (2011). *Unsafe abortion: global and regional estimates of the incidence of unsafe abortion and associated mortality in 2008* (6th ed.). Geneva: WHO.
Wujastyk, D. (2012). Bioethics. In K. A. Jacobsen et al. (Eds.), *Brill's encyclopedia of Hinduism. Vol. IV. Historical perspectives. Poets, teachers, and saints. Relation to other religions and traditions. Hinduism and contemporary issues* (pp. 633–640). Leiden/Boston: Brill.

Chapter 3
The Right to Life Among Chilean Youth

Jorge Manzi and Joaquin Silva

Religion is deeply connected to the understanding of life and death and, as a result, the right to life is central to most religions. This chapter addresses the role that religion and religiosity play in the protection of the right to life, as they are compromised in situations related to abortion, euthanasia and the death penalty. This chapter analyses this topic in the context of Chile, a traditionally Roman Catholic country that has been experiencing important changes in religious affiliation (especially an increase of Evangelicals and people who are non-religious). The first section of this study outlines the religious and legal context for the practice of abortion, euthanasia and the death penalty in Chile. Then it presents the conceptual framework for the analysis which includes social identities (religious and political) as well as psycho-social and attitudinal variables. The following empirical study is based on a survey study conducted in a sample of slightly over 1300 secondary school students in Chile. The main results indicate that the three expressions of the limitation of the right to life are only moderately correlated, indicating that rights to life are not highly integrated and consistent in the perception of our participants. Moreover, the three manifestations analyzed presented different relationships with religion and religiosity: abortion is the only case where religious affiliation plays a clear and significant role (with higher support for the rights to life among Catholics and Evangelicals). However, religiosity shows a consistent correlation with rights to life in the three contexts: more religious youngsters show increased opposition to abortion, euthanasia and the death penalty.

Religions express in an exceptional way the mystery of what life represents to human beings. Through a variety of actions, teachings, rituals and symbols, religious

The authors express their gratitude for the collaboration of Ignacio Silva in presenting the legal context of these rights in Chile.

J. Manzi (✉) · J. Silva
Pontificia Universidad Católica de Chile, Santiago, Chile
e-mail: jmanzi@uc.cl; jsilvas@uc.cl

H.-G. Ziebertz, F. Zaccaria (eds.), *Euthanasia, Abortion, Death Penalty and Religion – The Right to Life and its Limitations*, Religion and Human Rights 4, https://doi.org/10.1007/978-3-319-98773-6_3

groups propose an answer to the question of the origin and purpose of life. Natural life cycles are celebrated; community relationships supporting social coexistence are created; vital links which help intertwine past, present and future are established. Thus, religion contributes to the realization that human life is inextricably linked to life in the entire cosmos; it provides meaning to the profound question underlying the experience of the flimsiness of life, and the closeness and presence of death.

In religion, the question about life is not limited to a single aspect, but is all-encompassing: from the individual to the community; from past through present to future; from matter to spirit. Religion acknowledges the totality of life in relation to God. It not only provides a cognitive explanation, but also mainly celebrates and appreciates life as a gift to be shared, in the knowledge that what is referred to as "God" is a mystery that surpasses all human understanding and action.

The link between religion and life, however, is conditioned both by religious traditions and by the cultural contexts in which religions have taken shape throughout the centuries. Within a single tradition, such as the Judeo-Christian one, the same understanding and fostering of life has been a source of strong dispute on such questions as the origin of life, the value of life in the event of conflict and war, its inalienable dignity regarding foreign nationals, the sick, the poor, indigenous peoples, women or, simply, when the others think and believe differently from oneself.

Given the cultural roots underlying the link between religion and life, it becomes necessary to find out how the value of life is understood at a given time. The youth are privileged witnesses of an epoch. For one thing, they express and reproduce the culture they have received, but they also re-create it into new ways of thinking, feeling, and acting. In the young, perhaps more than in other age groups, past, present and future meet as a present-day realization, not only of what has been but also of what will be. Inquiring into how the youth value life and how life relates to their religiosity entails exploring the link between religion and life in privileged witnesses and active participants of the culture in question.

Life is threatened in many ways—by war, violence, terrorism, illness, poverty, old age; as well as by harassment, loneliness, and exclusion. Human efforts are not merely geared to survival, but also to living with ever-higher standards of economic, social and environmental well-being. However, the question about well-being is still associated with the more biological, fundamental meaning of life. Biological existence is the basic material condition for any psychological, spiritual or moral well-being. In this connection, it is worth inquiring into abortion, euthanasia, and the death penalty as practices—though not the only ones—that equate to a denial of the right to life. Determining whether or not these practices have a religious foundation among the youth will also be relevant for a better understanding of the link between religion and the right to life.

Before delving deeper into these questions, we will present the legal background and the doctrine of the Catholic Church that define core aspects of the regulatory framework governing current practices concerning abortion, euthanasia and the death penalty. This legal and doctrinal context will help us to better frame the question about how the right to life is asserted among Chilean youth.

This study consists of the following sections: (1) a description of the legal and doctrinal context for the practice of abortion, euthanasia and the death penalty; (2) the research questions; (3) the conceptual model that will be used for answering the aforementioned questions; (4) the method to be used; (5) the main findings of the study; and (6) our conclusions.

Legal and Doctrinal Context

It may be generally stated that the right to life is the first of the constitutional rights acknowledged by the Political Constitution of the Republic of Chile:

> *The Constitution guarantees that every individual has:*
>
> 1. *1st: The right to life and to physical and psychical integrity. The law protects the life of those about to be born. The death penalty may only be instituted for a crime dealt with by a law approved by a qualified quorum. All unlawful coercion is prohibited.*

In the Chilean legal system, the protection of the right to life is also endorsed by the different international treaties ratified by Chile and currently in force (Aldunate 2010).

On the other hand, a recent Pastoral Letter from the Chilean Bishops explains the basic understanding of the right to life that prevails in the Catholic sphere:

> *From the perspective of anthropology and Christian ethics, the Catholic Church acknowledges, respects and promotes the value of life and dignity of the human person as an essential and inalienable foundation of life in society. This right to life admits no discrimination* (Comité Permanente de la Conferencia Episcopal de Chile 2017b, p. 74).

The above assertion of the right to life is not only postulated with respect to being born (abortion) and dying (euthanasia), but it also reaches across every dimension of personal and social life:

> *Our option for the individual and his/her right to life*–the Chilean Bishops' statement continues—*implies seeking as a society, in addition to prohibiting all unfair attack against innocent life, for all individuals and their families with no exclusion, living conditions in accordance with their personal dignity: adequate housing, quality of education, a decent job, fair remuneration, a life-sustaining environment, comprehensive development opportunities, etc. By respecting and fostering human life in all its dimensions, we reject abortion, as well as the disgraceful and unfair social inequalities, usury, euthanasia, and arbitrary discrimination* (Comité Permanente de la Conferencia Episcopal de Chile 2017b, p. n°74).

On the other hand, and as a further general reference, in the Evangelic world some bishops and ministers have also declared that:

> *In defense of Christian values and principles, the church will actively participate in the issues of national interest by absolutely rejecting the agenda of legislative proposals being advanced in the Congress of the Nation, which directly threaten our principles and values based on respect for God and human life, integrity and commitment to the underprivileged, consolidation of marriage and the family, the basic unit of Chilean society. These values have governed our society from even before the dawn of our Republic* (Por un Chile para Cristo 2017, p. n°2).

It might be inferred from the above definitions that a life-enhancing legal and doctrinal-religious framework is in place in Chile since it acknowledges life as an inalienable right, both in its biological and its social, cultural and economic dimensions. As we shall see below, however, these very legal and religious definitions have been strongly challenged in the last few years, especially in the case of abortion.

Abortion

Abortion regulation in Chile has gone through different stages. Historically, abortion was included in the Criminal Code of 1875, where it was regulated and criminalized.

Later, in 1931, the passing of the Health Code set forth the possibility of performing therapeutic abortion. Then in 1968, the Health Code was rewritten, whereby therapeutic abortion remained legal but with less stringent requirements. This regulation remained in full force and effect until 1989, when a complete ban on abortion was instituted.

Until relatively recently, the regulation and criminalization of abortion was set forth in the Constitution, as well as in the Criminal, Civil and Health Codes. As stated in a report from the Chilean National Congress Library, "the current regulatory framework is clear in specifying the protection of life for those about to be born, and sanctions the interruption of pregnancy and all those involved in the deed" (Biblioteca Congreso Nacional 2015).

However, the above described legislative status underwent a significant modification with the enactment of the Law that *decriminalizes the voluntary termination of pregnancy on three grounds*. After intense legislative debate which had a far-reaching impact on public opinion, the proposed bill was passed in August 2017.

This legislative proposal modified the Health Code, the Criminal Code and the Criminal-procedure Code to enable abortion on three specific grounds as provided for through a modification of the Health Code. This code stipulates that "*Through the woman's will, a physician is authorized to terminate pregnancy whenever:*

1. *The woman is in vital risk, now or in the future, so that termination of pregnancy may prevent putting her life in jeopardy.*
2. *The embryo or fetus suffers a congenital structural alteration or genetic disorder incompatible with life outside the womb.*
3. *Pregnancy is the result of rape, provided that not more than 12 weeks of pregnancy have elapsed. In case of 14-year-old minors, termination of pregnancy may be performed provided that more than 18 weeks of pregnancy have elapsed.*"

As in many places in the world, the discussion that has arisen about abortion has been far-reaching: legal aspects have been followed by ethical-value, biological, medical, psychological and educational considerations, as well as those of a religious nature. The relevance of this issue and the various aspects involved in it have engaged specialists and citizens in general, thus becoming one of the most debated topics in public opinion in the last few years. The debate has also been accompanied by different citizen demonstrations, and religious and cultural acts.

The Chilean Catholic bishops firmly opposed the proposed bill by rejecting the decriminalization of abortion, claiming that it offended social awareness and the common good:

> *From an anthropological stance that places the right to life and respect for the dignity of every individual of the human species in the center of social coexistence, [...] the proposed abortion bill offends social awareness and the common good [...] some human beings about to be born are left unprotected by the State in what concerns this basic, fundamental right* (Comité Permanente de la Conferencia Episcopal de Chile 2017a, p. 2).

It should be noted that the Catholic Church hierarchy's opposition to the proposed abortion legislation was concurrently expressed by ministers from the main Evangelical churches in Chile, who were also against said draft bill.

Notwithstanding the Christian churches' clear calls to reject the decriminalization of abortion, it should be pointed out that the opinion of the Chilean public—who largely define themselves as Catholic—has evolved to a position that agrees with the recently-passed legislation. For example, a July 2017 survey revealed that nearly 70% of Chileans were in favor of decriminalizing abortion on three grounds (CADEM 2017). The 2016 National Bicentennial Survey already showed that 57% of respondents considered that abortion should be decriminalized "when the mother's health is at risk due to pregnancy;" 55% "when the woman has become pregnant as a result of rape;" and 49% "when the child has a serious defect that renders it inviable; in other words, when it is certain to die before being born or shortly afterwards" (Universidad Católica and GfK Adimark 2016). The 2017 National Bicentennial Survey, which compares data of the last 10 years, confirms that while in 2006 only 6% of the population agreed with abortion "under any circumstance," in 2017 this number stands at 14%. Moreover, only 28% of those who declare themselves Catholic agree with the Church in that abortion should not be sought "under any circumstance." By comparison, 56% consider that abortion is a woman's right "only under certain circumstances," and even 12% of Catholics consider that a woman has the right to have an abortion "under any circumstance."

Death Penalty

The legal and doctrinal-religious situation of the death penalty differs widely from that of abortion. The death penalty was in place in our country since the Colonial times (Arancibia Floody et al. 2003). However, it has been formally included in the legal system since 1875. The statistics show that 58 people were sentenced to death while the death penalty was in effect. The last execution took place in 1985. On the international scene (Amnistía Internacional 2017), Chile is among the countries where capital punishment is practically abolished, unlike others in which it is totally abolished, or still others where legislation allowing the death penalty not only is in place, but is also enforced.

In Chile, capital punishment was outlawed in 2001. Yet despite of this, some regulations establishing capital punishment remain, such as the Code of Military Justice which establishes the death penalty as a penalty that applies exclusively to some military offenses.

Moreover, the Political Constitution left open the possibility of reinstating the death penalty by enacting new legislation (which has not happened). In this context, a legal debate has arisen over whether the death penalty has been definitely abolished in Chile. The legal doctrine that has prevailed is the one that confirms such abolishment, something which is also backed by the fact that Chile signed the American Convention on Human Rights that stipulates *"The death penalty shall not be reinstated in those States that have abolished it"* (Nogueira 2009). This legal position has been ratified by Parliament after the discussion of this issue.

Within the religious-doctrinal context, Pope John Paul II positively acknowledged the "new cultural sensitiveness" that expressed "an ever-growing aversion" to the death penalty in his Encyclical letter *Evangelium Vitae*, as present-day society relies on more effective instruments to fight against crime and violations of human dignity (Juan Pablo II 1995, p. 27). This positive valuation of the new social sensitivity is based on the biblical tradition itself, particularly on the Gospel of Jesus, who in the Sermon of the Mount encourages people "to respect the inviolable nature of physical life and personal integrity," and culminates in the positive commandment to love one's neighbor as oneself: "Thou shalt love your neighbor as yourself" (Luke 19: 18) (Juan Pablo II 1995, p. 40). The commandment "Thou shalt not kill,"John Paul II argues, "included and delved more deeply in the positive rule of loving one's neighbor, [and] is *confirmed by Lord Jesus in all its validity*" (Juan Pablo II 1995, p. 41), extends to caring for others in all situation, especially when life is threatened by segregation, prepotency, false religiosity, and any other ways of exclusion from the banquet of life.

As Pope Francis has acknowledged, this evangelical doctrine has not always been understood as such and there have been times in the history of humanity—also shared by the Church—when capital punishment was accepted as normal, as an effective solution, as a practice that promoted the primacy of goodness and of truth (Cf. Giudice 2011).

Euthanasia

There is only one law in Chile that makes explicit reference to euthanasia (Law 20,584, 2012). This law regulates the rights and obligations of individuals in the context of healthcare, and prohibits all forms of euthanasia. Article 14, for example, provides that *"Refusal of treatment may under no circumstances have the goal of artificially accelerating death, performing euthanasic practices or assisting suicide."* Article 16 adds that *"Any person who is informed that his/her health condition is terminal, has the right to grant or deny his/her permission to undergo any treatment whose effect is to artificially prolong life, while retaining ordinary life-sustaining measures. Refusal of treatment may under no circumstances imply the goal of artificially accelerating the death process*."

Within public debate, euthanasia became relevant in 2015, in relation to the case of a young girl suffering from cystic fibrosis who requested the President of the Republic to authorize the performance of euthanasia on her. As a result of this case, the discussion of a proposed bill seeking to allow euthanasia in Chile was renewed in Parliament. This proposal, however, was not approved in the Health Committee of the Senate. The discussion of this draft bill revealed that there is no sufficient political consensus on this issue.

As the *Evangelium Vitae* (No. 3) reminds us, the Catholic doctrine considers euthanasia as one of the practices that "are themselves libelous, degrade human civilization, dishonor perpetrators more than the victims and militate against the honor due to the Creator" (GS, No. 27). In a narrow sense, euthanasia is understood by the Church as "an action or an omission which of itself or by intention causes death, in order that all suffering may in this way be eliminated. Euthanasia's terms of reference, therefore, are to be found in the intention of the will and in the methods used" (Congregación para la Doctrina de la Fe 1980). However, the proportionality of the means shall be judged "by studying the type of treatment to be used, its degree of complexity or risk, its cost and the possibilities of using it, and comparing these elements against the result that can be expected, taking into account the state of the sick person and his or her physical and moral resources." (Congregación para la Doctrina de la Fe 1980).

Pope Benedict XVI placed this stance in a wider context, arguing that "a pro-euthanasia mindset is making inroads as an equally damaging assertion of control over life that under certain circumstances is deemed no longer worth living" (Benedicto XVI 2009, p. n°75). Pope Francis sees this pro-euthanasia sentiment as being reflected in the "abandonment of the elderly: How many times are old people just discarded, victims of an abandonment that is tantamount to a hidden euthanasia!" (Francisco 2014).

This Catholic doctrinal perspective is generally shared by the Evangelical churches, even though "until now in the Evangelical world as a whole, and particularly among Presbyterians, there have been no official ecclesial decisions concerning euthanasia. It may be said that the notion is generally rejected, although there is a certain willingness to explore its pros and cons. The general idea that prevails is that of respecting life and doing everything possible for the patient, given that as a believer, even at the end of life the Lord does not forsake His followers" (Clemente Vázquez 2005, p. 316).

As to public opinion, the issue of euthanasia has not been systematically investigated. Nevertheless, several recent surveys reveal a relatively ambivalent stance towards euthanasia. For example, a 2012 survey showed that 52% of the Chilean population thought it justifiable to end the life of the terminally ill under certain circumstances, while 45% considered such a measure not at all justifiable (Universidad Católica and Adimark 2012, p. 30). In a more recent survey 57% of respondents considered that "euthanasia should only be allowed in special cases" (Centro de Estudios Públicos 2017). In the latter survey 54% of Catholics hold the same opinion, while in the case of atheists and agnostics the figure goes up to 67%.

Design of the Study

Research Questions

The specific questions guiding our investigation, and the configuration of the data analysis model that follows, were:

(a) What is the support for the right to life among the Chilean youth?
(b) Is the support for the right to life related to the support for other human rights?
(c) Is the support for the right to life related to religious and political identity?
(d) Is the support for the right to life related to psycho-social variables (interpersonal and political attitudes)?

Conceptual Model

The conceptual model used (see Fig. 3.1) aims to analyze the relationship between the roles of religion among Chilean youth and their attitudes towards civil human rights. The model includes religious identity as a key social identity, but also political orientation as there has been a clear political divide between the right-wing and the left-wing concerning the protection of rights to life in Chile. Especially during the highly debated case of abortion, the right-wing opposed any legal initiatives that would legalize abortion under some circumstances. The model also considers attitudinal variables that are related to religious and political orientation. These include religiosity, social values, authoritarianism, social dominance and empathy. It is expected that these variables will be significantly related to the support of the right to life, in addition to the role of the aforementioned social identities. In particular, it is hypothesized that religiosity, conservation values (according to Schwartz 1992)

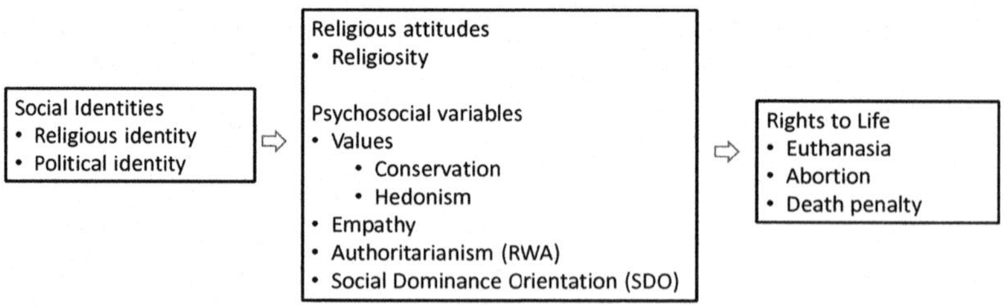

Fig. 3.1 Conceptual model

and empathy will be positively related to the protection of the right to life. Political attitudes such as authoritarianism and social dominance should be especially relevant in the case of the death penalty, predicting that people higher in those variables should provide more support to the use of this extreme punishment.

Methodology

Participants and Procedure

Our data was obtained from a sample of voluntary high school students (11th or 12th grade). The sample included seven middle-sized cities in Chile, selected because they all have a population between 100,000 and 200,000: Concepción, Copiapó, Iquique, La Serena, Melipilla, Quilpué, Talcahuano, Temuco and Villa Alemana. To increase the likelihood of reaching young people from different social contexts and from different religious affiliations, three to five schools were selected in each city, distributed as evenly as possible, according to type (municipal, charter or private school)[1] and religious denomination (Christian, Catholic, Protestant or non-religious), with a total of 36 institutions.

Participants answered a questionnaire in their classroom under the supervision of a person trained by the research team. A consent form had been signed by the principal of each school and by the legal guardians of the underage participants before the survey was conducted.

The total sample included 1307 young people. 62.2% were in 11th grade (the penultimate year of secondary education) and the remaining 37.7% in 12th grade (final year). Regarding the religious affiliation of the schools, 30.2% of participants attended a Catholic school, 23% attended a Protestant school, 5.5% attended a Christian-oriented school (without any specific denomination) and 38.1% attended a non-religious school.

The schools also varied according to their administrative type. Overall, 21.1% of the participants belonged to a municipal school, 55.8% belonged to a charter school and 20% attended a private school. Distribution by gender was even: 49.3% were females and 50.7% males. The average age of the participants was 16.6 years (DS = 0.83).

[1] Chile has a system of mixed provision of education, with three types of education establishment in primary and secondary education: municipal schools (financed in full by the State, and managed by municipalities); private charter schools (financed by the state, but privately managed); and privately-paid schools (financed in full by the families of students). The distribution of enrolment, at the national level, is around 38% in municipal schools, 54% in charter schools, and 8% in private schools.

Instruments

The questionnaire used in this study was developed as part of the international 'Religion and Human Rights' research project and translated and adapted to the national context by the Chilean research team. The survey was self-reported, and the majority of the items were answered by using a five-point Likert scale, from 1 (complete disagreement) to 5 (complete agreement). Among other items, the survey incorporated various measurements of the psychological, social, moral and religious aspects of the students.

1. Main dependent variables

This study concentrated on the three issues concerning the right to life included in the questionnaire, namely the death penalty, euthanasia and abortion). We factor-analyzed all items of this section of the questionnaire (12 in total), and found that a three factor solution best described the correlations among those items. As can be seen in Table 3.1, all items loaded in factor related to their content. Thus, we confirmed that the rights to life are not to be considered as a single dimension, but rather, as three separate constructs, related to the three contexts for those rights.

We then computed scores for the three dimensions and found that they are all reasonably reliable. Using Cronbach's alpha, it was observed that the Euthanasia scale (3 items) had $\alpha = .72$, the abortion scale (7 items) $\alpha = .86$ and the death penalty scale $\alpha = .63$. This last scale shows a lower internal consistency index, which is understandable given that it only contains two items.

Table 3.1 Rotated factor structure of rights to life

	Factor1	Factor2	Factor3
Euthanasia1		−.57	
Euthanasia2		.84	
Euthanasia3		.81	
Abortion1	−.59		
Abortion2	.68		
Abortion3	.69		
Abortion4	.68		
Abortion5	.67		
Abortion6	.79		
Abortion7	.81		
Death Penalty1			.82
Death Penalty2			.85

2. Independent variables

Religious affiliation. We considered the four dominant categories in the Chilean sample: Catholics (42.2%), Evangelicals[2] (23.1%), religious in a general sense (12%) and non-religious (22.8%).

Political self-identification. This is a 10-point scale anchored in both ends of the political spectrum: right-wing and left-wing.

Religiosity. This scale was computed by combining seven items. It resulted in a highly reliable scale ($\alpha = .87$).

Empathy. Four items were part of this scale, with a reliability of .61.

Right-wing authoritarianism was measured with four items, which were mildly consistent ($\alpha = .66$).

Social dominance orientation was also measured with four items, showing an internal consistency of .61.

Our analyses also included the support for other human rights. Table 3.2 indicates such rights, the number of items used to measure each one and the index of reliability observed. As Table 3.2 illustrates, one scale was highly consistent (women's rights), with an α index of .80, while three scales had a mild index (from .60 to .64). Finally, the scale of religious rights had the lowest internal consistency ($\alpha = .44$).

Results

In this section, we start with descriptive results before proceeding to test the hypotheses derived from the conceptual model previously presented.

Table 3.2 Descriptive information about scales that measure support for human rights

Scale	Items	Cronbach's alpha
Judicial rights	7	0.60
Political rights	6	0.64
Civil rights	4	0.63
Women's rights	3	0.80
Religious rights	3	0.44

[2] The category "Evangelicals" includes all denominations of the Reformed Church and their posterior referrals. In terms of the questionnaire, it combines the following categories: 'Lutheran', 'Pentecostal', 'Evangelical' and 'other Christian traditions'.

Table 3.3 Rights to life items and scale averages

Item/scale	Mean
Euth. should be permitted in the case of unbearable and irreversible suffering, if palliative care is exhausted. (rev)	3,84
Euth. should be permitted in the case of unbearable and irreversible suffering. (rev)	4,00
Euth. should be prohibited in all circumstances.	2,56
Euthanasia scale	**2,24**
Ab. should be permitted when the woman cannot afford any more children psychologically. (rev)	2,19
Ab. should be permitted when the woman cannot afford any more children economically. (rev)	2,11
Ab. should be permitted when the woman's own health is seriously endangered by the pregnancy. (rev)	3,47
Ab. should be permitted when there is a strong chance of serious defect in the baby. (rev)	3,17
Ab. should be permitted in cases of incest. (rev)	3,08
Ab. should be permitted in cases of rape. (rev)	3,51
Ab. should be prohibited in all circumstances because it terminates the beginning of human life.	3,10
Abortion scale	**3,08**
A death sentence should always be commuted to a life sentence.	3,73
The DP should be strictly prohibited because of the right to life.	3,03
Death penalty scale	**3,38**

Note: The mean for all items indicates the agreement with its original wording. However, scale scores are computed after items with "(rev)" were reverse scored. Therefore, in all scales the higher the mean, the higher the support for rights to life

Descriptive Information About the Rights to Life

Table 3.3 shows that support for Rights to Life is close to the middle point of the 1–5 response scale. The highest average is obtained in the case of the death penalty, and the lowest in euthanasia. As can be observed, two of the items of this scale (those that accept the possibility of permitting euthanasia in case of unbearable pain), receive high support. Support for the rights to life in case of abortion shows some variability among the items. Our participants agree less with abortions performed for economic or psychological reasons. On the other hand, support is the highest in cases of rape (which is one of the three conditions that are now accepted for legal abortion in Chile).

These results indicate that there is no overall strong support for the rights to life among our participants, and that their views depend on the specific circumstances, especially in the cases of euthanasia or abortion.

Moreover, the differential perception regarding these rights is also confirmed when scale scores are correlated. Table 3.4 indicates that although all correlations are positive and significant, they are relatively weak, especially when the death penalty is involved. This indicates that our participants do not hold a consistent view about protecting rights to life in the three contexts addressed in this study. They show more consistency when these rights concern the possibility of abortion or

Table 3.4 Correlations among rights to life scales

	RtL Abortion	RtL Death Penalty
RtL euthanasia	.45**	.18**
RtL abortion		.26**

** p<.01

Table 3.5 Correlations between support for the right to life and other human rights

	Euthanasia	Abortion	Death Penalty
Judicial rights	0.10**	−0.3	0.22**
Political rights	−0.02	−0.03	0.24**
Civil rights	−0.25**	−0.18**	0.08**
Women's rights	−0.18**	−0.04	0.13**
Religious rights	0.15**	0.22**	0.22**

** p<.01

euthanasia. However, the death penalty seems to occupy a different sphere, indicating that supporting or opposing this extreme sentence is not related to the possibility of ending life before birth or in cases where euthanasia is contemplated.

Relationship Between Support for the Right to Life and Other Human Rights

Considering that support for the three manifestations of the right to life was not highly correlated, it was important to find out whether it was related to the approval of other human rights. We consider in these analyses civil, political, judicial and religious rights. As can be observed in Table 3.5, there was a differential pattern of correlations for each of the rights to life. Euthanasia was mostly related to civil and women's rights, but the correlations were inverse in these two cases. This indicates that the more people support these two rights, the less they protect the rights to life in the case of euthanasia. On the other hand, religious and judicial rights had significant, but low, correlations, in this case in the expected direction: the more they supported these rights, the more they opposed euthanasia. Support for rights to life in the case of abortion was only correlated with religious and civil rights. Interestingly, women's rights were not associated with this manifestation of the right to life. Finally, the death penalty showed significant correlations with all other human rights: it was mostly connected with political, civil and religious rights, but their associations with women's and civil rights were also significant (but small). Altogether, we observe that the only right that consistently showed positive correlations with the three manifestations of the right to life was that of religious rights.

Test of the Conceptual Model

Our conceptual model assumes that two social identities are particularly relevant regarding the right to life: religious affiliation and political alignment. Religious identity focused on the four more frequent categories selected by the participants: Catholics, Evangelicals, religious in general and non-religious. Political alignment was measured with a bipolar 9-point scale, with the extremes labelled right-wing and left-wing.

As can be seen in Table 3.6, religious identity showed a consistent pattern in terms of support for the right to life. In the three contexts, religious affiliation was a significant factor in predicting support for the right to life: non-religious participants showed the lowest average in all three manifestations of this right, while Evangelicals, followed by Catholics, showed the highest support.

On the other hand, political alignment was significantly, but only mildly, correlated with the right to life in two of the cases: euthanasia ($r = .11$) and abortion ($r = .13$). In both cases the correlations were in the expected direction: people leaning towards the right-wing expressed higher support for the right to life.

The conceptual model also considered the role of a number of attitudinal variables. In order to test their role, we conducted a hierarchical multiple regression analysis. Consistent with the conceptual model, we first entered religious and political identities. We then added the attitudinal and psycho-social variables (religiosity, empathy, values, authoritarianism and social dominance orientation). The results are presented in Table 3.7. It can be seen that, although the general fit of the models is significant in all cases, and has a significant increment when attitudinal variables are added, the role of variables is not consistent across the three domains of the right to life. In the case of euthanasia, political and religious identities are significant in models 1 and 2. However, in model 2 religiosity is the only variable that had a significant effect, indicating that people with a higher religiosity expressed greater support for the right to life in the case of euthanasia. In the case of abortion, a similar pattern emerges regarding social identities. However, in this case only Evangelicals showed a significant difference with the reference category (non-religious). Religiosity and, in this case, empathy were also significant; empathy had a positive regression coefficient, indicating that participants who expressed more empathy showed higher support for the right to life as it pertains to abortion. Overall, this is the context where the models presented the best fit, with the R-square improving from .12 to .21 as we move from model 1 to 2. Finally, in the case of the death

Table 3.6 Support for the right to life based on religious identity

	Euthanasia	Abortion	Death Penalty
Catholics	2.23	3.13	3.39
Evangelicals	2.70	3.54	3.67
Religious in general	2.02	2.92	3.34
Non-religious	1.88	2.61	3.06

Table 3.7 Multiple regression analysis

	Euthanasia		Abortion		Death Penalty	
	Beta	Beta	Beta	Beta	Beta	Beta
Religious in general	0.05	−0.02	0.12	−0.01	0.06+	−0.01
Evangelicals	0.37**	0.22**	0.40**	0.10*	0.22**	0.05
Catholics	0.16**	0.06	0.25**	0.03	0.12*	−0.00
Political orientation	0.06+	0.05	0.08**	0.07*	–	0.05+
Religiosity		0.17**		0.32**		0.19**
Empathy		−0.04		0.06*		0.08*
Values (conservatism)		−0.02		0.02		0.04
Values (hedonism)		−0.12**		−0.10**		−0.10*
Authoritarianism		−0.00		0.02		−0.10**
Social dominance		0.02		0.01		−0.10**
R Square	0.10	0.13	0.12	0.21	0.03	0.10

* p<.05; ** p<.01

penalty, religious identities showed some significant effects in model 1, but it vanished when other variables were included in model 2. Similarly, political orientation did not reach statistical significance in model 2. The support for the right to life as it pertains to the death penalty was only related to attitudinal variables in model 2. Religiosity and empathy were also significant in the expected direction. However, in this case authoritarianism and social dominance were also significant, resulting in a negative coefficient. This indicates that participants who endorse order and authority in society are more willing to approve of the death penalty (something that is expected, considering that the traditional conceptualization of authoritarianism includes authoritarian aggression directed towards deviants). Social dominance orientation, on the other hand, indicates the degree to which people endorse hierarchical differences in society. In this case, the more that participants accepted this view, the more they were willing to approve of the death penalty.

Conclusion

The result of this study clearly indicates that the Chilean youth have a differentiated view about the right to life. They do not seem to perceive that different manifestations related to this right (abortion, euthanasia and the death penalty) belong to a single construct. This is evident when all items related to these rights are factor analyzed, as well as when their support for the three manifestations are correlated (they are positively, but only weakly, correlated).

In the introduction, we addressed the relationship between the right to life and the promotion of other human rights in the context of building a human rights culture in which all rights are recognized and supported. However, our results point to two aspects that are important to highlight, the first is the fact that our youth show a selective support concerning the right to life. None of the three instances of the right to life that were included in the questionnaire received high support. In relative terms, support was higher in the case of the death penalty and lower in the case of euthanasia. The second aspect, that suggests that our youth does not hold an integrated view concerning the right to life, is the fact that the correlations among the three manifestations of the right to life are only weak, especially the correlations involving the death penalty. Moreover, correlations with other human rights are also weak, indicating that our participants have not developed an integrated view about the protection of human rights. Within this context, the right to life in the context of abortion and euthanasia shows some connection with civil and religious human rights, whereas the death penalty is mostly related to judicial, political and religious rights.

This lack of integration indicates that our social institutions, especially schools, are not successful in fostering an understanding of different manifestations of human rights in a manner that would be expected based on the curriculum orientations of the Chilean educational system.

What is even more striking is the fact that these rights are only weakly related to religious identification. In spite of the fact that the Catholic Church and Evangelical denominations have been consistently promoting the right to life, especially as it pertains to abortion and euthanasia, our Catholic participants do not show a distinctive support for those rights. In fact, only Evangelical students showed higher support for those rights, whereas Catholics did not differentiate from non-religious participants. These results show a relevant distance between the Catholic community and the official Church doctrine.

In this sense, our results seem to indicate that new generations of Chileans are not embracing a view of human rights that is deeply rooted in religious teaching, not even in the case of the most fundamental rights according to Catholic doctrine.

Even though religious identification is not strongly associated with support for the right to life, religiosity does make a difference. In all manifestations addressed in this study, participants who expressed higher religiosity showed more support for the right to life. One possible explanation for these results is that more religious participants probably pay more attention to, and are more willing to accept, religious teachings from the Catholic and Evangelical traditions. If this is the case, the real problem is that only a minority of participants who identify themselves as Catholics actually hold high religiosity.

To conclude, our study shows that one of the most fundamental human rights, the right to life, has become contentious, having only mild support in our society. Young people are not developing a consistent view about this right based on relevant social identities, such as religious or political identification. In the absence of orientation based on social categories, participants´ religiosity, social values and ideological beliefs offer some bases to structure their support for rights to life, and the results of our study pose important challenges for religious and educational institutions involved in civic formation in our society.

References

Aldunate, E. (2010). La posición de los tratados internacionales en el sistema de fuentes del ordenamiento jurídico chileno a la luz del derecho positivo. *Ius et Praxis, 12*(2), 185–210.

Amnistía Internacional. (2017). *La pena de muerte en el mundo*. Recuperado 6 de noviembre de 2017, a partir de http://www.es.amnesty.org/en-que-estamos/temas/pena-de-muerte/?utm_source=facebook&utm_campaign=comp&utm_medium=social_com&utm_term=Death_penalty&utm_content=home

Arancibia Floody, C., Cornejo Cancino, J. T., & González Undurraga, C. (2003). *Pena de muerte en Chile colonial: cinco casos de homicidio de la Real Audiencia*. Santiago: Centro de Investigaciones Diego Barros Arana/RiL Editores.

Benedicto XVI. (2009). *Caritas in veritate*. Recuperado 15 de noviembre de 2012, a partir de http://www.vatican.va/holy_father/benedict_xvi/encyclicals/documents/hf_ben-xvi_enc_20090629_caritas-in-veritate_sp.html

Biblioteca Congreso Nacional. (2015). *La pena de muerte en el derecho internacional y en la legislación chilena y extranjera*. Recuperado a partir de www.bcn.cl/obtienearchivo?id=repositorio/10221/21317/1/pena_v7.pdf

CADEM. (2017, julio 24). *Track semanal de opinión pública*. Recuperado 6 de noviembre de 2017, a partir de https://www.cadem.cl/wp-content/uploads/2017/07/Track-PP184-Julio-S3-VF.pdf

Centro de Estudios Públicos. (2017). *Estudio Nacional de Opinión Pública*. Recuperado a partir de https://www.cepchile.cl/cep/site/artic/20170601/asocfile/20170601155007/encuestacep_abr_may2017.pdf

Clemente Vázquez, A. (2005). La eutanasia: aspectos religiosos. Punto de vista protestante. En F. Cano Valle, E. Díaz Aranda, & E. Maldonado de Lizalde (Eds.), *Eutanasia: aspectos jurídicos, filosóficos, médicos y religiosos* (pp. 311–317). México: UNAM, Instituto de Investigaciones Jurídicas, 2001.

Comité Permanente de la Conferencia Episcopal de Chile. (2017a, Agosto). *Siempre al servicio de las personas y la vida*. Recuperado a partir de http://documentos.iglesia.cl/documento.php?id=4464

Comité Permanente de la Conferencia Episcopal de Chile. (2017b, octubre 31). *Chile, un hogar para todos*. Recuperado a partir de http://documentos.iglesia.cl/documento.php?id=4484

Congregación para la Doctrina de la Fe. (1980). *Declaración Iura et bona sobre la eutanasia*. Recuperado 13 de noviembre de 2017, a partir de http://www.vatican.va/roman_curia/congregations/cfaith/documents/rc_con_cfaith_doc_19800505_euthanasia_sp.html

Francisco. (2014, septiembre 28). *Encuentro del Papa con los ancianos en la Plaza de San Pedro*. Recuperado 13 de noviembre de 2017, a partir de http://m2.vatican.va/content/francesco/es/speeches/2014/september/documents/papa-francesco_20140928_incontro-anziani.html

Giudice, H. (2011). Argumentos racionales y bíblicos sobre la pena de muerte en la patrística. *Teología y vida, 52*(1–2), 307–322. https://doi.org/10.4067/S0049-34492011000100017.

Juan Pablo II. (1995). *Evangelium Vitae*. Recuperado 6 de noviembre de 2017, a partir de http://w2.vatican.va/content/john-paul-ii/es/encyclicals/documents/hf_jp-ii_enc_25031995_evangelium-vitae.html

Nogueira, H. (2009). Informe sobre restablecimiento de la pena de muerte por Proyecto de Ley (Boletin No 6642-07). *Ius et Praxis, 15*(2), 306–316 https://doi.org/10.4067/S0718-00122009000200011.

Por un Chile para Cristo. (2017). *Declaración Pública de la Iglesia Evangélica Chilena*.

Schwartz, S. H. (1992). Universals in the content and structure of values: Theoretical advances and empirical tests in 20 countries. *Advances in Experimental Social Psychology, 25*, 1–65.

Universidad Católica, & Adimark. (2012). Encuesta Nacional Bicentenario. *Centro de Políticas Públicas UC, 7*(12), 11–58.

Universidad Católica, & GfK Adimark. (2016). *Encuesta Nacional Bicentenario 2016: Familia*. Recuperado a partir de http://encuestabicentenario.uc.cl/wp-content/uploads/2016/11/Encuesta-bicentenario-2016-Familia.pdf

Chapter 4
Human Dignity, Religious Ethics or Hedonism – What Can Predict Young People's Attitudes in Germany Towards the Right to Life in the Cases of Euthanasia and Abortion?

Hans-Georg Ziebertz

This paper argues that human life must be protected and any attacks on life must be negated: a right to life, and a right to live, exists. But is there a right to terminate life, specifically in the cases of euthanasia and abortion? These two topics inevitably lead to heated discussions, as has been observed in a number of societies. The question this paper asks is: how do young people in Germany evaluate the contradicting arguments surrounding the termination of life (i.e. whether the termination of life should be prohibited or permitted) and what motives determine their attitudes towards these topics? Given that it is a core value, human dignity is taken into consideration, as are respondents' religious convictions and the value orientation of hedonism. The research that forms the basis of this paper also asks whether young people with different religious backgrounds and religiously non-affiliated young people differ in their attitudes concerning the right to life. The empirical analysis was carried out with German young people (N = 1862) as the respondents. The findings show that young Germans legitimize the possibility of terminating life by euthanasia and, to a lesser extent, by abortion. The less student respondents are religious, the more they agree with these exceptions (i.e. euthanasia and abortion) from the rule that the right to life has to be protected. The value orientation of hedonism is the strongest predictor for a respondent having a permissive attitude towards euthanasia and abortion. The value of human dignity is found to be significant in only a few cases.

This paper presents empirical data concerning how young people in Germany think about the right to life. This right is guaranteed by the German constitution (Grundgesetz) in article 2: "Everyone has the right to life and physical integrity. The freedom of a person is inviolable." The right to life covers a wide range of topics,

H.-G. Ziebertz (✉)
Faculty of Theology, University of Würzburg, Würzburg, Germany
e-mail: hg.ziebertz@uni-wuerzburg.de

H.-G. Ziebertz, F. Zaccaria (eds.), *Euthanasia, Abortion, Death Penalty and Religion – The Right to Life and its Limitations*, Religion and Human Rights 4, https://doi.org/10.1007/978-3-319-98773-6_4

though this paper focuses specifically on euthanasia and abortion. These two cases can be understood as exceptions to the rule that life must be protected under all circumstances.

The question is to what extent do young Germans think that euthanasia and abortion should be prohibited or permitted and what influences their agreement or disagreement? The findings suggest that the understanding of human dignity, religious beliefs and a hedonistic value orientation can all influence a respondent's attitudes towards the right to life, and any possible exceptions.

The first section discusses the concepts used in this study. The second section explains the design of the study and the third section presents the findings; the paper ends with a discussion of our findings.

Introduction

The termination of life is a frequently-debated issue in many societies such as Germany. In these societies, certain interest groups have been, and are, trying to influence public discourse about this subject and the legislation and religious issues surrounding the subject. In the following sections the position of the Christian churches and the Islamic tradition regarding euthanasia and abortion will be briefly portrayed,[1] followed by a summary of previous research. At the end of this section, the concepts that may have an influence on young people's attitudes towards euthanasia and abortion will be explored.

Euthanasia in Christian Theology

The Catechism of the Roman Catholic Church[2] states clearly that direct euthanasia is morally unacceptable, regardless of any motives or means. Any acts that are directed at eliminating suffering, but which cause death, are regarded as murder and are a grave violation that is contrary to human dignity and God as the Creator of life (Catechism no. 2277). For the Church, indirect euthanasia is a form of euthanasia that does not cause the death of a person, but is aware of the medical incapability to save life. The Catechism stresses that sick people should be able to live their lives as normally as possible (Catechism no. 2276). Palliatives are understood as a form of charity and "painkillers to alleviate the sufferings of the dying, even at the risk of shortening their days, and can comply with the morality of human dignity if death is not willed as either an end or a means, but only foreseen and tolerated as

[1] This segment follows the comprehensive elaboration of these issues in: H.-G.Ziebertz and M. Reindl (2013).

[2] http://www.vatican.va/archive/ENG0015/_INDEX.HTM. With regard to Roman Catholic documents see also the chapter from Anthony and Sterkens.

inevitable" (Catechism no. 2279).[3] The Declaration on Euthanasia published by the Vatican Congregation for the Doctrine of Faith (5 May 1980)[4] offers a detailed justification of the referred position (see also Ernst 2007; Van der Ven 2013). This text puts the dignity and sanctity of any person at the forefront of the issue, and the text focuses on the right to life including the duty to protect life. The dignity and sanctity of human life are understood as universal values which cannot be disregarded, and any attack on life is a crime of the utmost gravity because it undermines the supremacy of God. An exception is made only for overarching reasons (e.g. martyrdom for the glory of God).

The Protestant Church in Germany emphasizes that the assisted suicide of a human being in the last stages of life is not consistent with Christian ethics, even if the act has been specifically requested.[5] From a Christian perspective, direct (active) euthanasia or assisted suicide has to be refused. No person may demand or receive a licence to kill another human being. However, the Protestant Church agrees that the medication of terminally ill patients may be discontinued if the patient has specifically expressed this. This form of passive euthanasia is, then, permitted. The Church does not defend the obligation to prolong life at all costs and to use the therapeutic potential of medicine to the fullest. The Church argues that it is part of the finiteness of life on earth to accept the approach of death when the time comes. The Protestant Church aims to assist people to reflect on the last period of life and to prepare a "living will", and, at the medical level, to expand palliative care that focuses on the treatment of pain and the relief of other symptoms. As far as the care of those facing the end of life is concerned, the Church supports the hospice movement, palliative care in the hospital, as well as family care and voluntary aid (W. Huber: Mainzer Allgemeine Zeitung, 10 July 2004).

Euthanasia in Islamic Theology

In Islamic theology, death is the boundary between this world and the afterlife. Death signifies the return to the Creator of life and the beginning of another state of being. The soul leaves the body until reunification at the Day of Judgment, and the time of death is fixed by God alone. This eschatological concept is a central Islamic principle of faith with a deep practical impact on the attitude of Muslim believers (Ilkilic 2008). The body of man is not his own, but a gift from God. There is,

[3] The catechism makes a distinction between euthanasia and suicide. In cases of suicide a person decides to terminate his or her own life with or without help of others. This is, in the Catholic view, clearly forbidden. "Suicide contradicts the natural inclination of the human being to preserve and perpetuate his life. (...) Suicide is contrary to love for the living God" (Catechism no. 2281). Voluntary co -operation in suicide is also contrary to moral law (Catechism no. 2282).

[4] http://www.vatican.va/roman_curia/congregations/cfaith/documents/rc_con_cfaith_doc_19800505_euthanasia_en.html

[5] http://www.ekd.de/EKD-Texte/44666.html (25th June 2010).

therefore, no justification at all for a theological legitimation of suicide or for an active support of euthanasia.

Cases of indirect or passive euthanasia are regarded as more complicated; such cases are the result of modern developments in medicine (Kellner 2010, 147 ff.). Jonathan Brockopp (2003a, b, 178 ff.) quotes the rector of the al-Azhar University in Cairo, Muhammad Tantawi, who distinguishes between (1) euthanasia "as killing" and as "letting die", (2) between the intention "to ease pain" and "to accept God's decree" and (3) between "actions of suicide" and "homicide and natural death". Death has no intrinsic importance in itself, "but rather gains importance due to the teleology of death, resurrection, and judgment [sic]" (Brockopp 2003a, b, 180). The moment of death is reflected in the larger context of the soul's life before and after the death of the body: death is a process of transition. Medieval sources in Islam contain a variety of opinions and argue more teleologically than deontologically. Thus, in this "liberal" tradition, it is possible to understand passive euthanasia as the working out of God's will, and so passive euthanasia is not regarded as assisting the process of dying, but as allowing death to occur.

Abortion in Christian Theology

A very clear and strict position on abortion has been developed by the Roman Catholic Church. The Church declares that "from the first moment of his existence, a human being must be recognized as having the rights of a person – among which is the inviolable right of every innocent being to life" (Catechism no. 2270). This statement is further reflected in the instructional document *Donum Vitae*, published 10 March 1987.[6] It declares that "the inviolability of the innocent human being's right to life 'from the moment of conception until death' is a sign and requirement of the very inviolability of the person to whom the Creator has given the gift of life" (*Donum Vitae* 1987, chapter 4). From this it follows that an embryo is a person from the moment of conception and "must be defended in its integrity, cared for, and healed, as far as possible, like any other human being" (Catechism no. 2273). Conducting abortion is understood as morally evil, as the Catechism argues: "This teaching has not changed and remains unchangeable" (Catechism no. 2271). Direct abortion is defined as "willed" either as "an end or as means", and is gravely contrary to the moral law. The Church also teaches that formal cooperation in conducting an abortion constitutes a serious offense and entails the canonical penalty of excommunication (Catechism no. 2272). The Church, referring to the basic principles of human life, argues that the right to life is inalienable and "must be recognized and respected by civil society and the political authority. These human rights depend neither on single individuals nor on parents; nor do they represent a concession made by society and the state; they belong to human nature and are

[6] http://www.vatican.va/roman_curia/congregations/cfaith/documents/rc_con_cfaith_doc_19870222_respect-for-human-life_en.html

inherent in the person by virtue of the creative act from which the person took his origin" (Catechism no. 2273).

The Protestant Church in Germany is believed to be less strict and fundamental regarding the abortion issue (Mantei 2004), although the Catholic and Lutheran Church have published common statements (cf. Sterbebegleitung 2003). Representatives of the Lutheran Church stress that human life, both the born and unborn, is at all times worth protecting.[7] At the same time the Protestant Church admits that during a pregnancy unpredictable conflicts may occur that leave seemingly no other choice than to terminate the woman's pregnancy. Such conflicts can result from the mother's age, her financial situation, a fear of the responsibility of taking care of a child, the child's disability, relationship problems, problems with employment, pressure from the social environment, the absence of a partner or non-existing family planning. These listed factors clearly exceed medical reasons to include social and economic factors. The Protestant Church respects these reasons and views the decision of the affected woman as decisive. The protection of the unborn child can only be warranted by the pregnant woman, not against her wishes.[8] A more critical position states that no one is allowed to interfere with human life – which includes the life of an unborn child.[9] Human self-determination does not constitute a right to dispose of the life of another human being. Abortion means terminating a human life, but God's commandment is clearly to preserve live and to prohibit killing, which means that abortion is always to be viewed as an offence. The Church is thus challenged to develop an office of counselling that takes all interests into account and moves within the limits of 'goal orientation' and 'open-endedness'.

Abortion in Islamic Theology

Although the Qur'an says nothing about abortion itself, Islamic theologians work with analogies based on verses about life, death and murder (Kellner 2010, 212–250; Bowen 2003, 53): "Do not kill the soul that God has made sacred, except for a just cause" (Qur'an 17:33 and 25:68). The Qur'an and Sunna talk about a stepwise and gradual creation of the human body in the womb, and the ethical and juridical valuation of abortion depends on these steps: "We first created the human being from an essence of clay: then placed it, a living germ, in a safe enclosure. The germ We made into a clot of blood, and the clot into a lump of flesh. This We fashioned into bones, then clothed the bone with flesh, thus bringing forth another creation" (Qur'an 23:12–14). The creation of life begins with the actual start of a pregnancy (phase one), then moving onto the material transition from embryo to man (phase two) and then to the moment of ensoulment (phase three). The shaping of the human

[7] http://www.ekd.de/vortraege/060329_huber_wfdl.html

[8] http://www.ekd.de/bevollmaechtigter/stellungnahmen/52400.html

[9] http://www.ekd.de/vortraege/6470.html

material in phase two takes place between the 40th and 45th day of pregnancy, and most legal schools do not detect the ontological existence of an individual being at this stage because the material body is still without a soul (cf. Bowen 2003, 54f). The status of a human being is reached when the soul is established, on around the 120th day. From this date onwards (excluding specific medical implications) abortion is forbidden and seen as equal to murder. However, this is only an overall picture and, as such, has to be differentiated depending on the different legal schools of thought and even different views within a given school.

Statements have been found which allow abortion before the 120th day, but this practice meets with grave disapproval (Brockopp 2003a, b; Kellner 2010). Another legal opinion prohibits abortion at all, but concludes at the same time that the degree of sin increases the later the abortion is performed. Some scholars perceive abortion as sin and avoid the term of murder because they do not want to relate abortion to a criminal act, while other legal schools allow abortion when a mother's pregnancy harms or may harm the child, under the condition that both partners agree to the abortion and that a doctor confirms that the abortion process will not hurt the mother. But there are also legal schools that reject abortion in all circumstances. They conclude that with fertilization a human being is shaped and no medical intervention is allowed. The ban, however, is also understood gradually: after the ensoulment abortion is equal to killing.

Seen from the outside, Islamic law is highly differentiated and heterogeneous (Kellner 2010, 220; Bowen 2003). Even conservative Islamic scholars who oppose abortion consider reasons that may justify a termination of pregnancy (economic reasons, health reasons, extramarital pregnancies and rape, eugenic reasons). After the 120th day, abortion is only legal when the mother's life is at risk because of the pregnancy. In all other cases, abortion is not only immoral but a legally punishable offence.

Euthanasia and Abortion in Secular Society

Young people in Germany grow up in a society where, in many fields, the state and religion cooperate. At the same time, though, this society has become increasingly secular. Public debates on euthanasia and abortion mirror a multitude of positions in which the Catholic Church is regarded as being extremely restrictive when it comes to defend any interventions on issues of the right to life. The clear deduction of norms from the natural law and a preference for deontological arguing distinguishes the Church as a bulwark against excessive liberalisation. On the other hand, humanistic groups campaign for the right of individual self-determination and the right to determine one's own life and death. In the public debate on the abortion laws, left-wing groups and women's movements were the strongest opponents of religious positions. In the centre of the argument is the concept of autonomy, which is set against the deontological reasoning that governs religious argumentation.

The German ethicist Eberhard Schockenhoff (2009, 536) perceives an increasingly liberal attitude in Germany. As such, human life is not regarded as intrinsically valuable as an end in itself. Instead, the argument is that life is loaded with instrumental and extrinsic values inasmuch as biological life is a prerequisite for the achievement of other values and goods: life is precious as far as it is individually valued. The subjective valuation of life accounts for the essential factor in debates concerning any issues about the termination of life. The individual assesses whether life is to occur and continue, and it is this individual assessment that is the key. Indeed, individualism is one of the key features of modern secular society (Dworkin 1993). Society is the framework of socialisation, and young people in German society are influenced by both religious and secular life perspectives when it comes to the issues of euthanasia and abortion. Thus, the question arises: how strongly do general socialisation and religious concerns influence young people's attitudes towards the question of life and death? Does religiosity matter – and to what degree – when the issue is forced (i.e. whether euthanasia and abortion should be prohibited or permitted)?

Previous Research

Similar research was undertaken in 2013. Ziebertz and Reindl (2013) showed that Christians and Muslims differ strongly when the importance of religion is on the agenda: Christian respondents do not consider religion as important in their lives, whereas Muslims do. However, the results on euthanasia and abortion differ: Christians had an ambivalent-positive attitude towards the legalisation of abortion and euthanasia. Muslims, however, were negatively-ambivalent with regard to abortion and euthanasia. These differences were found to be significant.

Another result was that the relationship between religiosity and the right to life was quite similar (i.e. between Christians and Muslims). In both groups, respondents were convinced that religious commitment and abortion are in conflict with each other, and Muslims felt the same for euthanasia.

The authors found a directly negative influence of religious affiliation on euthanasia and a weaker negative influence on abortion. Negative influences were mostly owing to the individual importance of religion. The more strongly respondents were religiously committed, the more they disapproved of abortion and euthanasia. The positive valuation of religion as a culturally open community that keeps up with trends in a society leads to the conviction that abortion and euthanasia in some cases might be allowed.

The conclusion was that religiosity has a major impact on life's "great decisions", especially when the protection of life is an issue. This 2013 study showed to what extent young people were socialised and educated within the context of their religion and to what extent they feel attached to their religion. This previous study did not include non-religious youth.

Predictors of Attitudes Towards the Right to Life

So far, it can be shown that religions have a vital interest in the right to life. In the following section, several concepts that can be reasonably expected to have an impact on people's attitudes towards the right to life will be discussed. These concepts are: human dignity, religious belief, and hedonism (i.e. a hedonistic value orientation). We shall also add the factors of age and sex as well as people's religious affiliation.

Human Dignity

Germany is probably the only country in the world that has declared human dignity to be a constitutional value (Grimm 2013). Article 1 of the 1949 German Constitution [Grundgesetz] says: "Human dignity is inviolable. To respect it and protect it is the duty of all state power [sic]. The German people therefore acknowledge inviolable and inalienable human rights as the basis of every community, of peace and of justice in the world." The background of the Holocaust was the motivational factor that led to human dignity as being regarded as a legitimising concept for all basic human rights.

Human dignity is also mentioned in international treaties. The *Universal Declaration of Human Rights* (UDHR, 1948) uses the term "inherent dignity" in its preamble and states that "recognition of the inherent dignity and of the equal and inalienable rights of all members of the human family is the foundation of freedom, justice and peace in the world". A similar wording can be found in the *International Covenant on Economic, Social and Cultural Rights* (ICESCR 1966) and in the *Charter of Fundamental Rights in the European Union* (1950).

The strong connection between human dignity and human rights has evoked criticism (cf. Ziebertz et al. 2017), where the precision, explicitness and unambiguity of the concept of dignity is questioned. Critics complain that it is not clear how dignity functions as the grounding for human rights, what rights it foregrounds, and if there is a direct link between dignity and such rights. According to these critics, the concept of human dignity is ineligible as a justification of such rights (Bagaric and Allen 2006; Rosen 2012).

This controversy is a challenge for empirical research. Is the concept of human dignity empirically important regarding attitudes towards the right to life? The concept of dignity has to be operationalised, and, in this research, a concept of dignity is used which is operationalised threefold. Firstly, individuals possess human dignity owing to their position or rank within society (dignity of merit) and, secondly, dignity is connected with personal achievement and moral behaviour (moral stature), and in these two cases dignity can be lost. The third meaning is in accordance with international covenants: dignity is inherent to all human beings, which means that dignity cannot be lost. Research will show if – and if so which – concept of human dignity predicts attitudes towards the right to life.

Belief

As was previously shown, the right to life is a key topic in both Christianity and Islam. The assumption is that young people who are religiously committed will not be unaffected by the teachings of their religious tradition. Although religious belief is not reducible to ethics, all religions see moral norms as important guidelines for human behaviour. Belief has an ethical component and it is part of religious socialisation and education to transmit the understanding of religiously motivated norms and values. To measure religiosity, religious affiliation is not a sufficient indicator because young people will tend to share the affiliation of their parents. However, this tells us little about their degree of intrinsic belief, meaning religious practice is also taken into account. Prayer and participation in worship can be interpreted as active commitment. In a liberal and secular society, there is only a low probability that extrinsic stimuli cause prayer and participation. In addition, religious belief should be experienced as valuable, enriching and important. In a self-description respondents should express how important their belief is when it comes to decisions in their daily life. Finally, should religious denominations play a social role? Should they function as an advocate for the underprivileged and for people who have no power to defend their interests (e.g. the unborn child and the person undergoing extreme suffering)? Does an appreciation of the churches and religious communities as performing a social function influence an evaluation of the right to life?

Hedonism (Values)

Those who adopt a liberal interpretation of euthanasia and abortion often stress the value of autonomy, that is, the value of self-direction. Shalom Schwartz (1994, 21) defines these values "as trans-situational goals, varying in importance, that serve as guiding principles in the life of a person or other social entity". Schwartz's values theory consists of two orthogonal dimensions of "self-transcendence vs. self-enhancement" and "openness to change vs. conservation". In this study, the focus is on the concept of self-enhancement, something defined as the motivation to enhance one's own personal interests, even at the expense of others. Personal claims are at the centre and it is these claims that should be satisfied primarily. Conceptually, this value orientation will be labelled as "hedonism".

Method

This section will explain the design of our study, which will include information about the research procedure and the sample, the conceptual model, and the instruments used in this study. This section will end with the research questions and hypotheses formulated.

Research Procedure and Sample

The context of this study is the international empirical research project "Religion and Human Rights" (2012–2019).[10] The purpose of the project is to explore the causal relationships that exist between religious affiliation, certain types of religious convictions, value orientations, worldviews and the social context of young people, and to what extent the former influences young people's attitudes towards human rights. Given the research question, this paper refers to a selection of instruments and to the data collected in the German survey.

The data collection took place from spring 2013 to winter 2013/14. The survey was conducted in 11 of Germany's 16 federal states, and included a total of 2157 students in their 10th and 11th grades. The interviews were conducted in 35 schools in 19 cities, and covered all parts of the country's geographical space. The schools were selected randomly (i.e. random sampling was used).

The data collection took place in cooperation with participating schools. Together with the questionnaires, detailed information and instructions for teachers were sent out on how to organise the survey in their classes. The total number of questionnaires sent to the schools was 3950, of which 2243 were returned and 2157 selected as suitable for evaluation. Of the participating students, 41% were male and 59% female. On average, participating students were 16 years old.

In this study, Catholics (N = 752), Protestants (N = 531), Muslims (N = 121) and non-religiously affiliated young people (N = 458) were selected (total N = 1862). Respondents belonging to other smaller communities have been excluded for the purpose of this analysis.

Conceptual Model

The dependent variables in this study are euthanasia and abortion. Both concepts represent cases in which the right to life is put to the test. As independent variables, human dignity is first included, with religious belief and a hedonistic value orientation as the second and third variables. The relevant control variables are age, sex and religious affiliation, it being assumed that these concepts predict attitudes towards the right to life. The conceptual model (Fig. 4.1) lists all of these concepts.

Conceptualisation and Operationalisation

All the concepts referred to in the conceptual model will be described in detail. When instruments are based on scales (instead of single items), we use a Cronbach's alpha of minimum .60 (DeVellis 2003) – in one case an alpha of .58 because the concept in question made this important.

[10] http://www.rhr.theologie.uni-wuerzburg.de

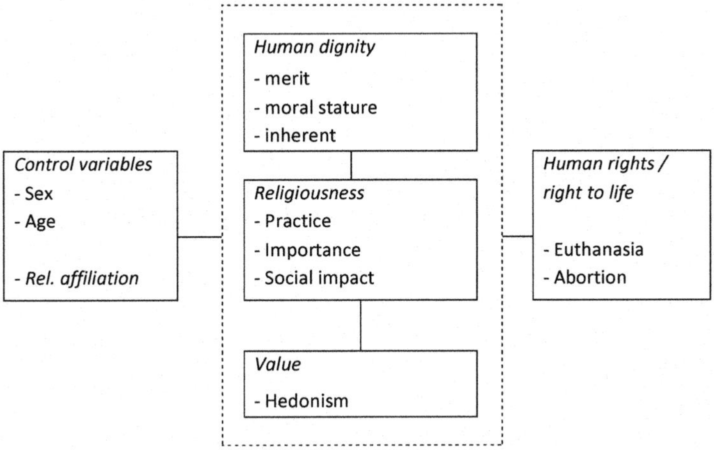

Fig. 4.1 Conceptual model

Euthanasia

In Germany, the term "euthanasia" is not often used. In the German language, the term "euthanasia" is not used since it refers to the extermination of "unworthy life" of the severely handicapped during the Nazi regime, instead the term "Sterbehilfe" (assisted suicide) was applied. The contemporary understanding of euthanasia means the act or process of terminating life by permitting death when healing cannot be expected. Sick people are assisted in dying as painlessly as possible for reasons of mercy. In the questionnaire this topic was introduced as follows: "*The situation: A woman, 99 years old, wishes to die because she feels she has lived long enough. She is tired of life. She is in full possession of all her mental faculties. She voluntarily asks her doctor to give her an injection to end her life.*" The respondents should indicate their agreement or disagreement to the statements: "Euthanasia should be prohibited in all circumstances" and "Euthanasia should be permitted in the case of unbearable and irreversible suffering". The analysis showed that the two items can be scaled when the first item is recoded (permission instead of prohibition). After this revision the meaning of the scale "euthanasia", which has an alpha of .60, is agreement or disagreement concerning the permission of euthanasia. The answering scheme to these items is based on a five-point scale: strongly disagree (1), disagree (2), not certain (3), agree (4) and strongly agree (5).

Abortion

The second case that shows a deviation from the position that life has to be protected under all circumstances is abortion. Many countries have experienced a heated debate on the issue of abortion, and religious communities in particular have often voted strongly against abortion. The respondents were able to express their position with regard to the following items: "Abortion should be permitted in cases of rape", "Abortion should be permitted in cases of incest", "Abortion should be permitted when there is a strong chance of serious defect in the baby", "Abortion should be permitted when the woman's own health is seriously endangered by the pregnancy", "Abortion should be permitted when the woman cannot financially afford to support any more children" and "Abortion should be permitted when the woman cannot psychologically cope with raising any more children". Together, these items build one factor that is to say that respondents do not differentiate between the contents. The reasons for this should be seriously discussed, though this cannot be done here. Answers could be given based on a five-point scale: strongly disagree (1), disagree (2), not certain (3), agree (4) and strongly agree (5). The alpha of the scale "abortion" is .78.

Human Dignity

According to Nordenfelt (2004), human dignity consists of three dimensions: dignity of merit, dignity of moral stature and inherent dignity (cf. Ziebertz et al. 2017). Merit was assessed using the following item: "The value of a person depends on the appreciation given to him or her by others". Moral dignity was assessed using the following statement: "The honour to be given to a person depends on his moral behaviour", and inherent dignity with "Each human being should be recognized just because he is a human being, irrespective of credit or moral behaviour". The answering scheme to these items is based on a five-point scale: strongly disagree (1), disagree (2), not certain (3), agree (4) and strongly agree (5).

Religious Belief

The first topic concerns religious practice. Compared with dogmatic religious convictions, it is the existence of a religious practice which is a strong indicator that religion has meaning for a person. Two items have been selected, the first being "How often do you pray?" Respondents could answer with "never, hardly ever, a few times a year, one to three times a month, once a week, more than once a week, once a day and several times a day" (1 to 8). The second item is "How often do you take part in religious services at a church or mosque or another place?" The answering scheme was "never, hardly ever, a few times a year, one to three times a month, once a week and more than once a week" (1 to 6). Together, the Cronbach's alpha of this scale ("religious practice") is .72.

The second topic in this area concerns the importance of religious belief for a person. The first item to assess this is "To what extent do you believe that God or something divine exists?" A five-point answering scheme has been selected: "not at all (1), not very much (2), moderately (3), quite a bit (4) and very much so (5)". The second item concerns experience: "How often do you experience situations in which you have the feeling that God or something divine intervenes in your life?" Answers are measured with "never (1), rarely (2), occasionally (3), often (4) and very often (5)". The third item runs as follows: "What is your position on the statement: 'My religion or worldview has a great influence on my daily life'"? The answering scheme was "totally disagree (1), disagree (2), not sure (3), agree (4) and fully agree (5)". Together, the three items reach a Cronbach's alpha of .84 and build the scale "importance".

The third topic is the function of religion in society. The selected items focus on the role of religion in influencing public opinion and as a prophetic voice, especially in its support for disadvantaged people. Items which assess the function of religion are: "Religions should try to influence public opinion on social problems"; "Religions should use their authority to intervene in societal affairs" and "Religions should take public responsibility for societal development." The possible answers were: strongly disagree (1), disagree (2), not certain (3), agree (4) and strongly agree(5). The Cronbach's alpha of this scale ("social religion") is .62.

Hedonism as a Value

In addition to human dignity and religion, respondents' value orientations could be relevant as far as their attitudes towards the right to life are concerned. In this study, the concept of the value of hedonism is selected. According to Schwartz's value theory, hedonism can be located around the centre of "self-enhancement" (Schwartz and Sagiv 1995). Schwartz's scale is based on the technique of respondents answering to items that ask if and to what extent the described person is "like me" or "not like me". The three items are: "It is important to him/her to be rich. He/she wants to have a lot of money and expensive things"; "Having a good time is important to him/her. He/she likes to "spoil" himself/herself"; and "Being very successful is important to him/her. He/she hopes people will recognise his/her achievements." The answering scheme runs from 1 (not like me) to 6 (like me). With an alpha of .58 and the internal consistency of "hedonism" being weak on this scale.

Control Variables

In the research that forms the basis of this paper, sex and age were included as control variables. To measure religious affiliation, "Roman Catholics", "Protestants", "Muslims" and respondents without any religious affiliation ("No religion") were selected.

Research Questions and Hypotheses

The first empirical question concerns the descriptive analysis: What is the attitude of young people towards euthanasia and abortion and to the other scales used in this study? Do Catholics, Protestants, Muslims and non-affiliated youth differ in their attitudes towards euthanasia and abortion?

Assumption: as far as the dependent variables are concerned, the assumption is that there is a large consensus among the German youth that both euthanasia and abortion are permissible. Given that the Catholic Church holds one of the strongest positions regarding euthanasia and abortion, it is not unlikely that Catholics, compared with other religious groups, have a more reserved attitude towards both these issues.

The second question is whether and to what extent respondents' understanding of human dignity, respondents' belief and their value orientation predict attitudes towards the right to life. Which of these concepts are the most significant and are there differences between the religious groups?

Assumption: as has been shown, human dignity is strongly connected with the right to life and, furthermore, human dignity has a specific meaning in the German context. Given this background, it is reasonable to expect respondents who agree with the understanding of human dignity as inherent to all human beings to be more cautious in accepting the termination of life via euthanasia and abortion. The same can be said with regard to respondents' religiousness, especially those who are Catholic. Respondents with stronger beliefs are more likely to be against a permissive stance on euthanasia and abortion. On the other hand, respondents with a hedonistic value orientation that is focused on one's own well-being and on self-directed decisions are more likely to accept euthanasia and abortion.

Empirical Findings

This section is divided into two parts (according to the research questions). The first section presents the descriptive findings and the second section analyses if and how strongly the chosen predictors explain the rights to life, including differences between religious groups.

Descriptive Analyses

The descriptive analysis starts with a presentation of the frequencies of the dependent and independent variables and is continuous with a correlation analysis between both groups of variables.

Descriptive Analysis

As expected, German young people show a high acceptance of the practice of euthanasia and abortion (see Table 4.1). The view that euthanasia is permissible (M = 3.95) is even higher than for abortion (M = 3.61). In both cases the standard deviation is moderate, which leads to the conclusion that there is little diversity among respondents. In Germany, the public discussion of the issue of abortion took place in the 1980s and 1990s and, as can be expected, the Catholic Church was a strong opponent against a liberalisation of the law. The compromise which was reached at that

Table 4.1 Means (M) and standard deviation (SD) of the dependent variables euthanasia and abortion

	Euthanasia		Abortion	
	M	SD	M	SD
Catholics	3.92	.78	3.55	.71
Protestants	3.96	.83	3.63	.75
Muslims	3.05	1.06	3.09	.79
Non-affiliated	4.22	.69	3.81	.76
All N	3.95	.83	3.61	.76

Table 4.2 Means (M) and standard deviation (SD) of the independent variables

	M	SD
Dignity – merit	2.28	1.10
Dignity – moral stature	3.35	1.10
Dignity – inherent	3.75	1.19
Religious practice	2.60	1.48
Importance of belief	2.56	1.07
Social religion	2.68	.80
Hedonism	4.40	.87

time is accepted by large parts of the German population. The empirical results probably mirror the widespread understanding that the abortion law allowing a termination of pregnancy within 3 months (with compulsory counselling beforehand). However, the discussion on euthanasia is a recent topic in public debate. Neighbouring countries, such as the Netherlands and Switzerland, adopt more liberal laws and some people move to these countries specifically in order to obtain assisted suicide. Given its Nazi history, Germany itself is more cautious regarding euthanasia. Young people could be aware of this debate and as it is shown in the data, they highly agree with the permissibility of the termination of life und the conditions mentioned in the items.

In both euthanasia and abortion, non-religiously affiliated youth show the highest acceptance. This is in accordance with the expectation that religion is significant when it comes to questions of life and death. The attitude of Muslim students regarding euthanasia and abortion is one of positive ambivalence, their mean being just above the middle of the scale. With regard to euthanasia there is a bigger divergence among Muslims, but not regarding abortion. The means for Catholics and Protestants are between Muslims and non-affiliated youth, while Catholics and Protestants agree with the permission to euthanasia (M = 3.92; M = 3.96) and less with the acceptance of abortion (M = 3.55; M = 3.63). Protestants mirror the average liberal attitude more clearly, while Catholics are slightly below this value – but the lowest are Muslim respondents. Religiously non-affiliated youth show an acceptance above the average.

We shall now analyse the frequencies of the independent variables (see Table 4.2). An examination of the concept of human dignity shows the results to be two positive and one negative. Dignity being understood as dependent on the appreciation given by others is clearly rejected (M = 2.28), while respondents have a slightly positive attitude towards dignity that is dependent on oral behaviour (M = 3.35). The strongest support is given to an understanding of dignity that is inherent to all human beings (M = 3.75), a view that is in line with international treaties. However, the idea that many respondents support the view that dignity is an outcome of moral behaviour is a finding that should not be overlooked. This is a contingent understanding of dignity because, according to this view, immoral conduct causes the loss of dignity. It is also obvious that, in all cases, the standard deviation is high, which indicates a certain degree of divergence within the group of respondents.

Three scales have been used to measure religiosity, and our overall result is that all means are in the negative half of the scale. The lowest mean concerns the importance of belief in daily life (M = 2.56). The standard deviation indicates differences between respondents, while religious practice shows the second lowest mean (M = 2.60), though it needs to be mentioned here that the standard deviation is very high (SD = 1.48). Divergence is highest when it comes to prayer and worship. Attitudes towards the social function of religion were also measured: should religion be the advocate of the underprivileged and should religion intervene in social affairs? The findings show that German young people are not convinced that this represents a valuable orientation (M = 2.68) and the difference between them is low.

Finally, by including hedonism, a specific value orientation was included. It is interesting that this concept received the highest acceptance (M = 4.40) and a moderate standard deviation. Having fun, becoming wealthy and being successful are all objectives that are highly appreciated by respondents.

To sum up, young Germans show a strong orientation as far as self-enhancement is concerned. They also support the concept of human dignity, particularly the interpretation of dignity that regards it as inherent to all human beings and less a moral concept of dignity, and they tend to have low religiosity.

Before we move on to the second research question, the correlation between dependent and independent variables should be analysed. Table 4.3 shows that there are several significant correlations. We will discuss the outcomes for euthanasia and abortion separately.

With regard to euthanasia there is only one significant positive correlation: hedonism. The meaning here is that the more respondents are hedonistic, the more they accept the view that euthanasia should be permitted (and vice versa). Four concepts show a negative correlation, and the strongest coefficients concern religion. The interpretation is that the less students are religious, the more supportive they are of euthanasia. Among the religious factors selected, religious practice is the most important. The fourth negative correlation concerns dignity of merit, with the rejection of this understanding correlating with the support of euthanasia.

As far as abortion is concerned, the strongest correlations concern religion. Religious practice and the individual importance of religion especially correlate negatively with abortion, with a lower coefficient, and this is also true for a social understanding of religion. The more students are non-religious, the more supportive they are of the legitimacy of abortion. Regarding religiosity, the overall picture is

Table 4.3 Correlations between independent and dependent variables (N = 1862)

	Euthanasia	Abortion
Dignity – merit	$-.097^{***}$	$-.012$
Dignity – moral stature	$.034$	$.065^{**}$
Dignity – inherent	$-.044$	$-.096^{***}$
Religious practice	$-.254^{***}$	$-.228^{***}$
Importance belief	$-.251^{***}$	$-.223^{***}$
Social religion	$-.200^{***}$	$-.157^{***}$
Hedonism	$.133^{***}$	$.156^{***}$
Age	$.000$	$.015$
Sex	$.034$	$.037$

Note: *, $p < .05$; **, $p < .01$; ***, $p < .001$

similar to euthanasia. Two concepts of dignity show significant correlations: one is the rejection of inherent dignity and the other is the acceptance of moral dignity – both views indicating support for abortion. The value orientation of hedonism is important: a hedonistic orientation and a permissive attitude towards abortion are connected.

Sex and age bear no relevance; no significant correlation could be found.

The correlation analysis (Table 4.3) indicates which concepts can be relevant when analysing how strong these concepts predict attitudes towards euthanasia and abortion. What is not documented in these tables is that there is a significant correlation of $r = .36$ between euthanasia and abortion.

Predictors of Attitudes towards the Right to Life (Regression Analysis)

With the second research question, the predictors of attitudes towards to the right to life enter the picture. Theoretically, the assumption was that human dignity will be a strong predictor, especially as far as the concept of inherent dignity is concerned. It was also assumed that religion makes a difference since most religions have a clear position on questions of life and death.

The analysis for all respondents is in line with the assumption that was made at the end of the correlation analysis in general and reveals some interesting nuances (see Table 4.4).

Our new insight is that hedonism has the strongest explanatory power with regard to euthanasia and abortion. It is the habit of self-enhancement that leads positively to a respondent adopting a permissive attitude towards euthanasia and abortion, and it is the absence of religious commitment that explains support for the view that it is permissible to terminate life via euthanasia and abortion. So far, religion counts in terms of non-religiosity. Furthermore, an acceptance of the concept of inherent human dignity has no significant impact on respondents' views concerning either

Table 4.4 Regression analysis between independent and dependent variables

	Euthanasia	Abortion
	Beta	Beta
Value dignity		
Dignity – merit	–.106***	–.030
Dignity – moral stature	.043	.054*
Dignity – inherent	.019	–.038
Religious belief		
Religous practice	–.126***	–.109***
Importance of religion	–.127***	–.115***
Social religion	–.105***	–.075**
Value		
Hedonism	.133***	.141***
Control variable		
Age	.001	.012
Sex	–.003	–.010
Adj. R^2	.113	.092
Significance	***	***

Legend: N = 1862; *$p \leq .05$; **$p \leq .01$; ***$p \leq .001$

euthanasia or abortion. The rejection of dignity of merit explains support for euthanasia and – with a low degree of significance – the view that dignity is linked to morality is connected to respondents supporting abortion. Again, age and sex bear no relevance. In both analyses the explained variance is low.

The next analysis focuses on religious differences. The question is if the predictors for attitudes towards the right to life differ when Catholics, Protestants, Muslims and non-religiously affiliated students are separated in the regression analysis. The same predictor variables as in the previous analysis will be considered here (see Table 4.5).

We come first to the outcomes for euthanasia. The results for Catholics and Protestants show a high degree of significance, although the explained variance is low. For Catholics, and even more for Protestants, hedonism is the most significant factor. An interesting finding is that hedonism is the only concept that explains the attitude of Protestants towards euthanasia, as no other significant predictor can be found. For Catholics, the weight of hedonism is slightly lower. The degree of non-importance of belief has the second highest impact. It should be mentioned that being Catholic does not mean being religious as the Catholic Church defines, as young people can formally share their parents' religious affiliation, without themselves being religiously committed in any way. Thirdly, the rejection of dignity as being dependent on the appreciation given by others is significant. Another interesting finding is that, although Muslim students show some relevant betas, the overall result is of only low significance. With regard to euthanasia, it is also worth noting that the attitude of non-religiously affiliated young people is predicted only by one negative beta. It is the explicit statement "not being religious" that explains the

Table 4.5 Regression analysis between independent and dependent variables by religious groups

	Euthanasia				Abortion			
	R.C.	Prot.	Musl.	No-R.	R.C.	Prot.	Musl.	No-R.
Value dignity								
Merit	−.103**	−.065	−.156	−.078	.014	−.020	−.060	−.060
Behaviour	.064	.032	.088	.022	.084*	.014	.037	.580
Inherent	−.032	.030	.156	.050	−.081*	.019	.023	−.044
Religious belief								
Practice	−.056	−.110	−.191	−.146**	−.051	−.136**	−.104	−.066
Importance	−.116**	−.081	−.117	−.029	−.074	−.078	−.113	−.006
Rel. social force	−.052	−.032	−.064	−.070	−.016	−.153**	−.101	−.037
Value								
Hedonism	.148***	.209***	.092	.029	.153***	.218***	.117	.056
Control variables								
Age	.001	.064	−.016	.009	.018	.019	−.038	.052
Sex	−.036	−.029	.015	.091	−.028	−.019	.056	.008
Adj. R^2	.063	.085	.154	.055	.064	.135	.083	.023
Significance	***	***	*	**	***	***	Ns	Ns

Legend: N = 1862; $*p \leq .05$; $**p \leq .01$; $***p \leq .001$; *ns* not significant, *R.C.* Roman Catholic, *Prot.* Protestant, *Musl.* Muslim, *No-R.* No religious affiliation

acceptance of euthanasia. For all groups, religion counts most as a framework that encourages a critical attitude towards the termination of life.

With regard to abortion, only the regression analysis for Catholics and Protestants shows a significant result. Again, the strongest predictor for both is hedonism; for Protestants hedonism counts even more. Interestingly, for Catholic respondents, the attitude towards abortion is not caused by religious commitment. Being religious has neither a positive nor a negative impact on respondents' attitudes towards abortion. In other words, Catholics' attitudes towards abortion are independent on their degree of religiousness. For Protestants, the absence of religious commitment and the rejection of the view that the Church has a social role is a predictor for respondents' adopting a permissive attitude towards abortion. The explained variance of 13.5% is the highest compared with all other regression analyses. For Muslims and religiously non-affiliated youth, the predictors in this analysis have no significant weight and the analyses are non-significant.

Conclusion

This paper sought to answer the questions of what young Germans' attitudes towards euthanasia and abortion are and whether there are differences between Catholics, Protestants, Muslims and religiously non-affiliated youth, as well as whether and to what extent respondents' understanding of human dignity, belief and value orientation can predict attitudes towards the right to life.

The expectation was that youth in Germany will generally share the moderate liberal position which is largely the dominant opinion in Germany. At the same time, it was assumed that religiously committed youth, especially Catholics, will be more restrained in accepting both euthanasia and abortion. Furthermore, it was expected that young people who agree with the concept of inherent human dignity will be more cautious in accepting the termination of life via euthanasia and abortion, while a hedonistic value orientation that is focused on one's own well-being and on self-directed decisions will predict a higher acceptance of euthanasia and abortion.

Our empirical findings show that there is slightly more acceptance of euthanasia than abortion. In both cases, Muslims are positive-ambivalent, while Catholics, Protestants and non-affiliated respondents support the view that it is permissible to terminate life. The hierarchy is similar: the lowest degree of support is given by Muslims, followed by Catholics, Protestants and – with the most positive attitude – the non-religiously affiliated youth. It is Muslims, not Catholics, who show the utmost restraint when it comes to the issues of euthanasia and abortion. This result suggests that religion does make a difference. However, religious affiliation is an ambiguous indicator and was supplemented in the empirical analysis by religious practice, the importance of belief and the social role of the religious community. The inclusion of these concepts confirms that religion is relevant when questions of life and death are raised.

If there were significant betas, the sign was always negative and the reason for this lies in the structure of the items. Theoretically, the statements run from prohibition to permission. Empirically, the construction of the scale resulted in two scales, each of which had only a permissive content. In other words, the theoretical differentiation of criteria for euthanasia and abortion was empirically irrelevant. Both scales expressed a general permissive orientation towards euthanasia and abortion. The reaction of respondents on these scales is therefore agreement or disagreement (i.e. with the statement that euthanasia and abortion should be permitted). However, if respondents perceived a tension between their religious commitment and the permissive orientation represented in the scales, the outcome was negative.

What is surprising is that the concept of inherent dignity showed less significance than was expected. There is only one case where the concept of inherent dignity became significant: Catholics who are critical of this concept tended to support abortion.

Another surprising finding was the importance of a hedonistic value orientation. This concept was included because some influence was expected, but our empirical analysis showed that, firstly, hedonism received the highest acceptance of all concepts used in this study and, secondly, that hedonism is the strongest predictor for respondents' having positive attitudes towards euthanasia and abortion. As has been stated, it is part of a hedonistic orientation to claim autonomy and self-directedness and, in the case of euthanasia, autonomy becomes relevant when the suffering person has decided that their life may be terminated. In the case of abortion, autonomy is often connected with the woman's decision not to continue her pregnancy. The idea that hedonism has a role to play is understandable, but it is the importance and the weight of this concept that is surprising.

In this study a limited number of concepts were used, and our study does not claim to have depicted a comprehensive picture of the attitudes of the youth towards the right to life and the predictors that influence young people's attitudes. Furthermore, the explained variance of most of the analyses is low, which is an indication that any future research needs to include alternative concepts. There is no clear answer why there are hardly any indicators explaining Muslims' attitudes towards euthanasia and abortion and, to some extent, the attitude of non-religiously affiliated youth in this sample.

References

Bagaric, M., & Allen, J. (2006). The vacuous concept of dignity. *Journal of Human Rights, 5*, 257–270.

Bowen, D. L. (2003). Contemporary Muslim ethics of abortion. In J. E. Brockopp (Ed.), *Islamic ethics of life. Abortion, war and euthanasia* (pp. 51–80). Columbia: University of South Carolina Press.

Brockopp, J. E. (2003a). The "good death" in Islamic theology and law. In J. E. Brockopp (Ed.), *Islamic ethics of life. Abortion, war and euthanasia* (pp. 177–193). Columbia: University of South Carolina Press.

Brockopp, J. E. (Ed.). (2003b). *Islamic ethics of life. Abortion, war and euthanasia*. Columbia: University of South Carolina Press.

Devellis, R. F. (2003). *Scale development: Theory and applications*. London: Sage.

Dworkin, R. (1993). *Life's dominion. An argument about abortion, euthanasia and individual freedom*. New York: Knopf.

Ernst, S. (2007). Verhältnismäßige und unverhältnismäßige Mittel. Eine bedenkenswerte Unterscheidung in der lehramtlichen Bewertung der Sterbehilfe. *Münchener Theologische Zeitschrift (MThZ), 58*, 43–57.

Grimm, D. (2013). Dignity in a legal context: Dignity as an absolute right. In C. McCrudden (Ed.), *Understanding Human Dignity* (pp. 381–391). Oxford: Oxford University Press.

Ilkilic, I. (2008). Medizinethische Entscheidungen am Lebensende in einer wertpluralen Gesellschaft am Beispiel muslimischer Patienten. *Zeitschrift für Evangelische Ethik, 52*, 34–49.

Kellner, M. (2010). *Islamische Rechtsmeinungen zu medizinischen Eingriffen an den Grenzen des Lebens. Ein Beitrag zur kulturübergreifenden Bioethik*. Würzburg: Ergon.

Mantei, S. (2004). Nein und Ja zur Abtreibung. In *Die evangelische Kirche in der Reformdebatte um §218 StGB (1970–1976)*. Göttingen: Vandenhoek & Ruprecht.

Nordenfelt, L. (2004). The varieties of dignity. *Health Care Analysis, 12*, 69–81.

Rosen, M. (2012). *Dignity – Its history and meaning*. Cambridge: Harvard University Press.

Schockenhoff, E. (2009). *Ethik des Lebens*. Freiburg: Herder.

Schwartz, S. H. (1994). Are there universal aspects in the structure and contents of human values? *Journal of Social Issues, 50*, 19–45.

Schwartz, S. H., & Sagiv, L. (1995). Identifying culture-specifics in the content and structure of values. *Journal of Cross-Cultural Psychology, 26*(1), 92–116.

Sterbebegleitung statt aktiver Sterbehilfe. (2003). *Eine Textsammlung kirchlicher Erklärungen*. (Eds.), Protestant Church in Germany (EKD) & Bishopsconference of the Catholic Church, Hannover/Bonn. http://www.ekd.de/EKD-Texte/44666.html

van der Ven, J. A. (2013). Euthanasia from the angle of law, morality and religion: A cross-cultural perspective. In E. Venbrux & Th. Quartier (Eds.), *Changing European death ways* (Death studies, Vol. 1). Münster: LIT.
Ziebertz, H.-G., & Reindl, M. (2013). Religion and attitudes towards euthanasia and abortion. An empirical study among young Christians and Muslims in Germany. In J. A. Van der Ven & H.-G. Ziebertz (Eds.), *Human rights and the impact of religion* (pp. 119–143). Brill: Leiden.
Ziebertz, H.-G., Döhnert, S., & Unser, A. (2017). Predictors of attitudes towards human dignity: An empirical analysis among youth in Germany. In H.-G. Ziebertz & C. Sterkens (Eds.), *Religion and civil human rights in empirical perspective*. Heidelberg: Springer.

Documents

Charter of Fundamental Rights in the European Union (1950).
Declaration on Euthanasia (Vatican 1980).
Donum Vitae (Vatican 1987).
International Covenant on Economic, Social and Cultural Rights (UN, 1966).
Universal Declaration of Human Rights (UN, 1948).

Chapter 5
The Impact of Religion on Attitudes Towards Abortion and Euthanasia. An Empirical Study Among Italian Students

Francesco Zaccaria, Francis-Vincent Anthony, and Carl Sterkens

Abbreviations

CCC	*Catechism of the Catholic Church.* Promulgated by Pope John Paul II (October 11, 1992)
COMECE	Commission of the Bishops' Conferences of the European Community.
DE	*Declaration on Euthanasia.* Congregation for the doctrine of the faith (May 5, 1980).
DV	*Donum Vitae.* Instruction of the Congregation for the doctrine of the faith on respect for human life in its origin and on the dignity of procreation (February 22, 1987).
EV	*Evangelium Vitae.* Encyclical letter of Pope John Paul II on the value and inviolability of human life (March 25, 1995).
GS	*Gaudium et Spes.* Pastoral constitution on the church in the modern world promulgated by Pope Paul VI (December 7, 1965).
VS	*Veritatis Splendor.* Encyclical letter of Pope John Paul II on some fundamental questions of the church's moral teaching (August 6, 1993).

All (English translations of) documents of the Second Vatican Council, Popes and Vatican Congregations have been taken from the Vatican website: www.vatican.va.

F. Zaccaria (✉)
Department of Practical Theology, Apulian Theological Faculty, Bari, Italy
e-mail: frazacc@yahoo.it

F.-V. Anthony
Department of Practical Theology, Salesian Pontifical University, Rome, Italy
e-mail: vincent@unisal.it

C. Sterkens
Faculty of Philosophy, Theology and Religious Studies, Radboud University Nijmegen, Nijmegen, The Netherlands
e-mail: c.sterkens@rs.ru.nl

H.-G. Ziebertz, F. Zaccaria (eds.), *Euthanasia, Abortion, Death Penalty and Religion – The Right to Life and its Limitations*, Religion and Human Rights 4, https://doi.org/10.1007/978-3-319-98773-6_5

Among the sensitive topics of the current public debate in Italy, bioethical questions are certainly to be found, more specifically those questions about the issues surrounding the beginning and the end of life, namely the ethical legitimacy and the legal boundaries of abortive and euthanasian practices. In this study we seek to explore the role of religion in this debate, not only at the level of church doctrine but also at the level of personal convictions and ideas of a Italian young people, which may shape the future of this debate. The empirical findings of this study, on a sample of secondary school students (N = 1087), show that religious beliefs and practices do have a significant impact on the students' attitudes on abortion and euthanasia and highlight a relevant role of religion in the current public debate on bioethical issues.

Introduction

Among the sensitive topics and the hot issues of the current public debate in Italy, bioethical questions are certainly to be found, more specifically those questions about the issues surrounding the beginning and the end of life, namely the ethical legitimacy and the legal boundaries of abortive and euthanasian practices. In this study we seek to explore the role of religion in this debate, not only at the level of church doctrine but also at the level of personal convictions and ideas of a sample of Italian students, which may shape the future of this debate. With this in view, we first take up bioethical issues in the framework of the human rights' discourse, secondly we address the position of the Catholic Church toward the issues of abortion and euthanasia. Then we present the conceptual framework the methods of our empirical research, and the empirical results. We shall conclude with a brief discussion on the findings of this study.

The Right to Life and Bioethical Issues

Enshrined since 1776 in the United States Declaration of Independence, the right to life is specified for the first time in international documents in 1948 both in the Universal Declaration of Human Rights and in the American Declaration of the Rights and Duties of Man. The 1953 European Convention on Human Rights, in Article 2, for the first time calls for legal enforcement of the right to life: "Everyone's right to life shall be protected by law", while stipulating a list of exceptions when intentional deprivation of life is permissible (e.g. death penalty). A similar compromise was reached by the 1966 International Covenant on Civil and Political Rights, where Article 6 states that "no one shall be arbitrarily deprived of his life", allowing for circumstances in which the right of life cannot be considered an absolute right. From these first formulations it appears that the affirmation of the right to life in human rights documents is open to ambiguous interpretations about its limitations and its rightful beneficiaries (Wicks 2012, 200–205). The ambiguity in declarations about the right of life mirrors the open debate about the application, the protection and the limitations of this right in current legislation; this debate in modern societies focuses mainly on the protection and the dignity of human life at its beginning and ending stages. This focus triggers current discussions about the ethical boundaries of abortion and euthanasia, which require the involvement of philosophical, juridical, political, religious actors and arguments in the public debate. Is a human embryo entitled to the right to life? How to balance the protection of human life and the principle of autonomy of sick people who wish to put an end to their suffering by choosing death? (Tiensuu 2015). Such dilemmas are faced by the general public and policy makers while addressing bioethical issues. With a view to shedding some light on the complex bioethical questions related to abortion and euthanasia, we shall examine their historical roots and their current relevance.

Abortion

The bioethical issue of abortion brings to the fore the protection of life at its early stages. An adequate comprehension of the abortion dilemma requires that we consider the cultural influence on the ethical evaluation of abortive practices both in the course of history and in the current public debate.

Diverse Views on Abortion in the Course of History

Moral evaluation of certain behaviours can change depending on cultural and historical influences; for example, no one today would be open to slavery as morally acceptable, as in some societies in the past. What is then the historical development of the moral stand with regard to abortion? Starting with the ancient Hellenistic culture we find that both Plato and Aristotle were open to the practice of abortion as a means of family planning and demographic control, although with some substantial differences. Plato was convinced that human life begins at the moment of conception, while Aristotle introduced an ontological difference between the foetus at the early and the one at later stages of pregnancy. Some Stoic thinkers condemned abortion, but also in their case the moral evaluation was not based on the embryo's right to live but rather on demographic and societal reasons (Schockenhoff 1997, 304–305). In brief, we can say that in ancient Hellenistic culture abortion was an undisputed medical practice (Jerouschek 1988). Roman Law did not considered the unborn child a subject of rights but rather a property of the mother, or more commonly of the father of the family; that is why terminating a pregnancy was considered a minor crime against property. In practice abortion was morally disapproved but very rarely prosecuted in court. Such a view of the Roman law on abortion has its parallel in the ancient Middle-eastern and Jewish juridical traditions: Babylonian and Sumerian codes of law, as also Talmud, Mishna and Palestinian Judaism

(Ex 21:22–25), considered abortion as a felony against property rather than a crime against an individual. Under the influence of Aristotelian philosophers who referred to the human foetus as "animated" at its later stages, meaning that the foetus had a soul (*anima*, in Latin), Greek Judaism began to consider abortion from the perspective of the embryo and hence as a crime against the unborn baby rather than against the society or the family's property. The Greek translation of Exodus 21 shows this shift and how abortion at later stages of pregnancy was compared to homicide (Schockenhoff 1997, 306–307).

Early Christianity made a further step in the moral condemnation of abortion, grounding it not much in the Hellenistic theory of the foetus' "animation" but rather in the protection of life in itself. According to the German theologian Schockenhoff (1997), early Christian thinkers found the arguments in favour of the protection of the unborn in respect of God, Creator of life, and his commandment not to kill, as mentioned in the *Didache*, but also in the positive commandment of Jesus Christ to love the neighbour, as the Letter of Barnabas recites. Christian doctrine condemning abortion and defending human life from the moment of conception, had a weak influence even when Christianity became State religion: sermons, synod and council decrees fiercely opposing abortion confirm that this was practiced during the middle ages. Secular jurisdiction on the matter of abortion increased in the modern era, in many cases the secularisation of the abortion's prohibition led to more severe punishments, in some cases even death penalty for the mother. Through the centuries, the legislation on abortion became an instrument of social and demographic control of the lower classes, oppressing peasants and especially women, who had to pay the heaviest penalties. With the age of Enlightenment there was a shift toward a progressive depenalisation of abortion, as death penalty was turned into imprisonment. Subsequently the enlightened juridical doctrine focused on how to prevent abortion rather than the practice of harsh punishments: a progressive decriminalisation of sexually "deviated" behaviours was put forward, together with a stronger fight against poverty and a plea for better education of the people (Schockenhoff 1997, 307–312).

This line of thought initiated by the Enlightenment which focused more on the prevention rather than the criminalisation of abortion, more on the autonomy of women's choice than on the defence of life in all circumstances, brought in the twentieth century to an increasing liberalisation of abortion in the Western democratic societies: United Kingdom legalised voluntary termination of pregnancy in 1967, Canada in 1969, USA at federal level in 1973, Austria in 1974, France in 1975 and so on. Of course, legislation varies from country to country in terms of reasons for which abortion is allowed and weeks of pregnancy in which its termination is legal. In Italy, elective abortion was regulated in 1978 with Law 194. According to this law, abortion must be carried out in a public hospital and can be performed for health-related, social, economic, family reasons within 3 months pregnancy, after which a woman could request the termination of pregnancy only if her health was at risk or a foetal abnormality was diagnosed. When a physician issues a certificate testifying that legal requirements for the abortion are met, the law prescribes a 7-day waiting period before the abortion can be carried out (Bo et al. 2015, 273), for, the rationale behind the law is to prevent and not to foster abortions, to protect human life and not to consider abortion as an instrument of birth control (Law 194/1978, Art. 1). Against this backdrop, we might wonder if abortions actually decreased during the last decades in Italy; official statistics of the Ministry of Health say they did: the ratio of elective abortions (number of abortions per 1000 live births) was 382 in 1983, 287 in 1991, 266 in 1997, 224 in 2007 and 198 in 2014. These results suggest that the purpose of the law, namely protecting life by reducing the number of abortions, might have been reached in the last decades, nevertheless abortion is a far too complex and multifaceted issue to explain decrease solely by the introduction of a law.

In the course of history abortion was differently considered in the light of the philosophical, theological and medical knowledge of the time, in general when the embryo started to be seen as "animated" life, abortion began to be considered as a crime comparable to killing a human being. With the Enlightenment a shift started toward decriminalisation of abortion which produced its legalisation in many countries during the twentieth century, nevertheless abortion never ceased to be considered an "evil" to prevent, therefore many issues continue to stay open in the current debate around the boundaries of abortion's practices and policies.

Open Issues in the Public Debate

Abortion is still a debated issue, in spite of the historic trend, which brought to its depenalisation and legalisation; it is vital for a democratic society to be aware of the voices within the public opinion which question current abortive policies. We confine ourselves here to three main debated issues, especially from the Italian point of view: the alleged rise of clashes between pro-choice and pro-life movements, conscientious objection of physicians, and abortion in the face of poverty.

Firstly, it is relevant to highlight the contrast between those who defend the right of women to choose about their pregnancy and those who defend the right to life of the unborn child. Those belonging to the first camp lament the failure of the United Nations' Rio Declaration in 2012 to recognise the "right of abortion", which was also rejected by the European Parliament in 2013, and they ascribe these moves to an alleged rise of influential political activism of right-wing movements and churches, namely of the Catholic Church in Poland and Southern Europe, of Evangelicals and Pentecostals in the USA and Latin America, and of Orthodox churches in Eastern Europe. In order to support this view different examples are cited: in 2013 Spain abolished the liberal abortion law which was approved 4 years earlier; in Poland a very restrictive law was passed in 1993 and further attempts to pass legislation which would prohibit abortion are being made; the increase in conscientious objection of physicians who refuse to perform abortion in Italy; a more restrictive law passed in Macedonia in 2013; Hungary's introduction in the Constitution of the "protection of the foetus" in 2011 and other such cases of harsh political battles in Latin America and the rise of pro-life movements and propositions in USA and Central-Western Europe (Heinen 2014). On the other hand, pro-life supporters underscore the juridical impossibility to talk of a “right of abortion” and lament about the increase of lobbying movements and legislation propositions, which soften abortion laws where it is already legal and introduce it where it is not, mostly in the global south (Sartea 2013; Villanueva Cañadas 2014). This brief overview brings to light that the debate on abortion is often locked up in contrasting arguments which do not seem to aim at effective communication and consensus but rather at endless ideological struggles.

As mentioned above, a crucial battlefield on abortion in Italy is the rather high number of physicians who refuse to perform termination of pregnancy appealing to conscientious objection, which is stipulated by Article 9 of Law 194/1978. Such objectors are exempted from performing any actions which may directly cause a termination of pregnancy, unless there is a medical emergency. Over the last years, the proportion of objectors has risen from 59.1% in 1983 to 69.3% in 2011; now it is stable around 70%. This phenomenon fuelled public debate about the legitimacy of conscientious objection because it might lead to certain difficulties and delays for women who wish to have access to abortion. In fact, the European Committee of Social Rights received a complaint against Italy requesting the Committee to declare that Law 194 does not ensure adequate and safe access to abortion. A first decision of the Committee was in favour of the complainer, stating that Article 9 violates the rights to health protection and non-discrimination enshrined in the European Social Charter, but in July 2016 the Committee of Ministers of the Council of Europe reversed this decision and promoted Italy for its handling of the matter. Nevertheless, the fact that Italy still remains under investigation, suggests that the issue of conscientious objection remains open. Furthermore, empirical data do not seem to offer a clear picture of this phenomenon: while in 2012 the statistics of the Italian National Committee on Bioethics concluded that no correlation exists between the number of objectors and the length of waiting time for abortion, a recent study of Bo et al. (2015) appears to challenge this conclusion. It means that public debate on abortion policies in Italy is in progress and that the media play an important role in this debate.

There is a third issue that fuels debate around abortion and its ethical legitimacy: economic reasons seem to increasingly condition the choice of performing termination of pregnancy. A closer look at the number of abortions in different European countries over the years shows that the declining trend between 2000 and 2009 reversed during the economic recession between 2010 and 2012, especially among younger generations (Lima et al. 2015). In Italy, the official data of the Ministry of Health released in 2015 indicate that the rate of abortions among immigrant women, notably in more difficult economic circumstances, is three times higher than the rate among Italian women. Different reports show that economic reasons are a major trigger of abortion. These data raise many questions: if the purpose of the legalisation of abortion was to ensure women freedom of choice and their medical safety together with a reduction of pregnancy terminations, how can we describe a choice as free when it is triggered by economic hardship? What is the role of the State in preventing abortions by fostering economic support for pregnant women in financial difficulties? How effective are policies in favour of life—the aim of Law 194 –

if so many women today in Italy have to choose abortion for these reasons? Is abortion for economic reasons ethically acceptable?

In this paragraph we have shown how legalisation of abortion did not end the debate about its ethical boundaries and legitimation. Many issues continue to be discussed and many actors and arguments engage in this debate: juridical, political, ethical and, not as least, religious ones. This explains the reason for conducting the present research on attitudes towards abortion and the factors that may influence these attitudes.

Euthanasia

Having considered the disputes referring to protection of life at its early stages, we now turn to those related to end-of-life, namely the ethical evaluation of euthanasia in the past and in the present context.

Diverse Views on Euthanasia in the Course of History

Unlike the case of abortion, one cannot find ethical debates on euthanasia dating back to ancient philosophy, as the term euthanasia ("good" or "beautiful death", in Greek) was applied to either a painless and easy death or to a glorious and honourable one, and not in the way it has been understood from the seventeenth century, namely as the conscious choice to accompany or induce a painless death, either by abstaining to do something to prevent death or to actively perform actions to accelerate it (Schockenhoff 1997, 314–315). Nevertheless, the theologian van der Ven points out how the arguments used today for supporting or rejecting the ethical legitimation of euthanasia are rooted in the ancient debate about the moral evaluation of the suicide. Referring to van der Ven's study we sketch the history of the ethical assessment of euthanasia starting from the premodern thinkers who laid down the background of a negative ethical evaluation of suicide against which modern thought developed the arguments supporting the legitimacy of euthanasia in Western society (Van der Ven 2010, 21–58).

In Hellenistic and Roman cultures suicide was justified and even praised by Stoic philosophers, who saw the conscious choice to take one's own life as a sign of strength, courage and the highest expression of the stoic virtue of *apatheia*, namely the ultimate liberation from all passions and sufferings. This idea was vehemently criticised by the early Christian thought, in a systematic way by Augustine. He described the choice of the Roman politician and thinker Cato, who preferred to die than to legitimise his political enemy, as an act of weakness in the face of political struggle rather than a courageous choice. Augustine challenged the religious arguments underlying Cato's stoic worldview, such as the atonement for past sins, by using the biblical argument of the fifth commandment – "You shall not kill" – and the necessity of accepting the will of God. The medieval Cristian philosopher and theologian Thomas Aquinas systematised at best the traditional arguments against suicide, both from a non-religious and a religious point of view, arguments which left a permanent trace in the discussion around euthanasia. The first argument is that suicide is against nature, namely the natural tendency to preserve and love oneself; secondly, suicide harms society of which everyone is a part; the third argument against suicide is that it goes against God's gift of life and his power to shape it. In line with Augustine, Thomas Aquinas did not think that suffering is an evil in itself to be avoided in all cases; sometimes it is possible to accept suffering as part of a larger divine plan; sometimes it can lead to greater good and spiritual perfection (Zaccaria 2010, 123–127). Being not an evil in itself but rather privation of good (*privatio boni*), suffering cannot justify death, which would be a larger privation of good. Such Christian scholastic thinking influenced the church doctrine condemning suicide and shaped the framework in which religious arguments against euthanasia are being developed today.

According to van der Ven (2010, 44–58), arguments legitimising euthanasia arose in Western society with modernity, not so much in direct reference to euthanasia as it is understood in our days, but more as an expression of a deeper development of social, cultural, religious, juridical shifts. We briefly mention here some of these shifts in order to understand the current debate on euthanasia and its decriminalisation, which is a consequence of this process. The first shift of modernity is functional differentiation, namely the loss of the medieval monopoly of religion in all fields of society and the consequent differentiation of society in systems with their own rules and regulations (for example the economic, the cultural, and the juridical system). This brought Francis Bacon in the seventeenth century to point out the role of the doctor at the deathbed, and not only of the priest, "when it may serve to make a fair passage" (Bacon 1973, 114). With the development of modern sciences in the sixteenth century a second shift gained strength, namely the one towards the desacralisation of nature: viewing nature and its laws as independent of God's intervention on the one hand, and human beings as capable of controlling the nature through science and technology, including life and death. Besides nature, other aspects such as the political and juridical were subtracted from the religious umbrella: sovereignty and political power were viewed as not deriving directly from the will of the personal God of Cristian revelation, but rather belonging to a social structure designed by a deistic type of divine architect. According to the seventeenth century thinker Hugo Grotius even justice should be administrated as if God did not exist (*etsi Deus non daretur*), suggesting the progressive emancipation of law from religion. In this vein, modernity promoted the notion that human beings are not God's property, neither their life nor their death, but rather that humans are in control of their individual and social reality. The deistic and pantheistic trends of modern philosophy brought into question God's commitment to human life, confining God to more abstract ideas and to areas far from concerns as suffering and death. While God loses grip with such matters in modern thinking, individuals gain control of them: in the final stages of life, human beings wish to keep their autonomy and steer the suffering and dying process in the most peaceful way possible. Such autonomy is affirmed by a further shift, namely, that of individualism. Individuals are retained autonomous not only from God but, in the light of the modern values of equality and freedom, also from the collective identity. The traditional argument against euthanasia as harmful to society cannot be used at a time when the clash between communitarian and personal interests would be in favour of the latter. This brings us to the last shift of modernity contributing to the moral legitimation of euthanasia, the shift toward utilitarianism. According to MacIntyre (2009) the shift toward utilitarianism begins with the substitution of the common good with the principal of utility: an action is as good as the production of total pleasure and reduction of pain for everyone affected by the consequences. Such a view can lead to questionable consequences, such as the possibility to accord less value to unproductive lives, for example of psychiatric or terminal patients. According to Habermas (1982) utilitarianism is an expression of economic colonisation of society, a mentality of utility and profit which is pervasive in all areas of society, in politics, in education, in health care and hence also in the care of terminal patients, raising the ethical question about the pressure which such an utilitarian environment can exercise on the will of the patient asking for euthanasia.

The short historical sketch of the ethical evaluations of euthanasia, presented above, shows the development from an initial condemnation of suicide by early Christianity to a growing acceptance of suicide and euthanasia as it is understood today. Such a stand results from the cultural shifts which associated with modernisation: functional differentiation of society, desacralisation of nature, politics and law, increasing control of life and death, individualism and utilitarianism. These developments induced the acceptance of euthanasia in the Western societies on moral grounds, to result finally in the decriminalisation of euthanasia under certain conditions in several countries: the Netherlands legalised euthanasia in 2000, Belgium in 2002, Luxemburg in 2009, Colombia in 2015 and Canada in 2016. The debate is currently open in many other countries. We address this debate, focusing on Italy, in the next paragraph.

Open Issues in the Public Debate

Currently in pluralistic Western society, both non-religious and religious arguments are used for and against the legalisation of euthanasia (van der Ven 2010, 59–157). In the case of Italy, in general those in favour of a regulation of euthanasia are mainly non-religious taking their arguments from the cultural shifts of modernity we mentioned above., They tend to justify euthanasia on the basis of the right to privacy of the terminally ill patients, their autonomy, and their "right to die". Privacy as a human right includes the right of individuals to their own vision of the meaning and value of their life, including the quality of their life. When a patient values his/her life well below the acceptable level of quality and meaning, when the painful situation of an incurable disease becomes unbearable, supporters of euthanasia justify the right to die on the basis of the right to privacy. The concept of autonomy is also put forward to legitimise euthanasia: when it can be reasonably verified by a third party that patients are free in their choice and have thoroughly reflected on their decision to terminate their life, their autonomy must be respected. In this vein, those in favour of legalising euthanasia, put forward the so called "right to die", although this right has never been officially recognised or codified. This right would imply that individuals are in full control of their body, that there is "informed consent" of patients about medical treatments they have to undergo. The supporters of the freedom to choose euthanasia apply this principle to all medical interventions as well as to refraining from them, thus including those actions which lead to the death of the patient. These arguments are debated under the critical scrutiny of counter-arguments, leaving open the discussion about the moral legitimacy of euthanasia (Van der Ven 2010, 100–140).

The debate reached a climax in the case of Eluana Englaro, with the national press influencing public opinion and political discussions on euthanasia. Ms. Englaro, a 37-years-old woman, was in a persistent vegetative state for 17 years, as a consequence of a car accident. Her father proposed the removal of artificial nutrition and hydration because his daughter had expressed before the accident the wish to die in case she found herself in a vegetative state. Since judges rejected his request three times, he started a campaign to mobilise public opinion in his favour. Euthanasia in Italy is treated as murder under Article 575 of the Criminal Code. Also in case when a patient agrees to the act that ends his or her life, everyone who contributes to the execution of such an act is punishable from six to 15 years of imprisonment. Nevertheless, in medical practice there is a general consensus in refraining from medical interventions that have no effect on the patient's illness. In November 2008, the Italian Supreme Court accepted Mr. Englaro's request to suspend artificial nutrition and hydration of her daughter Eluana. While affirming the principle that active euthanasia is prohibited, the Supreme Court compared artificial nutrition and hydration to a medical treatment, and concluded that withdrawing it expresses a right enacted by the Italian Constitution, namely the right of the patient's autonomy regarding health and, as in this case, life itself (Solarino et al. 2011).

Such a ground-breaking decision of the Court gave rise to public discussion on euthanasia in Italy. After many draft laws on euthanasia and on 'living wills' presented in the last years, on December 2017 the Parliament approved a law on living wills (Law 219/2017) which excludes euthanasia but gives adults of full capacity the possibility to formally indicate which medical treatments they wish to receive in case they will be no longer capable of making such choices. Longitudinal surveys show that the Italian public opinion is moving in the last decades toward more permissive attitudes towards euthanasia, like most of the European countries, and with a remarkable increase if we compare the data collected in the European Values Survey wave of 1999 with those collected in 2008 (Cohen et al. 2013, 2014). From the 2016 annual survey EURISPES conducted in Italy, it appears that about 60% percent of the population supports euthanasia. The Italian debate about a more comprehensive law on euthanasia is still open; Italian public opinion follows the trend of Western societies in the direction of its legitimisation and acceptance, provoked by the cultural shifts of modernity. As we shall see below, one of the most vocal actors in this debate voicing a contrary stand has been the Catholic Church.

The Position of the Catholic Church on Bioethical Issues

Generally religion is considered as a key cultural factor in shaping opinions and choices regarding abortion and euthanasia; nevertheless, empirical findings are ambivalent and do not always support such hypothesis: sometimes religious attitudes seem to have little or no effect on bioethical attitudes (Van der Ven 2010, 158–211), other times religious attitudes appear to play a major role in these issues (Gielen et al. 2011; Meñaca et al. 2012). This explains the relevance of our study on the role of religion in shaping the attitudes of Italian students on bioethical issues. Taking up such an empirical study requires that we first clarify the position of the Catholic Church on abortion and euthanasia.

Abortion

Building on the condemnation of abortion since the early Christianity, as we have seen in section "Diverse views on abortion in the course of history", the current Catholic official teachings reiterate the negative moral evaluation of abortion as an "intrinsically evil" act, to be avoided in all circumstances (*VS* 80; Sgreccia 2007, 567–571). John Paul II justifies this teaching on abortion as an evil act always and *per se* by quoting the Second Vatican Council, which underscores that "whatever is opposed to life itself, such as any type of murder, genocide, abortion, euthanasia or wilful self-destruction ... all these things and others of their like are infamies indeed. They poison human society, but they do more harm to those who practice them than those who suffer from the injury. Moreover, they are supreme dishonour to the Creator" (*GS* 27). Here the traditional arguments of Thomas Aquinas against suicide (cf. section "Diverse views on euthanasia in the course of history") are extended to include all attempts to harm or terminate human life: insofar as these acts are against the natural inclination to preserve life, they harm society and they offend God. The stand of the church against abortion is justified by the belief that human life must be protected from the very beginning, as *Gaudium et Spes* says: "from the moment of its conception life must be guarded with the greatest care while abortion and infanticide are unspeakable crimes" (*GS* 51). The official teaching of the Catholic Church did not consider the theoretical definition of the embryo as a person or the ancient debate on the "animation" of foetus, which did not find much consensus among early and medieval Christian thinkers. Nonetheless, the 1987 Instruction of the Vatican Congregation lead by Joseph Ratzinger *Donum Vitae* affirms that "the Magisterium has not expressly committed itself to an affirmation of a philosophical nature, but it constantly reaffirms the moral condemnation of any kind of procured abortion. This teaching has not been changed and is unchangeable" (*DV* I, 1). This teaching is reiterated by John Paul II in 1995 *Evangelium Vitae*: "Human life is sacred and inviolable at every moment of existence, including the initial phase which precedes birth" (*EV* 61). Human life is sacred and everyone is entitled to an "inalienable right to life" from the moment of conception, as the Catechism of the Catholic Church teaches: "Human life must be respected and protected absolutely from the moment of conception. From the first moment of his existence, a human being must be recognised as having the rights of a person – among which is the inviolable right of every innocent being to life" (2270). Therefore the church considers elective abortion a grave sin and punishes it with "excommunication" for all the people who are involved in the process (CCC 2272). Excommunication means that from a canonical point of view only some priests can grant absolution for abortion, depending on the diocesan guidelines. It is relevant to note here that Pope Francis in 2016 extended this faculty permanently to all priests, in order to enhance the mercy of God, which is taught by the church to be limitless also in case of grave sins.

Does this doctrine apply to all cases? What if we take the extreme case of a pregnancy that puts at risk the survival of the mother? How to solve the dilemma between two absolute values to be defended, namely the mother's life and that of the unborn baby? Here the theological interpretation of the Catholic doctrine might differ. On the one hand, a strict interpretation of the abortion as intrinsic evil would not permit any exceptions or circumstances, which would allow it: choosing the life of the mother to detriment of the life of the baby would assign a lower value to the weaker entity, which would not be ethically admissible (Sgreccia 2007, 574–581). However, a moral justification of abortion in this case may be possible on the basis of the principle that a life which can be saved should be given preference over a life which cannot be saved. When there is a moral certainty, in the light of the current scientific and medical knowledge, that not terminating a pregnancy would lead to the death of both the mother and the baby, it appears to be ethically acceptable to intervene in order to save the mother's life even if this intervention may have a deadly consequence for the child (Schockenhoff 1997, 337–338). This seems to be the only case in which church doctrine on abortion can be open to diverging interpretations, in all other circumstances there is a general consensus that in Catholic Church's teachings abortion is never to be justified.

Euthanasia

Church doctrine holds euthanasia among the "infamous" acts opposing life, like murder, genocide and abortion (*GS* 27). We have seen how this serious condemnation is rooted in traditional church teachings against suicide. Van der Ven (2010, 61–68; 74–78) shows how these teaching are substantiated both by philosophical and theological arguments. The philosophical arguments come mostly from the Scholastic thinking on suicide. Soliciting or performing euthanasia is not justifiable because it goes against the natural inclination of life to preserve itself; it is against natural law, namely against the cosmological and moral universal order which implies an absolute respect and protection for life. It goes against human dignity, insofar as human life has an absolute value and cannot be harmed or minimised by institutions or positive laws. Theological arguments against euthanasia in the Catholic teachings are based on the belief that human beings are created by God, their life is given by God and is in God's hands. Humans are custodians rather than owners of this gift. Moreover, they are created in the image of God (Gen 1:26), which places the value of their life above all other creatures: all human lives have absolute value, they are sacred and inviolable and every human life has to be protected, no matter how difficult or precarious it may be. A further argument in Catholic teachings against euthanasia is the biblical commandment "you shall not kill" (Ex 20:13). God's command is that human life be always respected and no one be allowed to put an end to another's life, even if motivated by good intentions. A final argument put forward is that suffering can have a profound Christian meaning; through suffering people can grow in their Christian faith, feel closer to God, be open to the hope of eternal life. This does not exclude that all efforts have to be made in order to provide relief to the sufferer, as the Catholic advocacy of palliative care indicates (COMECE 2016). It implies that terminating human life is the greatest evil, and not the pain in itself.

These core arguments that we have just sketched here underscore the Catholic Church teaching that euthanasia is an "intrinsic evil" (*VS* 80); that "to kill a human being, in whom the image of God is present, is a particularly serious sin" (*EV* 55). The 1980 *Declaration on Euthanasia* of the Congregation for the Doctrine of the Faith affirms: "no one can in any way permit the killing of an innocent human being, whether a foetus or an embryo, an infant or an adult, an old person, or one suffering from an incurable disease, or a person who is dying. Furthermore, no one is permitted to ask for this act of killing, either for himself or herself or for another person entrusted to his or her care, nor can he or she consent to it, either explicitly or implicitly, nor can any authority legitimately recommend or permit such an action" (DE, II). The same Declaration points out that particular circumstances may reduce or eliminate the individual guilt, while not changing "the nature of this act of killing, which will always be in itself something to be rejected". At the same time, church teachings reject medical treatments, which are disproportionate to the expected results or which are particularly burdensome for the patient: "When inevitable death is imminent in spite of the means used, it is permitted in conscience to take the decision to refuse forms of treatment that would only secure a precarious and burdensome prolongation of life, so long as the normal care due to the sick person in similar cases is not interrupted" (DE, IV). What would "normal care" mean, for example, in situations like that of Ms. Englaro's, whose lifesaving measure was artificial nutrition and hydration? Can such measures be understood as normal care? According to the authoritative interpretation of the Vatican Congregation responsible for these matters, the answer is yes: "A patient in a 'permanent vegetative state' is a person with fundamental human dignity and must, therefore, receive ordinary and proportionate care which includes, in principle, the administration of water and food even by artificial means" (Congregation for the Doctrine of the Faith 2007). This answer did not prevent Catholic theologians from reflecting further on this matter: some of them interpret strictly this prohibition to stop artificial nutrition and hydration always and in every circumstance (Sgreccia 2007, 901–902), while others hold the termination of such care in cases of permanent vegetative state as morally acceptable (Ernst 2007; Schockenhoff 2013). This appears to be an open issue among Catholic theologians, but is about the definition of "disproportionate" measures and the question if stopping artificial nutrition can be considered as a euthanasian act. In other words, a general Catholic theological consensus on rejecting euthanasia is not brought into question by this issue.

In the euthanasia debate, Catholic theological reflection not only puts forward traditional arguments and doctrines but also critically engages with the arguments put forward by supporters of its legalisation: the right to privacy of terminally ill patients, their autonomy and their "right to die" (Section "Open issues in the public debate"). Regarding the right to privacy and to decide about the quality of one's own life, the difficulty is to balance between the subjective judgment of the patient and some objective criteria which are necessary to evaluate the quality of the patient's life; for example, how to deal with depression which might influence this judgement? This question relates as well to the second argument: autonomy. How free and autonomous a patient can be while deciding between two opposing fundamental forces, conservation of life and termination of suffering? How are we to interpret the social influence on this decision, for instance the familial context, the economic situation, the caregiving setting? Thirdly, about the so-called "right to die", namely the right to have control over one's own life and body, it is asked if this idea does not reduce the human being to an object rather than a subject, if it does treat a human body like one's property rather than as one indivisible dimension of the whole person. Finally, we may add a further question: is euthanasia a real last help for the patient? Here one may wonder if legitimising euthanasia as an official medical procedure is not a shortcut to avoid other ways, maybe more time consuming or financially expensive, which could help the terminally ill person to go as peacefully as possible toward his/her death, such as the best palliative treatments and psychological support that current scientific knowledge can offer (Schockenhoff 1997, 342–348; Van der Ven 2010, 123–136). All these arguments and questions assign Catholic actors and voices a central role in opposing euthanasia in the current public debate.

The Role of the Catholic Church in the Italian Bioethical Debate

The presence of the Catholic Church in the public debate over bioethical issues has been rather intense in the last decades, especially if one takes the Italian case. According to Garelli (2013), the Catholic Church exercised a more direct political presence particularly since the collapse of the Christian Democratic party in the 1990s which caused the dissolution of the political unity of the Italian Catholics. In the face of the rapid changes in the recent years, especially on account of secularisation, pluralisation and a strong wave of immigrations, there seems to be a loss of church's public authority and a crisis of the Catholic traditional values. For these reasons the Catholic Church in Italy launched the "cultural project", namely a series of initiatives aimed at the proposition and justification of the traditional Christian values in the public realm, focusing especially on the defence of the so called "non-negotiable values" regarding the protection of life and of family, giving a central place for bioethical issues. According to the Italian sociologist, the Catholic Church started to behave as a lobbying group in the Italian politics as never before in history, in order to preserve a decisive role in the pluralistic culture and to defend the values the church believes essential for the Italian society. Such an effort on the part of the Italian bishops mirrors the indications and teachings of John Paul II, a leader who encouraged Catholics to confront openly the challenges arising from secularisation, revitalising the Catholic public presence in traditional Catholic countries, like Poland and Italy (Garelli 2013, 344–345). One example of such strong and direct church intervention in the political debate on bioethical issue was Law 40/2004 on *in vitro* fertilisation, which was considered one of the most restrictive laws in Europe because of the influence of the Catholic Church on lawmakers. The 2005 referendum, which attempted to loosen tight restrictions of this law, failed because it missed the requested 50% quorum, with a turnout of 26% of the electorate. During the referendum campaign, important representatives of the church hierarchy invited citizens to boycott the polls.

Such a model of direct intervention of the Catholic hierarchy in Italy appears to be in decline in the last years, one of the main reasons appears to be the change of church leadership which took place with the election of Pope Francis in 2013. In his teachings, speeches and actions one may note immediately a shift in concern and values, which are publically defended: a central role is now given to social issues such as poverty, war and immigration (Zaccaria et al. 2018). It does not mean a change of teachings, because on bioethical issues Pope Francis reiterates church's traditional condemnation of abortion and euthanasia, but rather a change of priorities of the church involvement in the public discourse. In an interview with Spadaro (2013) the pope said that one cannot insist only on issues such as abortion and contraceptive methods, and that the church has "to find a new balance" in the transmission of her moral teachings.

This new balance invoked by the pope might be at the origin of a new model of the Catholic presence in the public debate on abortion and euthanasia. The opposing rational arguments coming from "a Catholic and a secular bioethics", as the theologian Faggioli (2014) calls them, do not necessarily have to confront each other as in a battlefield, rather they can engage in a mutual critical dialogue. Through an exchange of reasonable arguments in a pluralistic and democratic society, legislative compromises which are acceptable for both sides can be reached. This goal can be achieved through a bottom-up participation of Catholics in the public debate, rather than on a top-down intervention of the church hierarchy on political actors. As Habermas (2011, 25) puts it, religions in a post-secular society can exercise their influence in the informal communication from below; in this way the Catholic Church can become a transformative force at the centre of a democratic civil society. It is for this reason that in this study we aim at verifying the impact of religion on young citizens' attitudes on abortion and euthanasia; it is on the basis of their convictions and their participation in public life that the influence of religion on bioethical issues in a pluralistic Italian society can emerge.

Conceptual Model and Research Questions

We have seen how bioethical questions referring to abortion and euthanasia are relevant in the current public debate. Focusing on Italy, we have shown how the policies which enforce Law 194/1978 raise some questions about the conscientious objection of physicians, the access of women to termination of pregnancy in public hospitals, the protection of life that the law aims at, and particularly the question of abortion for economic reasons. As regards euthanasia, we have observed have observed how, in spite of the recent law on living will, the public debate on this issue is still open. Questions on abortion and euthanasia mostly refer to determining the subject of the right to life and the dilemma between this right and other fundamental rights such as liberty and security: should the unborn child be a subject of the right to life? To what extent should his/her life be protected? How to balance this with the right of the mother to her physical and psychological health? How to balance the duty to save and protect life and the autonomy of the patient to decide about his/her medical treatments? How to ensure that patient's autonomous decisions are free from psychological or contextual constraints?

In all these situations, we have seen how the Catholic Church defends life as an absolute value, including the life of the foetus since the moment of conception and the life of the terminally ill patient until the medical therapies are found to be disproportionate measures compared to the expected results. These views can be defended in a pluralistic and democratic society not through a lobbying pressure of the church hierarchy on politicians, but through a bottom-up involvement of religious voices in public opinion, namely through the beliefs, attitudes and convictions of religious people participating in civil life. Previous researches show ambivalent results about the impact of religion on personal attitudes on abortion and euthanasia (Van der Ven 2010, 158–21; Van der Ven and Anthony 2008; Gielen et al. 2011; Meñaca et al. 2012), that is why it is important to explore this impact in the Italian context. We will do this on a sample of young people, who would be the main actors of this debate in the future Italian society.

In order to research the impact of religion on bioethical issues, we specify religion in terms of concrete religious attitudes, which we consider as independent variables. We can distinguish between personal and contextual religious attitudes. Personal religious attitudes may have a cognitive dimension (e.g. beliefs about God), an experiential dimension (e.g. religious experiences) and an operative dimension (e.g. religious practices). Contextual religious attitudes refer to the interaction between religions and between religion and society. Contextual attitudes can comprise convictions about how one's own religion relates to other religions, express confidence in one's own religion and the religion of others, or may describe the public function of religion in today's world, the effect of contemporary society on religion, and the relation between religious communities and the state. Thus the list of independent variables in our research model comprises personal religious attitudes (beliefs about God, beliefs about the relevance of God and religion, religious experiences and religious practices) and contextual religious attitudes (religious plurality, trust in religions, function of religion, religion in contemporary society, relation between religion and the state).

Background variables in our conceptual model are individual characteristics, which might influence their attitudes on abortion and euthanasia. First, we take into account personal characteristics: age, gender, geographical location; being a woman, for instance, can have a different impact on personal convictions about abortion; living in Southern Italy or in its capital city can relate more or less to traditional values. The religious socialisation of the respondents, such as being a church-goer and more often in contact with church teachings, can be related to the degree of support of abortion and euthanasia. Therefore we deem religious identity (affiliation and practice), family/peer religious influence and interreligious contacts to be background variables. Finally, we have considered the respondents' psychological and socio-political traits to be background variables in relation to social matters: psychological characteristics and ideas about society, cultural and political orientations that could influence the moral evaluation of abortion and euthanasia. The list of psychological traits includes the personality tendencies of authoritarianism, social dominance orientation and empathy. We have also added views on multiculturalism and political orientation as socio-political traits.

As shown in Fig. 5.1, the conceptual model underlying our empirical study among Italian students regarding the relation between religious and bioethical attitudes comprises three groups of variables: attitudes about abortion and euthanasia (dependent variables); personal and contextual religious attitudes (independent variables); and personal characteristics, religious socialisation, psychological traits and socio-political traits (background variables).

We intend to investigate the extent to which Italian secondary school students support or reject abortion and euthanasia. We begin by studying the relationship between these bioethical attitudes and religious attitudes, both personal and contextual, and then consider background characteristics – personal, religious, psychological and socio-political traits. The conceptualisation and operationalisation of these variables is part of the international research project Religion and Human Rights this volume reports about. We will therefore limit ourselves to a synthetic presentation of the operationalisation of the concepts from Fig. 5.1 in the next section. Our general aim is to understand the relationship between religion and attitudes towards abortion and euthanasia among Italian young people. Does religion make a difference in what young people think regarding bioethical issues? We can specify this research problem into five research questions.

1. How does our sample of students evaluate abortion and euthanasia?
2. Are there significant differences in attitudes towards abortion and euthanasia between student groups as defined by their religious affiliation and practice?
3. Is there a correlation between the students' views on abortion and euthanasia and their religious attitudes?

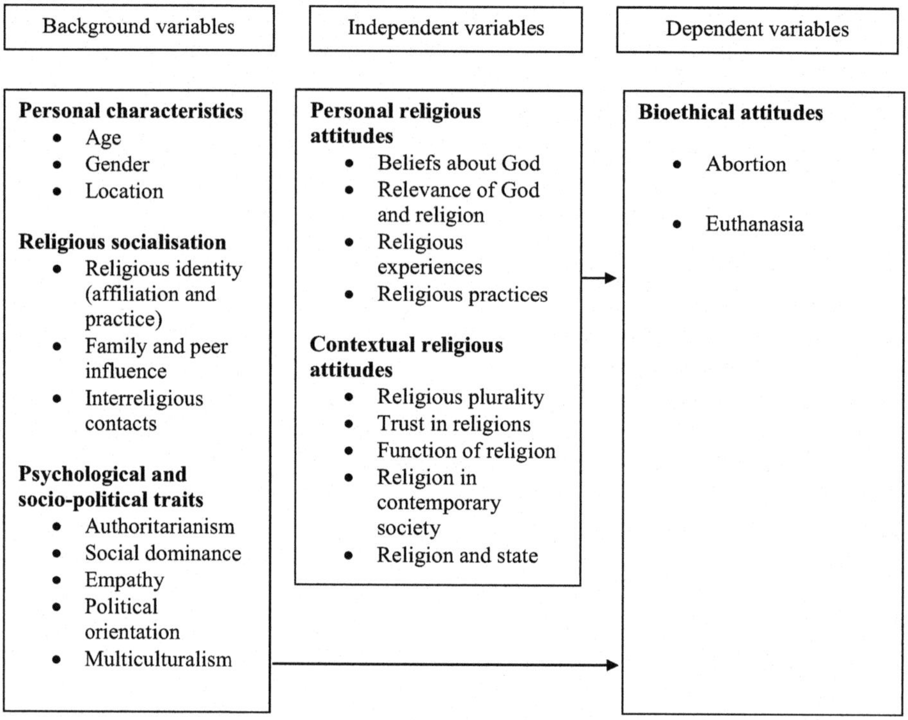

Fig. 5.1 Conceptual model

4. Is there a correlation between the students' views on abortion and euthanasia and their background characteristics?
5. What is the predictive strength of the students' religious attitudes and background characteristics with regard to students' attitudes towards abortion and euthanasia?

Research Methods

In this section we will briefly sketch the process of collecting data and the sample of this study, then the instrument we used and finally the statistical methods we chose for the data reduction and analysis.

Data Collection and Sample

In order to study the link between religion and bioethical attitudes among young Italians, we collected our data from students at the end of secondary education in state schools. We had teachers willing to participate and distribute our questionnaires in three areas with different geographical location and varied levels of urbanisation: Pordenone (a city in northern Italy with about 50,000 inhabitants), Rome (the capital in Central Italy; population approximately 2,800,000), and in Monopoli and Conversano (two cities in southern Italy with approximately 50,000 and 30,000 inhabitants respectively). A total of 1162 questionnaires were filled-in. As our focus was on religion, we needed religious groups within the sample of a sufficient size for the purpose of comparison. Given the monoreligious landscape of Italy, we decided to exclude from the sample all students belonging to religions other than the Catholic Church. Respondents belonging to other churches and religions made up about 5% of the sample in total. Our final sample therefore comprised 1087 students.

The sample of secondary school students comprises 54.7% women and 45.3% men. The age breakdown of students was as follows: 15 to 16 (4.6%), 17 (39.5%), 18 (41.4%), 19 (12.1%), 20 and 21 (2.4%). In terms of geographical location, 372 are from northern Italy, 348 from central Italy and 366 from the south of Italy. The students were classified by religious identity into four groups according to their self-declared church affiliation and frequency: Catholic churchgoers (30.8%), Catholic non-churchgoers[1] (39.3%), generally religious (9.2%) and non-religious (20.7%).

Measuring Instrument

The questionnaire we used in our study is an instrument designed by the group of international scholars involved in the Religion and Human Rights 2012–2019 research project. The questions used to determine the respondents' background, religious attitudes towards abortion and euthanasia were selected from the broader tool. *Background variables* comprise four groups of characteristics that could play a role in shaping students' bioethical attitudes: personal characteristics, religious socialisation, psychological traits and socio-political traits. *Personal characteristics* include age, gender and geographical location. *Religious socialisation* includes the religion to which respondents say they belong and their religious practice (religious identity), the faith of their parents and best friends, their parents' expectation that they should adopt their faith (family and peer influence), and time spent with people of other religions (interreligious contacts). *Psychological traits* refer to the respondents' psychological profile in terms of authoritarianism, social dominance orientation and empathy. *Socio-political traits* include valuation of multiculturalism and political orientation (left wing or right wing).

Independent variables refer to the religious attitudes of our students. Religious attitudes are assumed to include beliefs about religious sphere and religious activities. We divided religious attitudes into two groups: personal and contextual

[1] "Churchgoers" are defined as those who claim to go to church at least once a month; "non-churchgoers" claim to attend church a few times a year, hardly ever or never.

religious attitudes. *Personal religious attitudes* comprise beliefs about God, namely beliefs in a personal God (theism, panentheism), beliefs in a non-personal God (deism, pantheism), beliefs in a aniconic God (agnosticism); they also include convictions about the relevance of God and of religion in daily life, such as having a critical approach to religious beliefs, believing in the existence of God and in his intervention, and considering religion as influential in life. Personal religious attitudes also encompass behavioural issues, such as religious experiences (faith experiences and spirituality experiences) and religious practices (praying and attending religious services). *Contextual religious attitudes* include beliefs about religion in relation to other religions and society. For the purpose of our research, we have included beliefs about religious plurality (exclusivism and pluralism), trust in religions (trust in his/her own religion and in other religions), the function of religion (public function, cultural conformity and spiritual service), religion in contemporary society (relevance/irrelevance), and the relationship between religion and the state (strict separation and consultation).

Attitudes towards abortion and euthanasia constitute *dependent variables* in our model. Bioethical attitudes were operationalised using ten items (Table 5.1). Our respondents indicated whether and in which cases abortion should be permitted (items 1–7), and whether and under which circumstances euthanasia should be allowed (items 8–10).

Statistical Methods

The collected data were analysed with the help of statistical package SPSS. Means and standard deviations were calculated for each statement on abortion and euthanasia (Table 5.1), in order to explore the general evaluation of bioethical attitudes among the students, with a view to answering our first question. Factor analyses (principal axis factoring) were used for the purpose of data reduction and scaling.[2] We used variance analyses (ANOVA) and Scheffé's tests to answer the second research question. These calculations indicated variations in the mean scores for different groups of students on each scale of favourableness to abortion and euthanasia. The four religious groups taken into account here were Catholic churchgoers, Catholic non-churchgoers, generally religious and non-religious students. The relationships between religious attitudes and attitudes towards abortion and euthanasia (question 3) were investigated by calculating Pearson's r correlation coefficients; the same calculations were conducted in order to study the relationship between background characteristics and bioethical attitudes (question 4).[3] Finally, the fifth question, which refers to the predictive strength of our respondents' religious attitudes and background characteristics in view of their attitudes towards abortion and euthanasia, was answered by performing multiple regression analyses.

[2] For the authoritarianism measurement only, principal component analysis was applied.

[3] For the religious identity variable only, "eta" coefficients were calculated.

Table 5.1 Number of respondents (N), means and standard deviations *of items about attitudes towards abortion and euthanasia* among all students in descending order of average agreement

	N	Mean	s.d.
Abortion			
2. Abortion should be permitted in case of rape.	1085	3.77	1.14
5. Abortion should be permitted when the woman's own health is seriously endangered by the pregnancy.	1082	3.76	1.00
3. Abortion should be permitted in case of incest.	1085	3.35	1.18
4. Abortion should be permitted when there is a strong chance of serious defect in the baby.	1087	3.34	1.27
7. Abortion should be permitted when the woman cannot afford any more children psychologically.	1087	2.65	1.27
1.Abortion should be prohibited in all circumstances because it terminates human life at its beginning.	1087	2.63	1.30
6. Abortion should be permitted when the woman cannot afford any more children economically.	1083	2.58	1.24
Euthanasia			
10. Euthanasia should be permitted in the case of unbearable and irreversible suffering.	1086	3.95	1.01
9. Euthanasia should be permitted in the case of unbearable and irreversible suffering, if palliative care is exhausted.	1083	3.87	1.05
8.Euthanasia should be prohibited in all circumstances.	1087	2.36	1.16

Interpretations of means: 1.00–1.79: total disagreement; 1.80–2.59: disagreement; 2.60–2.99: negative ambivalence; 3.00–3.39: positive ambivalence; 3.40–4.19: agreement; 4.20–5.00: full agreement

Empirical Results

Following the order of the five research questions, we will first analyse the respondents' evaluation of abortion and euthanasia and then we will examine the relations between these bioethical attitudes, religious attitudes and background variables.

Question 1 How does our sample of students evaluate abortion and euthanasia?

As shown in the mean scores of Table 5.1, starting from the items referring to abortion, our students are favourable to abortion in the case of rape and health risks for the mother; positive ambivalence was expressed about the possibility of abortion in case of incest and serious defect of the baby, while negative ambivalence was expressed about abortion for psychological reasons of the mother and regarding the affirmation that abortion should be prohibited in all circumstances.[4] Instead, our students clearly disagreed with abortion for economic reasons. With regard to euthanasia,

[4] The score of this item ("Abortion should be prohibited in all circumstances because it terminates a human life at its beginning") was later inverted in view of data reduction and scale construction, because it was the only abortion item expressing prohibition of abortion.

our respondents expressed agreement with the two items allowing euthanasia and disagreement with the item that prohibited it.[5]

Factor analysis (PAF, oblimin rotation) of our seven items referring to abortion reduced the data to two factors, we called the first factor "attitude towards abortion for violence and health reasons", while the second factor was labelled "attitude towards abortion for psycho-economic reasons". This factor analysis explained a total variance of 56.8%, both scales we constructed from the two factors have a high reliability, respectively α .84 and α .81. Factor analysis on the three items about euthanasia formed one single factor, with an explained total variance of 53.2% and a fairly high scale reliability of α .72 ("attitude towards euthanasia") (Table 5.2 and 5.3).

These results show that the evaluation of abortion is differentiated in the mind of our students depending on the reason why abortion is performed: they tend to agree in case of violence and health risks while they tend to disagree with abortion triggered by psychological or economic hardships. Generally speaking, the attitude toward euthanasia, as it is explored by this instrument, is positive among our respondents.

Table 5.2 Factor analysis (PAF, Oblimin rotation), communalities (h^2), percentage of explained variance, and reliability (Cronbach's alpha) of *attitudes towards abortion* among students

	F1	F2	h^2
2. Abortion should be permitted in case of rape.	.845		.61
4. Abortion should be permitted when there is a strong chance of serious defect in the baby	.727		.56
3. Abortion should be permitted in case of incest.	.693		.49
5. Abortion should be permitted when the woman's own health is seriously endangered by the pregnancy	.651		.47
1.Abortion should be prohibited in all circumstances because it terminates human life at its beginning (item recoded).	.625		.47
7. Abortion should be permitted when the woman cannot afford any more children psychologically.		.869	.71
6. Abortion should be permitted when the woman cannot afford any more children economically.		.741	.67
Cronbach's alpha	.84	.81	
Number of valid cases	1078	1083	

Scale: 1 = totally disagree; 2 = disagree; 3 = not sure; 4 = agree; 5 = fully agree
Explained var. = 56.84%; F1 = Abortion: violence and health reasons; F2 = Abortion: psycho-economic reasons

[5] The score of this item ("Euthanasia should be prohibited in all circumstances") was also inverted for the same reasons mentioned in the previous footnote.

Table 5.3 Factor analysis (PAF, Oblimin rotation), communalities (h^2), percentage of explained variance, and reliability (Cronbach's alpha) of *attitudes towards euthanasia* among students

	F1	h^2
9. Euthanasia should be permitted in the case of unbearable and irreversible suffering.	.937	.88
10. Euthanasia should be permitted in the case of unbearable and irreversible suffering, if palliative care is exhausted.	.714	.51
8. Euthanasia should be prohibited in all circumstances (item recoded).	.454	.21
Cronbach's alpha	.72	
Number of valid cases	1082	

Scale: 1 = totally disagree; 2 = disagree; 3 = not sure; 4 = agree; 5 = fully agree
Explained variance = 53.15%; F1 = Euthanasia

Question 2 Are there significant differences in attitudes towards abortion and euthanasia between student groups as defined by their religious affiliation and practice?

As it is shown in Table 5.4, there are recurrent significant differences between the evaluation of bioethical issues expressed by non-religious students and the Catholics (both churchgoers and non-churchgoers). More specifically, in the case of abortion for violence or health reasons, non-religious students express agreement (mean = 3.96) and they differ significantly from all other groups which express ambivalence or less agreement (Catholic churchgoers: mean = 3.31; Catholic non-churchgoers: mean = 3.43; generally religious: mean = 3.59). Abortion for psycho-economic reasons is opposed by both Catholic churchgoers (mean = 2.42) and Catholic non-churchgoers (2.54), while an ambivalent stand is taken by non-religious respondents (mean = 3.02). All groups of respondents in average agree with euthanasia, but non-religious ones significantly support it (mean = 4.15) more than Catholic students (churchgoers: mean = 3.66: non-churchgoers: mean = 3.73). In short, we observe that Catholic respondents consistently express weaker support for abortion in case of violence and health reasons and for euthanasia than non-religious ones. Furthermore Catholic students disagree more than non-religious ones with regard to abortion for psycho-economic reasons.

Question 3 Is there a correlation between the students' views on abortion and euthanasia and their religious attitudes?

Table 5.5 presents significant correlations between personal religious attitudes of our respondents and bioethical attitudes. In presenting the results of the correlation analyses, we only comment on moderate ($.15 \leq r < .30$) and strong correlations ($r \geq .30$). Abortion for violence and health reasons correlates negatively with beliefs about God, both with the personal image of God (r – .40) and the non-personal image of God (r – .30); it also correlates negatively with the belief that God exists (r – 33.), that God can intervene in human life (r – .28) and that religion is important for respondents' daily life (r – .27). Similarly there is negative correlation with

Table 5.4 Levels of agreement (mean and standard deviation) with regard to *attitudes towards abortion and euthanasia* for Catholic churchgoers, Catholic non-churchgoers, generally religious and non-religious students; and comparison of means between groups of respondents (Scheffé's tests)

	N	mean	s.d.	Cath. non-churchgoers	Generally religious	Non-religious
Abortion: violence and health reasons						
Cath. churchgoers	335	3.31	.89			**
Cath. non-churchgoers	427	3.43	.91			**
Generally religious	100	3.59	.99			*
Non-religious	225	3.96	.80	**	*	
Abortion: psycho-economic reasons						
Cath. churchgoers	335	2.42	1.08			**
Cath. non-churchgoers	427	2.54	1.07			**
Generally religious	100	2.77	1.24			
Non-religious	225	3.02	1.26	**		
Euthanasia						
Cath. churchgoers	335	3.66	.90			**
Cath. non-churchgoers	427	3.73	.85			**
Generally religious	100	3.96	.76			
Non-religious	225	4.15	.75	**		

Interpretations of means: 1.00–1.79: total disagreement; 1.80–2.59: disagreement; 2.60–2.99: negative ambivalence; 3.00–3.39: positive ambivalence; 3.40–4.19: agreement; 4.20–5.00: full agreement

Intergroup differences are significant at $p < .01$ (**) or $p < .05$ level (*)

Scheffé's tests: *Abortion: violence and health reasons* (F-value: 26.76; sign. <.000); *Abortion: psycho-economic reasons* (F-value: 14.15; sign. <.000); *Euthanasia* (F-value: 19.90; sign. <.000)

faith (r – .25) and spiritual experiences (r – .18), frequency of prayer (r – .32) and participation in religious services (r – .34).

A similar pattern is found in the correlations between personal religious attitudes and abortion for psycho-economic reasons: respondents who believe more in a personal God (r – .31) or in something divine (r – .26) show less support of abortion in this case. The same thing can be said about those who think religion is more relevant in their lives (existence of God: r – .27; divine intervention: r – .21; influence of religion: r – .19) and respondents who had more frequently faith experiences (r – .23), who pray (r – .23) and go to religious services more often (r – .25).

The following religious attitudes also correlate negatively with euthanasia: belief in a personal God (r – .29), belief in a non-personal God (r – .20), belief in God's existence (r – .23) and divine intervention (r – .20), influence of religion in daily life (r – .19), faith experiences (r – .21), spiritual experiences (r – .16), prayer frequency (r – .27) and church attendance (r – .31). Only those who believe that God cannot be known or imagined by them, namely those who tend to agnosticism, show more support of euthanasia (r .17).

Table 5.5 Correlations (Pearson's r) between attitudes towards *abortion* and *euthanasia,* and *personal and contextual religious attitudes* among students

	% of variance explained	Cronbach's Alpha	Factor items	*Abortion: violence & health*	*Abortion: pyscho-economic*	*Euthanasia*
Personal religious attitudes						
Beliefs about God		.94	6	−.40**	−.31**	−.29**
Belief in a personal God						
Belief in a non-personal God		.87	4	−.30**	−.26**	−.20**
Belief in a aniconic God (agnosticism)		.51	2	.13**	/	.17**
Relevance of God and religion						
Critical approach to religious belief	43.4	.75	4	−.10**	−.10**	/
Belief in the existence of God				−.33**	−.27**	−.23**
Belief in divine intervention				−.28**	−.21**	−.20**
Influence of religion in life				−.27**	−.19**	−.19**
Religious experiences						
Faith	56.0	.88	2	−.25**	−.23**	−.21**
Spirituality	8.0	.64	2	−.18**	/	−.16**
Religious practices						
Prayer frequency				−.32**	−.23**	−.27**
Participation in relig. services				−.34**	−.25**	−.31**
Contextual religious attitudes						
Religious plurality						
Exclusivism	35.2	.55	2	−.29**	−.20**	−.28**
Pluralism	18.6	.81	2	/	/	/
Trust in religions						
Trust in ingroup				−.23**	−.14**	−.16**
Trust in outgroup				−.15**	/	−.09**
Function of religion						
Public function	25.3	.75	6	−.25**	−.17**	−.16**
Cultural conformity	9.6	.64	2	.20**	.10**	.19**
Spiritual service	8.9	.74	2	−.18**	−.12**	−.11**

(continued)

Table 5.5 (continued)

	% of variance explained	Cronbach's Alpha	Factor items	*Abortion: violence & health*	*Abortion: pyscho-economic*	*Euthanasia*
Religion in contemporary society						
Relevance of religion in society	53.7	.77	3	–.35**	–.29**	–.27**
Religion and state						
Strict separation				.25**	.16**	.21**
Consultation				/	–.08**	/

Correlations are significant at p < .01 level (**) or p < .05 level (*)
Interpretation of correlations: weak (r ≥ .14); moderate (.14 < r > .30); strong (r ≥ .30)

A number of contextual religious variables are also found to correlate with bioethical attitudes. Abortion for violence and health reasons is supported less by those who think their own religion is better than other religions (religious exclusivism: r – .29), by those who trust their religious group (r – .23) but also other religious groups (r – .15), by those students who agree more with the public function of religion (r – .25), with its spiritual mission for its members (r – .18) and with its relevance in today's society (r – .35). On the other hand, favourableness to abortion for violence and health reasons is supported by those who favour the adaptation of religion to contemporary culture (r .20) and the strict separation between church and state (r .25). Abortion for psycho-economic reasons correlates negatively with religious exclusivism (r – .20), with the public function of religion (r – .17) and its relevance in contemporary society (r – .29), while it correlates positively with the idea that religion and state should be radically separated (r .16).

Euthanasia is less supported among those with stronger sense of religious exclusivism (r – .28) and more trust in their religious group (r – .16), by those more in favour of the public function (r – .16) and the relevance of religion (r – .27) in society. A more positive attitude towards euthanasia is expressed, on the other hand, by those students who support more the idea that religion should adapt to culture (r .19) and should be strictly separated from the state (r .21).

Overall, we can say that abortion and euthanasia are less supported by those who are more religious on a personal level and those who support more strongly a meaningful role for religion in society, while they are more positively evaluated by those who support more a cultural adaptation of religion to the current trends in society and a strict separation between church and state.

Question 4 Is there a correlation between the students' views on abortion and euthanasia and their background characteristics?

We confine our comments here to the moderate (.15 ≤ r < .30) and strong correlations (r ≥ .30). As shown in Table 5.6, among the background characteristics of the respondents those which present more correlations with bioethical attitudes are the religious ones. Abortion for violence or health reasons is supported less by

Table 5.6 Correlations (Pearson's r) between attitudes towards *abortion* and *euthanasia* and *background characteristics* among students

	% of variance explained	Cronbach's Alpha	Factor items	*Abortion: violence & health*	*Abortion: pyscho-economic*	*Euthanasia*
Personal characteristics						
Age				/	/	/
Gender				/	/	/
Location (north, Centre, south) (eta)				.10*	/	/
Religious socialisation						
Father's belief and faith				−20**	−.15**	−.20**
Mother's belief and faith				−20**	−.17**	−.10**
Best friend's belief and faith				−.15**	−.19**	−12**
Father: Adopt his faith				−.28**	−.19**	−.25**
Mother: Adopt her faith				−.26**	−.20**	−.19**
Interreligious contacts	71.8	.88	3	−.11**	−.11**	−.06*
Psychological and socio-political traits						
Authoritarianism	40.7	.51	4	−.14**	−.14**	−.09**
Social dominance	34.6	.67	4	.11**	/	/
Empathy	38.5	.70	4	−.12**	−.16**	/
Political orientation				/	/	/
Multiculturalism	51.6	.74	3	/	/	/

Correlations are significant at $p < .01$ level (**) or $p < .05$ level (*)
Interpretation of Correlations: weak ($r \geq .14$); moderate ($.14 < r > .30$); strong ($r \geq .30$)

those who have more religious parents and peers around them (father's faith: r – .20; mother's faith: r – .20; best friend's faith: r – .15) and those who have parents who want them to follow in their religious footsteps (father: r – .28; mother: r – .26). Abortion for psychological and economic reasons is also more opposed by students who live in more religious families (father's faith: r – .15; mother's faith: r – .17; importance for the father that his faith be adopted: r – .19; importance for the mother that her faith be adopt: r – .20) and have more religious friends (best friend's faith: r – .19). Only in this case do we find a moderate correlation between a non-religious background characteristic, namely the tendency to psychological empathy which correlates negatively with abortion for psycho-economic reasons (r – .16).

Euthanasia is less supported among those students who have a more religious father (r – .20), and whose parents think it is important for their children to adopt their faith (father: r – .25; mother: r – .19). In short, this table shows how students

Table 5.7 Regression analyses for students' attitudes towards *abortion* and *euthanasia* with weights (β) for each variable and total explained variance (R^2 and Adjusted R^2)

	Abortion: violence & health	*Abortion: pyscho- economic*	*Euthanasia*
Religious socialisation			
Best friend's belief and faith	/	−.10*	/
Psychological and socio-political traits			
Empathy	/	−.08*	/
Personal religious attitudes			
Belief in a personal God	−.25**	/	−.08*
Belief in aniconic God (agnosticism)	/	/	.12**
Faith (religious experience)	/	−.13**	/
Participation in religious services	−.12**	/	−.19**
Contextual religious attitudes			
Exclusivism	/	/	−.13**
Public function of religion	−.11**		/
Cultural conformity as function of religion	.18**	/	.15**
Relevance of religion in society	/	−.21**	/
Strict separation (religion/state)	.09**	/	/
R^2	.23	.13	.16
Adj. R^2	.22	.12	.16

Standardised regression coefficients (β) are significant at $p < .00$ (**) or $p < .05$ (*) level

who experience a more religious family and circle of friends tend to be less supportive of abortion and euthanasia.

Question 5 What is the predictive strength of students' religious attitudes and background characteristics with regard to students' attitudes towards abortion and euthanasia?

We used regression analyses to explore the predictive strength of religious attitudes and background characteristics on students' attitudes towards abortion and euthanasia. We only analysed variables with at least a moderate correlation with the bioethical variable ($r \geq .15$), and we excluded after a first regression analysis those variables with a non-significant β value, the results of the final regression analysis for each bioethical attitude are shown in Table 5.7.

Results show some significant predictors of the attitude towards *abortion for violence or health reasons.* Interestingly all these predictors are religious variables. Personal religious attitudes such as the belief in a personal God (β − .25) and the participation in religious services (β − .12) affects negatively this bioethical attitude. Traditional beliefs and church practices seem to induce less agreement with abortion for violence or health reasons; so also the idea that religion has a public role in society (β − .11). Among the contextual religious attitudes two of them exercise a positive impact on agreement with abortion: cultural conformity of religion (β .18) and strict separation between church and state (β .09). These results may be explained by the fact that students with more traditional religious attitudes will tend to enhance the restrictive interpretation of the Catholic doctrine against abortion in all circumstances, while those students who wish more openness of the church to current cultural trends and its radical separation from the state will have a more permissive stance of abortion.

Regression analyses on the variable of *abortion for psychological or economic reasons* present the following findings: significant negative predictors are to be found among background characteristics, namely best friend's religious faith (β − .10) and the psychological characteristic of empathy (β − .08). It means that religious environment and tendency to empathic feelings (presumably with the unborn baby) can predict a stronger opposition to the idea that abortion can be requested because of the mother's difficult psychological or economic situation. A similar negative evaluation of abortion for these reasons can be induced by a stronger personal faith experience of the respondents (β − .13) and by the affirmation of religion's influence and relevance in contemporary society (β − .21). It appears that stronger religious environment and experiences, together with a more positive role of religion in society, tend to make students opposed to abortion practices, in tune with official church doctrine.

Finally, variables which predict students' evaluation of *euthanasia* are also religious ones, both personal and contextual. On the personal level, the Christian belief in a personal God (β − .08) and participation in church services (β − .19) have a negative impact. Similarly as in the case of the abortion for violence or health reasons, agnostic beliefs have a positive influence on openness to euthanasia (aniconic God: β .12). A negative impact on the variable of euthanasia is detectable among those who maintain the more traditional idea that only their own religion gives full access to a flourishing life (religious exclusivism: β − .13), while positive influence is exercised by the more liberal idea that religion should be at pace with current social trends (cultural conformity: β .15).

These data on euthanasia seem to confirm the previous findings in regression analyses, namely that a more negative evaluation of abortion and euthanasia among our students is induced by stronger religious setting and experience, a more orthodox idea of God, more regular church attendance, a more positive idea of their religion and of religion's role in society. On the other hand, we can also add that a more favourable attitude toward abortive and euthanasian practices is predicted by less traditional beliefs in God and more liberal ideas regarding religion and society. Overall, we can say that religious variables have some predictive strength on students' ideas on bioethical issues.

Discussion on Salient Findings

In the light of the findings on bioethical attitudes among Italian students we would like focus our discussion on three main areas of our research: the debate on abortion, the debate on euthanasia, and the role of religion in these bioethical debates.

In the first place we may underscore that the debate on abortion has its relevance also for young generations in Italy. In spite of Law 194 which broadly legalised abortion already since the 1970s, young generations today seem to have very different and nuanced attitudes towards this issue. While there is some consensus with regard to the possibility of abortion in case of violence against women and health risks for the mother or the baby, our findings show that students have some doubts regarding abortion for psychological and economic reasons. This means that the abortion debate cannot be reduced to two opposing fields, namely pro-life and pro-choice, but that a more nuanced presentation of the circumstances which induce women to ask for an abortion is needed and not all reasons for such a request can be evaluated in the same way. Law 194 introduces a differentiated picture on the reasons for allowing abortion only after the third month of pregnancy. Our findings suggest that this differentiation may be useful for the ethical evaluation of abortion in general, not only after the first stages of the foetus life. This is especially true in the case of abortion for economic reasons, which appear to be the first type of reason why abortion is requested today in Italy. At the same time it seems to be an unacceptable reason for abortion according to our young respondents. On the other hand, the importance of the circumstances in the ethical evaluation of abortion, expressed also by Catholic respondents, supports the idea of those Catholic theologians who take into account risk to mother's life as a morally acceptable circumstance in which abortion can be permitted. This encourages theological reflection to better define the understanding that even an evil act can have extenuating circumstances, which might reduce the moral responsibility of those carrying out this act.

As far as the debate on euthanasia is concerned, our findings seem to support the idea that the shifts of modernity which have brought some Western countries to legalise euthanasia have reached also the opinion of the young Italians in our sample. Principles such as privacy and autonomy in medical choices regarding the end-of-life phase seem to guide the attitudes towards euthanasia among our respondents, who in general agree with it. These findings underline once more the necessity of taking up the end-of-life issues in the public and political debate in Italy. On the other hand, we have to acknowledge also the limits of our findings on the issue of euthanasia: our research instrument was smaller and did not mirror the necessary differentiation we had in the items referring to abortion. More items could be added to our instrument: for example, items on euthanasia in the case of artificial nutrition and hydration in permanent vegetative state, as the heated debate in Italy in the case of Ms. Englaro showed, or items specifying underage or psychiatric patients, or items on euthanasia requested by elderly people in good health, as discussed in other European countries. Further research is needed in order to identify further differentiation in the case of euthanasia as in the case of abortion. Such differentiation might provide better insights into the attitudes of young generations of Italians regarding euthanasia, helpful in understanding the public debate on this issue and the role that religion might have in it.

The third area of our research focus concerns the role of religion in the debates on abortion and euthanasia. Our main research problem was to verify the impact of religious attitudes on bioethical attitudes among young Italians. Did we find this impact among our respondents? The answer in short is yes, religion does play a significant role when it comes to bioethical opinions. The differences between religious subgroups (Table 5.4) and the measurements of the correlations (Tables 5.5 and 5.6) bring to light less supportive attitudes towards abortion and euthanasia consistently present among Catholic respondents, if compared to non-religious ones. In other words, we have seen how abortion and euthanasia are supported less by more religious students (who believe in a traditional image of God, in its importance for their lives, who are more involved in religious experiences and practices) by those respondents with more religious families and friends, by those students who have a more traditional idea of religion (exclusivist toward other religions and spiritually oriented) and by those who defend the public significance of religion. The regression analyses brought out a sharper picture of this impact of religious variables on bioethical attitudes: more negative attitudes toward abortion and euthanasia are induced by a stronger religious environment and practice, by more traditional beliefs and by a more positive idea of religion, while more positive attitudes toward abortive and euthanasian practices are predicted by agnostic beliefs and more liberal ideas about religion and society. The fact that only religious predictors and virtually no other types (personal, psychological and socio-political characteristics) were present among those influencing bioethical attitudes, remarkably shows a different picture from the ones we obtained from similar analyses on other human rights attitudes of the same sample (Zaccaria et al. 2017, 2018), reinforces the idea that religion plays a significant role in shaping the evaluation of bioethical questions regarding abortion and euthanasia, even among young generations. These results might suggest that a different model of presence of the Catholic Church in the public debate on these issues is possible: not merely through the direct intervention of the hierarchy in the political arena, but rather through the participation of Catholics in civil society and in the political life of the country. This model appears to be more in tune with both the teachings of the church, which encourages social and political engagement of the laity rather than that of the clergy, and with the post-secular idea of democratic and pluralistic society, which allows the participation of religious voices in the public debate in a bottom-up movement, in what Habermas (2011, 25) calls informal communication from below. In this way, through the participation of Catholics in the public debate, through the use of rational arguments, religion can play a constructive role in revising existing laws or designing new ones in the bioethical sphere, taking into account Catholic traditional teachings in defence of life, and also paying attention to the circumstances and the societal context in which these teachings need to be transmitted and to the necessary legislative compromises which need to be reached in a pluralistic and multi-religious democratic society.

References

Bacon, F. (1973). *The advancement of learning*. London: Dent.

Bo, M., Zotti, C. M., & Charrier, L. (2015). Conscientious objection and waiting time for voluntary abortion in Italy. *The European Journal of Contraception & Reproductive Health Care, 20*(4), 272–282.

Cohen, J., et al. (2013). Different trends of euthanasia acceptance across Europe. A study of 13 western and 10 central and eastern European countries, 1981–2008. *European Journal of Public Health, 23*(3), 378–380.

Cohen, J., et al. (2014). Public acceptance of euthanasia in Europe. A survey study in 47 countries. *International Journal of Public Health, 59*, 143–156.

COMECE. (2016). *Opinion of the working group on ethics in research and medicine on palliative care in the European Union*. February 2016. Accessible online.

Congregation for the Doctrine of the Faith. (2007). Responses to certain questions of the US conference of Catholic bishops concerning artificial nutrition and hydration. August 1, 2007. Accessible online.

Ernst, S. (2007). Verhältnismäßige und unverhältnismäßige Mittel. Eine bedenkenswerte Unterscheidung in der lehramtlichen Bewertung der Sterbehilfe. *Münchener Theologische Zeitschrift, 58*, 43–57.

Faggioni, M. (2014). Bioetica secolare e bioetica cattolica. Modelli rivali? *Studia Moralia, 52*(2), 275–297.

Garelli, F. (2013). Catholiques, politique et culture. Le cas italien. *Social compass, 60*(3), 332–347.

Gielen, J., et al. (2011). The diverse influence of religion and world view on palliative-care nurses' attitudes toward euthanasia. *Journal of Empirical Theology, 24*, 36–56.

Habermas, J. (1982). *Theorie des kommunikativen Handelns*. Frankfurt: Suhrkamp.

Habermas, J. (2011). 'The political'. The rational meaning of a questionable inheritance of political theology. In E. Mendieta & J. Van Antwerpen (Eds.), *The power of religion in the public sphere* (pp. 15–33). New York: Columbia University Press.

Heinen, J. (2014). *Assauts tous azimuts contre le droit à l'avortement. La Pologne fait-elle école?* (Document de travail 7/2014). Genève: Pôle genre et développement/Programme Genre, globalisation et changements, Institut de hautes études internationales et du dèveloppement. Accessable online.

Jerouschek, G. (1988). *Lebensschutz und Lebensbeginn. Kulturgeschichte des Abtreibungsverbots*. Stuttgart: Ferdinand Enke Verlag.

Lima, J., et al. (2015). Austerity and abortion in the EU. *The European Journal of Public Health, 25*(3).

MacIntyre, A. (2009). Intractable moral disagreements. In L. Cunningham (Ed.), *Intractable disputes about moral law* (pp. 1–52). Notre Dame: Notre Dame University Press.

Meñaca, A., et al. (2012). End-of-life care across southern Europe. A critical review of cultural similarities and differences between Italy, Spain and Portugal. *Critical Reviews in Oncology/ Hematology, 82*, 387–401.

Sartea, C. (2013). Sulla problematica idea di "un diritto all'aborto". *Medicina e Morale, 62*(4), 767–784.

Schockenhoff, E. (1997). *Etica della vita. Un compendio teologico*. Brescia: Queriniana [original in German: (1993) *Ethiek des Lebens. Ein theologischer Grundriss*. Mainz: Matthias Grünewald Verlag].

Schockenhoff, E. (2013). Moraltheologische Überlegungen zur künstlichen Ernährung und Hydrierung. *Forschungsinstitut für Philosophie Hannover – Journal, 22*, 6–7.

Sgreccia, E. (2007). *Manuale di bioetica. Fondamenti ed etica biomedica* (Vol. 1). Milano: Vita e Pensiero.

Solarino, B., et al. (2011). A national survey of Italian physicians' attitudes toward end-of-life decisions following the death of Eluana Englaro. *Intensive Care Medicine, 37*(3), 542–549.

Spadaro, A. (2013). A big heart open to God. *America, 209*(8), 15–38.

Tiensuu, P. (2015). Whose right to what life? Assisted suicide and the right to life as a fundamental right. *Human Rights Law Review, 15*(2), 251–281.

Van der Ven, J. A. (2010). *Ondraaglijk lijden zonder uitzicht. Euthanasie vanuit religie, moraal en mensenrechten*. Budel: Damon.

Van der Ven, J. A., & Anthony, F.-V. (2008). Impact of religion on social integration from an empirical civil rights perspective. *Salesianum, 70*(317–338), 463–489.

Villanueva, C. E. (2014). A vueltas con el aborto. *Medicina e Morale, 63*(1), 117–120.

Wicks, E. (2012). The meaning of 'life'. Dignity and the right to life in international human rights treaties. *Human Rights Law Review, 12*(2), 199–219.

Zaccaria, F. (2010). *Participation and beliefs in popular religiosity. An empirical-theological exploration among Italian Catholics*. Brill: Leiden/Boston.

Zaccaria, F., Anthony, F. V., & Sterkens, C. (2017). Religion and civil rights in Italy. An empirical exploration among secondary school students. In H.-G. Ziebertz & C. Sterkens (Eds.), Religio*n and civil human rights in empirical perspective* (Religion and Human Rights 2, pp. 91–120). Berlin [etc.]: Springer.

Zaccaria, F., Anthony, F. V., & Sterkens, C. (2018 – forthcoming). Religion for the political rights of immigrants and refugees? An empirical exploration among Italian students. In C. Sterkens & H.-G. Ziebertz (Eds.), *Political and judicial rights through the prism of religious belief, Religion and human rights* (Vol. 3, pp. 45–70). Berlin: Springer.

Chapter 6
Religion, Human Rights and Matters of Life and Death: Exploring Attitude Toward Abortion and Euthanasia Among Adolescents in England and Wales

Leslie J. Francis, Ursula McKenna, and Abdullah Sahin

This study explores the association between attitude toward euthanasia and abortion and both religious practices (personal prayer and worship attendance) and self-assigned religious affiliation (Protestant, Catholic, Muslim, and non-religious) among a sample of 966 students between the ages of 14 and 18 years in England and Wales, after taking into account personal factors (age and sex) and psychological factors (extraversion, neuroticism, and psychoticism). The data demonstrate that religiously inclined students are less accepting of euthanasia and abortion. Religious practice is one key indicator with a significant negative correlation between prayer frequency and acceptance of euthanasia and abortion. In addition to prayer frequency, religious identity is a second key indicator. Muslim students and Catholic students are less accepting of euthanasia and abortion than Protestant students and non-religious students.

Introduction

The Right to Life

The right to life is fundamental to the spirit of Human Rights. According to the Universal Declaration of Human Rights (1948), all human beings are born free and equal in dignity and rights (article 1) and everyone has the right to life, liberty and security of person (article 3). According to the European Convention for the Protection of Human Rights and Fundamental Freedoms (1950), everyone's right to life shall be

L. J. Francis (✉) · U. McKenna · A. Sahin
Warwick Religions & Education Research Unit, Centre for Education Studies, University of Warwick, Coventry, UK
e-mail: leslie.francis@warwick.ac.uk

H.-G. Ziebertz, F. Zaccaria (eds.), *Euthanasia, Abortion, Death Penalty and Religion – The Right to Life and its Limitations*, Religion and Human Rights 4, https://doi.org/10.1007/978-3-319-98773-6_6

protected by law (article 2). According to the International Convention on Civil and Political Rights (1966), everyone has the inherent right to life, and that right to life shall be protected by law. In line with this human rights emphasis on the right to life, the Rome Statute of the International Criminal Court (1998) places under the jurisdiction of the criminal court the violation of human life, either by direct means (murder) or by indirect means (depravation of essential support for life).

This firm commitment to the right to life, however, is not unproblematic and is not without potential conflict with other notions of human rights. Two classic issues on which the right to life comes into conflict with other notions of human rights concern euthanasia and abortion. Issues of Euthanasia and abortion are often the subject of heated international debate. A number of writers discuss the arguments for and against both euthanasia and abortion from moral, social and political perspectives (Dworkin 1993; Weisstub and Pintos 2008; Toebes et al. 2012; Cook et al. 2014). A brief examination of legal cases and challenges in this area are explored.

Human Rights and Euthanasia

Euthanasia is a complex issue centred on questions regarding the role of government and the rights of individual citizens. Those who support euthanasia hold to the right of individuals to autonomy, and the belief that choosing where and when to die belongs to the individual as a human right. In contrast, arguments against euthanasia highlight the undesirability of any government supporting acts which violate the right to life of its citizens. The contrasting arguments appealing to human autonomy and civic duty of governments to protect the life of their citizens over euthanasia highlight a deeper ethical dilemma (individual ethics versus social or public ethics) within the wider narrative of secular modernity. It is these ethical ambiguities that appear to be shaping legal and political discussions over such issues.

While in the UK there may be a right to die, in that the Suicide Act (1961) made it legal for people to take their own lives, the Act also made actively taking action to end another's life illegal, even with consent. Though medically assisted suicide is legal in some European countries, including Belgium, the Netherlands and Luxembourg, a parallel right to die implied by the right to life is not recognised in UK law. However, as an outcome of the Bland ruling (1993), when the UK High Court ruled in favour of Tony Bland's doctors disconnecting the feeding tubes keeping him alive, 'assisted suicides', which involve 'omissions' that are principally the removal of life-saving care, are not illegal (BBC 1992).

During 2003–2006 Lord Joffe campaigned for an Assisted Dying Bill in the UK but this was rejected by the House of Lords in May 2006. Lord Joffe's bill would have given doctors the right to prescribe drugs that terminally ill patients could use to end their own life (BBC 2006). A further Assisted Dying Bill proposed by Lord Falconer was debated in the UK House of Commons in September 2015 with MPs voting overwhelmingly against doctors being allowed to help terminally ill people end their own life (Mason 2015).

Within the European Convention on Human Rights (ECHR) requests for recognition of a right to die through euthanasia or assisted suicide have been formulated mainly on the basis of article 2 (right to life), article 3 (that the denial of a right to release oneself from unbearable pain amounts to inhuman and degrading treatment), and article 8 (the protection of private and family life). The cases of Pretty v Director of Public Prosecutions (DPP), and Purdy v Director of Public Prosecutions (DPP) are two of the most famous in relation to this issue.

In 2001, Pretty lost her case in the UK High Court (2001) for the right to die. Pretty argued that the government's decision not to allow her to die breached article 3 of the UK Human Rights Act (1998), that no-one shall be subjected to torture or inhuman or degrading treatment or punishment. The case also challenged the DPP refusal to rule out a criminal prosecution if Pretty's husband helped her to die (Ashraf 2001). In 2002, Pretty then took her case to the European Court of Human Rights (ECtHR) but was again unsuccessful. Under article 2 (the right to life) Pretty argued that this right extended to a right to control the manner of her death, and therefore a right to commit suicide. The ECtHR held that this article imposed a duty on the state to protect life, but not a right to die. Under article 3 (the right not to suffer torture or inhuman and degrading treatment) Pretty argued that not allowing her husband to perform assisted suicide was inhuman treatment. The ECtHR held that even if the condition that she was suffering was inhuman, it was not the result of treatment by the state or inflicted by the state.

As a result Harmon and Sethi (2011) reflect that, while Pretty failed in what she sought to achieve in terms of the route to death she desired, the case broke new legal ground. While under articles 2 and 3 she had no right to die, article 8 was in some way supported as the Court accepted that respecting autonomy does include respecting one's decisions about dying (it was this that set a precedent). Similarly, in the case of Purdy v DPP (2009) interpretation of article 8 by the House of Lords led the DPP to produce a list of public factors that would be taken into account in cases of assisted suicide. Despite this move to a recognition of autonomy, the ECtHR supported the House of Lords in its refusal to agree with both Pretty and Purdy's requests: 'article 8 didn't overwrite article 2' (Harmon and Sethi 2011, p. 358). Hence, while a right to die is recognised by the ECHR, English and International courts have concluded that the right to life does not give any right to self-determination over life and death, since the provisions of the ECHR were designed for protecting and preserving life.

More recently, according to Puppinck and La Hougue (2014), the ECtHR seems to be progressively outlining a right to assisted suicide, which would fall in the scope of the right to private life and the right to respect for personal autonomy (article 8) claiming that through the judgement in the case of Haas v Switzerland (2011), the ECtHR went from assisted suicide as a quality of personal freedom to that of a conventional right. In contrast, Harmon and Sethi (2011, p. 359–60) claim that Haas sought more than Pretty and achieved less. Unlike Pretty, Haas wanted not just decisional scope to end his life but the state to facilitate that right (letting a physician issue a prescription to cause death). The ECtHR ruled that the existence of the right to make decisions concerning one's own death did not, and could not, impose an obligation on the state to assist in that death. As in the case of Pretty the ECtHR agreed with the right to respect private life and that time and circumstances of dying are protected under article 8 but that in cases where life was in the balance, as with Haas, article 2 which affirms the right to life and the states obligation to protect vulnerable individuals must be considered and must colour the interpretation and scope of article 8.

In a similar case, English (2015) reports on Lambert and Others v France (2014) with the Grand Chamber of the Strasbourg Court allowing the argument that the state's obligation to protect life also involves a duty to respect people's rights to exit life with dignity. It is an important step away from Pretty v DPP upholding that there would be no violation of article 2 (right to life) of the ECHR if artificial nutrition and hydration were to be withdrawn from a patient in a persistent vegetative state. English views this decision as an important step towards refining the Convention as a guardian of autonomy rather than the conservative position of defending life preservation above all other interests. It was not, however, a unanimous decision within the Court and a number of judges publicly disagreed with the decision. They used the case of Pretty v UK (2002) to insist that article 2 protects the right to life but not the right to die. Likewise, article 3 guarantees a right not to be subjected to ill-treatment, but no 'right' whatsoever to waive this right and to be, for example, beaten, tortured or starved to death (English 2015).

Human Rights and Abortion

At the international level recognition has been given of choice about child bearing being a basic human right. Finer and Fine (2013) assert that there has been a global trend toward the liberalisation of abortion laws. This trend reflects the recognition of women's access to legal abortion services as a matter of women's rights and self-determination and an understanding of the distressing public health implications of criminalising abortion. Likewise, according to Cook and Dickens (2003), the following factors require that women's choices for self-determination be legally respected and not criminalised: recognition that resort to safe and dignified healthcare is a major human right; respect for women's reproductive self-determination; and recognition of a women's rights to equal citizenship with men. According to Ireland (2013), pro-choice advocates assert that pregnancy and the decision either to continue or to end a pregnancy are private matters, which women should be able to decide for themselves without government intervention. Hence, the USA recognised abortion as part of the right to privacy in the case of Roe v Wade (1973) (Ireland 2013, p. 655).

The Universal Declaration on Human Rights (UDHR) (1948) gives recognition to the child before birth, including from the moment of conception. For Cook and Dickens (1999), legal recognition that human life begins at conception does not resolve conflicts between respect due to women's reproductive self-determination and respect due to prenatal life. Indeed, as outlined by Ireland (2013) in terms of article 2 (the right to life), "the ECtHR has not decided whether a foetus fits under Article 2's definition of a 'person'" (Ireland 2013, p. 668). On this issue Rothbard (2012) examines the arguments invoked by debates about when life starts and proposes that a foetus younger than 24 weeks is not a human life (when cerebral brain wave activity is detected) in the moral sense, and hence has no right to life (though it may have potential for human life). He concludes that abortion up to 24 weeks does not involve the violation of any human rights and a woman's right of self-ownership to abort a foetus should be supported.

National and international tribunals are increasingly called upon to resolve conflicts between state enforcement of continuation of pregnancy against women's wishes and women's reproductive choices. Many of the cases relate to challenges in countries where the influence of religion and the Catholic Church is strong such as Ireland and Poland. As Ireland (2013) points out, Ireland is the only country among those that recognise the ECHR that does not recognise a woman's right to terminate her pregnancy.[1] Poland is somewhere in the middle, in that it does not automatically grant women the right to terminate a pregnancy though Polish law does permit it in certain circumstances (Ireland 2013, pp. 655–656).

According to Weinstein (2012), article 8 of the ECHR guarantees the right to privacy, which the ECtHR has held to encompass, among other rights, the right to health and wellbeing. Weinstein reflects on the violation of the ECHR by Ireland's abortion law in the case of A.B.C. v Ireland (2010). Under article 8 European law guarantees women a fundamental right to abortion whereas in Ireland there is prohibition on abortion in all circumstances, except where there is a real and substantial risk to a woman's life. In this case the ECtHR had the opportunity to declare that article 8, the right to privacy, guarantees women a fundamental right to abortion. The court failed to do so and instead declared that Ireland did not violate the applicant's rights, even though their health and wellbeing – rights protected as part of the fundamental right to privacy – were at risk:

> The court concluded that the prohibition in Ireland on abortions sought for reasons of health and wellbeing does not exceed the state's margin of appreciation.... By finding that Ireland's restrictive abortion laws successfully balance Ireland's aim of protecting public morals and women's right to health and wellbeing the Court improperly deferred to Ireland's domestic legislation by granting Ireland a broad margin of appreciation – the ability to regulate a fundamental right guaranteed under the ECHR. (Weinstein 2012, pp. 394–395)

However, as Ireland (2013, p. 677) points out, in the case of A.B.C. v Ireland (2010) the ECtHR did declare Irish abortion practice to be problematic, since the country does not appropriately allow for abortions when women's lives are in danger – even though the law explicitly protects women in such circumstances. In a similar case, Amnesty International (2016) reported on the situation of Irish woman Amanda Mellet (2011) who had to travel to the UK for an abortion when she dis-

[1] This chapter was written prior to Ireland's Referendum on abortion laws held on 25 May 2018. Prior to this Ireland's abortion laws were some of the strictest in the world. The Referendum outcome was a vote in favour of repeal of the eighth amendment in the country's constitution that equates a foetus' life to that of the pregnant woman. The law will now be changed to allow abortion in the first 12 weeks of pregnancy.

covered the foetus had a fatal impairment. The UN committee found Ireland's abortion laws in violation of articles 7 and 26 of the International Convention on Civil and Political Rights (ICCPR) by subjecting her to cruel, inhuman and degrading treatment and also violating article 17 on the right to privacy.

According to Ireland (2013), while the case of A.B.C. v Ireland (2010) was unsuccessful, the case of R.R. v Poland (2011) illustrates how the ECtHR continues to expand the scope of rights available to women in asserting their reproductive freedoms. Discussing the ECtHR ruling in the case of R.R. v Poland in the context of international reproductive rights and domestic abortion laws, Ireland (2013) argues that rather than use article 8 advocates should use article 3 (no-one shall be subjected to torture or inhuman or degrading treatment or punishment) when pushing for greater reproductive freedoms. Hence, in the case of R.R. v Poland (2011), R.R. succeeded on a claim that she received insufficient medical treatment. The ECtHR concluded that her suffering reached the minimum threshold of severity meaning that her article 3 rights were violated.

In some ways all these cases illustrate two core conclusions: the difficulty of using human rights arguments for resolving disputes around issues of euthanasia and abortion which involve conflicting rights, and the central place of religion in studying the debates.

Theological Perspectives

Not surprisingly euthanasia and abortion are issues that have come under close scrutiny within religious traditions. Christian theology and Islamic theology all have insight to offer on these issues. In the Christian tradition the first clear teaching on the subject of abortion comes from the second century *Didache* which condemns the practice (2:2). Christian theologians and Church Councils have usually taken the same view. However, as Astley (2000) points out, Augustine made a distinction between abortions taking place before, and those administered after the 'animation' of the foetus when it received its soul (variously estimated at 40, 60 or 80 days). Aquinas held that the foetus cannot have a human soul until it develops a recognisably human shape, a view affirmed by the Council of Vienne (1311–1312).

In the Christian tradition the subject of euthanasia is often linked with the discussion of suicide. As in the case of abortion, with respect to both suicide and euthanasia Christian teaching appeals to the notion that life is a sacred gift from God. Thus suicide, and therefore voluntary euthanasia, becomes a deliberate rejection of the creative gift of life. This is regarded as an act of rebellious disobedience that precludes repentance.

While there are clear variations in teaching on abortion and euthanasia among the different streams within the Christian tradition, one clear strand of teaching is provided by the Catholic Church. The *Catechism of the Catholic Church* provides a core resource for formal Catholic teaching on both euthanasia and abortion. The Catechism declares that:

> Human life must be respected and protected absolutely from the moment of conception. From the first moment of his existence, a human being must be recognised as having the rights of a person – among which is the inviolable right of every innocent being to life. (*Catechism* no 2270)

A fuller discussion is provided in *Donum Vitae* (10 March 1987). This document argues that:

> From the moment of conception, the life of every human being is to be respected in an absolute way because man is the only creature on earth that God has 'wished for himself' and the spiritual soul of each man is 'immediately created' by God; his whole being bears the image of the Creator. Human life is sacred because from its beginning it involves 'the creative action of God' and it remains forever in a special relationship with the Creator, who is its sole end. God alone is the Lord of life from its beginning until its end: no one can, in any circumstance, claim for himself the right to destroy directly an innocent human being. (*Donum Vitae* 1987, Par 5)

The *Catechism of the Catholic Church* also holds a clear line on euthanasia, but in doing so makes a clear distinction between direct euthanasia and indirect euthanasia. Direct euthanasia is always unacceptable. Acts to eliminate suffering that cause death are regarded as murder. Indirect euthanasia recognises the limitations of medical procedures and interventions to prevent death. Thus, 'discontinuing medical procedures that are burdensome, dangerous, extraordinary, or disproportionate to the expected outcome can be legitimate… Here one does not will to cause death; one's inability to impede it is merely accepted' (*Catechism* no 2278). Within this context, palliative care is acceptable: 'painkillers to alleviate the suffering of the dying, even at the risk of shortening their days, can be morally in conformity with human dignity if death is not willed as either an end or a means, but only foreseen and tolerated as inevitable' (*Catechism* no 2279).

The *Declaration on Euthanasia* published by the Vatican Congregation of Faith (5 May 1980) defines euthanasia as follows:

> By euthanasia is understood an action or an omission which of itself or by intention causes death, in order that all suffering may in this way be eliminated. Euthanasia's terms of reference, therefore, are to be found in the intention of the will and in the methods used. (Chapter 2)

The *Declaration on Euthanasia* argues that the killing of an innocent life is not permissible 'whether a foetus or an embryo, an infant or an adult, an old person, or one suffering from an incurable disease, or a person who is dying.' Such an action is 'the violation of the divine law, an offense against the dignity of the human person, a crime against life, and an attack on humanity' (Chap. 2).

In his encyclical *Evangelicum Vitae* (1995) Pope John Paul II argued that 'extraordinary' care or medical treatment to prolong life need not be continued if it is futile, dangerous or burdensome to the patient, family or society. The administering of drugs such as morphine with the intention to prevent pain, even when they hasten death, was also accepted by the Pope in some circumstances, by appeal to the doctrine of double effect. The concern throughout is that there should be no *direct* attack on human life.

A good and detailed overview of Islamic teaching on abortion and euthanasia is provided by the essays edited by Brockopp (2003) in *Islamic ethics of life: Abortion, wars and euthanasia.* According to Islamic teachings, expressed within the Qur'an and the prophetic traditions, life is a Divine gift and therefore Islamic ethics is embedded in the fundamental principle affirming sanctity of all life. Moreover, Islam is often depicted as a 'rights'- based faith as the rights of humans *(huquq alebad)* and the Creator (*huquq alAllah*) are explicitly recognised. According to this, while God, as the giver of the gift life, has the right to be acknowledged, humans have the right to protect their dignity (*karama*). Classical Muslim scholars by working within the framework of this distinctive notion of human rights in Islam, which predates the modern secular-humanist notion of human rights, have identified the following five rights that they suggested to be summarising the ultimate ethos of Islamic ethics and law: right to protect life, family (progeny), property, religion and reason (human sanity) (Sahin 2011). As such the majority of Muslim theological and legal schools of thought agree that euthanasia is not allowed in Islam. This view is justified by the following reasons: The Qur'an explicitly forbids 'taking any human life that God has made sacred' (17:33) and the voluntary act of taking one's life, suicide (4.29). Furthermore, based on the Qur'anic verses (16:61/3:145), the mainstream Islamic theology asserts that the length of human life is decided by God. And finally, in Islamic Law euthanasia and suicide are not included among the reasons allowed for killing.

The Qur'an does not explicitly mention abortion. As such, the sanctity of life principle shapes Muslim theological and legal perspectives toward abortion which is seen to be wrong and forbidden. However, a majority of Muslim scholars accept that abortion may be permitted in certain cases invoking the well established legal maxim in Islamic law suggesting that sometimes 'necessities in life renders the unlawful lawful'. For example, abortion is permitted if continuing the pregnancy would put the mother's life in real danger. There are different scholarly opinions regarding the timing of the permitted abortion; some argue in the first 16 weeks of pregnancy, while others only permit it in the first 7 weeks. What is beyond dispute is the fact that in Islam a mother's life and well-being are taken seriously when considering the permissibility of abortion. In Islamic Law abortion is generally seen as a serious moral wrong but not a directly punishable act. Muslim jurists agree that after the foetus is completely formed and if the continuation of the pregnancy will not constitute a real danger to mother's life, abortion becomes a punishable crime because it constitutes an offense against a complete, living human being. Muslim jurists often insist that the payment of blood money (*diya*) becomes incumbent if the baby is aborted alive and then died.

Empirical Studies

Several strands of empirical research have mapped the connection between religiosity and attitudes toward abortion and euthanasia. One of these strands has focused on the connection between frequency of church attendance and levels of agreement with survey questions. In an early study of *The Religious factor in Australian Life*, Bouma and Dixon (1986) reported a strong association between frequency of church attendance and agreement with the statement that abortion is *never* justified: 17% of non-attenders, 26% of those who attend rarely, 26% of those who attend occasionally, and 51% of those who attend at least monthly. A similar pattern emerged in agreement with the statement that euthanasia is *never* justified: 17% of non-attenders, 16% of those who attend rarely, 17% of those who attend occasionally, and 43% of those who attend at least monthly. In his study of *Churchgoing and Christian Ethics*, Gill (1999), using British Social Attitudes Survey data, also recorded connections between frequency of churchgoing and attitudes to abortion and euthanasia. Also drawing on the British Social Attitudes Survey data, Curtice and Gallagher (1990) found that 25% of weekly attenders agreed that abortion should not be allowed in cases where there is a strong chance of defect in the baby, compared with 6% of those who attended less that twice a year. Donnison and Bryson (1996) constructed a scale to measure pro-euthanasia attitudes. They found significantly less acceptance of euthanasia among weekly attendees. Heath et al. (2007) examined the changing association between frequency of church attendance and attitudes toward abortion between 1984 and 2005. They found that the view that a woman should not be allowed an abortion if she did not want the child declined from 77% to 51% among churchgoers and from 67% to 32% among those who had a religious identity but did not attend church. Clery et al. (2007) created a scale of acceptance of euthanasia. They found higher acceptance among non-churchgoers than among churchgoers.

In the Teenage Religion and Values Survey, conducted among nearly 34,000 young people between the ages of 13 and 15 years, Francis (2001a) included the item, 'Abortion is wrong'. In an analysis crosstabulated against frequency of church attendance this study found agreement with this item among 47% of weekly churchgoers, compared with 33% of those who attend church less than weekly and 34% of those who never attend church.

A second strand of research has focused on the connection between self-assigned religious affiliation and attitudes toward abortion and euthanasia. Once again the British Social Attitudes Survey data has provided a useful source of data. For example, using their scale of acceptance of euthanasia, Clery et al. (2007) found highest acceptance among those who reported no religion, followed by Anglicans, Roman Catholics, other Christians, and non-Christian religious groups. Park and Rhead (2013), drawing on the 2012 British Social Attitudes Survey data, found that self-assigned religious affiliation continued to be closely associated with attitudes toward abortion. In 2012 Catholics were the least accepting, with 39% agreeing that abortion should be allowed when the woman does not wish to have the child, compared with 56% of Anglicans and 73% of non-affiliates. Park and Rhead (2013) also chart the growing acceptance of abortion among the religiously affiliated since the first British Social Attitudes Survey in 1983. For example, while in 1983 34% of Anglicans supported abortion when the woman does not want to have the child, the proportions rose to 54% in 1994 and to 56% in 2012.

The importance of self-assigned religious affiliation in shaping attitudes toward abortion has been explored by a series of studies drawing on the Teenage Religion and Values data (2001a). In the first of these studies, Francis (2001b) explored responses to the item 'abortion is wrong' through a sequence of analyses that gradually refined the notion of self-assigned religious affiliation. The first step dichotomised the participants into two groups, those who belonged to a faith group and those who did not: 38% of those who belonged to a faith group agreed that abortion is wrong, compared with 33% of those who did not belong to a faith group. The second step further dichotomised those who belonged to faith groups into Christian and other faiths: 38% of those who belonged to a Christian group agreed that abortion is wrong, compared with 46% of those who belonged to other faith groups. The third step distinguished among the non-Christian faith groups: 27% of Jews, 31% of Hindus, 40% of Sikhs, and 58% of Muslims agreed that abortion is wrong. The fourth step distinguished among different streams within the Christian tradition: 31% of Anglicans, 38% of Protestants, 50% of Catholics and 65% of those who belonged to the smaller Christian sects agreed that abortion is wrong. In the second of these studies, Francis (2008a) took a more detailed view on the ways in which young females affiliated with different Christian denominations responded to the item 'abortion is wrong'. This analysis found that the view that abortion is wrong was endorsed by 34% of Anglicans, 36% of Presbyterians, 37% of Methodists, 45% of Baptists, 53% of Roman Catholics, 68% of Protestants, and 82% of Jehovah's Witnesses. In the third study, Francis (2008b) also focused on young females, but compared the responses of those affiliated with different faith groups. The analysis found that the view that abortion is wrong was endorsed by 34% of Hindus, 40% of Christians, 43% of Sikhs, and 58% of Muslims, compared with 38% of non-affiliates.

Within the studies published on data generated by the International Empirical Research Programme Religion and Human Rights 1.0, van der Ven (2016) compared attitude toward euthanasia among Christians, Muslims, and non-religious across six nations (Belgium, England/Wales, Germany, Netherlands, Norway, and Sweden). The same pattern emerged in all six nations, with non-religious more supportive of euthanasia than Christians, and with Christians more supportive of euthanasia than Muslims.

A third strand of research has recognised the multidimensional nature of religiosity, within the context of the social scientific study of religion and set out to explore the contribution of different aspects of religiosity to explaining individual differences in attitude toward abortion. For example, a series of studies conducted in the USA, drawing on the General Social Survey's database have examined the religious, social (and sometimes psychological) predictors of individual differences in attitude toward abortion, including work reported by Emerson (1996), Sullins (1999), and Petersen (2001). One interesting example of the approach within the UK is provided by Francis (2004), again drawing on the Teenage Religion and Values data. After controlling for individual differences in sex, age and personality (extraversion, neuroticism, and psychoticism), Francis (2004) employed measures of church attendance, personal prayer, religious experience, belief in God, creationism, punitive God image, and denominational affiliation. Among these variables considered simultaneously, the strongest beta weight was associated with creationism ($\beta = .11$), followed by Catholic affiliation ($\beta = .09$) and a punitive God image ($\beta = .07$).

Within the studies published on data generated by the International Empirical Research Programme Religion and Human Rights 1.0, two studies employed a scale designed to measure attitudes toward permissions to lift the right to life as the dependent measure alongside multiple indices of religiosity. In the first of these two studies, conducted in Turkey, Ok and Eren (2013) created a nine-item scale that embraced the following themes and generated an alpha coefficient of .82:

- It should be possible for a pregnant woman to obtain a legal abortion:
  - if economically she cannot afford any more children;
  - if psychologically she cannot afford any more children
  - if there is a strong chance of serious defect in the baby;
  - if the woman's own health is seriously endangered by the pregnancy.
- A woman in the final stages of an incurable disease wants to end her life:
  - the doctor is allowed to do this;
  - the doctor is allowed to do this only if palliative care is exhausted.
- In regard to abortion politicians should take decisions independently of religious leaders.
- In regard to euthanasia politicians should decide irrespective of any religious leaders' will.
- Any form of sexual relations between adults should be their individual choice.

In their study designed to replicate Ok and Eren's (2013) study in England and Wales, Francis and Robbins (2016) argued that the last item listed in the original scale was problematic to locate within the theme concerned with permission to lift the right to life. Thus, they worked with an eight-item scale, generating an alpha coefficient of .76.

The original study in Turkey by Ok and Eren (2013) employed three measures of religiosity: a three-item scale of religious salience ($\alpha = .80$), a six-item scale of religious openness ($\alpha = .79$), and a six-item scale of religious stress ($\alpha = .87$). They also included three population characteristics in the model: sex, age and political preference. These data found positive associations between permissions to lift the right to life and both religious openness ($\beta = .16$) and religious stress ($\beta = .27$) and a negative association between permission to lift the right to life and religious saliency ($\beta = -.19$). The replication study in England and Wales by Francis and Robbins (2016) also employed three measures of religiosity: a four-item scale of religious saliency ($\alpha = .87$), a six-item scale of interreligious openness ($\alpha = .83$) and self-assigned religious affiliation, distinguishing between non-affiliates, Christians and Muslims. They also included in the model two personal variables (sex and age), three psychological variables (extraversion, neuroticism, and psychoticism) and a five-point measure of political preference (left, centre left, centre, centre right, and right). These data found a positive association between permissions to lift the right to life and interreligious openness ($\beta = .19$), and negative association between permissions to lift the right to life and religious saliency ($\beta = -.15$) and religious affiliation as Christian ($\beta = -.15$) and as Muslim ($\beta = -.19$).

Research Question

Against this background the aims of the present study drew on data generated by the International Empirical Research Programme in Religion and Human Rights 2.0 among young people in England and Wales in order to construct and to test a scale of attitude toward euthanasia and abortion and to test the general hypothesis that religiosity functions as a significant predictor among young people of individual differences in attitude toward matters of life and death. Within this general hypothesis the study is designed to differentiate between the effects of religious practice (personal prayer and worship attendance) and religious affiliation (Protestant, Catholic, and Muslim). The effect of these religious factors is contextualised within the effect of personal factors (sex and age) and psychological factors (extraversion, neuroticism, and psychoticism).

Such contextualisation is important because of the place given to these factors in previous research. The two personal factors (sex and age) are recognised as key predictors of individual differences in adolescent religiosity. Research tends to show that females record higher levels of religiosity than males (Francis and Penny 2014) and that levels of religiosity decline during adolescence (Kay and Francis 1996). The three psychological factors proposed by Eysenck's dimensional model of personality (Eysenck and Eysenck 1991) are also recognised as key predictors of individual differences in religiosity (Beit-Hallahmi and Argyle 1997). Eysenck's dimensional model of personality proposes three higher order factors defined as extraversion, neuroticism, and psychoticism. Empirical studies within the psychology of religion employing this model of personality have consistently shown an inverse association between psychoticism scores and religiosity, as crystalised by Francis (1992) and confirmed by more recent studies, including Francis et al. (2007), Francis et al. (2008), and Francis and Hermans (2009).

Method

Procedure

Selected schools within England and Wales in conurbations where there was evidence of Christian, Muslim and religiously-unaffiliated students were invited to participate in the study. Within participating schools complete classes of year 11, year 12, and year 13 students (15- to 18-year-olds) were invited to complete the questionnaire within the context of a normal lesson. Students were assured of confidentiality and anonymity. Although all students were given the choice not to present their questionnaire for analysis very few decided not to submit their response.

Measures

Attitude toward euthanasia and abortion was assessed by a newly constructed scale comprising three items about euthanasia and seven items about abortion. Each item was rated on a five-point Likert scale: disagree strongly (1), disagree (2), not certain (3), agree (4), and agree strongly (5).

Personal factors were assessed by two variables: sex, male (1) and female (2); and school year, year 11 (1), year 12 (2) and year 13 (3).

Psychological factors were assessed by the abbreviated form of the Eysenck Personality Questionnaire Revised (EPQR-A) as developed originally by Francis et al. (1992) and further modified by Francis et al. (2001). This instrument comprised three six-item measures for extraversion, neuroticism and psychoticism. Each item is rated on a two-point scale: yes (1), and no (0).

Religious practice was assessed by two items. Frequency of worship attendance was assessed by the question 'How often do you take part in religious services at a church or mosque or another place?' rated on a six-point scale: never (1), hardly ever (2), a few times a year (3), one to three times a month (4), once a week (5), and more than once a week (6). Frequency of personal prayer was assessed by the question 'How often do you pray?' rated on an eight-point scale: never (1), hardly ever (2), a few times a year (3), one to three times a month (4), once a week (5), more than once a week (6), once a day (7), and several times a day (8).

Religious affiliation was assessed by the question 'Do you belong to a religious community or would you describe yourself as non-religious?' followed by a check-list of religious groups and the final category 'non-religious'.

Participants

The analyses reported in this paper were conducted on the 966 students who self-assigned as Catholic, as Protestant, as Muslim, or as non-religious. This group comprised 370 males and 596 females, 360 students from year 11, 383 students from year 12, and 223 students from year 13; 101 Catholics, 145 Protestants, 35 Muslims, and 685 non-religious students.

Results and Discussion

The first step in data analysis examined the scale properties of the newly constructed Scale of Attitude toward Euthanasia and Abortion. The data presented in Table 6.1 demonstrates that each of the ten items contributed to a homogeneous scale with correlations between the individual items and the sum of the other nine items ranging from .35 to .70. Overall the item endorsements reveal a positive attitude toward

Table 6.1 Scale of Attitude toward Euthanasia and Abortion (SAEA): Scale properties

	r	%
Euthanasia should be prohibited in all circumstances[a]	.35	11
Euthanasia should be permitted in the case of unbearable and irreversible suffering	.59	72
Euthanasia should be permitted in the case of unbearable and irreversible suffering if palliative care is exhausted	.54	61
Abortion should be prohibited in all circumstances because it ends human life[a]	.51	13
Abortion should be permitted in the case of rape	.70	77
Abortion should be permitted in the case of incest	.67	68
Abortion should be permitted when there is a strong chance of serious defects to the baby	.63	56
Abortion should be permitted when the woman's own health is seriously endangered by the pregnancy	.68	77
Abortion should be permitted when the woman cannot afford more children economically	.58	49
Abortion should be permitted when the woman cannot afford more children psychologically	.65	56

Note: *r*, correlation between individual item and sum of other nine items
%, sum of agree strongly and agree responses
[a]these items were reverse coded to calculate *r* and the scale score

both euthanasia and abortion. In the case of euthanasia, 72% of the students agree that euthanasia should be permitted in the case of unbearable and irreversible suffering, and 61% agree that euthanasia should be permitted in the case of unbearable and irreversible suffering if palliative care is exhausted. Just 11% of the students agree that euthanasia should be prohibited in all circumstances. In the case of abortion, over three quarters of the students agree that abortion should be permitted in the case of rape (77%) and that abortion should be permitted when the woman's own health is seriously endangered by the pregnancy (77%). Two thirds of the students agree that abortion should be permitted in the case of incest (68%). Over half of the students agree that abortion should be permitted when there is a strong chance of serious defect in the baby (56%) and that abortion should be permitted when the woman cannot afford more children psychologically (56%). The proportion falls slightly to 49% who agree that abortion should be permitted when the woman cannot afford more children economically.

The second step in data analysis took an overview of the psychometric properties of the four scales employed in the study in terms of means, standard deviations, and alpha coefficients (Cronbach 1951). The data presented in Table 6.2 demonstrate that the ten-item scale concerned with attitude toward abortion and euthanasia and two of the three scales concerned with psychological factors (extraversion and neuroticism) recorded internal consistency reliability in terms of alpha coefficients in excess of the threshold of .65 commended by DeVellis (2003). The lower alpha coefficient recorded by the psychoticism scale is consistent with the known operational difficulties incurred in measuring this dimension of personality (Francis et al. 1992).

Table 6.2 Scale Properties

	N items	α	*M*	*SD*	Low	High
Euthanasia and abortion	10	.87	38.36	7.52	10	50
Extraversion	6	.79	3.98	1.96	0	6
Neuroticism	6	.72	3.86	1.78	0	6
Psychoticism	6	.47	1.02	1.18	0	6

The third step in data analysis explored the bivariate correlations between attitude toward euthanasia and abortion and the two personal factors (sex and age), the three psychological factors (extraversion, neuroticism and psychoticism), the two religious practices (personal prayer and worship attendance) and religious affiliation (Protestant, Catholic, Muslim, and non-religious). For the purpose of correlational analysis (and subsequent regression analysis) the categorical variable of religious affiliation was employed to create four dummy variables (Protestant, Catholic, Muslim, and non-religious). These correlation coefficients are presented in the first column of Table 6.3. They demonstrate that, when each of these factors is considered in isolation, the personal factors carry little predictive power in relation to attitude toward euthanasia and abortion: there is no significant sex difference, and a slight increase in acceptance of euthanasia and abortion with age. The psychological factors also carry little predictive power in relation to attitude toward euthanasia and abortion: there is no significant correlation with either extraversion scores or psychoticism scores, and a small positive correlation with neuroticism scores. Religious practice factors carry greater predictive power: there is a significant negative correlation between attitude toward euthanasia and abortion and both frequency of personal prayer and frequency of worship attendance. Religious affiliation also carry significant predictive power: there is a positive correlation between non-religious identity and attitude toward euthanasia and abortion, and significant negative correlations between Protestant affiliation, Catholic affiliation and Muslim affiliation and attitude toward euthanasia and abortion.

In light of these multiple correlations, the fourth step in data analysis constructs a series of regression models with attitude toward euthanasia and abortion as the dependent variable and with the independent variables being added incrementally in four steps (see Table 6.3). Model one begins by introducing the personal factors (sex and age). Model two adds the psychological factors (extraversion, neuroticism, and psychoticism). Model three adds the religious practices factors (personal prayer and worship attendance). Finally model four adds religious affiliation. In this model religious affiliation is added as three dummy variables (Protestant, Catholic, and Muslim) with non-religious identity standing as the reference point. It is the fourth model that is of greatest interest when all the predictor factors are taken into account. In this model, the factors of core importance are religious practice and religious affiliation. In terms of personal factors, age remains statistically significant ($p < .01$) when all other variables are in the equation: year 13 students are overall more accepting of euthanasia and abortion that year 11 students. In terms of psychological factors neuroticism scores remain statistically significant ($p < .05$) when all

Table 6.3 Regression models on attitude toward euthanasia and abortion

	r	Model 1	Model 2	Model 3	Model 4
Personal factors					
Sex	.06	.05	.02	.03	.04
Age	.08*	.07*	.07*	.09**	.10**
Psychological factors					
Extraversion	.04		.05	.04	.03
Neuroticism	.10*		.10**	.09**	.09*
Psychoticism	−.04		−.02	−.04	−.03
Religious practice					
Personal prayer	−.23***			−.21***	−.15***
Worship attendance	−.17***			−.05	−.03
Religious affiliation					
Protestant	−.09**				−.06
Catholic	−.16***				−.13***
Muslim	−.10**				−.07*
Non religious	.22***				
Total r^2		.009	.018	.076	.090

Note: *$p < .05$; **$p < .01$; ***$p < .001$

other variables are in the equation: higher neuroticism scores are associated with an attitude more accepting of euthanasia and abortion.

In terms of religious practice factors, while the correlation coefficients suggest that both personal prayer and worship attendance are significant predictors of a less accepting attitude toward euthanasia and abortion, the regression model demonstrates that personal prayer is the strongest predictor. When personal prayer is in the equation worship attendance accounts for no additional variance. Personal prayer remains a significant predictor when all other variables are in the equation. In terms of religious affiliation, even after personal prayer and worship attendance are in the equation, identities as Catholic and as Muslim carry additional predictive power, taking the non-religious as the reference point. Identity as Protestant, however, is not significant. This finding suggests that, irrespective of individual differences in religious practice, self-understanding as Catholic and self-understanding as Muslim carries higher rejection of euthanasia and abortion

Conclusion

Within the wider context of the human rights legislation, debates and controversies concerning the right to life and abortion and euthanasia, the present study set out to explore the connections among adolescents in England and Wales between attitude toward abortion and euthanasia on the one hand and religious identity and religious practice on the other hand, after taking into account personal and psychological factors. Three main conclusions emerge from this study conducted among 966 students between the ages of 14 and 18 years.

The first conclusion concerns the coherence between euthanasia and abortion within the minds of these adolescents. The development and psychometric examination of the ten- item Scale of Attitude toward Euthanasia and Abortion (SAEA) confirmed that the ten items, covering both issues, cohered to generate an homogenous scale with an alpha coefficient of .87. Acceptance and rejection of both issues concerning life and death work side-by-side in the adolescent mind.

The second conclusion concerns the connection between attitude toward euthanasia and abortion and personal religious practice. The correlation coefficients demonstrate significant negative associations between acceptance of euthanasia and abortion and both church attendance and prayer. The beta weights, however, demonstrate the primary role of personal prayer. After personal prayer has been taken into account no additional variance is accounted for by church attendance. This finding is consistent with the classic distinction, advanced by Allport and Ross (1967) and confirmed by Batson and Ventis (1982) and by Francis (2007), between intrinsic religious orientation and extrinsic religious orientation. Intrinsic religious orientation accesses the religion of the heart where religion is a master motivation or end in itself. Extrinsic religious orientation accesses a public face of religion where religion may serve other personal or social ends. Within this conceptual framework, personal prayer may serve as an indicator of intrinsic religiosity, less subject to social constraints, while church attendance may embrace aspects of extrinsic religiosity as well as intrinsic religiosity. In this sense, personal religiosity measured by frequency of prayer provides a sharper measure of the connection between religion and attitude toward euthanasia and abortion than offered by personal religiosity measured by frequency of church attendance.

The third conclusion concerns the connection between self-assigned religious affiliation and attitude toward euthanasia and abortion. This finding is important for two reasons. First the simple bivariate correlation coefficients confirm that the sense of belonging to a religious tradition continues to shape the attitudes of young people to core matters of life and death. In other words, the theological and religious teachings of the traditions to which they belong carry measurable implications for their lives and values. In secular and religiously diverse societies young people affiliated with Christian and Muslim traditions actually see matters of life and death through a different lens.

Second, the multiple regression model develops this insight regarding the connection between self-assigned religious affiliation and attitude toward euthanasia and abortion persists, after taking personal prayer into account, for two of the three religious traditions but not for the third. For young Protestants, the effect of self-assigned religious affiliation is mediated entirely through personal prayer. This suggests that young Protestants who have abandoned religious practice are undifferentiated in their attitude toward euthanasia and abortion from religiously unaffiliated young people. They retain no cultural resonance from their religious tradition. However, both for young Muslims and for young Catholics, the effect of self-assigned religious affiliation persists after taking individual differences in personal prayer into account. This suggests that young Catholics and young Muslims who have abandoned religious practice nonetheless continue to be influenced by their religious cultural heritage. This finding is consistent with the theories of religious identification developed and tested by Bouma (1992) in Australia and by Bibby (1985, 1987) in Canada, and re-presented by Fane (1999) in England. For example, Bibby's theory of encasement argued that Canadian Christians were 'encased' within the Christian tradition, and that the tradition retained an influence over both its active and latent members. The present data suggest that this remains the case for both Catholics and Muslims in England and Wales. In secular and religiously diverse societies young people who see themselves as Catholics or as Muslims continue to see matters of life and death through a different lens, even if they have abandoned the discipline of religious practice.

The weakness of the present study is that it was conducted on a small sample of only 966, among whom there were merely 101 Catholics and 35 Muslims. Further research within this tradition is needed in England and Wales among sufficiently large samples of young people that allow the smaller religious groups to become more fully visible.

References

Allport, G. W., & Ross, J. M. (1967). Personal religious orientation and prejudice. *Journal of Personality and Social Psychology, 5*, 432–443.

Amnesty International. (2016). *Ireland's ban on abortion violates human rights – Ground-breaking UN ruling*. Available online: https://www.amnesty.org/en/latest/news/2016/06/irelands-ban-on-abortion-violates-human-rights/. Accessed 23 Feb 2017.

Ashraf, H. (2001). UK woman's right-to-die case fails. *Lancet, 358*(9291), 1437.

Astley, J. (2000). *Choosing life? Christianity and moral problems*. Durham: Longman and Todd.

Batson, C. D., & Ventis, W. L. (1982). *The religious experience: A social psychological perspective*. New York: Oxford University Press.

BBC. (1992). *Hillsborough victim allowed to die (Bland Ruling, 1993)*. Available online: http://news.bbc.co.uk/onthisday/hi/dates/stories/november/19/newsid_2520000/2520581.stm. Accessed 2 Mar 2017.

BBC. (2006, May 12). *Lords block assisted dying bill*. Available online: http://news.bbc.co.uk/1/hi/health/4763067.stm. Accessed 2 Mar 2017.

Beit-Hallahmi, B., & Argyle, M. (1997). *The psychology of religious behaviour, belief and experience*. London: Routledge.

Bibby, R. W. (1985). Religious encasement in Canada: An argument for Protestant and Catholic entrenchment. *Social Compass, 32*, 287–303.

Bibby, R. W. (1987). *Fragmented Gods: The poverty and potential of religion in Canada*. Toronto: Irwin Publishing.

Bouma, G. D. (1992). *Religion: Meaning, transcendence and community in Australia*. Melbourne: Longman Cheshire.

Bouma, G. D., & Dixon, B. R. (1986). *The religious factor in Australian life*. Melbourne: Marc Australia.
Brockopp, J. E. (Ed.). (2003). *Islamic ethics of life: Abortion, war and euthanasia*. Columbia: University of South Carolina Press.
Clery, E., McLean, S., & Philips, M. (2007). Quickening death: The euthanasia debate. In A. Park, J. Curtice, K. Thomson, M. Philips, & M. Johnson (Eds.), *British social attitudes: The twenty-third report* (pp. 35–54). London: Sage.
Cook, R. J., & Dickens, B. M. (1999). Human rights and abortion laws. *International Journal of Gynaecology and Obstetrics, 65*, 81–87.
Cook, R. J., & Dickens, B. M. (2003). Human rights dynamics of abortion law reform. *Human Rights Quarterly, 25*, 1–59.
Cook, R. J., Erdman, J. N., & Dickens, B. M. (Eds.). (2014). *Abortion law in transnational perspective: Cases and controversies*. Philadelphia: University of Pennsylvania Press.
Cronbach, L. J. (1951). Coefficient alpha and the internal structure of tests. *Psychometrika, 16*, 297–334.
Curtice, J., & Gallagher, T. (1990). The northern Irish dimension. In R. Jowell, S. Witherspoon, & L. Brook (Eds.), *British social attitudes: The seventh report* (pp. 183–216). Aldershot: Gower.
Devellis, R. F. (2003). *Scale development: Theory and applications*. London: Sage.
Donnison, D., & Bryson, C. (1996). Matters of life and death: Attitudes to euthanasia. In R. Jowell, A. Park, L. Brook, & K. Thomson (Eds.), *British social attitudes: The thirteenth report* (pp. 161–183). Aldershot: Dartmouth.
Dworkin, R. (1993). *Life's dominion: An argument about abortion, euthanasia, and individual freedom*. London: HarperCollins Publishers.
Emerson, M. O. (1996). Through tinted glasses: Religion, worldviews, and abortion attitudes. *Journal for the Scientific Study of Religion, 35*, 41–59.
English, R. (2015). *Withdrawal of nutrition and hydration would not offend right to life – Strasbourg Court*. Available online: https://ukhumanrightsblog.com/tag/euthanasia/. Accessed 23 Feb 2017.
Eysenck, H. J., & Eysenck, S. B. G. (1991). *Manual of the Eysenck personality scales*. London: Hodder and Stoughton.
Fane, R. S. (1999). Is self-assigned religious affiliation socially significant? In L. J. Francis (Ed.), *Sociology, theology and the curriculum* (pp. 113–124). London: Cassell.
Finer, L., & Fine, J. B. (2013). Abortion law around the world: Progress and pushback. *American Journal of Public Health, 103*, 585–589.
Francis, L. J. (1992). Is psychoticism really a dimension of personality fundamental to religiosity? *Personality and Individual Differences, 13*, 645–652.
Francis, L. J. (2001a). *The values debate: A voice from the pupils*. London: Woburn Press.
Francis, L. J. (2001b). Religion and values: A quantitative perspective. In L. J. Francis, J. Astley, & M. Robbins (Eds.), *The fourth R for the third millennium: Education in religion and values for the global future* (pp. 47–78). Dublin: Lindisfarne Books.
Francis, L. J. (2004). Empirical theology and hermeneutical religious education: A case study concerning adolescent attitudes toward abortion. In H. Lombaerts & D. Pollefeyt (Eds.), *Hermeneutics and religious education* (pp. 355–373). Leuven: Peeters.
Francis, L. J. (2007). Introducing the New Indices of Religious Orientation (NIRO): Conceptualisation and measurement. *Mental Health, Religion and Culture, 10*, 585–602.
Francis, L. J. (2008a). Family, denomination and the adolescent worldview: An empirical enquiry among 13- to 15-year-old girls in England and Wales. *Marriage and Family Review, 43*, 185–204.
Francis, L. J. (2008b). Self-assigned religious affiliation: A study among adolescents in England and Wales. In B. Spalek & A. Imtoual (Eds.), *Religion, spirituality and the social sciences: Challenging marginalisation* (pp. 149–161). Bristol: Policy Press.

Francis, L. J., & Hermans, C. A. M. (2009). Psychological health and attitude toward Christianity: A study among pupils attending Catholic schools in the Netherlands. *Journal of Religious Education, 57*, 47–58.
Francis, L. J., & Penny, G. (2014). Gender differences in religion. In V. Saroglou (Ed.), *Religion, personality and social behaviour* (pp. 313–337). New York: Psychology Press.
Francis, L. J., & Robbins, M. (2016). Attitudes toward human rights and religiosity among adolescents in England and Wales: Replicating and extending a study in Turkey. In H.-G. Ziebertz & E. H. Ballin (Eds.), *Freedom of religion in the twenty-first century: A human rights perspective on the relationship between politics and religion* (pp. 105–129). Leiden: Brill.
Francis, L. J., Brown, L. B., & Philipchalk, R. (1992). The development of an abbreviated form of the revised Eysenck personality questionnaire (EPQR-A): Its use among students in England, Canada, the USA and Australia. *Personality and Individual Differences, 13*, 443–449.
Francis, L. J., Robbins, M., Louden, S. H., & Haley, J. M. (2001). A revised psychoticism scale for the revised Eysenck personality questionnaire: A study among clergy. *Psychological Report, 88*, 1131–1134.
Francis, L. J., Robbins, M., Ap Siôn, T., Lewis, C. A., & Barnes, L. P. (2007). Psychological health and attitude toward Christianity among Protestant and Catholic sixth-form pupils in Northern Ireland. *Pastoral Psychology, 56*, 157–164.
Francis, L. J., Robbins, M., Santosh, R., & Bhanot, S. (2008). Religion and mental health among Hindu young people in England. *Mental Health, Religion and Culture, 11*, 341–347.
Gill, R. (1999). *Churchgoing and Christian ethics*. Cambridge: Cambridge University Press.
Harmon, S. E., & Sethi, N. (2011). Preserving life and facilitating death: What role for government after Haas v. Switzerland? *European Journal of Health Law, 18*, 355–364.
Heath, A., Martin, J., & Elgenius, G. (2007). Who do we think we are? The decline of traditional social identities. In A. Park, J. Curtice, K. Thomson, M. Phillips, & M. Johnson (Eds.), *British social attitudes: The twenty-third report* (pp. 1–34). London: Sage.
Ireland, E. J. (2013). Do not abort the mission: An analysis of the European Court of Human Rights case of R.R. v. Poland. *North Carolina Journal of International Law & Commercial Regulation, 38*, 651–695.
Kay, W. K., & Francis, L. J. (1996). *Drift from the Churches: Attitude toward Christianity during childhood and adolescence*. Cardiff: University of Wales Press.
Mason, R. (2015, September 12). Assisted dying bill overwhelmingly rejected by MPs. *The Guardian*. Available online: https://www.theguardian.com/society/2015/sep/11/mps-begin-debate-assisted-dying-bill. Accessed 2 Mar 2017.
Ok, U., & Eren, S. (2013). Attitudes towards human rights and religiosity: A case of Turkish adolescents. In J. A. van der Ven & H.-G. Ziebertz (Eds.), *Human rights and the impact of religion* (pp. 145–165). Brill: Leiden.
Park, A., & Rhead, R. (2013). Changing attitudes towards sex, marriage, and parenthood. In A. Park, C. Bryson, E. Clery, J. Curtice, & M. Phillips (Eds.), *British social attitudes: The thirtieth report* (pp. 1–32). London: NatCen Social Research.
Petersen, L. R. (2001). Religion, strutures, and educations effect on attitudes toward elective abortion. *Journal for the Scientific Study of Religion, 40*, 187–203.
Puppinck, G., & de La Hougue, C. (2014). The right to assisted suicide in the case law of the European Court of Human Rights. *International Journal of Human Rights, 18*, 735–755.
Rothbard, M. (2012). *Abortion: Does the foetus have a right to life?* Available online: http://www.libertarianview.co.uk/general-principles/abortion-does-the-foetus-have-a-right-to-life. Accessed 23 Feb 2017.
Sahin, A. (2011). Islam, secularity and the culture of critical openness: A theological reflection. In Y. Birt, D. Hussain, A. Siddiqui, & H. Dilwar (Eds.), *British secularism and religion: Islam, society and the state* (pp. 3–24). Markfield: Kube.
Sullins, D. P. (1999). Catholic/Protestant trends on abortion: Convergence or polarity. *Journal for the Scientific Study of Religion, 38*, 354–369.
Toebes, B., Hartlev, M., Hendriks, A., & Hermann, J. R. (2012). *Health and human rights in Europe*. Cambridge: Intersentia.

van der Ven, J. A. (2016). On the brink of death: Euthanasia from the angle of law, morality and religion, a cross-cultural perspective. In H.-G. Ziebertz & E. H. Ballin (Eds.), *Freedom of religion in the twenty-first century: A human rights perspective on the relation between politics and religion* (pp. 257–299). Brill: Leiden.

Weinstein, B. (2012). Reproductive choice in the hands of the state: The right to abortion under the European Convention on Human Rights in light of A.B.C. v. Ireland. *American University International Law Review, 27*, 391–437.

Weisstub, D. N., & Pintos, G. D. (Eds.). (2008). *Autonomy and human rights in health care: An international perspective*. Dordrecht: Springer.

Chapter 7
The Right to Life: A Perspective of Young Palestinian Muslims

Raymond J. Webb and Fatma Jamal Asa'd

This paper examines the attitudes of 905 Bethlehem area Muslim males and females between the ages of 13 and 32 (M = 17.8) in regard to the right to life. Specifically, we examined three situations (and some variants) in which the right to life is at issue: abortion, euthanasia, and the death penalty. We found support for the statement that abortion is forbidden because it is the taking of human life. There is some ambiguity in this position, in that Islam allows abortion for serious reasons during the first 120 days of pregnancy, because God is not said to have infused humanness into the baby until after that time, when it is potentially human and must be respected. There was support for abortion to protect the life of the mother in regard to physical health but not to protect psychological health, prevent economic strain, or if the child would have serious problems. The attitude toward euthanasia was negative, even when there was immitigable suffering. Opposition to the death penalty was not supported, consistent with a certain Muslim position that, under specific conditions, the death penalty serves justice. There was the most explained variability in regard to the prohibition of abortion in general, the prohibition of euthanasia in general, and non-support of prohibiting the death penalty. We found attitudes basically consistent with Islamic teaching in regard to these life issues.

R. J. Webb (✉)
University of Saint Mary of the Lake, Mundelein, IL, USA
e-mail: rwebb@usml.edu

F. J. Asa'd
Researcher, Bethlehem, Palestine

H.-G. Ziebertz, F. Zaccaria (eds.), *Euthanasia, Abortion, Death Penalty and Religion – The Right to Life and its Limitations*, Religion and Human Rights 4, https://doi.org/10.1007/978-3-319-98773-6_7

Introduction

This paper examines the attitudes of Bethlehem area Muslims males and females between the ages of 13 and 32, with an average age of 17.8, in regard to situations in which the right to life is questioned. We consider abortion to be a process in which life in the womb is deliberately terminated. Besides a general prohibition of abortion, abortion in the case of violence or baby's health, abortion to save the life of the mother, abortion for psycho-economic reasons are also considered. Euthanasia is the intentional ending of life of a terminally ill person at their own request directly or by responsible others communicating the subject's putative will. The use of the death penalty is the deliberate taking of a life by the legitimate government as punishment for a certain crime. The background of the situation and human rights development in the general context is considered. The design, findings, conclusions, and suggestions for further clarification are presented. Age, gender, attitudes toward the relationship of religion and society, religious beliefs and experience, and psychosocial variables such as empathy are considered. Correlations are presented and regression analysis is used.[1]

After an overview of the civil and Bethlehem contexts as well as Islam, this chapter considers three areas in which life is at risk or challenged: abortion, euthanasia, and the death penalty. The structure of the presentation is that each area of these three areas is considered in each of several sections: civil and religious context (1), research method and research questions (2), empirical findings (3), discussion (4) and final observations (5).

Civil and Religious Context

Civil Context

In 1991, the Organization of the Islamic Conference issued the Cairo Declaration on Human Rights in Islam. Included is the position that Islamic Shariah (the right path) takes precedence over any other human rights declaration and prevails in disputes. In 2002, President Yasser Arafat ratified the Palestine Basic Law (Palestine Basic Law 2003), which had been passed by the Palestinian Legislative Council in 1997. Amendments were added in 2003 and 2005. The law applies to Palestinians living under the jurisdiction of the Palestinian (National) Authority, which excludes 62% of the West Bank as well as East Jerusalem, due to the Israeli occupation. The official religion of Palestine is Islam, although the sanctity of all other "divine religions" is to be respected. One of the principal sources of legislation is to be Shariah (Articles 4.1 and 4.2).

[1]The authors are grateful to Carl Sterkens for his assistance with technical and theoretical issues.

Abortion in general is prohibited in Palestine, but it is legal in Israel. Hence, it is said that some Palestinian seek abortions in Israel (Schwartz 2016).While the exception of abortion in order to protect the life of the mother is technically legal in Palestine, in practice, according to experts, it is impossible to get such a procedure. Abortion is not openly discussed in Palestine. There is some fear that pregnancy out of wedlock may result in the "honour killing" of the woman if her situation would become known (Shahawy 2016). Abortion statistics are difficult to find, although Hessini (2007) reports that there were 98,135 abortions in Palestine from 1995–2000, certainly not all from pregnancy outside of marriage. Advocates from outside of Palestine are more likely to be involved in open arguments for greater access to abortion; religious concerns are put to the side.

Euthanasia does not appear to be condoned or practiced in Palestine. Families care for the elderly, although there are some group facilities sponsored by religious groups. A sophisticated discussion of end-of-life issues is not widely available.

Judicial sentences of the death penalty in Palestine are to be reviewed and approved by the president. There have been executions in Gaza by the authorities (who are members of the de facto HAMAS government of Gaza as the result of a coup in 2007). These executions were not approved by the president, who has little de facto authority in Gaza. Since the summer of 2017 there has been an attempt to reconcile the HAMAS (an Islamic party) and Fatah (a nationalist party) Palestinian political factions. The effect on further use of the death penalty has yet to be seen.

Bethlehem Context

The city of Bethlehem has a Muslim majority with a strong Christian minority (who were in the majority two decades ago). The traditional site of the birth of Jesus draws a million visitors in years when there is no overt conflict. Of course, the Israeli occupation means that entrance and exit from Bethlehem are controlled by Israeli military, and the Palestinian government and police have limited control. Crime is very low, almost non-existent toward visitors. Hotels and tourist souvenir shops are the backbone of the economy. Church bells and the Muslim calls to prayer are heard several times each day. Major Muslim and Christian holy days are official holidays. Men pray at the mosque, women typically at home. Some males do not attend prayers in the mosque. Headscarves are usual for Muslim women after secondary school. Often, Muslim men wear beards. Some Christians wear small crosses. Bethlehem has the "flavour" of a modern Arab (not distinguishably Muslim) city. The context of Bethlehem is religious, but there are many secular aspects as would be found in any modern city of similar size – about 30.000.

Islam

Muslims believe that Allah revealed Islam (which means "peace") through the angel Jubril, who spoke to the Prophet Muhammed. The followers of Muhammed wrote down Muhammed's primary teachings (received from Allah) combined into Islam's holy book, the Qur'an. Other teachings were compiled by the first followers as the Hadith ("Sayings and Practices of the Prophet"). What was taught about Allah, life, the believer, and all things is the will of Allah. The content could have been different, had Allah willed it so. There are four "schools" of interpretation in Sunni Islam, much like modes of legal interpretation. The majority of Muslims are Sunni (including Palestinians), but about 10% of Muslims are Shi'ite. Both groups have scholarly authorities and tend to respect each other's' opinions. Shi'ites have authorities, such as the Ayatollahs in Iran who can make definite interpretations. Sunni scholars rely on judgments based on evidence in the Qur'an, from the hadiths, from logical reasoning and jurisprudence, and from analogy coming from a previous rule (Sachedina 1990). Specific rulings about particular situations are made by groups of learned persons, who come together in regional or national "Fiqh Councils." Learned persons can also make rulings called "fatwas." Rulings are to assist Muslims in following Shariah, the way that a good Muslim should live. It is not something Muslims seek to impose on everyone (Cf. also Webb and Asa'd 2015).

Abortion in Islam

According to Islam, every life belongs to God. And one has the right to God-given life. Abortion is the act of deliberately terminating a pregnancy. Islam is perhaps unique in its attention to fetal development with elaboration in the Qur'an (Hedayat et al. 2006). Abortion is not permitted after 120 days, although there are rare exceptions (Cf. Yacoub 2013). (There is a minority scholarly position that abortion is forbidden from the time of implantation [Hedayat et al. 2006]). Depending on the religious school of thought, the permitted period may be from 40–120 days (Tuell, 62–63; Alamri 2011). It is at that point that God infuses human spirit into the fetus (ensoulment) (Abdul Hussain 2011). Simply elective abortion is never permitted. Before the time of "ensoulment" abortion is permitted for a serious reason. One is a serious threat to the life of the mother. Another can be severe physical defects in the child (Al-Matary and Ali 2014). Al-Matary and Ali (2014) note that a child already dead in the womb or who would die shortly after birth could be aborted after 120 days. Some others would take into account economic reasons, and even that pregnancy would affect breast feeding of a recently born child (Hedayat et al. 2006). Even after 120 days, abortion may still be permitted to save the life of the mother. In the case of rape or incest, it is recommended that scholars and medical experts be consulted (Tuell 2010, 64). Abortion of a child conceived outside of marriage is not permitted. Hessini (2007) found that the average age for marriage is increasing and the age when women begin having sex is decreasing, with the number of "unwanted" pregnancies increasing. Hessini (2007) notes that "[secular] Interpretations that allow for abortion are based on fetal development, gestational age and the circumstances of the pregnant woman; they rarely mention fetal rights or when life begins." While there is some mention in the Qur'an of the life and rights of the child, in secular discourse only the woman's control of her body and the dangers of illegal or unsafe abortions are discussed. It is noted that the Muslim perspective on abortion is not at all the same as the strict Catholic prohibition (Bowen 1997).

Euthanasia in Islam

Rathor and Fauzi (2012) defines euthanasia as "a deliberate act, undertaken by a physician, to end the life of a person at his request in the name of compassion." But they qualify this into three categories: voluntary (patient has control), non-voluntary (patient is comatose or lacks decisional capacity) and involuntary (against the will of the patient). Additionally, they argues that "passive" euthanasia, the withdrawal or non-use of medical interventions which will not ultimately help the patient to live much longer, is not really euthanasia and reference to it only confuses the discussion. In these latter situations, a committee of two or three believing doctors should decide on appropriate treatment (Cf. also Nikookar and Sooteh 2014). For Tuell (2010) euthanasia ("mercy killing" as it is referred to) is simply forbidden in Islam. Interestingly, Rathor and Fauzi see euthanasia as a societal issue and further regrets the use of Western terminology in the Islamic discussion. Islam's principle of individual autonomy does not apply since life belongs to God and the rights of the individual are balanced with the rights of society as a whole as well as of the family and close friends and considerations of the harm which might also be caused to others. Nazila Isgandarova (2015) stresses the value of Muslim spiritual care for understanding the nuances of the issue of the end of life and appropriate Muslim responses. Rathor and Fauzi's (2012) research elaborates that the major motivation for euthanasia is not uncontrolled pain but rather depression, loneliness, hopelessness, and psychological distress. Abu Seir and Kharroubi (2017) urge continued discussion of palliative care, while strictly opposing euthanasia at either the patient's or the family's request. Aghababaei (2013) found that the strongest predictor of opposition to euthanasia was intrinsic religiosity. Chowdhury (2012) with a sample of 300 found that Muslims were more strongly opposed to the legalization and justification of assisted suicide than Christians and Jews, although all three groups were opposed.

The Death Penalty in Islam

The death penalty is permitted in Islam as a matter of justice. Schabas (2000) recognizes that the death penalty can be justified through Islamic religious principles and is found in the law of Islamic states, but contends that its practice is quite inconsistent among them and does not recognize the religious limitations. Greenberg and West (2008, 301–302) observe that countries whose legal systems are based on Islamic law are more likely to have the death penalty than others, while noting that in Islamic law there might be procedural impediments to its implementation. For example, in the case of murder a just punishment would be the execution of the killer. However, if the families involved were to settle on an agreement between to achieve justice in another way, for instance, the payment of a certain amount of money, then there would be no requirement of the death penalty. The death penalty has been considered as the appropriate punishment for apostasy. However, it is argued that this was because in earlier times, members of the community were of the same religion (Islam) and a change of religion could result in disunity and potentially great physical harm to the community because of its enemies (Peters and DeVries 1976). Saeed and Saeed (2004, 68, 86–87) find the argument from Islamic sources for the death penalty for apostasy to be weak and urge continued discussion of the restrictions, pitfalls, and great dangers in its availability and use. In agreement, Ahmadiyyeh (a ten million member Islamic religious movement) imam and scholar Mizra Tahir Ahmad (1986/2005) argues that the contention that apostates are to be killed as a baseless conviction found neither in the Qur'an nor the hadith but simply an originally invented political idea which gradually spread to a wider influence. (Unlike Shiites and Sunnis, Ahmadiyyeh Muslims are not considered "mainstream.") Schabas notes that, worldwide, two to three states every year abolish the death penalty (2015). Hood and Hoyle (2015) are optimistic about progress toward the gradual universal abolition of the death penalty, but refer with chagrin to Jordan's 2014 execution after an eight-year moratorium of 11 persons who had been on "death row" for ten years, this in response to a rising crime rate.

All young Muslims in the Bethlehem area have received religious instruction in Islam throughout their years of schooling up to the universal matriculation examination. This test includes a section on Islam. So we can say for sure that instruction in Islam is thorough for our sample. Western culture is evident from clothing and available advertising and other influences. But we expect that responses to the questionnaire will be in the general direction of consistency with Islam in regard to abortion, euthanasia, and the death penalty.

Research Method and Research Questions

Research Questions and Hypotheses

As noted above, Islam is generally opposed to abortion, especially after the first 40–120 days of pregnancy, after which God infuses a human spirit into the foetus. In any situation there would need to be a very good reason for an abortion, according to Islam. Euthanasia is never permitted, no matter the circumstances. The death penalty is allowed under strict circumstances in the name of justice, but these circumstances are disputed. However, the greater Bethlehem area is also influenced by non-Muslim attitudes and trends, so there is some question of the absolute conformity of the attitudes of young persons to Islamic belief. Nevertheless, our expectation is that the responses of the young Muslim to our questionnaire will be consistent with the general principles of Islam.

This paper investigates these research questions:

1. Do young Palestinian Muslims have a negative attitude toward abortion in general?
2. Does this negative attitude apply to all circumstances, including violence and baby's health circumstances, danger to the mother's health, and/or psycho-economic distress situations?
3. What demographic variables; personal and social religious attitudes, values and experience; psychological and socio-political traits predict this support?
4. Do young Palestinian Muslims have a negative attitude toward euthanasia in general?
5. Does this negative attitude apply to situations of severe and immitigable suffering?
6. What demographic variables; personal and social religious attitudes, values and experience; psychological and socio-political traits predict this support?
7. Do young Palestinian Muslims have a generally positive attitude toward the death penalty?
8. What demographic variables; personal and social religious attitudes, values and experience; and psychological and socio-political traits predict this support?
9. Do young Palestinian Muslims have attitudes generally consistent with Muslim religious beliefs in regard to abortion, euthanasia, and the death penalty?

Data Collection and Sample

The data were collected between January 15 and July 1, 2015 from ten governmental and private secondary schools and universities in the Bethlehem region of Palestine. Of the 1200 questionnaires which were distributed, 1060 were returned. 40 were discarded because of serious completion flaws. Late Middle and Secondary school children completed questionnaires under the supervision of teachers, who sometimes explained individual items. A few university students and "neighbours" also filled out the instrument. University students and some "neighbours" completed protocols on their own. Some teachers were given token gifts for their work. Some students were given refreshments. No person was required to complete the protocol.

The population from which the sample was drawn were male and female Muslim Palestinian Arabs from the ages of 13 to 32 (M = 17.8) who live and attend school in the greater Bethlehem area. They are Sunni Muslims, living in an area in which there is a significant Christian (less than 40%) population, as well as some foreigners.

Government, Christian, and Muslim schools were the loci of questionnaire completion. As noted above, Islam is practiced and lived in a variety of cultural contexts. There is no claim here that these results can be generalized beyond the greater Bethlehem area.

Only the 905 Muslim subjects were included in the present analysis, given the relatively small number of Christians, and the handful of others. 399 Muslims were male; 506 were female. It is the experience of the authors that Muslims were eager to complete the survey.

The instrument used was the questionnaire of the Religion and Human Rights 2.0 program, developed by Hans-Georg Ziebertz and Johannes Van der Ven, in collaboration with others. The questionnaire was translated into Arabic by two translators and later re-checked for accuracy. Most items were presented on a five point scale: strongly disagree, disagree, unsure, agree, and strongly agree.

Conceptual Model

Here we describe the concepts referred to in the conceptual model. Where we use a scale, a Cronbach's alpha of at least .60 is preferred, although in the case of psycho-economic reasons for abortion, we have accepted a lower alpha (Fig. 7.1).

Dependent Variables

Abortion

In our investigation of support for attitudes toward abortion, we used a single item regarding a general attitude toward abortion, "Abortion should be prohibited in all circumstances because it terminates beginning human life." But we were also interested in whether there was a different attitude toward abortion in certain circumstances: (1) the prohibition of abortion in all circumstances, (2) the permissibility of abortion in situations of rape, incest, or the baby having serious possibility of defects, (3) the permissibility of abortion in situations where the mother's health is endangered by the pregnancy, (4) the permissibility of abortion in situations of economic or psychological harm to the mother. The following three items made up the scale: abortion because of violence or baby health circumstances: *Abortion should be permitted in case of rape. Abortion should be permitted in case of incest. Abortion should be permitted when there is a strong chance of serious defect in the baby* (Cronbach's alpha = .68). The following two items make up the scale: mother's psychological or economic concerns: *Abortion should be permitted when the woman cannot afford any more children economically. Abortion should be permitted when the woman cannot afford any more children psychologically* (Cronbach's alpha = .53). There was also a single item for analysis: *Abortion should be permitted when the woman's own health is seriously endangered by the pregnancy.*

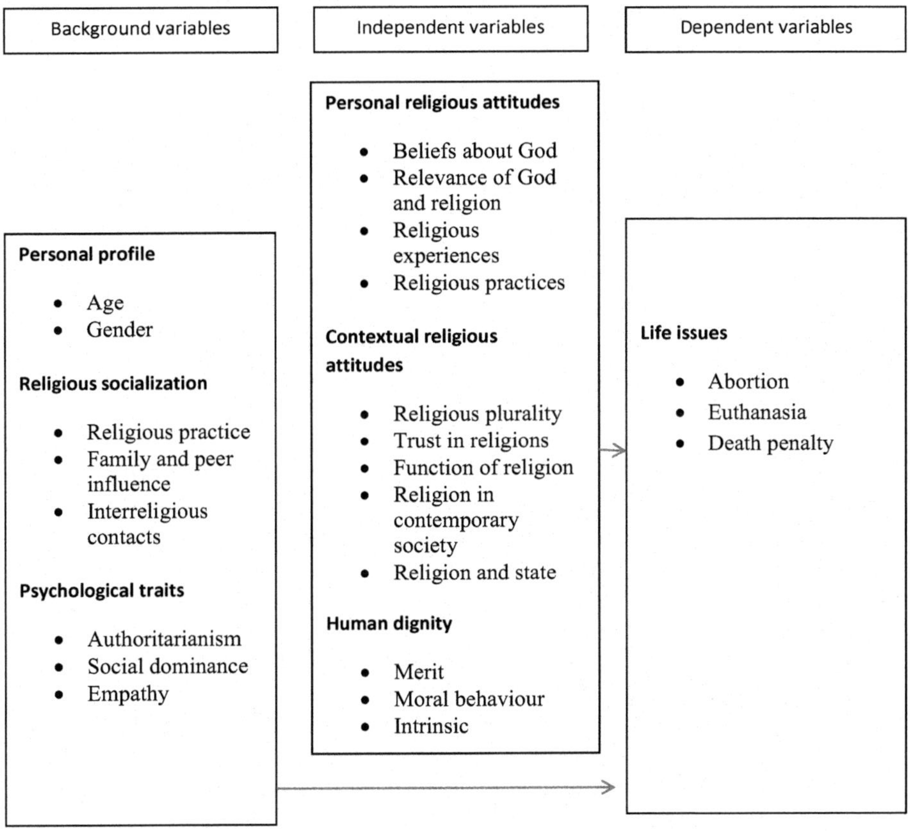

Fig. 7.1 Conceptual model

Euthanasia

In regard to the general attitude toward euthanasia, we used the single item "Euthanasia should be prohibited in all circumstances." We further measured the attitude toward euthanasia when the patient is undergoing unbearable, immitigable suffering. A scale measuring the subjects' position on euthanasia when suffering is unbearable was composed of two items: *Euthanasia should be permitted in the case of unbearable and irreversible suffering. Euthanasia should be permitted in the case of unbearable and irreversible suffering, if palliative care is exhausted.* (Cronbach's alpha = .62).

Death Penalty

The attitude toward the death penalty under consideration here is the position of our subjects in regard to the prohibition or commutation of the death penalty. A scale combining the following two items was used to measure attitudes toward the death penalty: *The death penalty should strictly be prohibited because of the right to life. A death sentence should always be commuted to a life sentence.* (Cronbach's alpha = .69).

Predictors of Attitudes Toward the Right to Life: Independent Variables

Abortion, euthanasia, and the death penalty are life issues around which there is considerable difference of opinion and controversy. Often, positions are based on a certain fundament, sometimes drawn from reason, sometimes from affect, sometimes from religion or worldview. Islam has positions on all of these issues. Some nuances may come from the situation of being in this particular area of Palestine. Bethlehem Muslims live in a religious atmosphere with many non-Muslim influences. It seems wise therefore to include both religious and non-religious variables in our analyses. In general, it can be supposed that demographic variables such as age and gender may have some effect on attitudes toward euthanasia, abortion, and the death penalty. Personal religious experience, convictions, and practice as well as views about the relationship of religion and society are important in our religious analyses. In the complex context, we also wonder if personal non-religious psychosocial tendencies and attitudes affect the attitudes under study.

We have presented in the conceptual model a number of variables in their relevant clusters in the hope of ultimately accounting for as much variability as possible. Below we list the variables found to contribute to explanation of variability in regression analyses. Later we discuss those significant relationships.

We consider independent variables, grouped as personal religious attitudes, contextual religious attitudes, and sources of human dignity (merit, moral behaviour, intrinsic). While we look at a number of correlations, only those independent variables which are significant in the account of variability explained (the regression equations) are named here. In regard to personal religious attitudes, belief in a personal God, belief in God as non-personal, perceived tension between races, perceived tension between sexes, the importance of religion in contemporary society, religion as spirituality, religious experience as faith, religious exclusivism, and religion in society are contributors. Among contextual religious attitudes are consultation between religion and the state, separation of religion and the state, and religious pluralism. Sources of human dignity considered are esteem by others, moral behaviour, intrinsic personal value. The background variables are grouped as personal profile (demographics), religious socialization, and psychological traits (authoritarianism, social dominance, and empathy).

Empirical Findings

In this empirical research section, we first describe the means and standard deviations of the dependent variables (Table 7.1). Then we present factor analysis regarding abortion, euthanasia and the death penalty (Tables 7.2a, 7.2b, 7.2c). Next, we report on the significant correlations between the attitudes toward abortion in general; abortion because of violence and baby health reasons; abortion because of mother's health; and abortion because of psycho-economic reasons and personal and contextual religious attitudes. Religious attitudes, and the background characteristics (Tables 7.3a and 7.3b). Then we present significant correlations between attitudes toward euthanasia, euthanasia in circumstances of immitigable pain and the death penalty and personal and contextual religious attitudes (Tables 7.4a and 7.4b). Finally, in the regression analyses we report on statistically significant betas, R, and adjusted R^2 (Tables 7.5 and 7.6).

Table 7.1 Number of respondents (N), means and standard deviations *of items about abortion, euthanasia* and the *death penalty* of respondents in descending order of average agreement

	N	Mean	s.d.
Abortion			
e. Abortion should be permitted when the woman's own health is seriously endangered by the pregnancy.	905	3.57	1.25
a. Abortion should be prohibited in all circumstances because it terminates human life at its beginning.	904	3.19	1.37
c. Abortion should be permitted in case of incest.	905	3.03	1.25
b. Abortion should be permitted in case of rape.	905	3.00	1.29
d. Abortion should be permitted when there is a strong chance of serious defect in the baby.	905	2.99	1.26
g. Abortion should be permitted when the woman cannot afford any more children psychologically.	905	2.56	1.23
f. Abortion should be permitted when the woman cannot afford any more children economically	905	2.52	1.25
Euthanasia			
a. Euthanasia should be prohibited in all circumstances	905	3.32	1.44
c. Euthanasia should be permitted in the case of unbearable and irreversible suffering, if palliative care is exhausted.	905	2.69	1.30
b. Capital punishment should be permitted in the case of unbearable and irreversible suffering.	905	2.59	1.29
Death penalty			
b. A death sentence should always be commuted to a life sentence.	905	2.86	1.34
a. Capital punishment should strictly be prohibited because of the right to life.	905	2.80	1.40

Interpretations of means: 1.00–1.79: total disagreement; 1.80–2.59: disagreement; 2.60–2.99: negative ambivalence; 3.00–3.39: positive ambivalence; 3.40–4.19: agreement; 4.20–5.00: full agreement

Table 7.2a Factor analysis (PAF, Oblimin rotation), communalities (h^2), percentage of explained variance, and reliability (Cronbach's alpha) of *attitudes towards abortion*

	F1	F2	h^2
c. Abortion should be permitted in case of incest.	.870		.44
b. Abortion should be permitted in case of rape.	.669		.73
d. Abortion should be permitted when there is a strong chance of serious defect in the baby	.429		.28
g. Abortion should be permitted when the woman cannot afford any more children psychologically.		.622	.39
f. Abortion should be permitted when the woman cannot afford any more children economically.		.590	.34
Cronbach's alpha	.69	.53	
Number of valid cases	905	905	

Scale: 1 = totally disagree; 2 = disagree; 3 = not sure; 4 = agree; 5 = fully agree
Explained variance = 43.56%; F1 = Abortion – Violence and health; F2 = Abortion – Psycho-economic reasons

Table 7.2b Factor analysis (PAF, Oblimin rotation), communalities (h^2), percentage of explained variance, and reliability (Cronbach's alpha) of *attitude towards euthanasia*

	F1	h^2
b. Euthanasia should be permitted in the case of unbearable and irreversible suffering.	.669	.45
c. Euthanasia should be permitted in the case of unbearable and irreversible suffering, if palliative care is exhausted.	.669	.45
Cronbach's alpha	.62	
Number of valid cases	905	

Scale: 1 = totally disagree; 2 = disagree; 3 = not sure; 4 = agree; 5 = fully agree
Explained variance = 44.75%; F1 = Attitude towards euthanasia

Table 7.2c Factor analysis (PAF, Oblimin rotation), communalities (h^2), percentage of explained variance, and reliability (Cronbach's alpha) of *attitude towards death penalty*

	F1	h^2
a. The death penalty should be strictly prohibited because of the right to life.	.726	.53
b. A death sentence should always be commuted to a life sentence.	.726	.53
Cronbach's alpha	.69	
Number of valid cases	905	

Scale: 1 = totally disagree; 2 = disagree; 3 = not sure; 4 = agree; 5 = fully agree
Explained variance = 52.64%; F1 = Attitude towards death penalty

Table 7.3a Correlations (Pearson's r) between attitudes towards *abortion in general, abortion because of violence and baby health reasons, abortion because of mother's health, abortion because of psycho-economic reasons,* and *background characteristics*

	No abortion in general	*Abortion violence and baby health*	*Abortion mother health*	*Abortion psycho-economic reasons*
Personal profile				
Age	–	–		−.08*
Gender (male)	−.12**	−.08*		.12**
Education			.07*	
Religious socialisation				
Father's belief and faith	−.08**	–		.07*
Mother's belief and faith	−.08**	.07*		.09**
Best friend's belief and faith	−.08*	–		.11**
Father: Important to adopt his faith	–	–		–
Mother: Important to adopt her faith	–	–		–
Interreligious contacts		–		.07*
Psychological traits				
Authoritarianism	.19**	.08*		–
Social dominance		–		.07*
Empathy	.19**	–	.12**	−.14**
Human dignity				
Dignity through merit	.10**	.13**		–
Moral behavior	.28**	.07*	.18**	−.20**
Intrinsic dignity	.11**	.12**		−09**

Correlations are significant at $p < .01$ level (**) or $p < .05$ level (*)
Interpretation of correlations: weak ($r < .15$); moderate ($.15 \leq r < .30$); strong ($r \geq .30$)

Means and Standard Deviations for Abortion, Euthanasia, and the Death Penalty

We find the strongest support for the permissibility of abortion when the woman's own health is thought to be endangered by the pregnancy (M = 3.57), although there is some diversity of opinion, given that the standard deviation is 1.25. The next strongest attitude (positive ambivalence) is the prohibition of abortion in all circumstances (M = 3.19), also with a diversity of opinion (s.d. = 1.37). The attitudes toward abortion in cases of incest, rape, and the baby having serious defects is right around the middle – evenly divided, "don't know" (M = 3.03, 3.00, 2.99). There is strong disagreement with abortion for psychological and economic reasons (M = 2.56, 2.52).

Table 7.3b Correlations (Pearson's r) between attitudes towards *abortion in general, abortion because of violence and baby health reasons, abortion because of mother's health, and abortion because of psycho-economic reasons* and *personal and contextual religious attitudes*

	No abortion In general	*Abortion violence and baby health*	*Abortion mother health*	*Abortion psycho-economic reasons*
Personal religious attitudes				
Beliefs about god				
Personal god	.29**	.14**	.12**	−.17**
Non-personal god	.26**	.16**	.16*	−.09**
Relevance of god and religion				
Critical approach to religious belief	.10**	–		.09**
Belief in divine intervention	–	–		.11**
Influence of religion in life	–	−.08*		–
Religious experiences				
Faith	.15**	–		−.16**
Spirituality	–	–	.07*	–
Experience of god			.12**	
Religious influence			.09*	
Religious practices				
Prayer frequency	–	–		.13**
Contextual religious attitudes				
Attitudes toward religious plurality				
Exclusivism	.14**	–	.12**	−.10**
Pluralism	.07	.11**	.09**	–
Trust in religion				
Trust in own religion	−.14**	–	−.15**	.08*
Trust in other religions	–	–		–
Function of religion				
Public function	−.18**	–	.12**	−.14**
Cultural conformity	–	.13**		–
Spiritual service	.17**	.11**	.13**	−.09**
Religion in contemporary society				
Relevance of religion in society	.28**	–	.18**	−.20**
Perceived tension between sexes	.09*	.17**		
Perceives tension between races				.10**
Religion and state				

(continued)

Table 7.3b (continued)

	No abortion In general	*Abortion violence and baby health*	*Abortion mother health*	*Abortion psycho-economic reasons*
Separation	–	–		–
Consultation	.20**	.13**		−.06

Correlations are significant at p < .01 level (**) or p < .05 level (*). Interpretation of correlations: weak (r < .15); moderate (.15 ≤ r < 30); strong (r ≥ .30)

Table 7.4a Correlations (Pearson's r) between attitudes towards *euthanasia, euthanasia in specific circumstances, the death penalty,* and *background characteristics*

	No Euthanasia in general	*Euthanasia-circumstances*	*No death penalty*
Personal profile			
Age	−.08*	–	−.08*
Gender (female)	−.13**	.07*	−.14**
Religious socialisation			
Father's belief and faith	−.13**	–	–
Mother's belief and faith	−.13**	–	–
Best friend's belief and faith	−.12**	–	–
Psychological traits			
Authoritarianism	.15**	–	–
Social dominance	−.11**	.14**	–
Empathy	−.23**	−.13**	–
Human dignity			
Dignity through merit	.10**	–	–
Moral behavior	.29**	.07*	.12**
Intrinsic	.13**	–	.18**

Correlations are significant at p < .01 level (**) or p < .05 level (*)
Interpretation of correlations: weak (r < .15); moderate (.15 ≤ r < .30); strong (r ≥ .30)

In our overall survey, the second strongest support was for the prohibition of euthanasia in all circumstances (M = 3.32), with also the largest diversity of opinions (s.d. = 1.44). The response to euthanasia being permitted in the case of unbearable suffering with palliative care being exhausted (M = 2.69) or simply unbearable suffering (M = 2.50) was negative. Both these findings are consistent with Islamic teaching.

Always commuting death sentences (M = 2.86) and prohibiting death penalty because of the right to life (M = 2.80) were not supported. As noted elsewhere, under certain circumstances, death penalty is seen as appropriate justice in the Muslim perspective.

Table 7.4b Correlations (Pearson's r) between attitudes towards *euthanasia in general, euthanasia in specific circumstances, the death penalty* and *personal and contextual religious attitudes*

	No euthanasia in general	*Euthanasia-circumstances*	*No death penalty*
Personal religious attitudes			
Beliefs about god			
Personal god	.24**	–	–
Non-personal god	.20**	–	–
Relevance of god and religion			
Critical approach to religious belief	–	–	.08*
Belief in divine intervention	.07*	–	–
Influence of religion in life	–	–.08*	–
Religious experiences			
Faith	18**	–.09*	–
Spirituality	–	.07*	.08*
Religious practices			
Prayer frequency	–	–	–
Contextual religious attitudes			
Attitudes toward religious plurality			
Exclusivism	.18**	–.07*	–
Pluralism	.10**	–	.17**
Trust in religion			
Trust in own religion	–.15**	–	–
Trust in other religions		–	–
Function of religion			
Public function	.18**	–.09**	–
Cultural conformity	.10**	–	–
Spiritual service	.20**	–.07**	–
Religion in contemporary society			
Relevance of religion in society	.28**	–.10**	–
Perceived tension between sexes		.14**	–
Perceived tension between races	–.13**	.16**	.10**
Religion and state			
Separation	–	.09**	.14**
Consultation	–.18**	–	.09**

Correlations are significant at $p < .01$ level (**) or $p < .05$ level (*)
Interpretation of correlations: weak ($r < .15$); moderate ($.15 \leq r < 30$); strong ($r \geq .30$)

Table 7.5 Regression analysis for attitudes towards *abortion in general, abortion because of violence and baby health reasons, abortion because of mother's health, abortion because of psycho-economic reasons* with weights (β) for each variable and total explained variance (R^2 and Adjusted R^2)

	No Abortion In general	*Abortion violence and baby health*	*Abortion mother health*	*Abortion psycho-economic reasons*
Personal religious attitudes				
Personal god	.167**			−.094**
Non-personal god		.155**	.084*	
Perceived tension between sexes		.162**		
Religion in contemporary society	.165**	–	.093*	−.117**
Religious experience – Faith	−.090*			
Religious exclusivism				
Trust in own religion			−.079*	
Contextual religious attitudes				
Religion and state – Consultation	.101**	–		
Psychological traits				
Authoritarianism	.088**	–		–
Empathy	–			
Dignity				
Moral behavior as source	.132**		.090*	−.095*
R^2	.155	.052	.060	.057
Adj. R^2	.149	.050	.056	.054

Standardised regression coefficients (β) are significant at $p < .01$ (**) or $p < .05$ (*) level

Structure of Attitudes Toward Abortion, Euthanasia, and Death Penalty (Factor Analysis)

We used factor analysis to investigate whether and what were the commonalities in our items concerned with abortion, with euthanasia, and with death penalty. In regard to abortion, we found two factors: a) abortion in the case of rape, incest, or strong chance of serious defect in the baby (violence and baby's health), and b) abortion when the woman cannot afford any more children psychologically or economically (psycho-economic). For the violence and baby's health factor, Cronbach's alpha was .68 with 905 valid cases. For the psycho-economic factor, Cronbach's alpha was .53, also with 905 valid cases. Explained variance was 43.56%. Abortion in general and abortion because of the mother's health were not included in the factor analyses due to low commonalities and low factor loadings. Abortion in general is considered later in the regression analyses, as is abortion in the case of serious

Table 7.6 Regression analysis for attitudes towards *euthanasia, euthanasia in specific circumstances, death penalty* with weights (β) for each variable and total explained variance (R^2 and Adjusted R^2)

Personal profile	*No Euthanasia In general*	*Euthanasia – circumstances*	*No death penalty*
Personal religious attitudes			
Personal god	.081*		
Perceived injustice between races		–.160**-	
Religion in contemporary society	.124**	–	–
Religion as spirituality			
Contextual religious attitudes			
Religion and state – consultation	.091**		.
Attitude toward religious plurality			
Religious pluralism			.146**
Psychological traits			
Authoritarianism	–	–	–
Empathy	.108**		
Social dominance			
Dignity			
Moral behavior as source	.150**		
Intrinsic			.148**
R^2	.138	.026	.051
Adj. R^2	.133	.024	.049

Standardised regression coefficients (β) are significant at $p < .01$ (**) or $p < .05$ (*) level

problems with the health of the mother. For euthanasia in the circumstance of immitigable pain, there was one scale of two items to be considered. The Cronbach's alpha was .619 with 44.75% of variability explained. In regard to the death penalty, the scale consisted of two items which had a Cronbach's alpha of .69. 52.64% of variability was explained.

Correlations Between Dependent and Independent Variables

In this section we consider only those relationships of r = .15 or higher, which are most likely to contribute to the explanation of variability in the regression analyses.

Abortion

Most significantly positively correlated ($r = .15$ or higher) with a prohibition against abortion in general were the position that human dignity comes from one's moral behaviour ($r = .28^{**}$), authoritarianism ($r = .19^{**}$), empathy ($r = .19^{**}$), belief in a personal God ($r = .29^{**}$), belief in a God described in non-personal ways ($r = .26^{**}$), the relevance of religion in society ($r = .28^{**}$), religion as faith ($r = .15^{**}$), the public function of religion ($r = -.18^{**}$), religion as spiritual service ($r = .17^{**}$), and a positive attitude toward consultation between religion and the state ($r = .20^{**}$).

In regard to allowing abortions in the cases of rape, incest, or because of serious health problems for the baby (violence and baby health), only belief in God described in non-personal ways ($r = .16^{**}$), and perceived tension between the sexes ($r = .17^{**}$) were correlated at a level of $r > .15$ or above with the dependent variable. Only moral dignity coming from moral behaviour ($r = .18^{**}$), belief in a non-personal God ($r = .16^{**}$), and religion being relevant to society ($r = .18^{**}$) were correlated above a level of .15 with support for abortion being permitted when the mother's health is in danger.

Permitting abortion for psycho-economic reasons was most strongly negatively correlated ($r > .15$) with belief in a personal God ($r = -.17$), faith as religious experience ($r = -.16$), religion as relevant in society ($r = -.20$), and human dignity coming from moral behaviour ($r = -.20$).

Euthanasia

The strongest correlations (.15 or above) with a general prohibition of euthanasia were human dignity coming from moral behaviour (.29**), the relevance of religion in society (.28**), belief in a personal God (.24**), belief in God as non-personal (.20**), religion as spiritual service (.20**), religion as faith (.18**), exclusivism (.18**), authoritarianism (.15**), and the public function of religion (.18**). Negatively related were empathy (−.23**), trust in one's own religion, and valuing consultation between religion and the state (−.18**). Also, the more empathy, the less support for the euthanasia prohibition.

Euthanasia in circumstances of extreme suffering was positively related at the level of .15 or above only to perceived tension between the races (.16**).

Death Penalty

Strong correlations with the non-use of the death penalty were only obtained with pluralism (.17**) and human dignity coming from one's intrinsic worth (.18**).

Predictors of Attitudes Toward the Right to Life: Regression Analysis with Weights (Betas) for Each Variable and Total Explained Variance (R and Adjusted R^2)

It should be noted that some of the variables with correlations greater than .20 in the correlation tables are not taken up in the final regression tables here. This is because these variables (although $r > .20$) had low significance in the regression analyses. In the regression analyses, we included only those independent variables that yielded relevant ($r = .15$ or higher) and significant correlations with the dependent variable concerned If a selected independent variable did not contribute significantly to the explanation of the dependent variable in the regression analysis, the regression analysis was generally re-done only with those independent variables which contribute significantly ($p < .05$) to the explained variance. The tables present these final analyses.

Abortion

We have analysed attitudes about the prohibition of abortion in all circumstances; as well as the permissibility of abortion in the case of rape, incest, and serious defects in the unborn baby; concerns about the mother's health; and attitudes about the permissibility of abortion for psychological and economic reasons.

14.9% of the variability was explained in regard to the prohibition of abortion in general. Significant predictors were belief in a personal God ($\beta = .167$**), the positive role of religion in contemporary society ($\beta = .165$**), human dignity coming from moral behaviour ($\beta = .132$**), a positive attitude toward consultation between religion and the state ($\beta = .101$**), and authoritarianism ($\beta = .088$*). The negative predictor was faith as religious experience ($\beta = -.090$*).

Only 5.0% of the variability was accounted for in considering abortion being permitted because of violence and baby's health reasons. Significant predictors were perceived tension between the sexes ($\beta = .162$**) and belief in a non-personal God ($\beta = .155$**).

5.6 % of variability was accounted for regarding the attitude that abortion should be permitted because of serious problems with the mother's health. Significant predictors were religion having a place in contemporary society ($\beta = .104$**), belief in a non-personal God ($\beta = .096$**), and human dignity coming from moral behaviour ($\beta = .105$**).

In regard to the attitude that abortion should be permitted for psycho-economic reasons, only 5.4% of the variability was explained. Belief in a personal God ($\beta = -.094$**), the positive place of religion in contemporary society ($\beta = -.117$**), and human dignity coming from moral behaviour ($\beta = -.095$**) all negative predictors. In other words, believers in a personal God and in the value of religion in contemporary society and in moral behaviour being the source of human dignity were significantly less likely to support abortion for psycho-economic reasons, perhaps because this reason is not adequate in the context of these believers.

Euthanasia

We looked at variables related to the prohibition of euthanasia in general and the permissibility of euthanasia in the case of extreme suffering. The significant predictors of opposition to euthanasia in general were human dignity based on moral behaviour ($\beta = .150^{**}$), a positive attitude toward the role of religion in contemporary society ($\beta = .124^{**}$), empathy ($\beta = .108^{**}$), religion and state in consultation (($\beta = .091^{*}$), and belief in a personal God ($\beta = .081^{*}$). 13.3% of the variability was explained. Opposition to euthanasia in general was second only to opposition to abortion in general in amount of variability explained in this study. Results were minimal in regard to euthanasia in the situation of unmitigated suffering since only one predictor variable was significant – perceived injustice between races ($\beta = .160^{**}$), with only 2.4% of the variability being accounted for. This relationship does not admit of ready explanation.

Prohibition of the Death Penalty

In the regression analysis, support for the prohibition of the death penalty was related to religious pluralism ($\beta = .146^{**}$) and human dignity being intrinsic ($\beta = .148^{**}$) 4.9% of the variance was explained in the analysis.

Discussion

In general, our findings are consistent with a Muslim understanding of the issues of abortion, euthanasia, and death penalty. The exceptions in regard to certain circumstances in regard to abortion are in keeping with Muslim understandings. Euthanasia admitted of no exceptions; this is also consistent with Muslim understanding. The death penalty is not prohibited, either in Islam or civilly.

Research Questions 1–2–3: Abortion

Opposition to abortion in general was slightly positively supported (3.19/5.00). 14.9% of the variability was accounted for. Opposition to abortion in general was related positively to believing in a personal God, valuing the place of religion in society, valuing consultation between religion and state, authoritarianism, and the view that human dignity comes from one's moral behaviour. It was negatively related to religious experience – faith, strength from faith. From these variables one might describe the person opposed to all abortion as one who believes strongly in his own Muslim religion and thinks that religion should influence society. How one lives one's life morally determines one's human dignity. This is consistent with Muslim belief in an emphasis on duties over rights. A reasonable amount of variability is accounted for but the proposition is only rated slightly positively. The young persons in the survey might be described as believers subject to other influences.

Support for abortion in the cases of violence and baby health issues was "neutral" (3.01/5.00). Total variability accounted for was low (5%) with belief in a non-personal god and perceived tension between the sexes as significant predictors. The issues related to "violence" certainly have an extremely negative sexual tension dimension.

Of all the abortion items, there was greatest agreement about the permissibility of abortion in cases of serious health problems for the mother (3.57/5.00), but in the regression analysis only 5.6% of the variability was accounted for. Believing a non-personal god, valuing the place of religion in society, and moral behaviour being the source of human dignity were significant predictors. Trust in one's own religion was a negative predictor. Perhaps support for abortion in this circumstance spreads across a wide range of persons with various qualities and attitudes. Islam widely allows abortion in cases of mother's health concerns.

There was disagreement with the notion that abortion could be permissible in the situation of not being able to afford any more children psychologically or economically (2.54/5.00). Support for abortion in these circumstances was consistent with low support for the valuing of the place of religion in society, for believing in God as personal, and not thinking that human dignity comes from moral behaviour. This profile would indicate a less religious person being more supportive of abortion for psychological and economic reasons. But only 5.4% of the variability is accounted for. While this might be consistent with secular values, some Muslim scholars may argue that psycho-economic situations could be stressful enough to endanger the life of the mother (Hedayat et al. 2006).

We find highest explained variability in the general prohibition of abortion ($R^2 = 14.9$) but a lower support for the item (3.13/5.00) than for abortion in the case of serious problems with the mother's health (3.57/5.00). However, there is little explanation for the latter item. One could opine that the general prohibition has foundation in one's believing in a personal God, the connection between religion and society and also between one's actions and one's human dignity. Where religion matters, there are negative concerns about abortion. No similar strength of association is found in regard to mother's health or any of the other abortion circumstance independent variables. Since Islam does in fact permit abortion for a good reason up to 120 days of pregnancy, it could be argued here that the opinion against all abortion presumes that "even early abortion is prohibited unless there is a good reason." How aware of the nuances of religious argumentation and discussion these 17-year-olds are could be questioned.

Research Questions 4–5–6: Euthanasia

Opposition to euthanasia in general is related most strongly to human dignity being based on moral behaviour, valuing the place of religion in society, empathy, and slightly less to believing in a personal God and religion and the state being in consultation. One could say that those who see religion as properly an influential factor in civic society most strongly oppose euthanasia. While 13.3% of the variability was accounted for, support for the prohibition of euthanasia in all circumstances was only moderately positive (3.32/5.00). There is disagreement (2.64/5.00) with allowing exceptions to the prohibition when there is immitigable suffering. Curiously, perceived injustice between the races was the only significant predictor ($\beta = .160$) but only 2.4% of the variability was accounted for. Euthanasia (mercy killing, so called in the society) has no support in Islam and in this Muslim cultural setting.

Research Questions 7–8: Death Penalty

Support for not using the death penalty was related to human dignity coming from simply being human as well as from an attitude of religious pluralism. 5.4% of the variability was accounted for. It seems that as one leans toward having a religious perspective wider than one's own religion and as one sees human dignity as simply intrinsic to every person as human, one may be more open to not using the death penalty.

Research Question 9: Consistency with Muslim Beliefs

In regard to abortion in general being forbidden, abortion in the situations of violence (rape, incest)and baby health problems, abortion to save the life of the mother, our subjects had views consistent with the teachings of Islam, although the support was not strong, except in the areas of the general prohibition of abortion, abortion to save the mother, and against abortion for psycho-economic reasons. Euthanasia was not supported in any circumstance. The prohibition of the death penalty was not supported, consistent with the general current position in Islam. So, all in all, we can say that the attitudes of the young Palestinian Muslims in our survey are quite consistent with the positions of Islam.

Final Observations

The young Muslims of this study live in a context where they are the majority religion but have frequent contact with both practicing and non-practicing people of their own and other religions. The "street" has a religious/secular flavour, but in general one could not tell the religion or practice pattern of a male from seeing him. The hijab of a woman would indicate her religion but not necessarily her level of practice.

According to Islam, every life belongs to God. And one has the right to God-given life. The respondents in our survey opposed abortion in general and supported abortion to save the life of the mother, support being at a moderate level, though higher in the case of the mother's health. This perhaps underscores the ongoing discussion within Islam about "serious reasons." Our respondents were evenly split about abortion in the case of rape, incest, and defects in the baby and disagreed with abortion for psychological and financial reasons. While this is consistent with Muslim religious belief in general, a minimal amount of variability is explained, except in regard to abortion in general.. Besides Qur'anic scholars, believing physicians and scientists are also in the discussion. They may be able to offer further enlightenment about means to save the life of both mother and baby. While in Islam, the abortion of babies conceived outside of marriage is prohibited, the threat of an "honour killing" or other reasons lead some to abort anyway. Ishaque (2008, 413–414) advocates further discussion among scholars of Islam in regard to what would be regarded in the West as adoption, with regard for the tradition of kafilah, inheritance, identity, family, and protection of the rights of the child.

All life belongs to God and one has "autonomy," but one does not have the "autonomy" do to with one's life as one wishes. The societal and familial dimensions and obligations complement this Qur'anic position. In addition, euthanasia obviously takes away one's future exercise of autonomy. Our respondents did not see immitigable suffering as a sufficient reason for euthanasia, thus not viewing "mercy killing" as "mercy." They were not asked about palliative care, which, as Muslim authors insist, is not a matter of euthanasia. Additionally, research has also indicated that remediable (at least partially) motives of loneliness, depression, and despair are the most likely reasons why patients might seek to end their lives. Brungardt (2017) suggests that end of life care would better attend to these dimensions.

As was pointed out, use of the death penalty is diminishing in the world, although both in neighbouring Jordan because of criminality and Palestine (Gaza) because of "treason," there have recently been executions. The executions in Palestine should have had the president's ratification, but did not. There is a disputed history of interpreting the Qur'an as permitting the death penalty under carefully defined conditions. Historically, one of these conditions has been apostasy, although there is discussion of whether a modern application is correct, since apostasy in days past could have been seen as a threat to the unity and survival of the state. Our respondents were slightly opposed to ending the death penalty. An attitude of religious pluralism and human dignity being intrinsic were consistent with opposition to the use of the death penalty. In Islam, certain offenses would be worthy of the death because of God's justice, but, in fact, the death penalty is not necessarily imposed; particular circumstances and Islamic governance of the jurisdiction are also required. A settlement between families involved in certain offenses would also commute the death penalty.

In our research, we believe we have provided evidence that the young Muslims in our sample are in accord with the general teachings of Islam in life areas. We can also say that Islam does not at all simply sanction "abortion on demand." Our subjects did not support euthanasia. Discussion within Muslim religious and medical circles continues to look at seeking positive support for patients nearing the end of life. The persons in our survey did not support an end to the death penalty. Islam recognizes many conditions and exceptions to any necessity to impose the death penalty.

References

Abdul Hussain, A. (2011). Ensoulment and the prohibition of abortion in Islam. *Islam and Christians-Muslim Relations, 16*(3), 239–250. Online April 12, 2011:. https://doi.org/10.1080/09596410500142999.

Abu Seir, R., & Kharroubi, A. (2017). Implementation of palliative care in Palestine: cultural and religious perspectives. *Palliative Medicine and Hospice Care. Open Journal, SE*(1), S4–S9. https://doi.org/10.17140/PMHCOJ-SE-1-102 Accessed 4 Nov 2017.

Aghababaei, N. (2013). The euthanasia-religion nexus: Exploring religious orientation and euthanasia attitude measures in a Muslim context. *OMEGA-Journal of Death and Dying, 66*(4), 333–341.

Ahmad, M. T. (Hadrat MirzaTahir Ahmad Khalifatul Masih IV). (1986/2005). T*he truth about the alleged punishment for apostasy in Islam.* Translation by Saleem-ur-Rahman and Mubachar Ahmad of Address at Jalsa Salana annual conference. Islamabad (1986). Tilford, Surrey: Islam International Publications, 2005 10.ion of 1986 address. https://www.alislam.org/library/books/Apostasy-in-Islam.pdf. Accessed 3 Oct 2017.

Alamri, Y. A. (2011). Islam and abortion. *Journal of the Islamic Medical Association, 43*, 39 http://scholar.google.com/scholar_url?url=http%3A%2F%2Fwww.scholarlyexchange.org%2Fojs%2Findex.php%2FJIMA%2Farticle%2Fdownload%2F5755%2F43_1-7&hl=en&sa=T&oi=gga&ct=gga&cd=7&ei=0woDWpiJKufXjgTUn56wBQ&scisig=AAGBfm09oc60Yb8TDN5WJ10w_xSaEAyr0Q&nossl=1&ws=1920x985. Accessed 7 Nov 2017.

Al-Matary, A., & Ali, J. (2014). Controversies and considerations regarding the termination of pregnancy for Foetal anomalies in Islam. *BMC Medical Ethics, 15*, 10. https://doi.org/10.1186/1472-6939-15-10 Accessed 3 Oct 2017.

Bowen, D. L. (1997). Abortion, Islam, and the 1994 Cairo population conference. *International Journal of Middle East Studies, 29*(2), 161–184 http://www.jstor.org/stable/164015. Accessed 3 Oct 2017.

Brungardt, M.. (2017). *Toward an understanding of loving accompaniment at the end of life*. Paper submitted for publication. Mundelein: University of Saint Mary of the Lake.

Chowdhury, R. (2012). *The role religion plays in attitudes toward euthanasia*. University of Central Florida, http://stars.library.ucf.edu/cgi/viewcontent.cgi?article=2323&context=honorstheses1990-2015&sei. Accessed 3 Oct 2017.

Greenberg, D. F., & West, V. (2008). Siting the death penalty internationally. *Law & Social inquiry, 33*(2), 295–343 http://www.jstor.org/stable/pdf/20108763.pdf Accessed 3 Oct 2017.

Hedayat, K. M., Shooshtarizadeh, P., & Raza, M. (2006). Therapeutic abortion in Islam: Contemporary views of Muslim Shiite scholars and effect of recent Iranian legislation. *Journal of Medical Ethics, 32*(11), 652–657 https://www.ncbi.nlm.nih.gov/pmc/articles/PMC2563289/ Accessed 5 Oct 2017.

Hessini, L. (2007). Abortion and Islam: Policies and practice in the Middle East and North Africa. *Reproductive Health Matters, 15*(29). http://www.tandfonline.com/doi/full/10.1016/S0968-8080%2806%2929279-6 Accessed 3 Oct 2017.

Hood, R., & Hoyle, C. (2015). Progress made for worldwide abolishment of the death penalty. *International Affairs Forum* 6(1) Death penalty around the World, 8–11. Accessed 2 Oct 2017.

Isgandarova, N. (2015). Physician-assisted suicide and other forms of euthanasia in Islamic spiritual care. *Journal of Pastoral Care & Counseling, 69*(4), 215–221.

Ishaque, S. (2008). Islamic principles on adoption: Examining the impact of Illegitimacy and inheritance related concerns in context of a child's right to an identity. *International Journal of Law, Policy and the Family,* **22(3)**, 393–420 http://citeseerx.ist.psu.edu/viewdoc/download?doi=10.1.1.818.2721&rep=rep1&type=pdf.

Nikookar, H. R., & Sooteh, S. H. J. (2014). Euthanasia: An Islamic ethical perspective. *European Scientific Journal, 10*(10).

Palestine Basic Law. (2003). http://www.palestinianbasiclaw.org/basic-law/2003-amended-basic-law.

Peters, R., & De Vries, Gert J. J. (1976). Apostacy in Islam. *Des Welt des Islams.* New Series, 17(1), 1–25. Brill. http://www.jstor.org/stable/1570336 Accessed 4 Oct 2017.

Rathor, M. Y., & Fauzi, M. (2012). Euthanasia and physician-assisted suicide: A review from Islamic point of view. *The International Medical Journal Malaysia, 11*(1), 63–68 http://iiumedic.net/imjm/v1/download/Volume%2011%20No%201/IMJM%20Vol11No1-2012-p63-68.pdf. Accessed 3 Oct 2017.

Sachedina, Z. (1990). Islam, procreation and the law. *International Family Planning Perspectives, 16*(3), 107–111 http://www.jstor.org/stable/2133308. Accessed 3 Oct 2017.

Saeed, A., & Saeed, H. (2004). *Freedom of religion, apostasy, and Islam.* Aldershot: Ashgate.

Schabas, W. (2000). Islam and the death penalty. *William and Mary Bill of Rights Journal, 9*(1), 223–236 http://scholarship.law.wm.edu/wmborj/vol9/iss1/13. Accessed 3 Oct 2017.

Schabas, W. (2015). Universal abolition of death penalty is drawing near. *International Affairs Forum* 6 (1) Death penalty around the World, 12–14. Accessed 2 Oct 2017.

Schwartz, Y. (2016). Palestine's abortion problem. *Foreign Policy Magazine.* https://www.yahoo.com/news/palestine-abortion-problem-213957968.html. Accessed 23 Oct 2017.

Shahawy, S. (2016). *Perspectives on elective abortion among Palestinian women: Religion, culture and access in the occupied Palestinian territories.* Doctoral Dissertation, Harvard Medical School. http://nrs.harvard.edu/urn-3:HUL.InstRepos:27007750. Accessed 8 Nov 2017.

Tuell, R.'u. S. (2010). *Islamic approaches to patient care: Muslim beliefs and healthcare practices for caregivers.* Beltsville: Amana Publications.

Webb, R., & Asa'd, F. J. (2015, December). *Young Palestinian Muslim support for judicial and political human rights.* Paper presented at the conference of the Religion and Human Rights 2.0 Project, Zagreb.

Yacoub, A. A. A. (2013). *The fiqh of medicine: Responses in Islamic jurisprudence to developments in medical science.* London: Ta-Ha Publishers.

Zabaneh, R. (2016). *Palestinian women deal with social stigma of abortion.* http://www.aljazeera.com/blogs/middleeast/2016/05/palestinian-women-deal-social-stigma-abortion-160505155316863.html. Accessed 23 Oct 2017.

Chapter 8
Attitudes Towards the Right to Life and the Religiosity of Young People in Lithuania

MildaIrena Ališauskienė and Aušra Maslauskaitė

This study analyzes the attitudes towards the right to life and the religiosity of young people (16–18 years old) in Lithuania. We will focus on euthanasia and abortion as two cases indicating attitudes of young people towards the possible limitation of the right to life. Abortion and euthanasia are rarely debated in public in Lithuania; from time to time conservative politicians and the Roman Catholic Church try to initiate such discussions, but they are not widely-supported. One of the public spheres open for this topic is religious education in public schools. Thus, the pupils are a relevant group to research attitudes to the right to life. The respondents of this empirical analysis were Lithuanian young people (n = 427). The findings indicate that respondents who regard religion as a personal matter show more liberal attitudes towards euthanasia and abortion, while those who have more traditional opinions about religiosity support its active participation in public life and express more conservative and prohibiting views on euthanasia and abortion. Contrary to our expectations, respondents who disapprove of abortion had a positive approach to women's rights.

Religion, Moral Values and Human Rights: The Main Encounters

Contemporary academic discourse on the origin of human rights includes discussions about the role of religion, particularly Christianity, in the process of the construction of the concept as well as the content of contemporary human rights. Even though, the relations between religion and human rights seem to be ambiguous as different religions and their dogmas are deemed to confront universal

M. Ališauskienė (✉) · A. Maslauskaitė
Vytautas Magnus University, Kaunas, Lithuania
e-mail: milda.alisauskiene@vdu.lt

H.-G. Ziebertz, F. Zaccaria (eds.), *Euthanasia, Abortion, Death Penalty and Religion – The Right to Life and its Limitations*, Religion and Human Rights 4, https://doi.org/10.1007/978-3-319-98773-6_8

human rights, particularly when they challenge patriarchal stances, as in the case of women's rights (van der Ven et al. 2004; Pace 2009; Wolterstorff 2012; Brewington 2013).

The complicated relationship between religion and human rights in contemporary society is influenced by a rapid social change and is related to a particular social context. Former communist countries have become an interesting case in understanding the perception of human rights in societies undergoing rapid social transformation from totalitarian regimes to liberal democracies, from state imposed monopoly of scientific atheism to a religiously diversified society. The significance of religion is particularly prevalent regarding the so-called national Churches, which play an important role in the nation-building process in post-communist countries and in many cases have a great impact on the everyday lives of these communities (Ališauskienė and Schroeder 2011; Simons and Westerlund 2015).

During Soviet times the Lithuanian Roman Catholic Church was an important agent in the battle for human rights, particularly freedom of conscience and religion (Streikus 2012). However, the situation changed in the 1990s after the collapse of the Soviet Union and the declaration of the independence of Lithuania. The assurance of human rights has been anchored in the 1992 Constitution of the Republic of Lithuania,[1] however, public perception of human rights and their assurance remains a challenge in the country. Lithuanian media analysis revealed that the Roman Catholic Church continues to be an important agent in the field of human rights even though it had shifted its focus from the individual's rights to freedom of conscience and religion to the rights to life, particularly rights of the fetus/unborn child and the right to life of the terminally ill people (euthanasia) (Ališauskienė and Kuznecovienė 2012). Since 2000 the Lithuanian Roman Catholic Church became an active participant in civil society and began to support different social initiatives promoting the right to life of the fetus. The Church objects artificial insemination procedures and the availability of contraception and promotes natural family planning, as analyses of the Lithuanian media disclose (Ališauskienė and Kuznecovienė 2012). In the last decade, public life in Lithuania was challenged by debates around traditional family values, artificial insemination, domestic violence and child abuse. Public debates on these issues indicated the formation of two opposing approaches in Lithuanian society. One approach represents the Roman Catholic Church (sometimes broader Christianity) values emphasizing traditional family values while the other is more associated with the values of the European Union. The latter approach was mainly presented as contradicting Christian values, primarily because of its emphasis on human rights, particularly women's, LGBT and children's rights. Both approaches were advocated by diverse politicians and non-governmental organizations participating in public debates.

[1] Constitution of the Republic of Lithuania, 1992. Internet access: http://www3.lrs.lt/home/Konstitucija/Constitution.htm, accessed on August 17, 2017.

However, religion is not the only factor influencing the approaches towards the universal culture of human rights; other factors are also embedded in local cultures and social contexts. Processes of modernization and secularization shifting attitudes towards liberalization occurred on the level of individual religiosity in many European societies, and Lithuania is no exception. The analysis of the 1990–2008 European Value Surveys in Lithuania demonstrated that, despite of a religious revival after the collapse of Soviet Union, the impact of religion on people's everyday lives was moderate (Juknevičius 2000; Žiliukaitė 2000). Further analysis of EVS data showed the constantly increasing justification of abortion, euthanasia, homosexuality and other private moral issues among the Lithuanian population. Although age and religiosity continued to be main variables indicating attitudes towards moral values in Lithuania – younger people declare more individualistic and liberal attitudes than older people (particularly cohorts raised during Soviet times) who expressed more conservative values and tend more towards collectivism. Gender also continues to be an important variable when evaluating the attitudes towards infringement of moral values in the public; men legitimate them more than women in Lithuania. Women are considered to be more religious than men, they are regarded as the carriers of tradition and as main agents within religious socialization in traditional societies (Trzebiatowska and Bruce 2016). However, this position is challenged by emancipation, secularization and the process of moral pluralism, factors influenced by modernization and individualization in contemporary society. The attitudes of the Lithuanian society towards family and women remains patriarchal, although the changes within family life have been affected by the aforementioned cultural and social factors (Maslauskaitė 2010). A particular cultural and social factor for the attitude towards women's rights in Lithuania is the Soviet gender equality policy that was forcefully implemented in the country. After the collapse of the Soviet Union attitudes towards gender roles in family life became more traditional. Between 1990–1999 some changes occurred, however, the tendency towards a greater implementation of gender equality in public life still remains. Nevertheless, traditional gender roles within the family are still maintained in Lithuania (Kraniauskas 2009).

At the end of this section, we would like to emphasize that religion and religiosity are an important factors, albeit not the sole ones, in influencing the population's attitudes towards human rights in contemporary society. The analysis of the Lithuanian population's attitudes towards moral values indicated that gender and age are also important factors and, together with cultural and social processes, they follow the trends of modernization in society. In the subsequent section we will provide a more detailed analysis of abortion and euthanasia in Lithuania that will be followed by the presentation of the design of our study, empirical data analysis and conclusion.

Abortion and Euthanasia in Contemporary Lithuania

Abortion

Abortion, i.e. the termination of a pregnancy, was legalized in Lithuania in 1955 (Daukšaitė 2015). It is currently regulated under the 1994 Order of the Minister of Health[2] and legal up to the 12th week of pregnancy. Under certain circumstances (incurable diseases, predictable birth defects etc.) it remains to be legal in the latter stages. The termination of a pregnancy should be conducted in a health care institution under the supervision of a medical doctor, according to the document. The Order of the Minister of Health insists that women should be informed about the possible physical, emotional and psychological consequences of terminating their pregnancy and they should provide a written consent for this procedure, if possible also of the husband. However, health statistics state that abortions are continuously decreasing in Lithuania, from 30,559 in 1997 to 7478 in 2016.[3]

Contrary to the situation in Poland, the ban of abortions was not introduced in the early 1990s during the change of political regimes in Lithuania (Grzymala-Busse 2015). Since the declaration of independence of Lithuania there was one attempt by conservative right-wing politicians in 2013, an attempt yet to be accomplished, to introduce a law regulating the termination of pregnancies, restricting the availability of the procedure and emphasizing the need to protect the life of a fetus from conception.[4] The latest public discussions about the law on termination of pregnancies were initiated in the autumn of 2016 after the Parliamentary elections, during the formation of a new political coalition within the context of the search for new political partners. Among these was the Polish minority party, the Electorial Action of Poles in Lithuania (recently extending its name to include the Union of Christian Families), a party committed to protecting such rights. This political party declares the views of a "Christian democracy" and follows political initiatives in Poland.

[2] Minister of Health of the Republic of Lithuania order 1994 01 28 No. 50 "Regarding the order of the termination of pregnancy operation" (in Lithuanian). Internet access: https://www.e-tar.lt/portal/lt/legalAct/TAR.9913EAF57AEA, accessed on August 17, 2017.

[3] Lietuvos sveikatos statistika. Lietuvos Respublikos Sveikatos apsaugos minsiterijos Higienos instituto Sveikatos informacijos centro svetainė. Internet access: www.sic.hi.lt, accessed on October 25, 2017.

[4] Lietuvos Respublikos gyvybės prenatalinėje fazėje apsaugos įstatymas (Republic of Lithuania Law on the Preservation of Life in the Prenatal Phase). 2013. Internet access: https://e-seimas.lrs.lt/portal/legalAct/lt/TAP/TAIS.444122?jfwid=wny8rlqxj, accessed on October 25, 2017.

Euthanasia

Euthanasia, i.e. the practice of intentionally ending a life to relieve insufferable pain, is not legal in Lithuania. In 2012 the liberal member of parliament Andrius Burba unsuccessfully attempted to register a law on euthanasia for a parliamentary debate. In 2014, and subsequently in 2015 after some corrections, a Lithuanian member of parliament, the social democrat Aušrinė Povilionienė, introduced a draft law legalizing euthanasia.[5] This initiative was grounded on the fact that the Lithuanian population (47%) had a favorable approach towards euthanasia.[6] The initiative was discussed in the public domain and revealed at least two groups of pro and contra opinions, though the majority of the population remained neutral. Public arguments as the dissemination of *the culture of death*, equating euthanasia to suicide or homicide, were made by religious groups against the draft law, a move that has not been included into the parliament's agenda.

The majority of the citizens of Lithuania (77.2%) declare that they are members of the Roman Catholic Church, however their approaches to the termination of pregnancy and euthanasia vary and do not necessarily correspond to the teachings of the Church (Lietuvos statistikos departamentas 2013:166). In 2012 the public evaluated euthanasia worse than abortion (N-1008)[7]: 13% stated that abortion can never be justified while 67% indicated that it could be justified in certain cases, 11% believed that it is always justified and 9% did not know. 20% of respondents did not know if euthanasia could be justified, 21% stated that euthanasia is never justified, 51% declared that euthanasia can be justified sometimes and 9% were sure that euthanasia is always justified. The attitudes towards abortion might be explained by analyzing public approaches to family planning, abortion and women's rights. During Soviet times abortion was generally a means for family planning as the accessibility of contraception was limited.

There is not much research data concerning the attitudes of young people towards the right to life, particularly on abortion and euthanasia, in Lithuania. The analysis of attitudes held by cohorts socialized during the post-communist period towards such moral values and their relationship to religiosity showed that these attitudes were more influenced by processes of modernization and globalization and thus tended to be more liberal (Žiliukaitė et al. 2016; Breskaya and Ališauskienė 2017). This social group also becomes an interesting case study due to the religious

[5] Lietuvos Respublikos eutananzijos įstatymas. (Republic of Lithuania Law of Euthanasia) 2014. Internet access: https://e-seimas.lrs.lt/portal/legalAct/lt/TAP/e03fae302208 11e4988dd8c7447f8ac 5?positionInSearchResults=47&searchModelUUID=884fe6fe-d270-49d1-8e36-a10672125b09 . accessed on October 25, 2017.

[6] Apklausa: Beveik pusė Lietuvos gyventojų pritaria eutanazijos įteisinimui (Inquiry: almost half of Lithuanian population supporst the legalization of euthanasia). 2012.

Internet access: https://www.15min.lt/naujiena/aktualu/lietuva/apklausa-beveik-puse-lietuvos-gyventoju-pritaria-eutanazijos-iteisinimui-56-225086 accessed on October 25, 2017.

[7] Report of 2012 public survey "The Peculiarities of Secularization in Lithuania" archived at Vytautas Magnus University.

socialization they might receive at public schools. The topics of abortion and euthanasia are analyzed within the school curricula during the classes of moral education and sexual education. However, it is difficult to assess the actual situation of this education, as it is not strictly regulated regarding the age of the pupils, what exact topics are discussed and how they are approached by the teacher. Even though, moral education is a compulsory subject in Lithuanian secondary schools. Pupils or their parents are free to choose between religious education and ethics within moral education. As the majority of children in Lithuania choose religious education, their attitudes towards abortion and euthanasia might be influenced by the topics and material discussed in these classes (Ališauskienė 2012). Thus, young people become a relevant group when researching the attitudes towards the right to life or, more accurately, towards the practices of abortion and euthanasia as two cases in which this right might be justly limited. Such a study can also contribute to a broader understanding of the perception of human rights in post-communist Lithuania.

Design of the Study

Research Questions and Assumptions

Our questions will not be examined in light of the situation previously discussed. The first two questions are similar, but in the second question women's rights are included given that these rights are often in conflict with a restrictive policy regarding abortion.

Question 1: How do young Lithuanians evaluate the termination of life through euthanasia and are their attitudes associated with religiosity and human dignity?

Question 2: How do young Lithuanians evaluate the termination of life through abortion and are their attitudes associated with religiosity, human dignity and women's rights?

Question 3: What is the strength of the predictors regarding the termination of life in the case of euthanasia and abortion? (Regression analysis)

The previously-discussed cultural and social context of Lithuania allows us to provide some hypotheses and pose some expectations for our empirical data. Firstly, we assume that young people will not have distinct attitudes towards euthanasia as this topic is not addressed at public discourses in Lithuania. Secondly, we expect that religious young people disapprove of euthanasia and abortion more than secular ones. Thirdly, we suppose that gender will have an impact on the evaluations of euthanasia and abortion: more precisely that women will be rather dismissive towards a prohibition. Fourthly, we expect that young religious people who have negative attitudes towards euthanasia and abortion will also have negative attitudes towards women's rights and their protection.

Conceptual Model

Several concepts will be used to answer the aforementioned questions by empirical analysis. The function of the concepts in the model is represented in Fig. 8.1. In the following section the concepts will be described.

Two main dependent variables are considered in the presented survey. They measure the subjective assessment of euthanasia and abortion. Three concepts are included that might influence the attitudes towards the limitation of the right to life: religiosity, human dignity and women's rights. Gender will also be included.

The Termination of Life Through Euthanasia and Abortion (Dependent Variables)

Euthanasia

Euthanasia is not widely discussed in the Lithuanian public domain and is a relatively new concept as we have already pointed out. The common perception is that euthanasia indicates the practice of intentionally ending a life in order to relieve insufferable pain. There are three statements in the questionnaire dedicated to the measurement of attitudes towards euthanasia. One of them expressed a more general evaluation of the phenomenon *(Euthanasia should be prohibited in all circumstances)*, while the two others articulated the justification of euthanasia under certain conditions (*Euthanasia should be permitted in the case of unbearable and*

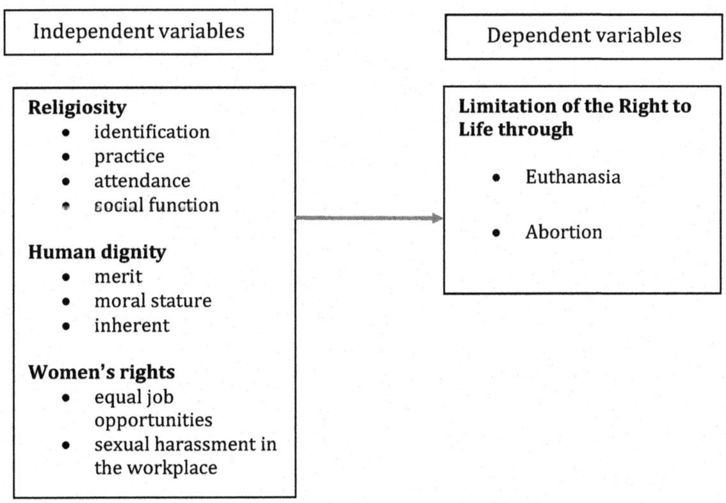

Fig. 8.1 Conceptual model

irreversible suffering and *Euthanasia should be permitted in the case of unbearable and irreversible suffering, if palliative care is exhausted).* In the following analysis, we included the first item, which measured the general attitude towards euthanasia. As discussed above, due to the lack of general public discussions on euthanasia, more nuanced and specific issues linked to euthanasia are apparently not commonly known among the Lithuanian youth.

Abortion

Abortion is another case surrounding the right to life issue in contemporary society, namely the debate between religious communities and other social groups concerning the clash between the debated right to life of a fetus and the so-called women's "reproductive rights", which include their right to request a termination of their pregnancy. As discussed above, abortion is legal in Lithuania and for a long time it had been considered to be a means of family planning.

The second independent variable is the indicator on the justification of abortion (*Abortion should be prohibited in all circumstances because it terminates the beginning of human life*). The questionnaire provided a scale of seven items to measure attitudes towards abortion. In this study we focus on one item, which unconditionally defines abortion as a termination of life. This methodological decision was influenced by such contextual factors as the laws on abortion are rather liberal and have a long tradition in Lithuania, meaning the issue is almost absent from public discourse.

Religiosity, Human Dignity and Women's Rights (Independent Variables)

The set of independent variables was developed based on the theoretical assumptions of the study.

Religiosity

First, we consider religiosity as the potential predictor of attitudes towards the right to life. In Lithuania the majority of the population consider themselves as believers (*statnuoroda*). Classical measurements of religiosity include belief, practice (prayer and participation) and intellectual, ideological and consequential dimensions (Glock and Stark 1965). In this analysis we assigned religiosity to the group independent variables by including the indicators on formal identification with a religious community (*Roman Catholic (1), other Christian (2), other religions (3), non-religious (4)*); participation in religious rituals, i.e. frequency of attendance of religious services (*never or hardly ever (1), a few times a year (2); one to three times a month or more frequently (3)*); personal religious practice, i.e. frequency of prayer (*never or hardly ever (1), a few times a year (2); at least once a month (3); at least once weekly (4); at least once a day (5))* and attitudes towards the function of religion in society. The last dimension was captured using the three items: *religions should try to influence public opinion on social problems, religions should use their authority to intervene in social affairs, and religions should take public responsibility for societal development.* All three items were measured with the 5-point Likert scale. Based on these items the summary index variable *Social function of religion* was created.

Human Dignity

According to Nordenfelt (2004), human dignity consists of three dimensions: dignity of merit, dignity of moral stature and inherent dignity (cf. Ziebertz et al. 2017). Dignity of merit was assessed using the following item: *the value of a person depends on the appreciation given to him or her by others.* Moral dignity was assessed using the following statement: *the honour to be given to a person depends on his moral behaviour* and inherent dignity with *each human being should be recognized just because he is a human being, irrespective of credit or moral behaviour.* All three human dignity dimensions were included as the other set of independent variables. In the questionnaire all items were also measured with the 5-point Likert scale. The additional independent variable included in the analysis is the gender of the respondent. Neither age nor place of residence were considered since the sample is homogenous in this characteristic. In the initial analysis we also used the indicators on the parents' education, but they were not relevant for the differentiation of the views on the right to life.

Women's Rights

Additional independent variables included into the analysis on abortion are the indicators on women's rights. Women's rights are a set of rights given to women and girls. They were based on the nineteenth century women's rights movement and twentieth century feminist movement. The women's rights movement was evident in Lithuanian in the early twentieth century, however, after the implementation of the Soviet gender equality policy the feminist movement, as every other social movement, was suppressed by the totalitarian regime. Only after the independence of Lithuania in the late twentieth century did the gender equality ideas together with the feminist movement emerge again in the public domain. Their main issues are: payment inequality, family and job reconciliation, domestic violence, etc. Since the feminist movement was only a recent development in Lithuania, women's rights are still under debate by the majority of the Lithuanian population, their perception being a relatively marginal phenomenon (*nuoroda*).

The first item expresses the views on women's rights regarding employment and the role of the state (*the state should protect women's right to adequate job opportunities*), while the second voices the protection of women against violence in the public sphere (*women should have the right to be protected from sexual harassment in the workplace*). Both items were measured on the 5-point Likert scale.

Sample and Methods

This research is based on the “Religions and Human Rights Survey” data, which was collected in 2014. The survey was conducted in secondary schools in rural and urban areas in Lithuania, including the three largest cities. The schools were selected according to practical criteria, i.e. the willingness of the teachers to participate in the survey. Within the schools the pupils were selected on the basis of participation in the classes of moral education. The sample includes 481 respondents between the ages of 16–18 years. The main limitation of the survey concerns the non-representative sampling strategy and the consequent restrictions, meaning that it was necessary to generalize the findings. However, being aware of it, we still believe that our results reveal a relevant, thorough, albeit partial, representation of the Lithuanian adolescents’ views on the rights to life.

Our analysis is based on the descriptive methods (one-way ANOVA) and linear regression models which were run separately for each dependent variable. The analytical strategy of our regression analysis is based on the theoretical considerations of the possible predictors of attitudes towards abortion and euthanasia.

In the following section we will present our main empirical findings. We begin with the descriptive results on the views of the prohibition of euthanasia and in the following section we will discuss our findings on the opinion concerning the prohibition of abortion. In the final section we will present the results of the regression modelling. Our analysis follows the previously-mentioned research questions (see par. 3.1).

Empirical Findings

Question 1: How Do Young Lithuanians Evaluate the Termination of Life Through Euthanasia and Are Their Attitudes Associated with Religiosity and Human Dignity?

Overall, almost half of the Lithuanian youth (44%) disagree with the prohibition of euthanasia and 38% have no clear idea about the matter. In addition, 18% adhere to the prohibition of it (combined responses “totally agree” and “agree”). Thus, the opposition to euthanasia among the Lithuanian youth is rather marginal. However, many respondents are ambivalent and have no clear position on the issue. We will now give an overview of the variation in the assessment of euthanasia across and within the dimensions of religiosity.

Table 8.1 provides information on the mean values and the test of significance between group comparisons for each variable of religiosity.

In considering formal religious identity, the results show the highest support for the prohibition of euthanasia among the Roman Catholics and other Christian denominations, while it is much lower among the non-religious group and among

Table 8.1 Assessment of prohibition of euthanasia by the dimensions of religiosity (mean values, standard deviation and F-test values)

	Mean	SD
Formal religious identity		
Roman Catholic	2.68	1.11
Other Christian	2.69	1.30
Other religion	2.39	1.23
Non-religious	2.44	1.21
Total	*2.59*	*1.18*
Between group comparison (F-test, F-value)	F = 1.9; p = 0.11 (ns)	
Religious practice (prayer)		
Never, hardly ever	2.45	1.20
A few times a year	2.41	1.18
At least once a month	2.64	1.01
At least once weekly	2.84	1.26
At least once a day	2.75	1.39
Total	*2.53*	*1.20*
Between group comparison (F-test, F-value)	F = 1.74; p = 0.14 (ns)	
Religious service attendance		
Never, hardly ever	2.34	1.23
A few times a year	2.58	1.14
At least once a month or often	2.84	1.27
Total	*2.54*	*1.21*
Between group comparison (F-test, F-value)	F = 4.84; p = 0.008	
Religion, social function (index min = 3, max = 15)[a]		
Lowest support of the active social function of religion (index value = 3)	2.20	1.28
Highest support of the active social function of religion (index value = 15)	4	1
Total	*2.59*	*1.18*
Between group comparison (F-test, F-value)	F = 3.1; p = 0.000	

[a]The assessment of the social function of religion is measured on the interval scale with the lowest value of 3 and highest 15. We provide mean values of the dependent variable by categories of independent variable. All descriptive statistics for this variable could be provided upon the request. In this table we provide only the descriptive statistics for the lowest and highest values of the index variable

members of religious groups other than Christianity. However, the between group differences are not statistically significant, and as a result the formal religious identity seems not to be the most important factor regarding attitudes towards euthanasia according to the participants of the survey.

The intensity of personal religious practice (frequency of personal prayer) does not show significant differences between the groups regarding euthanasia, even though we observed a gradual increase in the more restrictive assessment of euthanasia with every group of more intense personal religious praxis, the differences between the groups are not statistically significant.

In discussing the views on euthanasia and the attendance of religious services, the results indicate a positive association. Respondents with a higher frequency of participation in religious services are more in favour to prohibit euthanasia. For those who do not attend any religious services the mean value is 2.34, while for those with monthly or more frequent attendance it is 2.84. This dimension of religiosity differentiates the views on euthanasia in a statistically significant way. Thus, the descriptive results suggest that the attendance of religious services has more influence on the assessment of euthanasia if compared to personal religious practice.

The last dimension of religiosity considered in our analysis is the attitude towards the social function of religion. The findings reveal that they considerably shape young people's views on euthanasia: approval of the active role of religion in society increases the support for the prohibition of euthanasia. Those in favour of the active role of religion express more rigorous views on euthanasia, while respondents who regard religion only as a personal matter have more liberal attitudes on this issue. The differences between the groups with different attitudes towards the social function of religion are statistically significant.

Table 8.2 presents the results of the descriptive statistics for the attitudes towards euthanasia by the views on human dignity and also by the gender of the respondents. Considering human dignity, we observe that views on the prohibition of euthanasia are associated with the ideas on human dignity based on merit. Surveyed adolescents with more restrictive views on euthanasia (i.e. agree with the prohibition of it) are more inclined to support the view that the value of a person depends on the appreciation given to him/her by others. On the other end of the spectrum, those disagreeing with the prohibition of euthanasia approve more of the idea that a person's value should not depend on the appreciation of others. Similarly, but more clearly, we observed commonalities between the assessment of euthanasia and human dignity based on moral stature. Those more in favour of the prohibition of euthanasia in all circumstances are also more convinced that the honour given to a person depends on his or her moral behaviour. However, the association between the assessment of euthanasia and of human dignity as inherent to the person has no clear direction.

Table 8.2 Assessment of prohibition of euthanasia by the human dignity variables, gender of the respondent (mean values, standard deviation and F-test values)

	Mean	SD
Dignity-merit		
Totally disagree	2.24	1.26
Disagree	2.33	1.14
I am not sure	2.91	1.04
Agree	2.69	1.18
Totally agree	2.64	1.41
Total	*2.59*	*1.18*
Between group comparison (F-test, F-value)	F = 6.7; p = 0.000	
Dignity – moral stature		
Totally disagree	2.32	1.41
Disagree	2.83	1.16
I am not sure	3.40	1.02
Agree	3.71	1.12
Totally agree	3.98	1.19
Total	*3.57*	*1.20*
Between group comparison (F-test, F-value)	F = 15.6; p = 0.000	
Dignity-inherent		
Totally disagree	3.66	1.56
Disagree	3.49	1.33
I am not sure	3.46	1.05
Agree	3.63	1.08
Totally agree	3.81	1.27
Total	*3.57*	*1.20*
Between group comparison (F-test, F-value)	F = 1.23; p = 0.29 (ns)	
Gender		
Female	3.78	1.18
Male	3.30	1.17
Total	*3.57*	*1.20*
Between group comparison (F-test, F-value)	F = 19.5; p = 0.000	

In addition, gender is relevant in defining the views on the prohibition of euthanasia. Young Lithuanian women express more rigorous views on euthanasia compared to men: they are more inclined to prohibit euthanasia than young men.

Question 2: How Do Young Lithuanians Evaluate the Termination of Life Through Abortion and Are Their Attitudes Associated with Religiosity, Human Dignity and Women's Rights?

There are clear divisions in the assessment of the prohibition of abortion among the Lithuanian youth. 37.2% of respondents disagreed with the view that abortion should be prohibited. 34.9% have no clear views and 27.8% agree that abortion should be prohibited because it terminates beginning human life. Based on our theoretical considerations we further outline the associations between the views on abortion and independent variables. We begin with the indicators of religiosity and afterwards discuss human dignity and women's rights indicators.

Formal religious identity seems not to contribute to the assessment of abortion (Table 8.3). Even if Roman Catholics and people from other religious groups in our sample are more prone to support the prohibition of abortion (mean for Roman Catholics = 2.98, for non-religious = 2.63), the differences between the groups are not statistically significant.

The intensity of the personal religious practice (prayer) is positively linked with support for the prohibition of abortion; those cultivating prayer as part of their religiosity are more in favour of the prohibition of abortion and the between group differences are statistically significant. We also observed a similar effect of the attendance of religious services. More frequent participation in religious services is associated with the justification of the prohibition of abortion. For example, the mean value on the assessment of abortion is 3.02 for those attending religious services at least once a month, while the mean value for the item of never participating is 2.64. Moreover, the between group comparison test reveals that differences are statistically significant. An additional indicator is the understanding of the social role of religion. Young people in favour of a less active role of religion in society are also more inclined to disagree with the prohibition of abortion, while proponents of the active role of religion express more support for this argument.

Views on human dignity are linked with attitudes towards the prohibition of abortion in a rather ambiguous manner. Table 8.4 illustrates that understanding of human dignity based on merit does not differentiate the views on abortion. Support for the idea that human dignity depends on one's moral behaviour is positively associated with support for the prohibition of abortion. A similar link can also be observed regarding the idea of human dignity as being inherent to the person. Those more in favour of prohibiting abortion are also more inclined to support the notion that the recognition of a person should not depend on their credit or moral behaviour.

The gender of respondents does not influence the views on abortion. Young women and men are very similar in their believes on the prohibition of abortion.

In addition to the previously-discussed indicators we also considered the attitudes towards the protection of women's rights. Table 8.5 presents the mean values

Table 8.3 Assessment of prohibition of abortion by the dimensions of religiosity (mean values, standard deviation and F-test values)

	Mean	SD
Formal religious identity		
Roman Catholic	2.98	1.23
Other Christian	2.73	1.18
Other Religion	2.93	1.34
Non-religious	2.63	1.30
Total	*2.86*	*1.26*
Between group comparison (F-test, F-value)	F = 2.05; p = 0.1 (ns)	
Religious praxis (prayer)		
Never, hardly ever	2.57	1.24
A few times a year	2.95	1.26
At least once a month	3.18	1.40
At least once weekly	3.12	1.20
At least once a day	3.08	1.38
Total	*2.86*	*1.30*
Between group comparison (F-test, F-value)	F = 3.99; p = 0.003	
Religious service attendance		
Never, hardly ever	2.64	1.26
A few times a year	2.98	1.30
At least once a month or often	3.02	1.30
Total	*2.86*	*1.29*
Between group comparison (F-test, F-value)	F = 3.95; p = 0.02	
Religion, social function (index value, min = 3, max = 15)[a]		
Lowest support of the active social function of religion (index value = 3)	2.20	1.20
Highest support of the active social function of religion (index value = 15)	2.7	0.5
Total	*2.86*	*1.2*
Between group comparison (F-test, F-value)	F = 3.4; p = 0.000	

[a]The assessment of the social function of religion is measured on the interval scale with the lowest value of 3 and highest – 15. All descriptive statistics for this variable could be provided upon the request. In the Table 8.1 we provide only the descriptive statistics for the lowest and highest values of the index variable

for the assessment of abortion by the women's rights variables. Contrary to our expectations, the findings show that young people in favour of the prohibition of abortion are also positive about the protection of women's rights regarding job opportunities and rights to be protected from sexual harassment in the workplace. Interestingly, the more active role of the institutions in protecting women's employment rights or security is positively associated with the reduction of women's reproductive rights.

Table 8.4 Assessment of prohibition of abortion by the human dignity variables, gender of the respondent (mean values, standard deviation and F-test values)

	Mean	SD
Dignity-merit		
Totally disagree	2.87	1.39
Disagree	2.78	1.30
I am not sure	2.99	1.06
Agree	2.68	1.22
Totally agree	3.32	1.62
Total	*2.86*	*1.25*
Between group comparison (F-test, F-value)	F = 2.02; p = 0.08	
Dignity – moral stature		
Totally disagree	2.21	1.27
Disagree	2.71	1.16
I am not sure	3.01	1.08
Agree	2.96	1.30
Totally agree	2.74	1.35
Total	*2.86*	*1.25*
Between group comparison (F-test, F-value)	F = 2.44; p = 0.04	
Dignity-inherent		
Totally disagree	2.33	1.43
Disagree	2.80	1.24
I am not sure	2.93	1.16
Agree	2.95	1.23
Totally agree	3.00	1.40
Total	*2.86*	*1.,25*
Between group comparison (F-test, F-value)	F = 2.52; p = 0.04	
Gender		
Female	2.81	1.29
Male	2.94	1.20
Total	*2.86*	*1.25*
Between group comparison (F-test, F-value)	F = 1.24; p = 0.26 (ns)	

Table 8.5 Assessment of prohibition of abortion by women's rights (mean values, standard deviation and F-test values)

	Mean	SD
The state should protect women's right to adequate job opportunities		
Totally disagree	2.04	1.04
Disagree	2.67	1.27
Not sure	2.86	0.90
Agree	2.95	1.12
Fully agree	2.95	1.46
Total	*2.86*	*1.26*
Between group comparison (F-test, F-value)	F = 3.1; p = 0.01	
Women should have the right to be protected from sexual harassment in the workplace		
Totally disagree	2.33	1.43
Disagree	2.63	1.19
Not sure	2.90	0.98
Agree	3.10	1.20
Fully agree	2.79	1.45
Total	*2.86*	*1.26*
Between group comparison (F-test, F-value)	F = 2.59; p = 0.03	

Table 8.6 Linear regression analysis for dependent variable – views on euthanasia and views on abortion, standardized coefficients (beta) and total explained variance (R^2 and Adjusted R^2)

	Euthanasia	*Abortion*
Religiosity		
Formal religious identity	−0.13	−0.17
Religious practice (prayer)	0.04	0.1
Religious service attendance	0.09	0.02
Religion, social function	0.14**	0.16**
Human dignity		
Dignity-merit	0.18*	0.01
Dignity – moral stature	−0.02	−0.07
Dignity – inherent	0.16**	0.1*
Gender	0.17*	0.08
Women's right to employment		−0.03
Sexual harassment		0.15*
R^2	0.11	0.10

Standardized regression coefficients are significant at $p < .00$ (***) or $p < .05$ (*) level

What Is the Strength of Predictors Regarding the Termination of Life in the Case of Euthanasia and Abortion? (Regression Analysis)

Firstly, we will present the results of the linear regression models for the views on euthanasia and abortion. The coefficients of the linear regression models are presented in Table 8.6. It should be noted in advance that the level of variance explained in our models is not very high.

Euthanasia

Overall, the regression analysis shows that views on euthanasia are predicted by the perception of the social function of religion, human dignity and by the gender of the respondent. The results contradict our expectations that views on euthanasia will be determined by religiosity. Our results prove that there is only one significant predictor out of the set of all indicators measuring the religiosity, i.e. the understanding of the social role of religion. Respondents who prefer a more active role of religion in society are also more in favour of the prohibition of euthanasia. Indicators of religiosity linked with religious practice (prayer, attendance of services) are not relevant in predicting the views on euthanasia. This partially corroborates the results already presented; however, we have to add that the attendance of religious services also turns out to be insignificant, and thus it was the compositional effect.

Ideas concerning human dignity are also relevant predictors of the view on the prohibition of euthanasia. More support for ideas on human dignity, as depending on merit or as inherent to the person, result in higher support of the prohibition of euthanasia. The regression analysis reveals the significant effect of human dignity as inherent to the person, something which was not reflected in the descriptive analysis. Gender also seems to be relevant in defining views on euthanasia. Thus, the regression analysis corroborates the descriptive findings on the effect of gender and proves that females are more in favour of the prohibition of euthanasia than male respondents.

Abortion

The third column in Table 8.6 presents the results of the regression analysis for the assessment of the prohibition of abortion. Our analysis proves that there are only three relevant predictors. Again, among the indicators of religiosity the only significant predictor is the understanding of the social role of religion: those who believe that religion should have a more active social role are also more inclined towards the prohibition of abortion, while other religious indicators are not relevant for the prediction of the attitudes towards abortion. Regarding human dignity indicators, the only relevant indicator is the understanding of human dignity as inherent to the person. The association between these two value statements is positive, thus, the more human dignity is understood as being inherent to the person, the more actively the prohibition of abortion is supported. Two other views on human dignity are not significant in predicting the attitudes towards abortion. Views on abortion are determined by the opinion towards the women's protection against sexual harassment in the workplace in a statistically significant way. Contrary to our expectations we found that support for the right of women to be protected against sexual violence is positively associated with support for the prohibition of abortion.

Conclusion

This chapter aimed to analyse young people's attitudes towards rights to life, particularly towards abortion and euthanasia, in Lithuania, and the relationship between these attitudes and religiosity, human dignity and women's rights. The limitations of this study do not allow us to make generalizations for all young people in Lithuania, however the study still provides some insights.

Our primary expectation was that young people will have more open and tolerant attitudes towards abortion and euthanasia and that these attitudes will have a low correlation with their religiosity as the tendencies of secularization are evident in Lithuanian society. The analysis of empirical findings showed that more religious young people tend to be more supportive of the prohibition of abortions and euthanasia, and the frequency of religious practices was also connected with the justification of prohibition. Research data showed that women were more inclined to prohibit euthanasia, however there were no gender differences in the attitudes towards abortion. Interestingly, the research data revealed that young people favouring the prohibition of abortions were positive in their assertion of women's rights to employment and protection from sexual harassment in the workplace.

This explorative study leads to the formulation of one hypothesis for further research, rather than a final conclusion: religiosity, understood more as participation in religious services and attitudes about the public role of religion than any personal religious practices, might be one of the factors shaping the attitudes of young people in Lithuania towards the right to life, or more precisely, towards the limitation of this right in the cases of abortion and euthanasia. Although there is a lack of public debate concerning abortion and euthanasia it seems that religious education classes and religious services might become important agents in the secondary socialization on attitudes towards abortion and euthanasia in Lithuania.

References

Ališauskienė, M. (2012). Religious education in Lithuania. In D. H. Davis & E. Miroshnikova (Eds.), *The Routledge international handbook of religious education* (pp. 212–216). Oxon: Routledge.

Ališauskienė, M., & Kuznecovienė, J. (2012). "Katalikų bažnyčios vaidmuo viešajame Lietuvos gyvenime: dalyvavimo formų kaita (1990–2010)" [The role of Catholic Church in public life of Lithuania: the change of forms of participation]. *Filosofija. Sociologija, 23*(2), 102–110.

Ališauskienė, M., & Schröder, I. W. (Eds.). (2011). *Religious diversity in post-soviet society. Ethnographies of Catholic hegemony and the new pluralism in Lithuania*. Farnham: Ashgate.

Breskaya, O., & Ališauskienė, M. (2017). Sociologizing religious freedom: Comparative study of attitudes among young people in Belarus and Lithuania. *Religioni e Società, 87*(1), 67–77.

Brewington, D. V. (2013). Religion. In D. L. Brunsma, K. E. Iyall, & S. B. K. Gran (Eds.), *The handbook of sociology and human rights* (pp. 213–222). Boulder/London: Paradigm Publishers.

Daukšaitė, I. (2015). Baudžiamųjų įstatymų, reglamentavusių atsakomybę už neteisėtą abortą Lietuvoje, raida. *Teisė, 96*, 25–37.

Glock, C. Y., & Stark, R. (1965). *Religion and society in tension*. Chicago: Rand McNally.

Grzymala-Busse, A. (2015). *Nations under god: How churches use their moral authority to influence policy*. Princeton: Princeton University Press.

Juknevičius, S. (2000). Lietuvių moralinės vertybės: tarp Dievo ir Mamonos. *Kultūrologija, 6*, 192–211.

Kraniauskas, L. (2009). Vyriškas ir moteriškas šeimos pasaulis: struktūros poveikis artapatumo konstravimo strategija? In S. V. Stankūnienė & A. Maslauskaitė (Eds.), *Lietuvos šeima: tarp tradicijos ir naujos realybės* (pp. 169–219). Vilnius: Socialinių tyrimų centras.

Lietuvos statistikos departamentas (Statistics Lithuania). (2013). *Lietuvos Respublikos 2011 metų gyventojų ir būstų surašymo rezultatai* [Results of the 2011 Population and Housing Census of the Republic of Lithuania]. Vilnius: Lietuvos statistikos departamentas.

Maslauskaitė, A. (2010). Lietuvos šeima ir modernybės projektas: prieštaros bei teoretizavimo galimybės. *Filosofja. Sociologija, 21*(4), 310–319.

Nordenfelt, L. (2004). The varieties of dignity. *Health Care Analysis, 12*, 69–81.

Pace, E. (2009). The sociocultural and socio-religious origins of human rights. In P. B. Clarke (Ed.), *The Oxford handbook of sociology of religion* (pp. 432–448). Oxford: Oxford University Press.

Simons, G., & Westerlund, D. (Eds.). (2015). *Religion, politics and nation-building in post-communist countries*. Oxon: Routledge.

Streikus, A. (2012). The history of religion in Lithuania since the nineteenth century. In M. Ališauskienė & I. W. Schröder (Eds.), *Religious diversity in post-soviet society. Ethnographies of catholic hegemony and the new pluralism in Lithuania* (pp. 37–76). Farnham: Ashgate.
Trzebiatowska, M., & Bruce, S. (2016). *Why women are more religious than men?* Oxford: Oxford University Press.
van der Ven, J. A., Dreyer, J. A., & Pieterse, H. J. C. (2004). *Is there a god of human rights?* Leiden/Boston: Brill.
Wolterstorff, N. P. (2012). Christianity and human rights. In J. White Jr. & C. M. Green (Eds.), *Religion and human rights. An introduction* (pp. 42–55). Oxford: Oxford University Press.
Ziebertz, H.-G., Döhnert, S., & Unser, A. (2017). Predictors of attitudes towards human dignity: an empirical analysis among youth in Germany. In H.-G. Ziebertz & C. Sterkens (Eds.), *Religion and civil human rights in empirical perspective*. Heidelberg: Springer.
Žiliukaitė, R. (2000). Religinių vertybių kaita Lietuvoje 1990–1999 metais. *Kultūrologija, 6*, 213–251.
Žiliukaitė, R., Poviliūnas, A., & Savicka, A. (2016). *Lietuvos visuomenės vertybių kaita per dvidešimt nepriklausomybės metų* [The changes of Lithuanian population values throughout the twenty years of independence]. Vilniaus universiteto leidykla.

Chapter 9
Death Penalty and the Right to Life. A Comparative Empirical Study in Tanzania and Nigeria

Clement Fumbo, Modestus Adimekwe, and Hans-Georg Ziebertz

This is a comparative study on the attitudes of the youth in Tanzania and Nigeria. The main concentration in this area is the right of life in cases of crimes against humanity (the death penalty). The data was collected in 2014 and 2015 among selected students in secondary schools, high schools, and universities in Tanzania (N = 1286) and Nigeria (N = 1191). The expectation is that the younger generations in both Tanzania and Nigeria may have some similarities on appreciating a human rights culture and, within this context, that they will show a high support for the right to life. Previous studies indicate that attitudes towards human rights are contextually-biased. Capitalizing on the context of these two countries, our study will take two areas into account which may influence young people's attitudes towards the right to life. Firstly, the place of religion in moulding individuals' attitudes in Tanzania and Nigeria as well as the global quest for a human rights culture across Africa. The second is the socio-cultural background of each country and individuals. The assumption is that the perception of the role of religion in society has impact on young people's attitudes towards human rights and the right to life in particular. Personality is an additional characteristic. While some similarities can be observed in the general attitudinal patterns of the respondents in the two countries, the findings of this study do not show the expected high support for the right to life from them. However, their perception of religion tends to be the main variable.

C. Fumbo (✉)
Eckernforde Tanga University, Tanga, Tanzania
e-mail: cfumbo@gmail.com; gfumbo@yahoo.co.uk

M. Adimekwe · H.-G. Ziebertz
University of Würzburg, Würzburg, Germany
e-mail: hg.ziebertz@uni-wuerzburg.de

H.-G. Ziebertz, F. Zaccaria (eds.), *Euthanasia, Abortion, Death Penalty and Religion – The Right to Life and its Limitations*, Religion and Human Rights 4, https://doi.org/10.1007/978-3-319-98773-6_9

Introduction

This study will investigate and compare the attitudes of the youth towards the right to life in Tanzania and Nigeria. In both countries, the society is an accumulation of various ethnic groups mainly formed by kinship (cf. Mbiti 1970, 3; Fumbo 2011, 8). In that sense, human rights in Tanzania and Nigeria are often interpreted from the perspective of the beliefs and traditions of strong collectivist communities, as well as of the particular interests these communities serve (Fumbo 2012; cf. Schilder 1994). On the other hand, religion in its plurality (i.e. Islam and Christianity) with socio-cultural ingredients make a vital contribution to the moulding of an individual's attitude on different perspectives of life (Fumbo 2013; cf. Oduyoye 2001). In general, human rights exist under a community-based umbrella with the religions around them.

Despite the fact that human rights are embraced fully in theory, actual compliance is highly problematic in practice, including the exercising of the right to life. Therefore, our focus is to scrutinize and compare civil rights and liberty in Tanzania and Nigeria, the main concentration being the right to life, especially in cases of crimes against humanity which trigger the death penalty. The role of religion in society is another important aspect, as well as personality characteristics and their influence on young Tanzanians' and Nigerians' attitudes towards the right to life. Our goal is to identify similarities and differences of attitudes of young people in Tanzania and Nigeria regarding the right to life, and how those differences and similarities in religion(s) and other factors influence the attitudes of these young people. Firstly, our study will give a theoretical introduction on the situation in each country (1), followed by an explanation of our research method (2). In the third segment we will present our findings (3) followed by a discussion of the results (4) and a conclusion.

Theoretical Context of the Right to Life in Tanzania and Nigeria

In this section, before embarking on the questions raised, the study briefly provides a general overview of the political and social background of Tanzania and Nigeria, giving definitions of civil rights and liberties, the status of the right to life and the role of religion in Tanzanian and Nigerian societies. The last part of this section will address the youth and their relation to civil rights, liberties and religion.

Political and Social Background of Tanzania

Tanzania is a constitutional, secular, united republic with a multi-party political system. Present-day Tanzania is the result of the unification of two countries, Tanganyika and Zanzibar, in April 1964.

In terms of religious affiliation, Tanganyika's population comprised 30% Christians, 35% Muslims and 35% having indigenous believers during the colonial period. Zanzibar's population was virtually entirely Muslim. Three years after unification, however, religious affiliation had changed somewhat: according to the 1967 National Census, 34% of the population were Christian, 31% Muslim, and 35% belonged to other religious traditions (CIA Report 2005). According to 2009 statistics, 60% of the current population of mainland Tanzania are Christian, 36% Muslim, and 4% belong to other religious traditions (PEW 2010a, b). The situation in Zanzibar has remained almost unchanged since 1964, meaning that the population of 984,625 people (Census 2002) is almost completely *Ibadi* Muslim (Fumbo 2015).

The constitution guarantees freedom of religion, thus helping to limit religious conflicts (Article 19 and 20; cf. DIIS Report 2006). Every individual has the right to freedom of worship and is free to be affiliated with any religious group, as long as one does not infringe the freedom of others, and the leadership succession in Tanzania can be seen as an indicator that tensions between religious groups are limited (Fumbo 2015). The first president, Julius Kambarage Nyerere (1961–1984), was Catholic; his successor, Ally Hassan Mwinyi (1985–1995), a Muslim from Zanzibar. President Benjamin William Mkapa (1995–2005) was Anglican; and Jakaya Mrisho Kikwete (2005–2015) a Muslim. Current president John Joseph Pombe Magufuli is Catholic (2015–2020).

Tanzania has some distinctive characteristics in terms of peace and unity compared with other related communities in Africa (cf. Kobia 2003, 35). Despite Tanzania being one of the poorest nations in Africa and the third-poorest country in the world, the government tries to stimulate dialogue between different cultures and religions, also trying to adapt its policies to suit the diverse Tanzanian context. This dialogue has resulted in peace, unity, tranquillity, and relatively few ethnic and religious conflicts – an achievement that is partially the result of the consistent use of *Swahili* as a unifying language for the country in the last 50 years (cf. LHRC 2012, 3). The late *Mwalimu* (teacher), Julius Kambarage Nyerere, the founding father of the nation, made the Swahili language (*Kiswahili) a unifying factor,* not only to Tanzania but to Africa as a whole. On the eve of Tanzania's independence in the late 1950s and early 1960s, he noted that the country's diversity (approximately 126 ethnic groups and languages) could potentially jeopardise Tanzanian unity and the struggle for independence (Fumbo 2015 cf. Tajfel 1981; Petzell 2012). Although there are so many languages, no one language is taken as the native language by a majority or even a large proportion of the population. Nyerere introduced *Swahili* as the first language of the prospective new nation.

Swahili is now an official language, next to English, in all official communication, having been taught as a compulsory subject at every public school and college for more than 50 years. It is the official language in business, for national and international political affairs, and for instruction in primary schools. The country has also influenced the spread of Swahili to other jurisdictions across East Africa and beyond. Swahili is taught in various universities across the world and is seen as an important language, and the African Union recognises it as an official language.

Around 80% of the total population of 44,928,923 people (census 2012) speak Swahili (Tanzania National Statistics, population 2013, VI cf. UNFPA 2012). The use of one common language is vital for Tanzania's state policy, and also helps to maintain social cohesion, stability and peace – essential elements of meaningful political freedom and social and economic change – as well as for the realisation of a culture of human rights in Tanzania. However, several human rights are still under threat due to specific and persistent ethnic traditions.

Political and Social Background of Nigeria

Nigeria was formed in 1914, with the British amalgamation of the northern and southern protectorates into the Colony and Protectorate of Nigeria, and later became a sovereign state in 1960. The Nigerian population is drawn from more than 250 ethnic groups, which vary considerably in terms of their socio-political, cultural and religious backgrounds. Politically, Nigeria is a federal republic with a presidential system of government operating under a multi-party system. For a total of 28 years, the country had been under several military dictatorships before political liberalisation was ushered in by the return of civil rule in 1999. Prior to this period, the country's socio-political climate did not favour a meaningful human rights programme (Dada 2012a, 70; Ojo 2006, 23–26).

With about 182 million inhabitants (Nigerian Population Commission 2016), Nigeria is easily the most populous African country. According to a recent report by the World Bank (2015), it is also the largest economy on the continent, even though around 66% of its population lives on $1.90 or less per day (The Nigerian Observer 2015).

As far as religion is concerned, Nigeria is a multi-religious nation. According to the PEW Report (2010a, b), the 1963 Nigerian census found 36% of the population to be Christian, 48% Muslim, and 16% belonging to other faith groups. Similarly, other sources suggest that Muslims constitute approximately 50% of the population, Christians 40%, while the adherents of the indigenous religions make up the remaining 10% (CIA Report 2001; Democracy Web 2010; Nigeria Religion Statistics 2011; PEW 2010a, b). More recent reports appear to contradict such data, estimating that the Christian population is slightly larger than the Muslim population.[1] The remarkable growth of the Christian faith in Nigeria in the last two decades, especially of the Pentecostal churches, could account for this new assessment, among other considerations. However, accurate official statistical figures are lacking,

[1] The Pew Forum (2010) compared reports of the religious affiliations of Nigerians, from several sources and came out with following: the 2008 Nigeria Demographic and Health Survey (DHS) found 53% Christian, 45% Muslim, and 2% other; in the 2008 Afrobarometer poll, it is 56% Christian, 43% Muslim, and 1% other. Later, the 2012 PEW Report stated that in 2010, 49.3% of Nigeria's population were Christian, 48.8% Muslim, and 1.9% for adherents of indigenous and other religions, or unaffiliated. Furthermore, the 2010 census of Association of Religion Data Archives reported these figures: 46.5% for Christians, 45.5% for Muslims, and 7.7% for other religious groups.

meaning it is safe to consider the country as nearly equally divided between Christianity and Islam.

One other notable fact about these two religions in Nigeria is their peculiar geographical distribution. Whereas most Nigerian Muslims are Sunni and are concentrated in the northern area of the country, Christians dominate in the Middle Belt and the south (Ojo 2006, 25). As such, religious and ethnic affiliations tend to coincide. These identities are often politicized and interfere intensely in the affairs of the nation. Nigeria is, then, arguably a secular state. Section 10 of Nigeria's Constitution prohibits the establishment of a state religion, though experience does not seem to correspond with this provision (Constitution of Federal Republic of Nigeria 1999).

Civil Rights and Liberties in Tanzanian and Nigerian Law

Tanzanian Law Concerning Civil Rights and Liberties

Tanzania is one of many countries around the world that accepts instruments of international human rights which address civil rights and liberties. On the domestic level, the Bill of Rights guarantees civil rights and liberties, becoming part of the 1977 text of the *Constitution of the United Republic of Tanzania* through the Fifth Constitutional Amendment Act in 1984 (Act No. 15 of 1984), more specifically in articles 12 to 29. *Black's Law Dictionary* defines civil liberties as 'freedom from undue governmental interference or restraint'. It refers to freedom of speech, freedom of the press, freedom of religion, freedom of association, and other liberties associated with the Bill of Rights (*Black's Law Dictionary* 2009, 280). In Tanzania, civil rights refer to the individual rights of personal liberty, which are guaranteed by the *Constitution of the United Republic of Tanzania (originally* 1977*),* more specifically in Part III, known as the *Bill of Rights [of Tanzania] (LHRC & ZLSC* 2014, *14). The Basic Rights and Duties Enforcement Act (Act No. 33, 1994)* was enacted with the aim of facilitating the enforcement of the provisions provided under the *Bill of Rights*. In essence, civil rights especially include the right to vote, the right to due process, and the right to equal protection under the law (*Black's Law Dictionary* 2009, 281). Both civil rights and civil liberties fall under the category of negative rights (cf. LHRC Report 2013, 14) which entitle a person to refrain from doing an act that might harm the person that is entitled to these rights (*Black's Law Dictionary* 2009, 1437). The simple distinction between the two is that civil liberties are a protection against governmental actions and seek to restrict the government from abusing its powers, while civil rights refer to basic human rights to which every citizen should be entitled. Nevertheless, they also need support and protection from the government, which some stakeholders say must still be granted (Fumbo 2015).

Civil rights ensure a citizen's ability to participate in the civil and political life of the country. While civil liberties are protective in nature, civil rights are a broader concept. The founding documents, such as the constitution, grant both of these, and they are both sets of basic legal rights that each citizen possesses and which any person should possess. However, this distinction between civil liberties and civil rights may not always be very clear, and can at times create confusion. As such several laws have been under revision and others face similar constant challenges (cf. *Nyalali Commission Report*, April 1994 & Maina, Peter (Undated).

The newly proposed constitution draft of 2014 has also preserved the provision for civil rights and liberties (Constitution Draft 2015, Part 4.1, Article 23–48). The constitutional referendum was due to take place in 2015 but has been postponed several times. Tanzania has also signed the following treaties: *International Covenant on Civil and Political Rights (1966)*; the *African Charter on Peoples' and Human Rights (1981);* and the *UN Convention on the Rights of Persons with Disabilities (2006),* to mention a few (cf. LHRC & ZLSC 2014, 14). Furthermore, the right to life is enshrined under Article 6 of *the International Covenant on Civil and Political Rights, 1966*, and in Africa, Article 4 of the *Charter on Peoples' and Human Rights (ACHPR) of 1981* also guarantees the right to life. Despite the existence of such founding documents such as Tanzania's constitution that at least guarantee these rights as noted above, the modern world demands awareness of human dignity among humankind in all aspects of life, including the right to life. However, Tanzania faces a number of challenges when it comes to the implementation of these civil rights and liberties

Nigerian Law Concerning Civil Rights and Liberties

The 1999 Constitution of the Federal Republic (CFRN) is Nigeria's most current constitution and its major instrument of human rights. In this document, human rights are recognized and two chapters (namely Chapters II and IV) deal with human rights issues. Under the general title of *Fundamental Objectives and Directive Principles of State Policy*, Chapter II deals mainly with economic, social and cultural rights. However, these rights are regarded in section 6(6)(c) of the same document as non-justiciable, which simply means that they are not enforceable (Dada 2012b, 37). The body of rights of citizens is contained in Chapter IV of this document, widely known as the Bill of Rights, or simply as fundamental rights in the CFRN (Odoeme 2011, 32).

All the civil rights and liberties that are granted in Nigeria's constitution are covered under the section concerning fundamental rights. The catalogue of enforceable fundamental rights in Nigeria's constitution is as follows: right to life, right to dignity of the human person, right to a fair hearing, right to private and family life, right to freedom of thought, conscience and religion, right to freedom of expression and freedom of the press, right to peaceful assembly and association, right to freedom of movement, right to freedom from discrimination, right to acquire and own immovable property, etc. (CFRN, chapter IV, sections 33–44; Odoeme, 33; Ojo 2006, 20; Dada 2012b, 37). In any case, Nigeria has subscribed to many human rights instruments, most importantly the *Universal Declaration of Human Rights (1948),* the two covenants, namely the *International Covenant on Civil and Political Rights (1966)* and the *International Covenant on Economic, Social and Cultural*

Rights (1966), the African Charter on Peoples' and Human Rights (1981), etc. all of which boost the range of constitutional provisions. Therefore, as with many other nations around the world, the notion of human rights is entrenched in Nigeria's constitution. However, the keenness of this entrenchment does not automatically lead to practical application of these basic rights and liberties (Dada 2012a, 68–69; Ojo, 21).

Status of the Right to Life in Tanzania and Nigeria

The right to life is the supreme right from which no derogation should be permitted, even in times of public emergency that threaten the life of the nation. Quite literally, life can never be recovered when lost. Therefore, it should never be tampered with at any time and under any circumstances. This section will describe and attempt to analyse the status of the right to life in Tanzania and Nigeria respectively.

The Right to Life in Tanzania

The right to life in Tanzania, as in many parts of the world and especially in Africa, is a fragile term that remains under constant threat. The threat mostly involves individuals, communities, societies, state policies, state instruments, state organs, culture, traditions and, as a rule, religions and their teachings. The problem can at times be beyond limits, insofar as it suppresses those rights at the expense of the victims to such an immense degree. Furthermore, the available options mentioned above such as state policies, instruments, organs, culture, traditions, religions and others need desirable commitment from the different people involved in order to fulfil standard expectations. In this section we consider the death penalty as one of the practical threats to the right to life.

The death penalty in Tanzania is retained as a punishment in the *Penal Code, Cap 16 [R.E 2002] of the Laws of Tanzania* for crimes of murder and treason[2]; and *the National Defence Act, Cap. 192 [R.E 2002]* for the crime of misconduct on any military service in the presence of an enemy, to be imposed on a person who has been convicted and sentenced to death for such criminal offences that attract capital punishment.,[3] The method used in Tanzania being hanging. However, the death penalty does contradict Articles 14 and 13(6)(b) and (e) of the *Constitution of the United Republic of Tanzania* 1977 which guarantee the right to life and the right not to be subjected to cruel, inhuman or degrading punishment. Literarily, the death penalty is a violation of fundamental human rights that advocate the right to life. The Tanzania Human Rights Reports (LHRC & ZLSC) of years 2008–2009, 2012–2015 indicate that since receiving independence Tanzania has executed 238 people.

[2] Sections 196, 197 Cap 16 [R.E 2002] of the Laws of Tanzania.

[3] Section 39, 40, 196 and 197 of the Penal Code Cap 16.

There are no clear statistics of death row inmates in Tanzanian prisons, however by the year 2007 there were 2562 convicts on death row (LHRC & ZLSC 2013, 17). Moreover, records indicate that Tanzania is an abolitionist country of the death penalty in principle but has not yet implemented this.

There are several cases of efforts to litigate against the death penalty, but these always face a number of challenges in the form of objections, hindrances and delays of the matter from political and judicial state organs. For instance, there were arrangements for Constitutional Petitions against the death penalty in the Tanzanian High Court which were filed in 2008 and were supposed to be determined by a panel of three Judges (Section 10 of the *Basic Rights and Duties Enforcement Act, Cap 3 of Laws of Tanzania [R.E 2002]*). However, the petitions failed to take place – failing even to have a single hearing – until December 2013. Some of the reasons given for this failure include the disruption of the panel by way of retirement, transfer to another registry or promotion to the Court of a Judge in the panel, which meant the matter had to be referred to the Judge in charge for reassignment (LHRC & ZLSC 2013, 19). In fact, the matter had experienced several undesired delays at the expense of the right to life of individual victims and their relatives in the country.

The Right to Life in Nigeria

The CFRN as amended guarantees the right to life. Section 33(1) of the Constitution makes the following provision: "Every person has a right to life, and no one shall be deprived intentionally of his life ***save*** in execution of the sentence of a court in respect of a criminal offence of which he has been found guilty in Nigeria."

The right to life is recognized as the foremost and pivotal of all rights (Odoeme 2011, 37; Mendie 2014, 155). The idea of the right to life existed in pre-colonial Africa because the indigenous belief system held life, even the life of animals, to be sacred. Among the native Nigerian population, a lack of respect for the value of human life or to kill a human person, even in error, was frowned upon, and life-threatening situations such as war and violent conflicts were highly restricted. Of course, violations of a human right to life existed in such practices as the custom of killing twins which was seen as a bad omen for the tribe, yet "it is wrong to kill except in cases of need" (Mbiti, in Ojo 2006, 19–20).

The above provision reveals that Nigeria's Constitution guarantees the right to life, though in a qualified manner (Dada 2012b, 42). In section 33(2) some lawful exceptions to this right are outlined: a person may be deprived of his life in order to execute a death sentence for capital offences by a court of competent jurisdiction, in defence of property, in order to effect lawful arrest, to prevent the escape of a suspect from lawful custody, or to suppress a riot, insurrection or mutiny, and, with added reference to section 45(2), in order to deal with situations of emergency or situations of lawful acts of war. The practical implication is that Nigeria's security operatives had the discretionary power to kill in such situations as affecting an arrest (cf. section 24 of the Police Act, 2004; section 271 of the Criminal Code Act, 2004).

Furthermore, under section 34(a), the CFRN prohibits torture and inhuman or degrading treatment. However, it can be deduced from the above constitutional provision that killing as a result of the use of "force as is reasonably necessary" [section 33(2)] does not constitute a violation of the right to life. However, scholars argue that the scope of this lawful exception is so wide as to tantamount to utter derogation of the aforementioned right (Dada 2012b, 42; Odoeme 2011, 37). Even though this provision has been repealed in section 8(1) (a) and (b) of the Administration of Criminal Justice Act, 2015 (from now on, ACJA 2015), it is left to be seen how much of this would apply in reality. Hence, it could be said that the right to life is sacrosanct in Nigerian law, but also that its sacrosanctity may be tampered with under due process of the same law (Mendie 2014, 156–157).

Put more concretely, the death penalty is a legal practice in Nigeria, the Supreme Court of Nigeria upholding it as a lawful process in *Kalu v. State 1998 13 NWLR*[4] *PT 583531* (Babalola 2014). Nigerian law prescribes the death penalty for a wide range of offences, such as murder, terrorism-related offences, armed robbery and treason. The scope of capital punishment has recently been extended to include kidnapping (Umoru and Erunke 2016). In any case, under Shari'a law crimes such as apostasy, sexual offences like adultery, homosexual sodomy and incest are eligible for the death penalty. The constitutional execution methods are hanging and shooting, with lapidation (rajm) and crucifixion (salb) permissible under the Shari 'a Penal Code.[5] The Death Penalty Database (2014) reports that more than 2626 people had been executed in Nigeria between 1970 and 2013. The last known executions took place in 2013, involving four inmates. Amnesty International (2013) estimates in the same year that out of the some 1233 individuals on death row in Nigeria, no less than 141 death sentences were executed.

It has been suggested that no moratorium has been imposed on capital punishment in Nigeria to date, though efforts in this regard have not been lacking. For example, in 2007 the Presidential Commission on Reform of the Administration of Justice recommended a moratorium on the death penalty but the federal government did not implement it (Death Penalty Database 2014). The most common argument advanced for the continued retention of the practice is that of deterrence. But with empirical and classical arguments, for instance, the logic of inherent imperfection of the judicial system as exemplified in instances of miscarriages of justice across the world, human rights groups continue to refute this position, proposing instead that death sentences be commuted to long terms of imprisonment in Nigeria (Babalola 2014).

[4] NWLR: Nigeria Weekly Law Report.

[5] Information about the Shari 'a law is obtained from the Harmonized Shari'a Penal Code Annotated, as contained in the Death Penalty Database (2014) on Nigeria. This document grew out of the compilation of the Shari'a law of the Northern states with the Penal Code applicable in the same region.

Role of Religion(S) in Tanzania and Nigeria

Religion falls under almost all three generations of rights, namely the first generation of human rights that consists of civil and political rights, the second generation of rights which are economic, social and cultural and the third generation of rights which consist of collective rights (van der Ven et al. 2004, 163). In the context of Africa, a simple definition of the collective rights category is those rights which protect a group of people, while individual rights protect the individual (Fumbo 2015, 185).

Religion in Tanzania

In Tanzania, as in many other African countries, religion is part of the culture of people and religious pluralism has existed for many years, most kingdoms in Tanzania having previously recognised and experienced such pluralism. As such, African religions were common in every kingdom, and the king or chief, as the supreme authority of the kingdom or chiefdom, guaranteed the freedom of every religion even to the newly conquered ethnic groups, provided they would promote the common good of the kingdom (Fumbo 2015 cf. Pirouet 1991). This was the basis for future religions to enter into Tanzanian society without objection by the people, the kings or the chiefs (Fumbo 2015 cf. Gunnar 2001).

As noted above, the Constitution of the United Republic of Tanzania, 1977 provides for enjoyment of the right to freedom of religion and association (Articles 19 and 20). This means that Tanzanians enjoy freedom of religion, as there are diverse religions but with a high degree of tolerance that generally allows peace and tranquillity to prevail. This existence of a relatively high level of religious tolerance among believers of different religions and denominations gives ample room for negotiations in times of misunderstanding (Nyerere 1967). The main official religions are still Christianity and Islam (Cf. LHRC & ZLSC 2012 & 2013, 4; Fumbo 2015, 189), but there also other religions like Hinduism, Buddhism and African Traditional Religions present in the country. Therefore, every individual has the right to freedom of worship and to be affiliated with any religious group as long as one does not infringe the freedom of others on basis of religion.

Over the years, religious institutions have contributed a lot to Tanzanian society. The most vivid example concerns the making of leaders. The most prominent leaders in the country, including the founding nation leader the late Julius Kambarage Nyerere, and others who followed after him like the retired presidents Benjamin Mkapa and Jakaya Mrisho Kikwete, were raised in Church-managed schools and institutions, and such prominent leaders and others who served in such state organs are products of mission schools and colleges. However, after the Arusha Declaration in 1967 and the following years, the above option ceased to be available after the government confiscated almost all religious schools and colleges. The move had negative effects which Tanzanian society is still struggling to rectify to this day, even with the returning of some of the schools and colleges to their original owners after the failed attempt by the state to run these institutions. One of the effects of this is the dramatic drop of education standards in the country. In some cases, people who can afford to do so opt to send their children abroad or overseas for quality education that is lacking in their own country. A second noticeable negative effect is moral decay among the youth and an increase in crime.

The country also faces the challenge of a high rate of human rights violations from those with traditional religious beliefs. Examples of such violations include the recent escalation of killings of people with albinism and old women, as well as female genital mutilation (FGM) (cf. Fumbo 2015 & UNICEF 2013). Hence, some blame traditionalists and other minority religions that actively function within these main religious organs, namely Christianity and Islam. Sometimes these killings can have implications that prevent the presiding state organs from abolishing the death penalty for convicted criminals of such barbaric killings and murders (cf. Fumbo 2013, Suleyman 2013, Matandiko 2013). Nevertheless, religion occupies a relevant place in Tanzania in terms of advocating human dignity and of regulating the attitudes of young people towards mutual respect while encouraging a culture of human rights.

Religion in Nigeria

Nigeria has been described as a deeply divided state (Osaghae and Suberu 2005). Many factors account for this state of affairs, one of which is religion. The religious landscape of Nigeria is dominated by Muslims and Christians, with the adherents of the African Traditional Religion forming a significant minority. Interactions between these religious identities, especially the two main religious groups, are not always smooth; some scholars describe these in very strong terms as "the test case of the clash of civilizations [sic]" (Paden 2007). Based on this, Nigeria's Constitution guarantees the right to freedom of thought, conscience and religion (section 38). If anything, this provision avails of the platform on which efforts to foster tolerance and pluralism could rest.

Studies have demonstrated the saliency of religion in Africa (Mbiti 1989, 15; 1991; Van der Tuin and Fumbo 2012, 204), and Nigeria is no exception to this finding (Odoeme 2011, 79). Instead, religion is a very sensitive issue in Nigeria, and from the outset one gets the impression of a strong influence of religion on both the constitution and the judicial system. It is relevant to point out that Nigeria operates under a plural legal system, in which the informal functions alongside the formal system (Obilade 1979, 169), the Shari'a court being constitutional and being part of the informal system (see CFRN sections 230–283). However, between Shari 'a law and the Constitution, there are some discrepancies with respect to the Penal Code, among others. Death sentences for offences such as adultery and sodomy constitute a violation of the right to life (Gwangndi1 2016, 62). The constitutionality of these Shari'a provisions have been the subject of public debates, though without many practical implications.

Institutions of learning are another area where the influence of religion as a societal actor can be felt in Nigeria. Originally, Nigerian schools were established by religious groups for the purpose of proselytization. Before the advent of the Europeans in Nigeria, Islamic Qur'anic schools had already been established by Islamic scholars in the northern areas of the country. Thus, the formal educational system in the region was Islamic. Later, Christian missionaries set up mission schools in the south. These schools were largely western-like and Christian-oriented (Lemu 2014), and the most renowned public schools in Nigeria belong to this category. The gains of these religious institutions cannot be overemphasized. Nevertheless, it is believed that this double-barrel arrangement of the education sector is significant in the context of wide social distances between the diverse identities in Nigeria. Even with the government take-over of schools in 1970, introduced in order to instill secular values into the system, this project of secularisation appears not to have succeeded (Igwe 2008), as the evidence of the influence of these religions on Nigeria's students has persisted.

Young people's Relation to Civil Rights, Liberties and Religion in Tanzania and Nigeria

As previously mentioned, the different communities in Tanzania and Nigeria are an accumulation of various ethnic groups mainly formed by kinship with strong beliefs and traditions. The collectivist communities do necessarily influence individuals under those particular interests that include commonality in traditions and culture (Fumbo 2012 cf. Hiebert 1992 & Vanhoozer 1993). The commonality that includes religion in its plurality (i.e. Islam and Christianity) with socio-cultural ingredients plays a major role in Tanzania and Nigeria and, in a broader sense, the global quest for a human rights culture across Africa does not exempt the youth who are the majority in Tanzania and Nigeria (cf. Mbunda 2014). The quest for fostering human rights does from time to time necessitate reviews of the laws in both Tanzania and Nigeria in terms of their coming closer to complying with International treaties from time to time, the issue of the right to life being a part of such reviews (cf. Mesaki 2010). The aforementioned social and religious context is vital for the establishment of human rights in both countries and for understanding the attitudes of their youth towards the right to life.

Research Design

This study is a comparative research survey on the attitudes of young people in Tanzania and Nigeria. The main concentration in this area is the right of life as it pertains to cases of crimes against humanity. The focus is to scrutinise the role of religion and personality characteristics in Tanzanian and Nigerian society and their influence on young Tanzanians' and Nigerians' attitudes towards the death penalty. From the study so far, one gets the impression that both societies share some similarities in terms of cultural values and orientations, such as the respect for the value of human life and respect for the other. Such values predate the present status of these societies as civil societies and are relevant for appreciating a human rights culture. Based on this assumption, we expect that the young generation in both Tanzania and Nigeria will show a similar high support for the right to life. It is also expected that the perception of the role of religions in these societies has a strong positive relationship with young people's attitudes towards human rights and the right to life in particular. This idea is premised on the notion that the major religions support human dignity as a foundation of the right to life. Furthermore, we hypothesise that the perception of religion is a more important predictor of the respondents' attitudes than the other selected possible predictor-variables, namely the respondents' perception of their respective societies, their personality and their socio-demographic characteristics. Based on these, the research questions are: (1) what are the attitudes of the youth regarding the right to life in Tanzania and Nigeria? (2) How do the attitudes of young people relate to their perception of the state and of religion, their personality traits and their socio-demographic characteristics? (3) Can their attitudes towards the right to life in Tanzania and Nigeria be predicted by their perception of the state and the role of religion in society, personality and socio-demographic characteristics?

In addressing these questions we will begin with a description of research design which includes the method of data collection, size, description of the sample and our conceptual model. Then, different concepts within the model will be presented before discussing the measuring instruments and the procedures for statistical analysis that we used.

Data Collection

The collection of the present data is within a large, international research project and focuses on samples in Tanzania and Nigeria. The data collection took place in late 2014 and early 2015 in both countries. Young students from high schools, colleges and universities from five regions in Tanzania participated in the study, while only senior secondary students from seven states took part in the study in Nigeria. The researchers gave assurance to the participants on confidentiality and anonymity and informed them that participation was voluntary.

Some schools, colleges and universities were from two regions of the north of Tanzania, the other students were from the eastern, central and the southern part of the country. All schools, colleges and universities were of mixed background in terms of gender and religious affiliations, and the students of all five regions have an indigenous background, that is to say they belong to or come from a particular ethnic group found in Tanzania. It is the consideration of the study that the participants are partly or fully socialised in particular indigenous cultural and religious beliefs and practices. Hence, almost all of them communicate using the common '*Swahili*' language. Therefore, the questionnaire was essentially translated into *Swahili* so that as many young people as possible could respond. In Nigeria, of all the states that we covered, three are located in the north while the others are in the southern part of the country. Also, most of the sampled schools have a mixed student population in terms of gender, religion and ethnic affiliations, which is in line with the exigencies of our study. The questionnaire already exists in English, which was used, though with very minimal grammatical adjustments.

Sample

More than 2443 high school, senior secondary school, college and university students in Tanzania (N = 1286) and Nigeria (N = 1191) agreed to fill in the questionnaire, and around 2800 questionnaires came back fully completed (97%). After data cleaning 2443 questionnaires could be used (86%), meaning the sample includes 1286 young Tanzanians aged 16 to 25 and 1191 young Nigerians within the age-bracket 14 to 22. For Tanzania, the average age is 19.9 years. 66.9% are male and 33.1% are female, and the sample contains 77% Christians and 23% Muslims. The available statistics of religious affiliation for 2009 indicate that there are 60% Christians, 36% Muslims and 4% others (PEW 2010a, b). For Nigeria, the average age is 17.36 years. 55.1% of the sampled students are female, the remaining 44.9% are male. 65.8% described themselves as Christians, while 34. 2% are Muslims. Therefore, in this survey, Christians are slightly overrepresented and Muslims underrepresented. However, it is important to say that there are no official reliable statistics for the respective national representations of denomination because of some limitations highlighted earlier (see part 1).

Conceptual Model

This conceptual model represents the concepts of our study and how they are ordered and related. The dependent variable comprises attitudes towards right to life, while our independent variables are understood as potential predictors of attitudes towards rights to life. Sex, age, and religious affiliation function as control variables (see Fig. 9.1).

Measuring Instruments

In the following section we will describe the concepts used in this study.

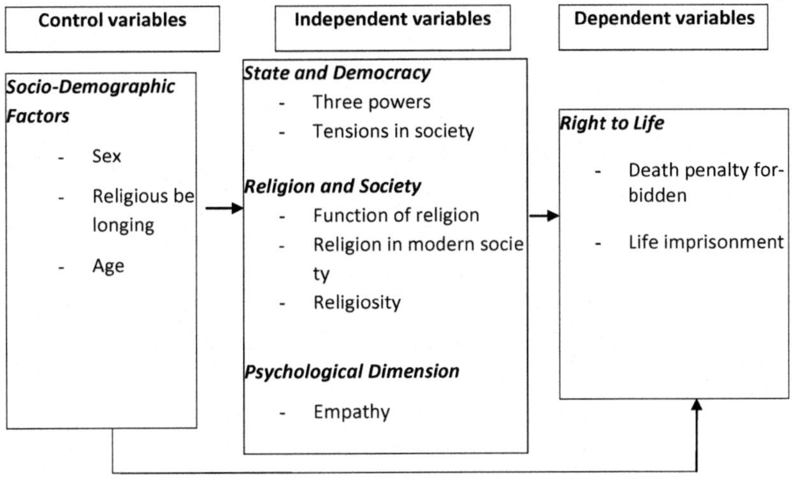

Fig. 9.1 Conceptual model

Right to Life – Death Penalty (Dependent Variable)

In this conceptual model, the study considers university students', and high school and secondary school students' attitudes towards our dependent variable – the right to life. The latter is expressed through prohibiting the death penalty and commuting the death penalty to life sentence. In this study, therefore, the right to life is measured with the following instruments:

(Right to life)

Death penalty should strictly be prohibited because of the right to life.
Death sentence should always be commuted to a life sentence.

Answer scheme: 1 = I totally disagree; 2 = I disagree; 3 = I am not sure; 4 = I agree; 5 = I fully agree.

Independent Variables

Independent variables in this study cover attitudes towards state and democratic institutions, sources of tensions in society, religion and personal characteristics. The word 'independent' here signifies that the study is not interested in how these attitudes are developed or socialised, rather it takes them as they are and its interest is if and to which degree these variables show any impact on the dependent variables.

State and Democracy

The first group of independent variables concerns the state as a societal actor. The subject under study involves the state and democratic institutions as the custodian of the lives and rights of its citizens. Accordingly, the study has so far shown the state's involvement in issues pertaining to the right to life in Tanzania and Nigerian via provision of laws that promote, but at the same time curtail, the enjoyment of this right. The items on these three powers provide statements about the functioning of the government in a democratic society. We consider the functioning of the state as a possible predictor of the attitudes of young people towards right to life and include it, here as operationalised in the following three items:

Items of the Concept State and Democracy
(Three powers)

Parliament succeeds in making laws for political refugees
The government manages the country's economic crisis well
The courts act impartially, they decide cases of different ethnic groups equally

Answer scheme: 1 = strong disagreement; 2 = disagreement; 3 = uncertain; 4 = agreement; 5 = strong agreement.

Tensions in Society

This set of variables includes items about the possible causes of conflicts and tensions in society. These instruments are meant to test the respondents' awareness of their contexts, with reference to the sources of conflicts and their own personal experiences of injustice. With this variable, we target two possible areas of information. First, we intend to find out what the respondents consider to be the 'hot spots' of tensions in their communities. Secondly, it is also our intention to know whether this perception of tension (if it is present) among the main institutions of their society, as well as their personal experiences of injustice, predispose them to support corrective measures not excluding capital punishment, especially in cases of very serious conflicts.

Items of Tensions in Society
(Perceived tensions)

In your view:

To what degree are there tensions or conflicts in society between the rich and poor?
To what degree are there tensions or conflicts in society between religions?
To what degree are there tensions or conflicts in society between political sympathies?

(Perceived injustices)

In your view:

How often have you been personally treated in an unjust manner because you are rich or poor?
How often have you been personally treated in an unjust manner because of your religion?
How often have you been personally treated in an unjust manner because of your political sympathies?

Answer scheme: 1 = never; 2 = very seldom; 3 = occasionally; 4 = often; 5 = very often.

Religion and Society

The saliency of religion in Africa as a societal actor cannot be overemphasised (Mbiti 1989, 15; Odoeme 2011, 79; Van der Tuin and Fumbo 2012, 204). Thus, we include here a group of variables concerning the perception of religion as possible predictors. Under this group, the first set of questions contains items about the role of religion in society, including five dimensions: religion as a social force, religion as a spiritual movement, religion as being focused on national identity or on societal issues, and religion as something that always tries to be up-to-date and conform to cultural trends in society.

In addition, four items offering statements about the relationship between religion and modern society are included. The first two statements express that religion is still relevant in modern society, while the other two say that religion is a relic from the past.

Scales and Items of Religion and Society
(Influence on public opinion)

Religions should try to influence public opinion on social problems.
Religions should use their authority to intervene in societal affairs.

(Public prophetic voice)

Religions should publicly stand up for the lower classes.
Religions should take public responsibility for societal development.

(Cultural conformity)

Religions should go along with changing ideas in society.
Religions should always keep up with current social trends.

(Spiritual service)

Religions should take responsibility for their members' spiritual growth.
Religions should create places for deep spiritual experiences.

(National culture)

Religions should take a joint responsibility with the state for our national culture.
Religions should consolidate nation against alien influences and deprivation of its originality.

(Religion in contemporary society)

Contemporary society will further rather than hinder quests for religious meaning.
For the morality of contemporary society, it is good that there is religion.
Religious convictions, rituals and symbols do not fit into these modern times. *
Religion is a "leftover" from times past. *

Answer scheme: 1 = I totally disagree; 2 = I disagree; 3 = I am not sure; 4 = I agree; 5 = I fully agree.

* Items could be recoded in further analyses

Religiosity

Religion's primary concerns are individual beliefs and the importance of these beliefs to the individual. Again, based on the contexts of this study, we consider individual religiosity as a possible predictor of attitudes towards human rights, particularly the right to life. The variables below include items that discuss the concept of religiosity. The items derive from the Glock and Stark (1965) study, in which they arranged the different ways in which individuals can be deemed to be religious under intellectual, ideological, experiential, consequential and ritual dimensions.

Items of Religiosity
(Intellectual dimension)

How often do you think about religious issues?

(Ideological dimension)

To what extent do you believe that God or something divine exists?

(Experience-dimension)

How often do you experience situations in which you have the feeling that God or something divine intervenes in your life?

(Consequence-dimension)

What is your position on the statement: "my religion or worldview has a great influence on my daily life?"

(Ritual dimension)

How often do you pray?
How often do you take part in religious services at a church or mosque or another place?

The Answering schemes are different.

Psychological Dimension

The third group of independent variables includes one concept that focuses on the ability of students to empathise with the sorrows of another person. The ability of empathy could show support for the right to life, and studies indeed show that empathy predicts inherent dignity, a fundamental principle upon which the entire structure of human rights is based (Ziebertz et al. 2018). Therefore, empathy is included as one of our explanatory variables.

Items of Psychological Dimension
(Empathy)

I often have tender, concerned feelings for people less fortunate than myself.
When I see someone being taken advantage of, I feel somewhat protective toward him or her.
I am often quite touched by things that I see happen.

Answer scheme: 1 = I totally disagree; 2 = I disagree; 3 = I am not sure; 4 = I agree; 5 = I fully agree.

Socio–Demographic Characteristics

Finally, the socio-demographic characteristics such as age, sex and religious belonging are included as control variables.

Items of Socio-demographic Characteristics
(Religious belonging)

Answer scheme: 16 religions/denominations and the categories "other religions" and "non-religious".

Empirical Findings

In this section we report on the results relating to the two research questions that directed our investigation, analyses and discusses the results accordingly.

Firstly, we conducted T-tests because two groups are being compared in the study, namely the youth in Tanzania and Nigeria. We did this for all our variables to enable us to answer our first research question. Then we ran the correlations analysis using Pearson. By far, the latter is the most common correlation coefficient that is used in most tests to measure the degree of the (linear) relationship between two variables, which was used to answer our second question. Lastly, we turned to the regression analysis, conducting such an analysis with the intention to find out what the predictors of the youth's attitudes towards the right to life are.

Respondents' Attitudes Towards the Right to Life in Tanzania and Nigeria

With respect to the first research question, we intend to find out about the attitudes of the young generation in Tanzania and Nigeria regarding the right to life. The results as reported in Table 9.1 show, in general terms, that the youth approve of the abolition of the death penalty. However, their approval dangles between mere agreement and positive ambivalence. The Tanzanian respondents lend more support for the prohibition of the death penalty via the two items (mean = 3.47 and mean = 3.63) than their Nigerian counterparts (mean = 3.27 and mean = 3.32, respectively). Put

Table 9.1 Death penalty (T-test)

Country	Tanzania (N = 1252)		Nigeria (N = 1191)			
Item	Mean	SD	Mean	SD	Df.	T-value
Death penalty forbidden	3.47	1.50	3.27	1.30	2418.73	3.54***
Life imprisonment	3.63	1.43	3.32	1.14	2367.64	6.02***

***p ≤ 001

more concretely, young people in Tanzania tend to support the right to life more than their counterparts in Nigeria.

Based on circumstances which we considered to be similar, we expected the youth in both countries to have considerably similar attitudes to the death penalty as a violation of the right to life. The results in Table 9.1 also show the outcome of the T-test. As we can see, there is a statistically significant positive difference in the evaluation of the death penalty among the youth in Tanzania and Nigeria. Obviously, this development could be attributed to a host of structural and compositional factors, some of which are not covered in this study.

It is really surprising to note that the youth in both countries are not as highly supportive of the right to life as was expected. In Tanzania, the high rate of barbaric killings of people with albinism and of the elderly as well as an increase of criminal offences that result in killing innocent people could be employed to explain this tendency. In the case of Nigeria, the culture of "executive lawlessness" (Ojo 2006, 15) and "impunity" (Dada 2012,70) which was mentioned earlier in connection with prolonged military rule in Nigeria, could be part of the reason for the youth's ambivalent stance on the prohibition of capital punishment.

Before we address the second question our study will first show the respondents' attitudes towards all other explanatory variables.

State and Democracy

Table 9.2 presents the sample's attitudes towards the state and democratic institutions in the two countries. In two of the items that investigate the functioning of the three powers in a democratic society, precisely the first and third item, it can be seen that the respondents differ significantly but negatively in their evaluation of the functioning of the parliament and the courts. On the other hand, they differ positively in their assessments of the functioning of the executive arm.

On a general note, the means in this table are very low, indicating a very negative perception of the state and its organs among the students of both countries. Whereas the youth in Tanzania disagree more (mean = 2.46 and mean = 2.35) than the Nigerians (mean = 2.93 and mean = 2.56) in terms of the good functioning of parliament and the impartiality of the courts respectively, the reverse is the case with reference to the executive. That is to say, the Nigerians disagree more (mean = 2.06) with the good functioning of the latter than their Tanzanian counterparts

Table 9.2 Three powers (T-test)

Country	Tanzania (N = 1252)		Nigeria (N = 1191)			
Item	Mean	SD	Mean	SD	Df.	T-value
Parliament_good refugee law	2.46	1.09	2.93	1.14	2441	−10.44***
Government_good economic policies	2.35	1.26	2.06	1.02	2385.11	6.32***
Courts_impartial	2.35	1.28	2.56	1.13	2427.58	−4.34***

***p ≤ 001

Table 9.3 Tensions in society (T-test)

Country	Tanzania (N = 1252)		Nigeria (N = 1191)			
Item	Mean	SD	Mean	SD	Df.	T-value
Perceived tensions:						
Between rich & poor	3.60	1.21	3.77	1.09	2435.70	−3.76**
Between religions	3.70	1.26	4.23	.94	2309.27	−12.00***
Between political sympathies	4.06	1.19	3.80	1.10	2441	5.56***
Perceived injustices:						
Because rich/poor	2.21	1.19	2.43	1.15	2441	−4.49***
Because of religion	2.26	1.35	2.68	1.20	2431.22	−8.18***
Because of political sympathies	2.05	1.36	1.80	.10	2296.42	5.21***

**$p \leq .01$; ***$p \leq 001$

(mean = 2.35). The malfunctioning of state organs in a number of issues and discrepancies in the law-making process at times make individuals less satisfied and come up with such notions as above. In the case of Nigeria, the reason for this dissatisfaction could be traced to some instances of corruption, which the government is often accused of by citizens (see Global Corruption Barometer 2013).

Table 9.3 shows the responses of the students to questions concerning tensions and conflicts in their respective contexts, chiefly concerning the sources of such conflicts and the extent of the proneness of the sources in causing such tensions. Furthermore, they are required to relate their own experiences of injustice. With regard to tensions based on social status (rich/poor), on religious affiliation and on political affiliations, the two groups of respondents differ significantly in their evaluations. Their attitudes in terms of the first two aforementioned items are negatively significant, but positive in the third. This pattern repeats exactly in the section for personally perceived injustices, though unlike in the section for perceived tensions the students tended to choose the negative category in their responses.

A more interesting finding here is that the responses clearly indicate the tension-prone institutions in the two countries. While Nigerian students perceive that religious crises dominate the corpus of conflicts in their society (mean = 4.23), for the students in Tanzania, tensions between political affiliations are more on the high side in their society (mean = 4.06), compared to all other tensions. The response of the Nigerian students somehow confirms what we already said in our theoretical discussion on rivalry between religious groups in Nigeria. The "winner-takes-it-all" mentality that mostly characterises the ruling parties in these two countries could be one of the reasons for the high results on the item concerning tensions between political factions, which seems to be more apparent for the young Tanzanians.

Religion and Society

Next, we examine the relevance of religion as it pertains to the evaluation of the right to life. In Table 9.4 we have two scales with which to assess the youth's perception of the function of religion in society, namely the socio-spiritual and cultural

Table 9.4 Function of religion (T-test)

	Country					
	Tanzania (N = 1252)		Nigeria (N = 1191)			
Religion	Mean	SD	Mean	SD	Df.	T-value
Socio-spiritual	4.25	.62	3.80	.58	2441	18.18***
Cultural	3.06	1.28	3.04	1.04	2383.05	.37

Legend: A factor analysis of the items yielded two factors with an explained variance of 46% for all respondents (Tanzania and Nigeria). Factor 1 contains 8 items in which religions function as a socio-spiritual value provider (from now on, socio-spiritual religion). The Cronbach-Alpha is .75. The second factor is made up of 2 items (from now on, cultural religion). This factor expresses that religions should be in tune with the times. The Cronbach-Alpha is .68
***$p \leq 001$

Table 9.5 Religion in contemporary society (T-test)

Country	Tanzania (N = 1252)		Nigeria (N = 1191)			
Item	Mean	SD	Mean	SD	Df.	T-value
Religion unfit for society	2.63	1.24	2.87	1.33	2441	−4.61***
Religion good for morality	4.31	.94	4.25	.98	2441	1.46

***$p \leq 001$

roles. Here we see a positive difference in attitudes between the student groups with regards to the socio-spiritual role of religion. While both groups express their support for religion with a socio-spiritual focus in society, the item appears to be more important for the students from Tanzania (mean = 4.25) than for those in Nigeria (mean = 3.80). The two groups, however, do not differ in their perception of the function of religion as having a cultural emphasis.

We also consider the relevance of religion in modern society. The following two statements express antithetical views about the place of religion as being unfit for modern society, on the one hand, and on the other hand, as good for society (see Table 9.5). In the variance analyses of these items the attitudes of the students differ significantly (with a negative coefficient) in the first, but not in the second. Between the Tanzanian and Nigerian respondents, the former disagrees more with the item (mean = 2.63) than the latter (mean = 2.87). From these responses, we get an indication of the importance of religion, which is typical of African countries. This is also consistent with our earlier position on religion as a strong societal factor in both countries. A clearer picture of this claim could be seen in the religiosity variables.

A closer look at Table 9.6 shows that the answers of the students on their own religiosity in its varied dimensions are generally positive. Nevertheless, their collective attitudes differ significantly. In terms of ideological dimension and ritual participation (ritual dimension), the Tanzanian and Nigerian students differ significantly in their attitudes, with the latter agreeing more (mean = 4.74 and mean = 5.21) to the items than the former (mean = 4.57 and mean = 4.71, respectively). Unlike these two items that have negative significance, the attitudes of respondents towards the other dimensions of religiosity – namely intellectual, experiential and consequential dimensions, and the prayer aspect of the ritual dimension – differ significantly, in a positive way. In addition, these latter dimensions are more important to the Tanzanian students than their Nigerian counterparts.

Table 9.6 Religiosity (T-test)

	Country					
	Tanzania (N = 1252)		Nigeria (N = 1191)			
Dimension	Mean	SD	Mean	SD	Df.	T-value
Intellectual	4.14	.83	4.05	1.03	2278.83	2.58**
Ideological	4.57	.75	4.74	.69	2439.73	−6.05***
Experience	4.54	.72	4.33	1.03	2107.64	5.85***
Consequence	4.40	.71	4.10	.82	2441	9.66***
Ritual: Prayer	7.21	1.35	7.05	1.41	2441	2.82**
Ritual: Participation	4.71	1.51	5.21	1.18	2352.99	−9.12***

**p ≤ .01; ***p ≤ 001

Table 9.7 Empathy (T-test)

Country	Tanzania (N = 1252)		Nigeria (N = 1191)			
Item	Mean	SD	Mean	SD	Df.	T-value
Empathy	4.30	.66	4.06	.75	2365.04	8.39***

Legend: the three items are used as a scale, with a Cronbach's Alpha of .60 for all respondents (Tanzania and Nigeria)
***p ≤ 001

Table 9.8 T-test for Death penalty and sex (Tanzania & Nigeria)

Items	N	Mean	SD	Df.	T-value
Death penalty is forbidden	1071	Female 3.40	1.37	2352.55	.94
	1372	Male 3.35	1.44		
Life imprisonment	1071	Female 3.44	1.25	2361.68	−1.13
	1372	Male 3.50	1.34		

Psychological Dimension

The ability to empathize with others is considered as a possible predictor of attitudes towards the right to life in this study. As in the religiosity concept above, the students' answers are generally positive, indicating a tendency towards empathy on their part. However, answers differ significantly between the two groups (T-value =8.39***). Once again, empathy is more important for the Tanzanians (mean = 4.30) than for the Nigerians (mean = 4.06). Among others, this difference could be explained based on contextual factors, such as the socio-political backgrounds of the two countries (Table 9.7).

Socio-Demographic Characteristics

Sex is included in the study as a control variable. In Table 9.8 sex is not statistically significant, simply meaning the students in both countries do not necessarily differ along this line in their attitudes towards the death penalty.

Table 9.9 Death penalty and religious belonging (T-test)

	Tanzania					Nigeria				
Country	N	Mean	SD	Df.	T-value	N	Mean	SD	Df.	T-value
Death penalty forbidden										
Christians	967	3.52	1.50	1250	2.26*	774	3.36	1.30	1175	3.12**
Muslims	285	3.29	1.51			403	3.11	1.29		
Life imprisonment										
Christians	967	3.72	1.39	441.19	4.15***	774	3.36	1.12	1175	1.87
Muslims	285	3.31	1.49			403	3.23	1.17		

*p ≤. 05; **p ≤ .01; ***p ≤ 001

The picture is somewhat different with regards to religious belonging. In another result not shown here, the respondents differ positively in their attitudes to the two items concerning the death penalty (T-value = 4.17*** and T-value = 5.09***) based on their religious belonging. But in order to get a clearer picture of the groups' attitudes on an intra-national basis, we conducted another analysis, the results of which are outlined in Table 9.9. As can be seen, there are positive differences in attitudes towards the right to life between Christian and Muslim students in Tanzania based on their responses to the items, with the Christian students agreeing slightly more (mean = 3.52 and mean = 3.72) than the Muslims (mean = 3.29 and mean = 3.31, respectively), who are positively ambivalent. In Nigeria, Christian and Muslim students exhibit positive ambivalent attitudes towards the right to life, and they do not differ in their evaluation of the item that death sentences should be commuted to life imprisonment. However, they show positive significant differences in their assessment of the prohibition of the death penalty, with Christians agreeing with this notion slightly more (mean = 3.36) than Muslims (mean = 3.11).

Comparatively, Christian students tended to support the right to life more than the Muslims in both countries. As we saw above, the death sentence forms part of the Shari'a punishments for criminal offences. This, perhaps, could explain the weaker support of this fundamental right by the Muslim respondents in this study.

Findings on Interrelationships

Our second research question concerns the relationships between the respondents' attitudes towards the right to life, operationalised in our study in terms of the death penalty (i.e. 'the death penalty should be forbidden' and 'the death sentence should be commuted to life sentence'), and the independent variables, namely the respondents' perceptions of the state and religion, their personality traits and their socio-demographic characteristics. In line with Pearson's correlation, we distinguish between three types of relationship: positive, negative and no relationship. The positive relationship expresses that the higher scores on the values of the independent variables are associated with higher scores on the values of the dependent variable, and vice versa. In contrast, the negative relationship indicates that higher scores on the coefficients of the independent variables are associated with lower scores on the coefficients of the dependent variable, and vice versa. No relationship simply indicates that there is no predictable relationship at all between the two sets of variables. Table 9.10 reports on the relationships between our independent and dependent variables.

Table 9.10 Correlations (Pearson's r) between the dependent variable of right to life and independent variables

	Death penalty forbidden		Life imprisonment	
Items/country	Tanzania	Nigeria	Tanzania	Nigeria
State and democracy				
Three powers				
Parliament_good refugee law	−.02	.14**	−.05	.05
Government_good economic policies	.11**	.04	.09**	.09**
Courts_impartial	.12**	.02	.05	.06*
Tensions in society				
Perceived conflicts				
Between rich & poor	.05	.09**	.05	.05
Between religions	.02	.00	.02	−.05
Between political sympathies	.08**	.01	.06*	−.02
Perceived maltreatments				
Because rich or poor	−.03	.10**	−.04	.07*
Because of religion	−.02	.03	−.03	−.03
Because of political sympathies	.09**	.07*	.03	−.03
Religion				
Function of religion				
Socio-spiritual religion	.16**	.05	.14**	.04
Cultural religion	.04	.15**	.06*	.09**
Religion in society				
Rel. Unfit for society	.04	.07*	.05	.02
Rel. Good for morality	.10**	−.01	.12**	.02
Religiosity				
Intellectual	.15**	.01	.11**	.03
Ideological	−.01	−.00	.11**	.01
Experience	.14**	.01	.18**	−.00
Consequence	.12**	−.01	.20**	−.02
Ritual: Prayer	.10**	−.01	.21**	−.02
Ritual participation	.13**	.01	.05	.01
Psychological dimension				
Empathy	.11**	.07*	.08**	.09**

All correlations are significant at $p < .01$ (**) or $p < .05$ (*) level (2-tailed). Interpretation of correlations: weak ($r < .15$), moderately strong ($r < .15 \leq r < .30$); strong ($r \geq .30$) associations

With reference to the perception of the state we can see a mixture of weak correlations and instances where there are no correlations between the attitudes of young Tanzanians and Nigerians towards the right to life. The same goes for the second set of variables, that is, the awareness of tensions in society and the respondents' personal experiences of maltreatment. The relationship between attitudes to capital punishment and some of the items related to this concept in the survey is also very weak.

The picture is somewhat different when we consider the perception of religion in both countries. Under this concept, we notice very slight improvements on the correlation coefficients relative to the two groups of respondents. Firstly, the perception of the role of religion with a socio-spiritual focus shows a moderately strong positive correlation with the attitudes of Tanzanian students to the prohibition of the death penalty (r = .16**). But it does not correlate at all with the Nigerian students' attitudes to the same issue. We interpret this to mean that the more the role of religion is expressed in socio-spiritual terms in Tanzanian society and is accordingly perceived by the students, the more they support the right to life. Similarly, the perception of the cultural role of religion reveals a moderate positive relationship with the respondents' attitudes towards the same right (r = .15**). This is true for the Nigerian students more than it is for their Tanzanian counterparts. In other words, the perception of the cultural role of religion significantly relates to the attitudes of the Nigerian students to the prohibition of capital punishment. Therefore, the more the respondents in Nigeria consider that religion is in line with the Zeitgeist, the more they tend to support the prohibition of capital punishment.

Furthermore, the two items, "religion is good for morality" and "religion is unfit for society" show partly weak correlations, and also a lack of any relationship to some extent, with attitudes towards the right to life. Religiosity is another important variable in our study, especially for the Tanzanian students given the concept largely exhibits moderately strong correlations (r = .15**; r = .18**; r = .20**; and r = .21**) with their attitudes towards the right to life, meaning that the more the Tanzanian students try to be religious, the more they lend support to this right. In contrast, and to our surprise based on the findings above (see Table 9.6), none of the dimensions of the religiosity concept correlate with the attitudes of the Nigerian students towards the right to life. Lastly, empathy is also positively related to the right to life but with rather weak correlation coefficients.

Thus, very few of our selected variables correlate significantly with the right to life via the two items regarding the death penalty. Comparatively, the perception of the role of religion shows a relatively stronger correlation with the respondents' attitudes towards the right to life in both countries.

Factors Predicting Young People's Attitudes Towards the Right to Life in Tanzania and Nigeria

In the following section we will investigate the factors that predict the student respondents' attitudes towards the right to life in line with our third research question. For this purpose, we conducted a regression analysis, and it is appropriate to point out here that we included only those items which show significant correlations in the regression analysis. We feel it is justified to do so because in the first instance, we conducted two regression models with all the predictor-variables and they yielded the following r-squares for Tanzania (adj. $R^2 = .092$; adj. $R^2 = .102$) and for Nigeria (adj. $R^2 = .043$; adj. $R^2 = .018$) respectively. The results of the adjusted R^2 saw no significant change when we conducted a smaller regression analysis with only the items that have significant correlations, as we can see in Table 9.11. Hence, we chose to adopt this approach here.

Table 9.11 contains the results of this analysis. The table has four columns containing the selected variables with their corresponding beta-values. The first two columns show the results of the item (the death penalty is forbidden) for Tanzania and Nigeria respectively, while the results of the second item (a death sentence should be commuted to a life sentence) are found in the last two columns. That is to say, the regression analysis has two sets of models for the purpose of this comparative study. From the betas, we get to know the impact of the selected variables on the attitudes of the respondents towards the right to life.

The Table shows that our list of selected variables generates largely low beta values. First, the results indicate that the perception of state and democracy has some effects on the attitudes of Nigeria's youth towards the right to life. In other words, the perception of the functioning of parliament has a positive impact on the item on the prohibition of the death penalty (Beta = .109***), but the latter with a beta-value of lower than .15 exhibits merely a weak impact on the dependent variable. Likewise, the notion that the governments of their respective countries have good economic policies shows some positive impact on the students' attitudes towards the right to life in the second pair of models (Beta = .117*** for Tanzania; and Beta = .065* in the case of Nigeria), but these are also lower beta-values. The only statistically significant impact we see on the first column (model 1), and in fact in the whole of the table, is in connection with the perception of the functioning of the courts, which has a moderately strong positive impact on the attitudes of Tanzania's students to the prohibition of capital punishment. We interpret this to mean that, the more the students perceive the courts to be impartial, the more they approve of the right to life. When considered holistically, in spite of the low beta-values, these findings can be viewed as potentially hinting towards the situations we reported in our earlier theoretical discussion of the poor socio-economic situation in Tanzania and the culture of impunity in Nigeria. Whereas Nigeria tends to require more or less good laws to stem the tide of impunity in its society, Tanzania appears to have more socio-economic concerns, hence the need for socio-economic justice, among others.

Table 9.11 Regression analyses for right to life (Betas)

Item/country	Death penalty is forbidden		Life imprisonment	
	Tanzania	Nigeria	Tanzania	Nigeria
State and democracy				
Three powers				
Parliament good refugee law	–	.109***	–	–
Government_good economic policies	.040	–	.117***	.065*
Courts_impartial.	.154***	–	–	.045
Tensions in society				
Perceived conflicts				
Between rich & poor	–	.043	–	–
Between pol-sympathies	.072*	–	.032	–
Perceived injustices				
Because rich or poor	–	.042	–	.053
Because-pol-sympathies	.044	.054	–	–
Religion				
Function of religion				
Socio-spiritual religion	.122***	–	.066*	–
Cultural religion	–	.114***	.051	.066*
Religion in society				
Rel. Good for morality	.043	–	.066*	–
Religiosity				
Intellectual	.074*	–	−.009	–
Ideological	–	–	.009	–
Experience	.049	–	.066*	–
Consequence	.037	–	.093**	–
Ritual: Prayer	.021	–	.134***	–
Ritual: Participation	.067*	–	–	–
Psychological dimension				
Empathy	.002	.054	−.023	.092***
Socio-demographic characteristics				
Sex *(ref. male)*				
Female	–	.062*	–	–
Religious belonging *(ref. Christians)*				
Muslims	–	−.054	−.089***	–
Age	.048	.021	.068*	–
Adj. R^2	*.080*	*.052*	*.093*	*.022*
F =	*9.389****	*8.259****	*10.846****	*6.386****
N = 2443	*1252*	*1191*		

***Reference*:** sex = male; religious belonging = Christians
*p ≤. 05; **p ≤ .01; ***p ≤ 001

The second group of variables, that is, the awareness of tensions in society, does not contribute much in explaining the attitudes of respondents towards the right to life. The same applies to the perception of religion, with the perception of the socio-spiritual role of religion accounting for almost the same amount of influence on the Tanzanian students' attitudes towards the right to life (Beta = .122***) as the cultural function of religion on the Nigerian students' attitudes towards the same right (Beta = .114***), in models 1 and 2 respectively. However, the strength of the influence is again very minimal.

Religiosity is not an important predictor as it pertains to the attitudes of our respondents towards the right to life, as we had imagined, as the variable does not have any impact on the Nigerian students' attitudes towards the right to life. It has some weak, positive effects on the Tanzanian students' attitudes towards the right, via the ritual dimension (Beta = .134***), among others. Furthermore, as with religiosity it is somewhat surprising that empathy did not contribute much to explaining the students' attitudes towards the right to life.

Lastly, the socio-demographic variables, sex and age, have only a very weak effect on attitudes towards the right to life, as is the case for religious belonging, though the Muslim respondents tend to evaluate this right less than their Christian counterparts.

On the whole, with these predictor-variables we could only account for 8% and 9% of the variance of the fundamental right to life among our Tanzanian respondents, and a paltry 5% and 2% with reference to the Nigerian students. The implication is that these variables do not explain much of the attitudes towards the right to life, as operationalised in our study. Comparatively, all the variables contributed minimally to explaining the attitudes of our study population towards this fundamental right. As far as Tanzania is concerned, the perception of state and democracy contributes relatively more than the other variables, whereas for Nigeria the perception of religion tends to be a more likely predictor of the students' attitudes.

Conclusion

In this study, we tried to compare the attitudes of young people towards the fundamental right to life in Tanzania and Nigeria. We first looked at their different backgrounds to see what the human rights situations in these two countries are, especially with regard to the fundamental right to life. It was clear to see from their political patrimonies and socio-cultural backgrounds that they share considerable similarities, for instance, in their basic values and orientations, particularly in their respect for the value of human life. Based on this, we expected both a high support for the right to life and some similarities in their attitudes towards it. However, this expectation did not correspond to the empirical findings and could be explained using several other compositional and structural factors, most of which are not covered in this study. Examples of such factors would include the poor state of the nations' economies which renders people economically poor and makes them susceptible to corruption and all forms of outlandish value systems, their educational level, their perception of the activities of politicians and state security agencies and their lack of social cohesion among the diverse ethnic nationalities, child-trafficking and prostitution, oppression, terrorism, to mention just a few. These factors contribute to the desecration of human life not just in these two countries, but also in most of Africa. As much as the difference in attitudes between the two groups did surprise us, it was more surprising that the right to life was not as highly supported as we had imagined. Reasons for this may be better explained by the factors already mentioned. Secondly, we also expected a strong relationship between the respondents' perception of religion and their attitudes towards the right to life. Again, this expectation was not confirmed. We saw only moderately strong correlations between the two variables, with Tanzanian respondents accounting for this correlation more than the Nigerians. Thirdly, we had further expected the same variable – the perception of religion – to be the strongest predictor of the attitudes of the respondents towards the right to life. This hypothesis did not correspond to our empirical findings.

Our study has both limitations and difficulties. Firstly, apart from the normal difficulty of comparing realities at such a level, our study has the additional difficulty of the paucity or even lack of empirical studies on this topic in Tanzania and Nigeria. If anything, this hindered us from further comparisons or wider verification of our findings. Secondly, this limitation of our study becomes more noticeable when one considers the fact that our independent variables did not account for much of our dependent variable. That simply means, among other things, that a better explanation of this reality would entail expanding the list of predictor-variables to include some of the factors mentioned above that could amply help to explain the negative attitudes towards the right to life in our almost completely different African context. To identify all such relevant variables can therefore be considered as a matter for further research. In the meantime, the findings of this study afford us a veritable and tentative insight into the subject matter.

References

Babalola, A. A. (2014). *The Constitutionality of death penalty: Need to amend the law*, (& II). URL: Retrieved 1 June 2016.

CIA World Factbook. (2001). *Religions*. URL: https://www.cia.gov/library/publications/the-world-factbook/fields/2122.html#ni. Retrieved on 1 June 2016.

CIA World Fact-Book Report. (2005). http://www.cia.gov/library/publicatiions/the-world-fact-book/geos/tz.html. Accessed 22 May 2014.

Constitution of Federal Republic of Nigeria. (1999).

Constitution of United Republic of Tanzania. (1977).

Dada, J. A. (2012a). Impediments to human rights protection in Nigeria. *Annual Survey of International and Comparative Law, 28*, 67–92.

Dada, J. A. (2012b). Human rights under the Nigerian constitution: Issues and problems. *International Journal of Humanities and Social Science, 2*(12), 33–43.

Death Penalty Database. (2014). *Nigeria*. URL: https://www.deathpenaltyworldwide.org/index.cfm. Retrieved on 30 September 2016.

Democracy Web. (2010). URL: http://www.democracyweb.org/about/democracyweb.php. Retrieved on 1 October 2014.

DIIS Report, 2006.

Fumbo, C. D. (2011). The Interface between human rights and the African concept of community, with special reference to the Ndali people of Tanzania. *Teofilo Kisanji University Journal, 2*(1), 1–15.

Fumbo, C. D. (2012). *The Moravian Church response to domestic abuse in Tanzania: A case study of Mbeya Municipality*. A PhD Dissertation. Dares salaam.

Fumbo, C. (2015). Human rights from a Tanzanian perspective. In H.-G. Ziebertz & G. Crpic (Eds.), *Religion and human rights, An international perspective* (pp. 183–194). Heidelberg: Springer.

Garner, B. A. (Ed.). (2009). *Black's law dictionary* (9th ed.). West: Thomson Reuters.

Global Corruption Barometer. (2013). URL: https://www.transparency.org/gcb2013/country/?country=nigeria. Accessed on 1 Dec .2015.

Glock, C. Y., & Stark, R. (1965). Religion and Society in Tension. In H. G. Ziebertz & T. Benzing (Eds., 2012). *Menschenrechte: Trotz oder Wegen Religion?* Berlin: Lit-Verlag.

Gunnar, N. (2001). *Islam and its world*. Usa-River: Makumira University Publication.

Gwangndi, M. I. (2016). The socio-legal context of the Nigerian legal system and the Shariah controversy: An analysis of its impact on some aspects of Nigerian Women's rights. *Journal of Law, Policy and Globalization, 45*, 60–66.

Hiebert, P. G. (1992). *Cultural anthropology* (2nd ed.). Grand Rapids: Baker Book House.

Igwe, L. (2008). Nigeria's educational system needs free thought. URL: http://www.secularhumanism.org/library/shb/igwe_19_2.htm. Retrieved on 25 September 2014.

Legal and Human Rights Centre [LHRC]. (2013). *Human rights opinion survey*.

Legal and Human Rights Centre [LHRC] & Zanzibar Legal Services Centre [ZLSC]. (2012). *Tanzania human rights report 2012*. Dar es Salaam/Zanzibar: LHRC& ZLSC.

Legal and Human Rights Centre [LHRC] & Zanzibar Legal Services Centre [ZLSC]. (2014). *Tanzania human rights report 2013*. Dar es Salaam / Zanzibar: LHRC & ZLSC.

Lemu, B. A. (2014). *Religious education in Nigeria – a case study*. URL: http://folk.uio.no/leirvik/OsloCoalition/AishaLemu.htm. Retrieved on 3 October 2014.

Maina, P. (Undated). A Paper on the Independence of the Judiciary in Tanzania: Many Rivers to Cross (unpublished).

Matandiko, K. (2013). Mauaji ya kutisha mkoani Simiyu Mwananchi Newspaper, 10 September 2013.

Mbiti, J. S. (1969/1989). *African religions and philosophy*. Oxford: Heinemann Educational Publishers.

Mbiti, J. S. (1970). *Concepts of God in Africa*. London: S.P.C.K.

Mbiti, J. S. (1991). *African religion and philosophy* (2nd ed.). Oxford: Heinemann.

Mbunda, L. (2014). Securing human rights through the rule of law in Tanzania. In P. T. Zeleza & P. J. Mc Connaughay (Eds.), *Human rights, the rule of law, and development in Africa* (pp. 144–156). Philiadelphia: University of Pennsylvania Press.

Mendie, A. (2014). Status and limit of human rights: Right to life under Nigerian constitution, 1999 with focus on rural women in Akwa Ibom state. *Mediterranean Journal of Social Sciences, 5*(26), 154–160.

Mesaki, S. (2010). Review of witchcraft and the law in Tanzania. *International Journal of Sociology and Anthropology, 1*(8), 132–138.

National Population Commission. (2016). Nigeria's population now 182 million. *Vanguard Newspaper*, November 10, 2016. http://www.vanguardngr.com/. Retrieved 10.11.2016.

Nigeria and the World Bank Poverty Index. *Where does that leave us?* The Nigerian Observer, March 27, 2015. URL:http://www.nigerianobservernews.com/2015/03/nigeria-and-the-world-bank-povertyindex-where-does-that-leave-us/#.V-hSd8lDqNE. Retrieved: 30 August 2016.

Nigeria Religion Statistics. (2011). URL: http://www.nationmaster.com/country/ni-nigeria/rel-religion. Retrieved on 1/8/2012.

Nigerian Administration of Criminal Justice Act. (2015). URL: http://www.justice.gov.ng/documents/CriminalJustice.pdf. Retrieved on 30 September 2016.

Nigerian Criminal Code Act. (2004).

Nigerian Police Act. (2004).

Nyerere, J. K. (1967). Freedom and Development. Dar es Salaam: United Republic of Tanzania, the Government Printer.

Obilade, A. O. (1979). *The Nigerian legal system*. Ibadan: Sweet & Maxwell.

Odoeme, P. C. (2011). *Human rights and the mission of the Church in Nigeria*. Tübingen: Lit-verlag.

Oduyoye, M. (2001). *Introducing African Women's theology*. Cleveland, Ohio: The Pilgrim Press.

Ojo, E. O. (2006). Human rights and sustainable democracy in Nigeria (1999 – 2003). *Journal of Social Science, 13*(1), 15–29.

Osaghae, E., & Suberu, T. (2005). *A history of identities, violence, and stability in Nigeria* (CRISE Working Paper 6). Oxford: Centre for Research on Inequality, Human Security and Ethnicity (CRISE).

Paden, J. (2007). Comments at the symposium on religious conflict in Nigeria: Contemporary religious dynamics in Nigeria'. In E. Okpanachi (Ed., 2012). *Ethno-religious identity and conflict in northern Nigeria*. URL: http://www.cetri.be/spip.php?article2470&lang=fr. Retrieved on 1 October 2014.

Petzell, M. (2012). The linguistic situation in Tanzania. *Moderna språk, 2012*(1), 136–144.

Pew Research Center's Religion and Public Life Project. (2010). http://www.pewforum.org/files/2010/04/sub-saharan-africa-appendix-b.pdf. Retrieved 1 June 2016.

Pew Research Center's Religion and Public Life Project. (2015). The future of world religions: Population growth projections, 2010–2050. URL: http://www.pewforum.org/2015/04/02/religious-projections-2010-2050/. Retrieved 1 June 2016.

Pew Research Centre [PEW]. (2010a). *The Pew forum on religion and public life*. http://www.pewforum.org/files/2010/09/Muslim-networks-full-report.pdf. Accessed 22 May 2014.

Pew Research Centre [PEW]. (2010b). *Muslim networks and movements in Western Europe*. Washington: Pew Research Centre's Forum on Religion and Public Life.

Pirouet, L. (1991). *Christianity worldwide: A.D. 1800 onwards*. London: SPCK.

Schilder, K. (1994). Quest for self-esteem. State, Islam, and Mundang ethnicity in northern Cameroon. African Studies Centre Research Series.

Suleyman, M. (2013). Are they the Law unto themselves? In *The Citizen Newspaper*, 8th February 2013.

Tajfel, H. (1981). *Human groups and social categories*. Cambridge: Cambridge University Press.

Tanzania Criminal Procedure Act, 1985 Cap. 20 [R.E. 2002].

Tanzania Labour Institutions Act, 2004 (Act No. 7 of 2004).

Tanzania Land Act, 1999 Cap 113 [R.E. 2002].

Tanzania Local Government (Elections) Act, Cap. 292 [R.E. 2002].

Tanzania National Census, 2012.

Tanzania National Defence Act, Cap. 192 [R.E. 2002].

Tanzania Penal Code, Cap 16 [R. E. 2002]. *www.geographia.com/tanzania/*. Accessed on 8 May 2016.

Umoru, H., & Erunke, J. (2016). Senate okays death penalty for kidnappers. *Vanguard Newspaper*, May 5, 2016. URL: http://www.vanguardngr.com/. Retrieved 01.06.2016.

UNFPA [United Nations Population Fund]. (2012). *Ageing in the twenty-first century. A celebration and a challenge*. London/New York: UNFPA.

Unicef. (2013). *Female genital mutilation/cutting, a statistical overview and exploration of the dynamics of change*. New York: Unicef.

United Republic of Tanzania. (1994). The law reform commission: Final report on designated legislation in the Nyalali Commission Report, April 1994.

United Republic of Tanzania. (2012) Population and housing census; population distribution by administrative areas, March 2013.

United Republic of Tanzania. (2013). *Population distribution by age and sex.* (i.e. Tanzania National Statistics, population 2013).
Van der Tuin, L. W. J. M., & Fumbo, C. D. (2012). Human rights and religion among Christian and Islamic students in Tanzania. In J. A. Van der Ven & H. G. Ziebertz (Eds.), *Tensions within and between religions and human rights*. Brill: Leiden.
Van der Ven, J. A., Dreyer, J. S., & Pieterse, H. J. C. (2004). Is there a god of human rights? The complex relationship between human rights and religion. In *A south African case*. Leiden: Brill.
Vanhoozer, K. J. (1993). The world well staged? Theology, culture, and hermeneutics. In D. A. Carson & J. D. Woodbridge (Eds.), *God and culture* (pp. 1–30). Grand Rapids Michigan: William B. Eerdmans Publishing Company.
Ziebertz, H. G., Döhnert, S., & Unser, A. (2018). Predictors of attitudes towards human dignity: An empirical analysis among youth in Germany. In H. G. Ziebertz & C. Sterkens (Eds.), *Religion and civil human rights in empirical perspective*. Cham: Springer.

Chapter 10
Religion and Attitudes Towards Abortion and Euthanasia Among Young People in Poland and Norway

Pål Ketil Botvar, Claudia Sarti, Katarzyna Zielińska, and Marcin K. Zwierżdżyński

This article compares attitudes towards abortion and euthanasia in two countries with different Christian traditions. Poland is a former communist country with a strong Catholic tradition. Norway is a highly secularized Scandinavian country with a dominating Lutheran Church. The two countries have different legal frameworks regarding abortion and euthanasia. We aim here to investigate the connection between religion and attitudes towards abortion and euthanasia. Our methodological approach is "most different systems design". If one finds similar patterns in countries with different religious and political cultures, there is reason to believe that the findings will also apply to other countries. Though the two countries differ with respect to political and religious culture, we find interesting similarities between them. In both countries, religiosity has a negative impact on attitudes towards abortion and euthanasia; this means that the most religious people also have the most negative attitudes regarding these issues. Views regarding the role religion should perform in society are also strong predictors of attitudes. In both countries, those who think that church and religion should actively influence society have negative attitudes towards abortion and euthanasia while those who think church and religion should adapt to trends in society support both abortion and euthanasia as a right.

P. K. Botvar (✉)
KIFO Institute for Church, Religion, and Worldview Research, Oslo, Norway
e-mail: pal.ketil.botvar@kifo.no

C. Sarti
Emory University, Atlanta, GA, USA

K. Zielińska
Jagiellonian University, Kraków, Poland
e-mail: katarzyna.zielinska@uj.edu.pl

M. K. Zwierżdżyński
Jagiellonian University, Kraków, Poland

H.-G. Ziebertz, F. Zaccaria (eds.), *Euthanasia, Abortion, Death Penalty and Religion – The Right to Life and its Limitations*, Religion and Human Rights 4, https://doi.org/10.1007/978-3-319-98773-6_10

Theoretical Introduction

Changing Social Role of Religion and Impact on Individual Attitudes

The societal impact of religious traditions and level of religiosity has been the subject of a variety of theoretical discussions and empirical investigations. In the following, we summarise some of the main outcomes of these deliberations and set up a theoretical background for our investigation, focusing on a comparison of students' attitudes towards right to life (i.e., abortion and euthanasia) in countries with different religious traditions: namely, Catholic-dominated Poland and Lutheran-dominated Norway. Though we stress different 'religious traditions', the two countries in fact share biblical and traditional teachings on abortion and euthanasia. This means that, when we refer to religious students and the impact of religion on their attitudes about abortion and euthanasia, we are mainly talking about a comparison of Lutheran Christians and Catholic Christians.

Weber and the Protestant Ethic

Max Weber's study of the social distinctions of Protestantism and Catholicism is a classic investigation of a link between religious confessions and social practices (Weber 1904/2011). One of his conclusions is that the work ethic underpinned by Protestant doctrines played a crucial role in the development of capitalist economy. Weber argued that the spread of a Puritan ethic in Northern Europe paved the way for entrepreneurship, for accumulation of resources and eventually for modern capitalism. Many Protestants thought that hard work was an indication of salvation and thus a good afterlife. On the opposite side, the Catholic Church assured salvation to all those who accepted the sacraments of the Church and submitted to clerical authority.

Much water has run into the sea since Weber made his famous analysis. Along with secularisation, the spread of social and economic rights has undermined some of the cultural differences rooted in different religious traditions in Europe. One important change that has occurred in the last century is the establishment of welfare states which provide social security to their inhabitants. Even if very few traces of the so-called Protestant work ethic remain, religious cultures tend to leave a mark on societies by influencing adherence to certain values, beliefs and practises.

Max Weber was one of the first scholars to proclaim that modernisation would lead to secularisation. During the 1960s to 1980s, this was the dominating paradigm within the sociology of religion. Based on what was happening in many countries during the 1980s and 1990s, more nuanced theories were brought to the fore. One of the most prominent critics of traditional secularisation theory is the Latin-American scholar, José Casanova (1994). He criticises traditional secularisation theories for being too simple and linear.

Casanova's De-privatisation Thesis

The development of multicultural societies in the West has given religion a more prominent place in the public sphere. It is becoming both more visible and more contested. Casanova (1994, 2003) describes this process as the *de-privatisation* of religion. New forms of *public religion* are emerging primarily because religious actors are protesting against the marginalization of religion (Casanova 1994: 5). The new visibility of religion has led to heated debates in the mass media and disputes between religious and non-religious people. It also translates into more general questions about the border between the sacred and secular and about the role of secular and religious citizens in liberal democracies (see e.g., Habermas 2008; Rawls 1997; Weithman 2002; Wolterstorff 1997).

Casanova (1994) discusses the relations of three different theories of secularisation: the differentiation theory, the privatisation theory and the decline theory. According to him, the differentiation of religion from other fields of society does not necessarily lead to privatisation and decline. This view contradicts classical secularisation theory as represented, for example, in the work of Peter Berger (1967). In the 1960s, Peter Berger predicted a growing privatisation of religion. Casanova's empirical examples, on the contrary, point in the direction of religion becoming more public (or de-privatised) in recent decades.

One of the aspects of Casanova's theory of public religion is the role of religious actors. Based on empirical examples, Casanova shows how religious actors played an active role in the process of making religion relevant in the public sphere during the 1980s and 1990s. Based on empirical data from countries as diverse as the United States, Spain, Brazil and Poland, Casanova postulates a continued 'politicisation' and de-privatisation of religion in Western societies. This means that religion and political matters have become more and more intertwined and that religion has gained a more prominent place in the public sphere.

Pippa Norris and Roland Inglehart: Religion and Country Characteristics

Two other scholars who have discussed and criticised traditional secularization theory are Norris and Inglehart (2004). They refer to Weber's idea that the rise of a rational worldview has undermined the foundations of faith in the supernatural. From this perspective, the era of the Enlightenment generated a rational view of the world based on empirical standards of proof, scientific knowledge of natural phenomena, and technological mastery of the universe.

Norris and Inglehart agree with scholars who criticise theories of inevitable religious decline. Their own theory of secularisation based on existential security rests on two axioms: The first is that rich and poor nations differ sharply in their conditions of human security and thereby differ with respect to religiosity; the other is the assumption that religious traditions have shaped the cultures of each nation in an enduring fashion, and that these values are transmitted to citizens even if they are not active in a church, mosque, or the like. Norris and Inglehart predict that the level of religiosity depends on the level of *perceived security*. Both the level and type of religiosity in a country reflect the religious tradition that has historically dominated it. According to Norris and Inglehart, the major faiths of the world express divergent teachings and doctrines regarding many moral values and normative beliefs – such as those surrounding the roles of women and men, the sanctity of life, and the importance of marriage and family. This means that religious traditions still have potential to influence social questions in contemporary society – especially those questions that are related to private morality and family matters.

Max Weber was one of the first scholars to stress the differences between Catholics and Protestants. His work on differences in work ethic is a classic in the sociology of religion. Moreover, even if some of the differences related to work ethic have diminished, dominant religious cultures tend to influence societies even after a long period of secularization. One of the themes of this article is to consider the extent to which Catholics and Protestants still differ in their views on moral questions. José Casanova introduces views regarding the role of religion in society as a factor behind the new visibility of religion in the public sphere. In this article, we look at role of religion as a possible explanatory factor *vis-à-vis* moral questions. Norris and Inglehart argue that, even in highly secularised societies, religion may influence moral questions – especially those related to life and death or family matters. According to Norris and Inglehart, the impact of religion is connected to the level of security in a given society.

Historical Background and Legal Situation of Euthanasia and Abortion

To understand the different empirical results in the two samples, we present some background information related to the political and legal situations of the two countries in what follows.

Poland: Background Information

Compared to Norway, Poland is much more religiously homogenous and less secularised. The Roman Catholic Church holds a dominant position in Polish society both demographically and symbolically. As of 2012, approximately 93% of the population self-identify as belonging to the Roman Catholic Church, and about 4.2% identify as non-believers, atheists or agnostics. About 8% identify themselves as belonging to other religions (mostly Orthodox or Protestant Churches) (Boguszewski 2012, 1). The political and symbolic position of the Roman Catholic Church in Polish society results from certain historical developments. Roman Catholicism became interwoven with Polish national identity, and the Church played the role of an institution representing the nation in opposition to foreign (i.e., during the partition of Poland between Prussia, Russia and Austria-Hungary in XIX c.)

or illegitimate (i.e., communist times) rule (Casanova 1994, 92–93; Zubrzycki 2006, 36–39; Borowik 2002, 241).

However, Catholicism has been a dominant religion in Poland for centuries. At the beginning of the twentieth century, many religions co-existed on Polish ground. In 1918, Poland regained its sovereignty. According to a second general census of the population taken in 1931 (which counted almost 32 million inhabitants), Poland was a multi-religious country[1] with over 20.5 million Roman Catholics, over 3 million Easter Rite Catholics, more than 3.5 million Orthodox, over 3 million Jews, almost 1 million Protestants (mostly Lutheran Evangelical) and others. This census provides insight into the historical religious pluralism of Polish society.

After the fall of the Communist regime, the Roman Catholic Church had a very strong and respected position in Polish society. This authority was used in the Church's craving for more political power – especially at the beginning of the 1990s (e.g., in case of religious education in public schools, see Zielińska and Zwierżdżyński 2013). However, the public presence and religio-political activity of the Roman Catholic Church in Poland still proves the re-publicization of religion in Poland (Herbert and Fras 2009) or the existence of a clerical democracy (Ramet 2007, 120). Examples include the church's presence in the mass media, links to right-wing political parties, the episcopate's guidance of voters in the EU accession referendum, strong support for the inclusion of a reference to God in the EU constitutional preamble, recent fierce opposition to *in-vitro* fertilization, and support for pro-life movements.

The existing data also indicate the high level of religiosity of the Polish population. As noted above, in 2012, 94% of population identified as believers; only 8% identified as non-believers. This identification is accompanied by a relatively high level of religious practice. More than 50% of the population goes to church at least one or more times per week (Boguszewski 2015). Among the youth (18–24 years old), religiosity also remains at a relatively high level (especially in comparison to many other European countries). In recent years, however, we can see a decline in the number of youth who identify themselves as believing (from 86% in 2004 to 77% in 2014). At the same time, we can notice a growing number of non-believers (from 6% in 2005 to 15% in 2014) (Boguszewski 2014).

Abortion and Euthanasia: The Legal Situation in Poland

Since 1993, Poland has had one of the most restrictive abortion laws in Europe, and the issue is subject to intense political controversy. However, abortion was readily available before 1993. The Polish code of 1932 allowed induced abortion after rape, incest, or certain medical indications. This liberalization of abortion—especially

[1] Original title: *Drugi Powszechny Spis Ludnośći z dnia 9 grudnia 1931 r.* Główny Urzad Statystyczny Rzeczypospolitej Polskiej, Statystyka Poslki, Seria C, Zeszyt 94a. The original document from 1931 is available at: http://statlibr.stat.gov.pl/exlibris/aleph/a22_1/apache_media/VUNVGMLANSCQQFGYHCN3VDLK12A9U5.pdf

with regard to various medical indications for abortion—was due to the struggle in 1920s intellectual circles against the 'Women's Hell' (a phrase which refers to 'botched, back-street abortions'). The communist government changed the law on abortion in 1956, enacting the *Abortion Admissibility Law* in April of that year. Under the new provision, abortion within the first trimester was allowed upon demand based on a woman's difficult economic or social circumstances. Moreover, in 1959, the Ministry of Health issued a regulation that allowed abortion on request. Even though the pro-life Catholic groups tried to restrict this law, abortion was widely accessible until 1991. Already in the period of the first democratic elections in 1989, during which the *Solidarność* party won, experts of the episcopate prepared a draft of a new law to criminalize abortion, forbidding this procedure under any circumstances. This church initiative and several bills outlawing abortion were discussed in the Polish parliament. In April of 1990, the Ministry of Health enacted a regulation limiting abortion. Before the eventual Unborn Child Protection Bill was voted on, the Senate's Commission on Human Rights (Jankowska 1991) rejected the draft. The first public debate on the Unborn Child Protection Bill took place in 1990, just a year before the visit of Pope John Paul II. It is often seen as a gift to the Polish pope, who paid tribute to the criminalization of abortion by the state. Eventually, in January of 1993,[2] the Act on Family Planning, Human Embryo Protection and Conditions of Permissibility of Abortion was passed by the Parliament. Abortion is allowed in the first trimester and may only be obtained in the following circumstances (Section 4 (a)):

1 *An abortion can be carried out only by a physician when,*
   a) *pregnancy endangers the mother's life or health;*
   b) *prenatal tests or other medical findings indicate a high risk that the foetus will be severely and irreversibly damaged or suffer from an incurable, life-threatening disease;*
   c) *there are strong grounds for believing that the pregnancy is a result of a criminal act.*
2 *In the cases listed above under b), an abortion may be performed until such time as the foetus is capable of surviving outside the mother's body; in cases listed under 3) above, an abortion may be performed until the end of the 12th week of pregnancy.*

Despite the restrictive abortion law, which is still in force, there are many underground abortion clinics, and an increasing number of Polish women travel to surrounding countries for this procedure – often to Germany. According to the Polish Federation of Women and Planned Parenthood, there are around 27,000 teenage pregnancies and more than 150,000 abortions yearly; most of them occur in the 'Polish abortion underground'. In 2008, there were 499 lawful, registered abortions in the hospitals and no record of unlawful abortion.[3]

In the past decade, pro-life movements and right-wing politicians, supported by representatives of the Roman Catholic Church in Poland, have attempted to further tighten the law to outlaw abortion completely, or at least to impose further limitations

[2] This restrictive law was briefly liberalized by an amendment in 1996 which allowed abortion on social grounds; however, this amendment was found unconstitutional in 1997 by the Constitutional Tribunal.

[3] See: http://wyborcza.pl/1,76842,7218275,Raport_o_aborcji_w_2008_roku.html

(e.g., to ban abortion in case of the foetus' deformation). The references to the right to life for every person (for 'unborn children' and disabled people), guaranteed by both the Polish constitution and the UDHR, serve as justifications for such claims. On the other hand, the feminist movement has mobilized to liberalise the existing law (or, as in the case of the recent 'Black Protest', it mobilised a much broader group of women, often indifferent to feminist claims, just to maintain already restricted access to abortion).[4] The movement legitimises its claims by references to human rights, stressing women's rights to self-determination, health and life.

Like abortion, euthanasia is also stirring public discussion. Euthanasia used to be seen as a question of public morality, but it has now turned into a question of the rights of the individual. In Poland, euthanasia is a crime against life, as is stated in Article 150 of the Criminal Code: "Whoever commits a killing of a human being at his/her request and under the influence of compassion for the person, shall be sentenced to 3 months and up to 5 years of imprisonment. In special cases, the court may exceptionally avoid the sentence and even waive the punishment". These exceptions relate, for example, to the case of persistent therapy which makes agony longer or to MDs actions aimed at reducing patient's pain. Article 151 anticipates, that "who by persuasion or by helping another human being makes him/her take their own life, is subject to imprisonment from 3 months up to 5 years". Commentary on the Criminal Code, which includes the interpretation of this paragraph, treats euthanasia as any action aimed at taking away someone's life under influence of compassion and individual demand (Pacian and Kulik 2011).

Polish criminal law treats euthanasia as a murder at somebody's request and because of empathy. So, two conditions must be fulfilled to speak about euthanasia in Poland: the request of the initiator (victim), and the compassion of the executor (lawbreaker). The former is clearly defined: The request has to be clear, conscious, firm and free of any pressure, made by a person who is able to recognize his/her condition. It means that mentally ill people, adolescents and those who are under custody cannot submit the demand. The latter is much harder to determine; compassion, an emotion, cannot be defined by objective qualifications.

Polish juridical literature distinguishes between passive and active euthanasia (Barnard 1985). The former (called negative) is defined as a discontinuation of medical treatment while the latter (called positive) means an act causing someone's death by delivering drug or poison, etc. However, the Polish Penal Code has a problem distinguishing passive euthanasia from withdrawal of persistent therapy (Śliwka and Gałęska-Śliwka 2011). As Marek Safjan, former president of Polish Constitutional Tribunal, states, "there are moral and ethical reasons to state that disconnecting a human being from artificial nutrition system in such situation is not euthanasia but only the discontinuation of an already initiated – through temporally extended – dying process".[5]

[4] "Black Protest" is the name of the massive protests across Poland in 2016 against a proposal to ban abortions in almost all circumstances. Many women dressed in black to mourn the death of women's rights.

[5] http://www.roik.pl/wieloletnie-sztuczne-odzywianie-nie-jest-uporczywa-terapia-w-polsce-zaprzestanie-go-wobec-osoby-w-satnie-wegetatywnym-byloby-eutanazja/

The legal regulations concerning euthanasia in Poland raise many doubts. The problem is deepened by the fact that the legal aspects are frequently mixed with ethical and medical ones. However, euthanasia in Poland, unlike abortion, is discussed scientifically (especially with respect to 'living will' institutions) rather than socially. It is not the subject of Polish parliamentary discourse; it does not bring any emotional public statements, organised group protest or social-media campaigns. Polish literature distinguishes between discontinuation of care (which means euthanasia) and discontinuation of treatment (which is not euthanasia). The legalisation of euthanasia faces two main obstacles: (1) conscious and free consent, and (2) respecting a person's dignity, which is presumed in Polish Constitution (Szeroczyńska 2004).

Norway: Background Information

According to opinion polls, Norwegians are among the least religious people in Europe; they are surpassed only by Estonia, the Czech Republic, Denmark and Sweden (Norris and Inglehart 2004). The relation between church and state in Norway could until recently be described as a state-church system. However, in 2012, this system was formally abandoned when the Norwegian Parliament voted to amend the 1814 Constitution. The state-church system favouring the national Lutheran church had come under pressure because of the country's growing religious diversity. The close relation of church and state was thus seen as problematic *vis-à-vis* the principle of religious freedom.

Nonetheless, around 75% of the Norwegian population still belong to the national Lutheran church, and a significant number use church services such as baptism, confirmation, church marriage and church burial. At the same time, a growing number of people belong to other religious organisations or do not belong to any religious organisation at all. In recent years, Muslims have become the largest religious group outside the national church; they today account for about 6% of the Norwegian population and about 20% in the capital of Oslo. The situation in the large cities of Norway differs from that of the rural areas when it comes to the effects of ethnic and religious pluralisation. Norway has been a parliamentary democracy since the 1880s.

Abortion and Euthanasia in Norway

Current Norwegian legislation and public-health policy provides for abortion on demand in the first 12 weeks of pregnancy, by application up to the 18th week, and thereafter only under special circumstances until the foetus is viable, which is presumed to be at 21 weeks.

Gradually, the laws on abortion underwent liberalization thanks to activism from pro-choice groups in society. A milestone for the issue of abortion on demand came in 1978 when the Labour Party and Socialist Left party passed the current law with a one-vote majority, which provides for abortion upon request up to 12 weeks of pregnancy and after that with the agreement of a medical commission, taking the woman's own views into consideration.

The Lutheran national church has frequently protested the liberalization of the abortion law. In 1978, the bishops wrote a pastoral letter (*'hyrdebrev'*) to the Norwegian people and the government against the 1978 law. The letter was read from the pulpit in all the churches. This is the first time such a letter had been written since World War II. When the parliament voted in favour of the new liberal law, one of the bishops resigned as an act of protest. In addition, the Christian People's Party has fought for a more restrictive abortion law. Because of the activism of the Christian party, political discussion about the abortion law has continued every year.

However, not much has changed in the law on abortion in recent decades. New technology allowing pregnant women to detect abnormalities in the foetus at an early stage of pregnancy has, however, caused new debate about abortion. In 1994, the Christian People's party tried to introduce a clause defining the foetus as a human being with its own rights from the moment of conception, but the other parties turned the proposal down. In reality, the main discussions have concerned so-called selective abortion. *Selective abortion* refers to choosing to abort a foetus because the foetus is likely to be born with some birth defect or impairment or the mother does not prefer the sex of the foetus. The two left-wing parties, the Labour and Socialist Left parties, have had different views on this matter. While the Labour Party has generally applied its views on abortion to selective abortion, the Socialist Left has expressed fears that permissive diagnostic procedures could send out wrong signals: e.g., that the disabled are of less value than the able-bodied.

Euthanasia is illegal according to Norwegian law. However, there have been some court-cases, and the result is that the caretaker (doctor) receives reduced punishment for taking the life of someone who consents to it. Euthanasia is heavily discussed in the media, and public opinion has become more and more permissive on the topic. The right-wing Progress Party want to legalize some forms of euthanasia and has put this question into the party program.

Even if the two countries differ with regard to the political history and legal situation, one might find a similar pattern when it comes to the role of religion *vis-a-vis* attitudes towards ethical and political issues such as abortion and euthanasia.

Conceptual Elaboration of Key Terms

The Dependent Variables

In the empirical analyses, we use attitudes towards abortion and euthanasia as dependent variables. Attitudes toward abortion and euthanasia are sometimes seen as indicators of views regarding the right to life. However, this way of interpreting the matter is controversial. Both pro-life and pro-choice groups in society refer to the discourse on human rights, often offering different interpretations. The strong public presence and influence of a given religion may help to institutionalise and give hegemony to certain religious interpretations (Minkenberg 2003). This implies a specific interpretation of Article 3 of the Universal Declaration of Human Rights (UDHR). The right to live means the right to live from conception until natural death. Many active Christians regard abortion as against the principle of a human being's right to life. However, churches differ in their opinions and official positions on the issue; their views range from the Catholic and conservative evangelical churches' support for a complete ban on abortion to the much more liberal approach of some liberal Protestant Churches. The strong political position of the Roman Catholic Church has had a significant impact on Polish law regarding abortion. The situation differs in the case of Norway. Though the Lutheran majority church in Norway sees the unborn child as created by God with a right to live, it still believes that abortion is sometimes morally acceptable – for example, when the health of the woman is at risk or the baby is suffering from a serious disability. On the other hand, the pro-choice side of the debate seems to focus on the rights of women to life and self-determination, bodily integrity, and health. The absolutisation of the right to life of an 'unborn child' is seen as a ground for potential conflict between the rights of the foetus over the rights of a woman (Zielińska 2015: 147).

Besides the national penal-law regulations, the prohibition of active euthanasia in most countries is based on numerous legal regulations regarding human rights. For example, Article 6 of the International Covenant on Civil and Political Rights states that, "Every human being has the inherent right to life. This right shall be protected by law. No one shall be arbitrarily deprived of his life". In turn, Article 2 of the European Convention on Human Rights states that, "Every human being has the inherent right to life. This right shall be protected by law. No one shall be arbitrarily deprived of his life".

As in case of abortion, discussions of euthanasia illustrate the clash between different dimensions of human rights: the right to life (ECHR Article 2) and the right to respect for private and family life (ECHR Article 8). The cases brought to the European Court of Human Rights concerning the right to a dignified death or the right to end of life often invoke three articles in addition to Article 8 of the ECHR: Article 3, prohibition of inhuman or degrading treatment; Article 9, freedom of conscience; and Article 14, prohibition of discrimination.

Arguments supporting euthanasia are rooted in a fundamental right to decide whether to end one's own life, which can be seen as a matter of human dignity, autonomy, privacy and safety (Shala and Gusha 2016). On the other hand, those who regard the sanctity of life to be undebatable support the ban on euthanasia. Religion plays an important role in strengthening such interpretations of human rights with regard to euthanasia. This applies to both the Catholic Church and the National Lutheran Church in Norway.

In the empirical analyses, we look at factors which explain attitudes towards abortion and euthanasia in both countries. The questions regarding abortion in the questionnaire are all concerned with the circumstances in which abortion can be justified. Respondents answer on a five-point Likert scale (1 = disagree completely, 5 = agree completely).

The seven statements are as follows:

- Abortion should be prohibited in all circumstances because it terminates a human life (reversed).
- Abortion should be permitted in case of rape.
- Abortion should be permitted in case of incest.
- Abortion should be permitted when there is a strong chance of serious defect in the baby.
- Abortion should be permitted when the woman's own health is seriously endangered by the pregnancy.
- Abortion should be permitted when the woman cannot afford any more children economically.
- Abortion should be permitted when the woman cannot afford any more children psychologically.

These seven questions are highly interrelated, which means that they can be used in an additive index. Based on the Polish sample, the reliability score of the abortion index was .90 (Cronbach's alpha) and .87 in the Norwegian case.

Three questions in the questionnaire deal with euthanasia. Two of them are rather similar and are therefore not properly understood in both countries. Because of this, we had to stick to two of the questions when making the index. In this case, the Cronbach's alpha is .73 in the Polish sample and .67 in the Norwegian one.

- Euthanasia should be prohibited in all circumstances (reversed).
- Euthanasia should be permitted in the case of unbearable and irreversible suffering.

Based on reliability analyses of the variables, we construct similar indices for the two countries. One measures attitudes towards the permission of abortion (based on seven items), and one measures attitudes towards the permission of euthanasia (based on two items). The variables are organized such that low values indicate no acceptance of abortion/euthanasia while high values indicate acceptance. In the empirical analyses, we shall see how the two indices relate to each other and what factors are best suited to explain attitudes towards abortion and euthanasia.

The Independent Variables

Based on the theoretical considerations, we are mainly interested in four sets of independent variables: affiliation with major Christian traditions (Protestantism vs. Catholicism), religiosity, view regarding the role of religion in society, and security orientation. Religious affiliation is operationalised as religious group membership and is measured by religious self-identification. Individual religiosity is measured by using the Huber and Huber (2012) religiosity index based on five items: namely, interest in religious questions, belief in God, religious experiences, praying frequency and service participation.

Five questions are used in the questionnaire:

- How often do you think about religious issues?
- To what extent do you believe that God or something divine exists?
- How often do you experience situations in which you have the feeling that God or something divine intervenes in your life?
- How often do you pray?
- How often do you take part in religious services at a church or mosque or another place?

The Cronbach's alpha for the religiosity index is .89 for Poland and .81 for Norway.

In addition to these variables, we introduce one more variable related to religion: namely, views on the role of religion in society. This variable is intended to tap views regarding the preferred role of churches and other religious organizations in society: i.e., to what extent one thinks religious organisations should perform an active versus a passive role in society and whether or not churches should try to influence political decisions. Attitudes regarding these questions are related to what one thinks about religion in the public sphere (cf., Casanova 1994).

In the questionnaire, ten questions/statements are used to measure five different views on the role of religion in society. Based on the whole sample, the reliabilities of four of the indices are acceptable (Cronbach's alpha >.60). The view that religion should be a 'public prophetic voice' exhibits low alpha values. We therefore have to use only one indicator for this dimension. The nine statements are as follows:

(a) Influence on public opinion

  - Religions should try to influence public opinion on social problems.
  - Religions should use their authority to intervene in societal affairs.

(b) Public prophetic voice

  - Religions should take public responsibility for social development.

(c) Cultural conformity

  - Religions should go along with changing ideas in society.
  - Religions should always keep up with current social trends.

(d) Spiritual service

  - Religions should take responsibility for their members' spiritual growth.
  - Religions should create places for deep spiritual experiences.

(e) National culture

  - Religions should take joint responsibility with the state for our national culture.
  - Religions should consolidate the nation against alien influence and the deprivation of its originality.

To follow up the theory of Norris and Inglehart, we introduce a variable we call security orientation. Based on Schwartz and Sagiv (1995), ten different individual values are measured: self-direction, power, security, hedonism, benevolence, achievement, stimulation, conformity, universalism and tradition. The values 'security' and 'stimulation' are opposite orientations. The first one describes a person who seeks security and safety; the other is about seeking risk and adventure. To have a robust measure of security orientation, we have made an index based on the two questions. The value regarding risk seeking is reversed before we use it in the index.

As background variables, we use gender, age of student, the educational level of student's parents and political preferences.

Conceptual Model

The conceptual model displays the following three groups of variables: first, the dependent variables (in this case, the students' attitudes towards abortion and euthanasia); second, the independent variables (in this case, the religious variables including the view regarding the role of religion in society and security orientation); and lastly, the control variables (in this case, the students' population characteristics, such as gender, age, political preference, and parents' educational level). The conceptual model also displays the relationships between these groups, symbolised by the arrows indicating the impact of one group on the other – in this study, the impact of the religious variables and values on attitudes towards abortion and euthanasia, controlling for the impact of the population characteristics (Fig. 10.1).

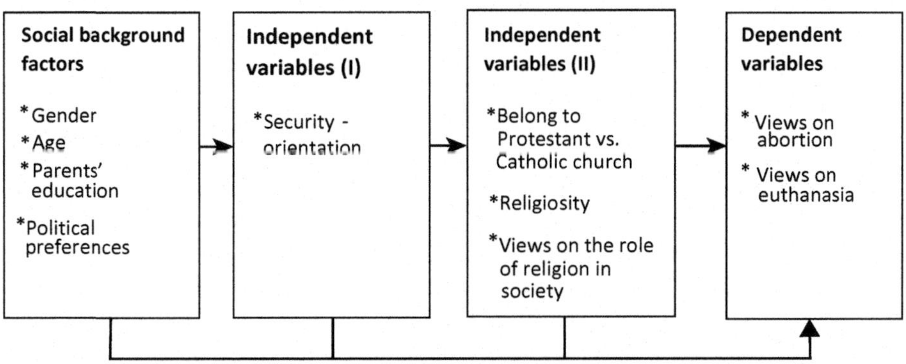

Fig. 10.1 Conceptual model

Research Questions, Method and Sample

Research Questions

In this section, we identify our research questions, describe our data-collection process, and describe the research sample, data collection, and statistical methods to be used in what follows.

Based on the theories of José Casanova (1994) and Norris and Inglehart (2004), we formulate the following research questions:

(a) Do Catholics and Protestants have different views on moral questions? (Weber)
(b) Are views regarding the role of religion in society important as explanatory factors *vis-à-vis* moral questions? (Casanova)
(c) Is religiosity an important factor in explaining attitudes towards moral questions? (Norris & Inglehart)
(d) Is security orientation an important factor in relation to religiosity and moral questions? (Norris & Inglehart)

Method

The selection of the two countries reflects one of two different strategies used in comparative research: the most different systems design (MDSD). In this approach, the aim is to maximise the number of variables with respect to which the system differs in order to isolate the phenomenon being studied (Anckar 2008). If one finds similar patterns related to certain selected areas in very different countries, there is good reason to believe that the findings will also apply to other countries. We have chosen to look at two countries that differ both with respect to Christian tradition (Roman Catholic vs. Lutheran-Protestant) and with respect to political culture and democratic history.

Data Collection

This study was conducted in the period 2014–2015 in or around large cities in Poland and Norway. The Polish sample consists of two integrated datasets.

The first was collected from different types of schools (technical, vocational and general high schools) in Krakow and in small cities of the Malopolska *voivodeship*. In addition, we also contacted schools located in different parts of Poland which offer religious education other than Catholic (we used this as an indication of the presence of religious minorities). The data was collected via an electronic, online version of the questionnaire. To gather the data, we sent letters to schools addressed to pupils; these letters were then delivered to the students by the schoolteachers. In the letters, we explained the aim of our study and provided access to the online version of the questionnaire. We received 443 completed surveys.

The second dataset, which consists of 1211 respondents, was collected from seventeen upper-level secondary schools and one university. The students came from Warsaw (34.8% of participants), Poznań (32.6% of participants) and Olsztyn (32.5% of participants). Between June and December of 2015, the students filled in paper questionnaires in various classes, including classes in religion, philosophy, history and society. Because the directors needed to give permission to allow this research in most of the schools, the schools were contacted in person by the researcher. Every school received clear information about the intention of the study and how the survey had to be conducted. Because of the sensitive topics discussed in the questionnaires, most of the directors allowed the study to take place only in the last class of the secondary school, as these students are mature and it is not necessary to ask parents to allow them to participate. Consequently, 77.2% of the students surveyed are 18 years of age and older.

The Krakow sample includes some students from rural areas outside of Krakow. The Krakow students are somewhat younger on average than the Warsaw/Poznań/Olsztyn students. There are also some differences between the two Polish samples when it comes to the parents' education. The Warsaw/Poznań/Olsztyn students have parents who are educated at the university level more often than the Krakow students. When it comes to religiosity, Krakow students are on average more religious than Warsaw/Poznań/Olsztyn students. We expect these differences to be real differences related to the urban/rural dimension. Taken together, the two datasets are comprised of students between 15 and 24 years of age who are living in or near large cities in Poland.

In Norway, the sample was collected from 20 upper-secondary schools in the Oslo area – on average, from two classes from each participating school. The survey was conducted in the classrooms, resulting in a response rate of around 90%. The pupils completed the questionnaires in regular religious-education or social-studies classes during the school day with pencil and paper. The sample consists of students aged 16 to 20 attending this level of public school. Most of the students had studied religion and ethics during the previous year. This probably made them more prepared than other students to answer questions related to human rights and religion.

Population Description

Comparison of the two samples shows a much more religiously diversified sample in Norway than in Poland. In addition, the Polish group declares religious belonging and practices more often than the Norwegian sample. The Norwegian sample has a higher percentage of youth who identify as non-religious.

First, we compare the mean scores on the social-background variables. Females are overrepresented in the Polish sample (60%) but not in the Norwegian one (50%). In addition, the two country groups differ with respect to political preferences and

Table 10.1 Sample characteristics, Poland and Norway. Percent (except age)

	Poland (N = 1657)	Norway (N = 1001)	Sign.
Mean age	18.0	18.2	**
Female	60.0	50.5	**
Father born on another continent	1.0	15.1	**
Mother born on another continent	0.4	15.3	**
Father with education at university level	52.1	64.1	**
Mother with education at university level	40.9	64.0	**
Leaning to the political left	46.6	38.2	**
Leaning to the political right	53.4	61.8	**
Identify with Catholicism	61.9	2.1	**
Identify with Protestantism	1.0	31.8	**
Identify with Islam	0.5	6.9	**
Identify as non-religious	22.0	46.8	**
Believe in God or higher power	63.7	36.0	**
Pray at least weekly	29.7	12.6	**
Attend religious rituals at least monthly	45.2	9.6	**

**Sign on the 0.001-level (two-tailed)

the education level of parents. Norwegian students generally have more highly educated parents than Polish students. However, this may be a result of different sampling methods in the two countries. The Polish sample was collected in metropolitan areas (Warsaw, Kraków and Poznań) and in medium or small towns across Poland whereas the Norwegian sample is limited to the capital city.

The Polish students lean more to the left side of the political spectrum than the Norwegians do. When it comes to the religious variables, the Polish students have a higher score than the Norwegians on all variables which measure religiosity and are included in the religiosity index. The difference between countries in percentage of parents born on another continent also suggests a much higher level of cultural diversity among Norwegian than Polish participants. This also holds if we compare the religious diversity of the samples (Table 10.1).

Statistical Methods

We used variance analysis to compare the means for both control variables and dependent and independent variables among the subpopulations of Christians and Muslims.

We used ordinary linear regression analysis to investigate the impact of religiosity and security orientation on attitudes towards abortion and euthanasia. The methods are described briefly in what follows.

Anova

Polish youth and Norwegian youth were compared. We also compared those who identify as Catholics, Protestants and non-religious. Most measurements use a five-point Likert scale (1 for low value to 5 for high value).

Regression Analysis

Regression analyses are used to examine what impact the religious variables and other personal values have on support for abortion and judicial euthanasia. For this article, a limited number of independent variables (i.e., religiosity and security orientation) and control variables (i.e., population characteristics) are selected.

The scales used in the regression analyses are all on the ordinal level (except for gender, religious affiliation), but they may be analysed on an interval level. We conducted four regression analyses, analysing attitudes towards abortion and euthanasia in Poland and Norway.

Empirical Research

In this part, we report the scores for Polish and Norwegian youth with respect to the different variables and indices in the model. In some cases, we also compare religious groups within each country. Then we report two step-wise regression analyses with abortion and euthanasia as dependent variables.

Comparisons of Polish and Norwegian Youth

We compare the scores with respect to indicators used to construct the dependent variable before we show the scores with respect to independent variables.

Table 10.2 shows that the Norwegian students are more permissive than the Polish students on all questions related to abortion. The largest differences between the two countries have to do with abortion on social criteria: i.e., when the mother is unfit to have a/another child. The attitudes are more similar when it comes to euthanasia. In both countries, a clear majority is open to euthanasia in cases of irreversible suffering.

Table 10.3 compares Protestants and Catholics with the group of non-religious students in each country. When it comes to abortion, there are clear differences in both countries between the non-religious and those identifying with the majority churches. Both groups are more permissive in Norway than in Poland. Regarding euthanasia, the differences between Catholics and non-religious persons in Poland are striking. In Norway, on the other hand, the two groups more or less share attitudes.

Table 10.2 Comparing views on life and death questions, Polish and Norwegian sample

Percent agreeing with statement	Poland (N=1657)	Norway (N=1001)	Sign.
Abortion should be prohibited in all circumstances because it terminates a human life.	26.0	8.8	**
Abortion should be permitted in case of rape.	62.6	92.0	**
Abortion should be permitted in case of incest.	49.3	86.4	**
Abortion should be permitted when there is a strong chance of serious defect in the baby.	54.5	65.7	**
Abortion should be permitted when the woman's own health is seriously endangered by the pregnancy.	63.4	89.1	**
Abortion should be permitted when the woman cannot afford any more children economically.	20.3	59.2	**
Abortion should be permitted when the woman cannot afford any more children psychologically.	28.8	64.3	**
Euthanasia should be prohibited in all circumstances.	19.2	12.3	**
Euthanasia should be permitted in the case of unbearable and irreversible suffering.	65.1	76.5	**

**Sign on the 0.001 level (two-tailed)

Table 10.3 The scores of Protestants, Catholics and non-religious

Percent agreeing with statement	Catholics Poland (N = 1011)	Non-religious Poland (N = 360)	Protestants Norway (N = 312)	Non-religious Norway (N = 460)
Abortion should be prohibited in all circumstances because it terminates a human life.	35.1	5.0	8.6	1.8
Euthanasia should be prohibited in all Circumstances.	26.4	3.9	9.2	9.0

The two indices are positively correlated both in Poland and in Norway, but the correlation is weaker in Norway (Pearson's r .44) than in Poland (Pearson's r .65). This means that, especially in Norway, people who are supportive of abortion (as a right) are not positive towards euthanasia as often as in Poland.

The independent variables in the empirical analyses are religious factors and security orientation. Religiosity is measured by the use of the Huber and Huber (2012) scale mentioned earlier. To measure views regarding the role of churches and religious organisations in society, we used a set of questions designed to tap five different attitude dimensions or roles. These are called 'influence society', 'prophetic role', 'conformity', 'service provider' and 'national culture supporter'. We have compared the scores on these five indices in the two countries. There is no difference in the first two indices, but the differences are significant for the last three. More Norwegian than Polish students want church/religious organisations to conform and adapt to trends in society. On the other hand, the Poles have the highest scores regarding the church/religious organisations as service providers and supporters of (traditional) national culture (Table 10.4).

Table 10.4 Scores on view of religion's role in society, Poland and Norway

	Poland (N = 1642)	Norway (N = 1000)	Diff. sign
Influence society (1–5)	2.43	2.51	N.s.
Prophetic role (1–5)	2.60	2.52	N.s.
Conformity (1–5)	3.06	3.57	**
Service provider (1–5)	3.63	3.09	**
National culture Supporter (1–5)	2.85	2.48	**

**Sign on the 0.001-level (two-tailed)

Table 10.5 Scores on security orientation and risk-taking orientation, Poland and Norway

	Poland (N = 1650)	Std. dev.	Norway (N = 1000)	Std. dev.	Diff. sign
Maximising security	4.04	1.34	4.11	1.35	n.s.
Seeking risks & adventure	4.25	1.37	4.34	1.34	n.s.
Security/no-risk-index	3.39	1.01	3.39	1.00	n.s.

To follow up the assumption of Norris and Inglehart (2004) – that perceived security has an impact on religiosity and probably on religiosity-related attitudes – we have constructed an index based on questions about security orientation and risk-taking orientation which represents the opposite. Norris and Inglehart also predict that perceived security is related to the objective level of security. This means that the level of religiosity will vary with welfare systems and social-security provisions across countries. With only two countries in the analyses, we must focus on security at the individual level. Before using the variable in the regression analyses, we compare the mean scores in the two countries. Contrary to what we expected, there were no significant differences between the Polish and the Norwegian students regarding security. In Table 10.5, the Norwegians score somewhat higher than the Polish students with respect to willingness to take risks. The next step is to use security as a variable in the regression analyses.

Regression Analyses

In this section, we do a stepwise regression analysis of the two samples. In the first step, background characteristics are analysed. Step two introduces orientation towards security and low risk. In the third step, the religious variables are included. This enables us to analyse the effects each predictor has on the dependent variable when controlling for all the other variables. It is of theoretical interest to see if security orientation has a direct effect on the dependent variables or if the effect is indirect via the religious variables. Also of special interest are the variables which measure views regarding the role of religion in society. If there has been a process of de-privatization of religion, as Casanova predicts, the public role of religion is potentially an important predictor of attitudes towards moral questions such as abortion and euthanasia.

In the first step, we analyse the impact of the background factors on attitudes towards abortion among Polish students. All four variables have significant effects. They remain significant through Step 2. However, in Step 3, only age and political preference are significant when religion is taken into account. In the Polish sample, males tend to be somewhat more permissive towards abortion than females. This effect probably has to do with females being more religious than males. The same is true for parent's level of education. Those with highly educated parents are more permissive towards abortion. Students in their twenties are a little more permissive than teenagers are. The effect of age is, however, still significant after control for religion. The political variable has a significantly negative effect after controls; this means that students who identify with the left side of the political spectrum are more in favour of the right to abortion than are students who identify with the right side of the political spectrum. All four background variables taken together explain 10% of the variance in the dependent variable.

Step two introduces security orientation. According to Norris and Inglehart (2004), this factor is important in explaining religious attitudes and possibly related values as well. In the study, security orientation has no effect on attitudes towards abortion among Polish students. This becomes clear when we introduce the religious variables. However, as we shall see later, security orientation has some effect *vis-à-vis* attitudes towards euthanasia in Poland.

In Step 3, we include the religious variables in the analyses. The whole set of variables explains a great deal (39%) of the variance in the dependent variable. Affiliation with the Catholic Church, however, has no effect on attitudes towards abortion. This is somewhat surprising when we take into account the church's high profile on the issue. The result can probably be explained by the fact that the Poles are often nominal Catholics and so are not necessarily very involved in the church. In addition, as other polls show, regardless of the very strict and clear teachings of the Catholic Church on abortion and the existing restrictive law, a majority of Polish citizens oppose the criminalization of abortion. According to 2008 polls from the World Public Opinion on Abortion, a majority of Polish society rejects penalizing abortion. As much as 66% of the population is at odds with the existing law, agreeing that this matter should be 'left to the individual'. 16% agrees that government should discourage abortion by 'using only non-punitive methods,' and 6% agrees to governmental use of 'criminal enforcement.'[6]

When two thirds of the students feel that they belong to the Catholic Church, they tend to reflect the whole sample. This means that affiliation is a very rough way of measuring religious orientation in the case of Poland. Huber's religiosity scale,

[6] In Poland the research was made by the Public Opinion Research Center, for more information see: http://www.federa.org.pl/dokumenty_pdf/aborcja/WPO_Abortion_Jun08_packet.pdf

on the other hand, has a clear (negative) effect on attitudes towards abortion. The same goes for variables which measure views on the role of the church in society. The view that the church should follow current trends in society is positively related to permissive attitudes on abortion. Three of the variables which measure views regarding the role of the church in society have negative effects on abortion attitudes. The opinions that the church should try to influence public opinion, take responsibility for societal development, and take responsibility for national culture have negative effects. The view that the church should focus on the spiritual growth of its members has no effect on attitudes. The analysis of attitudes towards abortion in Poland supports the hypothesis that religion has become de-privatised and that the role of religion in society is important for moral questions. This is something we will follow up in the analysis of attitudes towards euthanasia in Poland.

The model explains a little less of the variance in attitudes towards euthanasia than it does in the previous analyses of abortion. Step 1 shows that all four background variables have a significant impact on attitudes towards euthanasia. The relations between social-background factors and attitudes are more or less the same as in Table 10.6. Again, males are more permissive than females. However, the effect of gender disappears when religion is taken into account. The fact that the males are less religious than the females can explain this. This time age also has a small but significant impact (on the 10% level), which means that older students are somewhat more permissive than younger ones. Again, the effect of parents' education disappears when religion is taken into account. Political preferences, however, also have a significant effect after control, but the effect is weakened when religion is

Table 10.6 Three-step regression analyses with attitudes towards abortion (index, 1–5) as dependent variable. Beta values, explained variance. Poland, N = 1650

Variables	Step 1 (Social background)	Step 2 (Security-orientation)	Step 3 (Religious variables)
Gender (men = 2)	.063**	.062**	.012
Age 15–24	.059*	.060*	.054*
Parents' education	.063**	.063*	.032
Political preferences	−.311***	−.311***	−.103***
Security orientation		−.018	.003
Catholic affiliation			−.021
Religiosity			−.273***
Church-role: Influence			−.140***
Church-role: Prophetic			−.088***
Church role: Conformity			.240***
Church role: Service			.016
Church role: National culture			−.105**
R square	.100	.100	.393

*** sign. on 0.001-level, ** sign. on 0.01-level, * sign. on 0.05-level, # sign. on 0.10-level

Table 10.7 Three-step regression analyses with attitudes towards euthanasia (index, 1–5) as dependent variable. Beta values, explained variance. Poland, N = 1650

Variables	Step 1 (Social background)	Step 2 (Security-orientation)	Step 3 (Religious variables)
Gender (men = 2)	.077**	.072**	.031
Age 15–24	.044#	.046#	.040#
Parents' education	.048#	.045#	.009
Political preferences	−.263***	−.263***	−.068**
Security orientation		−.092***	−.070***
Catholic affiliation			−.043
Religiosity			−.242***
Church-role: Influence			−.147**
Church role: Prophetic			−.091***
Church role: Conformity			.199***
Church role: Service			.069**
Church role: National culture			−.098**
R square	.071	.079	.325

*** sign. on 0.001-level, ** sign. on 0.01-level, * sign. on 0.05-level, # sign. on 0.10-level

introduced. Those on the left side of the political spectrum are the most permissive. This seems to be the situation when 'life values' are on the agenda (Table 10.7).

In the second step of the analyses, we include security orientation. In the case of euthanasia, this variable has a significant, albeit moderate effect on attitudes. As expected, those who are most oriented towards security are those who have the most traditional and preserving attitudes towards the issue at stake. Security orientation continues to have a significant effect even after the religious factors have been taken into account. Security orientation is related to religiosity, as predicted by Norris and Inglehart, but it also seems to have some effect on other types of values. Security was, however, not an important variable in the analyses of abortion. It will be interesting to see if this variable has an effect in the Norwegian sample. If Norris and Inglehart are right, security should play a smaller role in societies where the level of welfare is high, as in Norway.

In the third step of the analyses, we include the religious variables. All twelve variables in the model explain 32% of the variation in the dependent variable. The religious variables have the same effects on attitudes towards euthanasia that they had on abortion. Affiliation with the Catholic Church exhibits no significant effect. Again, the religiosity-index is a strong predictor of attitudes. Highly religious people tend to be much more sceptical about euthanasia than those who are less religious or not religious at all. It is interesting to note that the role of religion in today's society is an important predictor of attitudes towards moral questions. The picture is like this: Those who support a church or a religion that actively tries to influence public opinion, to offer a prophetic voice or to preserve traditional national culture tend not to support euthanasia (nor abortion). On the other hand, those who want the

Table 10.8 Three-step regression analyses with attitudes towards abortion (index, 1–5) as dependent variable. Beta values, explained variance. Norway, N = 1000

Variables	Step 1 (Social background)	Step 2 (Security-orientation)	Step 3 (Religious variables)
Gender (men = 2)	−.082**	−.085**	−.120***
Age 16–20	.067*	.066*	.029
Parents' education	.194***	.190***	.093***
Political preferences	.070*	.071*	.062*
Security orientation		-.052#	−.014
Protestant affiliation			.025
Religiosity			−.299***
Church-role: Influence			−.121***
Church role: Prophetic			−.087**
Church role: Conformity			.212***
Church role: Service			−.017
Church role: National culture			−.053
R square	.056	.059	.287

church to be adaptive and focus more on providing services to its members are more positive about euthanasia as a way of preventing term suffering. It will be interesting to see if these variables have the same effects in Norway, which is a country that differs from Poland in many respects – not least regarding religion (Table 10.8).

In the Norwegian case, the model explains less of the variance (29%) in abortion attitudes than it did in the Polish case (39%). Still, almost all the variables have significant effects in at least some steps. All four background variables have a significant effect in the first and second steps of the analysis. Some of the variables, however, have different effects than they had among Polish youth. This is the case with gender, for example. Among Norwegian students, females are more permissive towards abortion than males. Older students tend to be somewhat more permissive than younger ones, but this effect disappears when religion is taken into account. The level of education among parents has a significant effect on attitudes. This effect is weakened when religion is controlled for, but it is still significant. Political preference has some impact on abortion attitudes, but this time it is a positive one. This means that people who identify with the political right are somewhat more permissive than those on the political left. The left-wing party in the parliament has been critical of the new technology which makes it possible to detect all sorts of defects in a foetus. The leftist party is worried about a society without disabled people ('*sorteringssamfunnet*' in Norwegian). People who vote for the rightist parties seem to be more individualized and concerned with an individual's freedom to form his or her own destiny. However, the right-wing parties in Norway are not very concerned about religion. Religion is the main priority for the small Christian Democratic party in the middle of the political spectrum.

Security orientation is introduced into the analysis in Step 2. This variable has a small but significantly negative effect on abortion attitudes. This corresponds with what we found when we looked at attitudes towards euthanasia in Poland. The effect of security orientation disappeared when we took the religious variables into account in Step 3, however. According to Norris and Inglehart, security is an important factor in explaining religiosity but not necessarily other value orientations. In the Norwegian analysis, security orientation is negatively correlated with abortion attitudes, but this effect disappears when religion is introduced.

In Step 3, we use affiliation with a Protestant church instead of Catholic affiliation. This variable does not have a significant effect. The explanation for this is not that the group belonging to a Protestant church constitutes a majority and tends to look a lot like the whole population; the reason for the lack of effect has more to do with the fact that the Protestant church is rather liberal regarding private morality – not least related to sexuality and family matters. Another element which could explain the lack of effect for church affiliation is the Lutheran dogma of the two kingdoms. For some members of the national Lutheran church, it is up to the state to decide about the laws and the church should not protest against the laws that have been decided upon by legitimate state authorities.

Even if affiliation is not an important factor for explaining attitudes on abortion, religiosity is. As in the Polish case, those who are most religious are also those who are most against abortion rights. As in Poland, we find that one's view on the role of religion also has explanatory power. When all other variables are controlled for, three of five variables which measure religion in society have significant effects. These effects form the same pattern as was detected for Poland. Those who think that the church should influence society are generally more negative about liberal abortion laws than others are. The same goes for those who subscribe to a prophetic role for the church. On the other hand, those who think that the church should follow trends in society are positive about liberal abortion rights (Table 10.9).

We go on to look at attitudes toward euthanasia in Norway. In this case, the model explains only 14% of the variation in attitudes. This is much less than in Poland (32%). Still, the four background variables have a significant effect on attitudes in steps 1 and 2. Some of the variables have effects opposite those they had when abortion was the focus. We now find that, for example, gender has a positive effect on euthanasia as a right. This means that boys are more supportive than girls. We found the same tendency earlier for Poland. However, the effect of gender disappears when religion is introduced. As we saw in Table 10.6, age has a positive effect in the first two steps but loses its explanatory power in Step 3. Students in their twenties tend to be a little more permissive towards euthanasia than teenagers are. The educational level of the parents is pushing in the direction of allowing euthanasia to take place under certain circumstances. Political preference has a significantly positive effect, which means that those on the right side of the political spectrum are the most permissive. This is the same tendency we found when we studied abortion attitudes in Norway, but it is the opposite of what we found in the Polish case. In Poland, political preference had a negative effect on attitudes. One reason for this is that the right-wing parties in Norway are not very concerned with the church as they

Table 10.9 Three-step regression analyses with attitudes towards euthanasia (index, 1–5) as dependent variable. Beta values, explained variance. Norway, N = 1000

Variables	Step 1 (Social background)	Step 2 (Security-orientation)	Step 3 (Religious variables)
Gender (men = 2)	.066*	.060#	.040
Age (16–20)	.064*	.063*	.050
Parents' education	.103**	.096**	.033
Political preferences	.126***	.128***	.126***
Security orientation		−.102**	−.078*
Protestant affiliation			.033
Religiosity			−.210***
Church-role: Influence			−.081*
Church-role: Prophetic			−.028
Church role: Conformity			.113***
Church role: Service			−.014
Church role: National culture			−.046
R square	.038	.048	.143

are in many other European countries. In Norway, those who identify with the political right are not more religious than those who belong to the leftist parties. The most religious people often vote for the parties in the middle of the political spectrum: the Agrarian Party, the Christian People's Party or the Liberal Party. In addition, the right-wing Progress Party is the only party in Norway that has actively campaigned to change the laws legalizing euthanasia as in the Netherlands and Switzerland.

As expected, security orientation has a negative impact on attitudes towards euthanasia. Those most security oriented are more negative about euthanasia than are others. When the religious variables are introduced in Step 3, the effect of security orientation is weakened, but it still has some effect. All background variables lose their effect in Step 3 – except for the political variable. Regarding the religious variables, the pattern remains the same as before. The religiosity variable has a significantly negative impact on attitudes toward euthanasia. This time, only two of the variables which measure views regarding the role of religion in society have significant effects: the influence variable (negative effect) and the conformity variable (positive effect). The religious variables have more or less the same effect on life-and-death questions in the two countries we are studying.

Discussion and Conclusion

In the following, we shall repeat the main findings and relate them to the research questions. This leads us to the following discussion: In what way do religiosity, one's view of the role of religion in society and security orientation explain attitudes towards abortion and euthanasia in the two countries, and are the findings in line with the theoretical assumptions?

First, the overall outcome of the regression analyses is that religiosity, as expected, has an impact on attitudes towards life and death questions. The religious variables have more or less the same effect in both countries despite different religious traditions. On a general level, these findings confirm what can be expected on the basis of the theoretical perspectives. Despite secularisation processes, religion continues to play a role when it comes to moral questions – especially when these are related to life and death. Our findings confirm the views of Casanova (1994) and Norris and Inglehart (2004) regarding the persisting significance of religious orientations in contemporary societies. As expected, the findings support the common view that Poles and Norwegians differ in their attitudes towards abortion as a right. The country with the most religious population is also the one with the most restrictive views on abortion. Regarding euthanasia, the differences are less striking – perhaps because the question has not yet been politicized and included in public debate like abortion. In Norway, the two questions are not as interconnected as they are in the Polish case, which means that not all of those who have a liberal view on abortion are also ready to accept euthanasia.

Some of the findings in the analyses are in line with the theoretical assumptions we presented at the beginning; others are not. Both Casanova (1994) and Norris and Inglehart (2004) have predicted that religion would continue to play a role *vis-à-vis* attitudes towards moral questions. Casanova is most interested in the role of religion on the societal level while Norris and Inglehart stress that religion has the greatest impact in the fields of private morality and family matters. Abortion and euthanasia can be seen as belonging to both public and private spheres. Abortion and euthanasia involve families but are also relevant in a wider political setting. In all four regression tables, religiosity is the variable with the strongest and most consistent effects on these attitudes. This effect remains the same regardless of what Christian tradition dominates. On the other hand, the similarities of some of the findings to some extent contradict the perspective of Norris and Inglehart (2004), who stress that the type of religious tradition is of crucial importance and will influence the whole society and not only those who see themselves as religious.

Though the two countries we have studied have different religious traditions, both variables related to religiosity and role of religion in society tend to have the same type of effects. This means that the religious variables are robust predictors when the object of study concerns moral questions related to life and death. Based on the theoretical perspectives presented at the beginning of the article, we also wanted to see if security orientation has any impact. According to Norris and Inglehart, security is a factor which explains the level of religiosity. In order to see if 'security' has an effect which is independent of the religious factors, we made stepwise regressions. The results do not clearly support the theory. In some cases, security orientation has an impact on attitudes; other times it does not. Both in Poland and in Norway, security orientation has a significantly negative effect on attitudes towards euthanasia after religious variables are controlled for. In the case of abortion, security orientation did not, however, have a significant impact either in

Poland or in Norway. In order to investigate the hypothesis that feeling of security is important *vis-à-vis* religiosity and religion-related values, we probably need to include both more countries and factors on the macro level such as BGP per capita and welfare-state systems.

The two countries we have compared have different political and democratic histories. This is reflected in the way the political variable works in the analyses. In Poland, those who lean to the right are the most restrictive. In Norway, the leftist group exhibits restrictive views towards both abortion and euthanasia. This difference in political culture is related to differences in religious tradition. In the Protestant – especially Lutheran – tradition, those who go regularly to church and feel that they belong to the church tend to be sceptical of a tight connection between religion and politics. According to the Lutheran concept of the two kingdoms, the church should respect the decisions made by legitimate state authorities. According to our data in both countries, there are different views on the role that religion should play in society. Some people want the church and religious organisations to be active in the political field and try to influence public opinion. Others want religion to keep up with trends in society and not try to challenge political authorities. Both Casanova and other scholars have pointed to the public role of religion as a new field of research. This study of attitudes towards abortion and euthanasia in Poland and Norway shows that the idea of de-privatisation adds a promising perspective to ongoing research regarding the social impact of religion.

The relation between the legal right to abortion and human rights is problematic. On one hand, some (especially religious people) think that abortion represents a violation of human-rights principles. Others argue that human rights have to do with protection of human life that is already born and that abortion can be seen as part of women's rights to control their own bodies and to decide about their lives. It is easier to argue that euthanasia is in conflict with basic human rights, as it violates the principle of right to life and protection of vulnerable people. However, even in this case, there are good arguments favouring the possibility of some kind of euthanasia in certain cases. In this article, we have in fact studied attitudes towards legal rights to abortion and euthanasia without articulating a definite position on how they are related to the human-rights package.

References

Anckar, C. (2008). On the applicability of the most similar systems design and the most different systems design in comparative research. *International Journal of Social Research Methodology, 11*, 389–401.

Barnard, C. (1985). *Good life, good death: Doctor's case for Euthanasia suicide*. London: Peter Owen Publishers.

Berger, P. (1967). *The sacred canopy: Elements of a sociological theory of religion*. New York: Doubleday.

Boguszewski, R. (2012). Zmiany w zakresie wiary i religijności Polaków po śmierci Jana Pawła II. BS/49/2012. *Aktualne problemy i wydarzenia*. Warszawa: CBOS. http://www.naukairozwoj.uksw.edu.pl/sites/default/files/Nag%C3%B3rska.pdf

Boguszewski, R. (2014). Religijność a zasady moralne. 15/2014. *Aktualne problemy i wydarzenia*. Warszawa: CBOS. http://www.cbos.pl/SPISKOM.POL/2014/K_015_14.PDF

Boguszewski, R. (2015). Zmiany w zakresie podstawowych wskaźników religijności Polaków po śmierci Jana Pawła II. 26/2015. Warszawa: CBOS. http://www.cbos.pl/SPISKOM.POL/2015/K_026_15.PDF

Borowik, I. (2002). The Roman Catholic Church in the process of democratic transformation: The case of Poland. *Social Compass, 49*(2), 239–252. https://doi.org/10.1177/0037768602049002008.

Casanova, J. (1994). *Public religions in the modern world*. Chicago: University of Chicago Press.

Casanova, J. (2003). What is a public religion? In H. Heclo & W. M. McClay (Eds.), *Religion returns to the public square* (pp. 111–141). Washington, DC: Woodrow Wilson Center Press.

Habermas, J. (2008). Notes on post-secular society. *New Perspectives Quarterly, 25*(4), 17–29.

Herbert, D., & Fras, M. (2009). European enlargement, secularisation and religious re-publicisation in central and Eastern Europe. *Religion, State and Society, 37*(1–2), 81–97. https://doi.org/10.1080/09637490802693668.

Huber, S., & Huber, O. W. (2012). The Centrality of Religiosity Scale (CRS). *Religions, 3*, 710–724.

Jankowska, H. (1991, Autumn). Church and politics in Poland. *Feminist Review*, 39, 174–181. Shifting Territories: Feminism & Europe.

Minkenberg, M. (2003). The policy impact of Church-State relations: Family policy and abortion in Britain, France, and Germany. *West European Politics, 26*(1), 195–217. https://doi.org/10.1080/01402380412331300267.

Norris, P., & Inglehart, R. (2004). *Sacred and secular: Religion and politics worldwide*. New York: Cambridge University Press.

Pacian, A. J., & Kulik, T. B. (2011). Practicing Euthanasia in Poland – Necessity or freedom of introducing and application of legal regulations? – Discussion on the legal matters. *Romanian Journal of Bioethics, 9*(4), 74–84.

Ramet, S. P. (2007). *The liberal project and the transformation of democracy: The case of East Central Europe*. College Station: Texas A&M University Press.

Rawls, J. (1997). The idea of public reason revisited. *The University of Chicago Law Review, 64*(3), 765. https://doi.org/10.2307/1600311.

Schwartz, S. H., & Sagiv, L. (1995). Identifying culture-specifics in the content and structure of values. *Journal of Cross-Cultural Psychology, 26*(1), 92–116.

Shala, I., & Gusha, K. (2016). The debate over Euthanasia and human rights. *European Scientific Journal, 12*(8), 73–81.

Śliwka, M., & Gałęska-Śliwka, A. (2011). Regulating end-of-life decisions in Poland: Legal Dilemmas. *Advances in Palliative Medicine, 10*, 49–56.

Szeroczyńska, M. (2004). *Eutanazja i wspomagane samobójstwo na świecie*. In *Studium prawnoporównawcze*. Kraków: Universitas.

Weber, M. (2011/1904). *The protestant ethic and the spirit of capitalism*. New York: Oxford University Press.

Weithman, P. J. (2002). *Religion and the obligations of citizenship*. Cambridge, MA: Cambridge University Press.

Wolterstorff, N. (1997). The role of religion in decision and discussion of political issues. In R. Audi & Wolterstorff (Eds.), *Religion in the public square: The place of religious convictions in political debate* (pp. 67–120). Maryland: Rowman & Littlefield.

Zielińska, K. (2015). The Roman Catholic Church and human rights in Poland. In H.-G. Ziebertz & G. Črpić (Eds.), *Religion and human rights* (pp. 137–149). Cham: Springer.

Zielińska, K., & Zwierżdżyński, M. K. (2013). Religious education in Poland. In D. H. Davis & E. Miroshnikova (Eds.), *The Routledge international handbook of religious education* (pp. 264–271). London: Routledge.

Zubrzycki, G. (2006). *The crosses of Auschwitz: Nationalism and religion in post-communist Poland*. New ed. University of Chicago Press.

Chapter 11
Religion, Trust in Institutions and Attitudes Towards Abortion: A Comparison of Lutheran and Orthodox Countries

Olga Breskaya, Pål Ketil Botvar, Anders Sjöborg, and Silviu Rogobete

This article compares students' attitudes towards human rights in countries with different religious traditions, namely Lutheran-dominated Scandinavian countries and Christian Orthodox countries in the eastern part of Europe. The four countries involved in this study are Belarus, Romania, Norway and Sweden, and our focus is on students' attitudes towards human rights—especially reproductive health and women's rights. The effect religion has on attitudes to such rights is a central part of our analysis. In addition, the article will examine the relationship between trust in institutions and support for human rights. Previous studies report that trust in institutions correlates positively with values that stress stability, protection, and preservation of traditional practices, correlating negatively with values that emphasise independent thought and change. On this basis we expect that trust in governmental institutions will have different effects in countries with democratic and authoritarian regimes.

O. Breskaya (✉)
University of Padova, Padova, Italy
e-mail: olga.breskaya@phd.unipd.it

P. K. Botvar
KIFO Institute for Church, Religion, and Worldview Research Oslo, Norway
e-mail: pal.ketil.botvar@kifo.no

A. Sjöborg
Uppsala University, Uppsala, Sweden
e-mail: anders.sjoborg@teol.uu.se

S. Rogobete
West University of Timisoara, Timişoara, Romania

H.-G. Ziebertz, F. Zaccaria (eds.), *Euthanasia, Abortion, Death Penalty and Religion – The Right to Life and its Limitations*, Religion and Human Rights 4, https://doi.org/10.1007/978-3-319-98773-6_11

Introduction

This paper investigates the connection between attitudes towards religion and human rights, with a special focus on legal abortion and women's rights, comparing attitudes towards human rights in Lutheran-dominated Scandinavian countries and Christian Orthodox countries in the eastern part of Europe. Moreover, we investigate the role of trust in institutions in relation to human rights attitudes in democratic versus semi-democratic and authoritarian regimes. We draw on the theoretical perspectives of Casanova (1994, 2003, 2009), Norris and Inglehart (2004) and Devos et al. (2002).

The 'right to life' is a moral concept and a fundamental freedom enshrined in international human-rights declarations and treaties.[1] It is an umbrella concept that combines various dimensions and is related to such issues as capital punishment, abortion, and euthanasia. Abortion has a strong moral connotation, as it questions the moments at which personhood and life begin and end and influences the conditions of their termination.

In the discussion and implementation of human-rights principles, legal access to secure abortion is often regarded as part of a woman's right to sexual and reproductive health. The term 'reproductive health' tends to be a key term in UN programmes and conferences on women's rights. Churches and other religious institutions have, however, remained sceptical about sexual and reproductive rights, partly because they see human life as sacred from conception to natural death but also because they support family values based on distinct roles for males and females. Given this background, it is interesting to investigate the relationship between religion and attitudes towards abortion and women's rights.

Abortion, then, can be seen as a key issue in the debate on women's rights and the overall right to life. It raises questions concerning family planning, population control, the right to privacy and the concepts of bodily integrity and subjectivity with respect to pregnant women. As such, abortion is an issue not only of legal importance but also of importance in the gender debate and in the political and ethical spheres. Over time, reproductive health has become a central issue in the discourse on women's rights and its content and implications, even if the theme is still controversial in certain milieus.

The heterogeneous and conflicting structure of rights, freedoms, and moral principles related to abortion has revitalised the public-private divide in the gender, religious, legal, and family spheres. Our study takes the 'de-privatisation of religion' thesis introduced by Jose Casanova (1994) as the point of departure. The idea of a de-privatisation of private moral and religious spheres—together with a re-normalisation of the public socio-political agenda—must be considered when discussing the importance of religion in the process of rethinking moral and gender-sensitive problems such as abortion. For our study, this means exploring the

[1] All human beings are entitled to the right to life according to Art. 3 of the Universal Declaration of Human Rights: "everyone has the right to life, liberty, and security of person". Cf. also the European Convention on Human Rights (Art. 2), and in the International Covenant on Civil and Political Rights (Art. 6).

relationship between such factors as gender, religiosity, and views on abortion and women's rights in diverse cultural contexts.

Considering that our empirical study of abortion implies the comparison of different religious and political traditions (Lutheran and Eastern Orthodox, democratic and transitional democracy, and authoritarianism), we believe that the thesis of Inglehart and Norris (2004), which argues that religious traditions have shaped the cultures of each nation in an enduring fashion, and that values embedded in religious traditions are transmitted even to those citizens who are not themselves active in religious groups, is a relevant one.

Religious institutions have traditionally played a strong role of moral authority and set standards regarding questions of life and death. Generally, the Orthodox Churches forbid abortion. The Russian Orthodox Church condemns abortion in its social teaching "Basis of Social Concept", adopted in 2000. The document argues that "Under no circumstances can the Orthodox Church bless abortion" (Basis 2000) XII.2.[2] The Romanian Orthodox Church, claiming to follow Holy Scripture and Holy Tradition, supports human life in all its forms, including the rights of the unborn. However, its position is nuanced: the church finds it acceptable to practice abortion when the mother's life is under serious threat, and in the case of a well-established genetic malformation of the unborn child, the responsibility for such a decision being left to the family. In all other cases, abortion is forbidden.[3] Nevertheless, despite its high level of religiosity, Romania continues to rank very highly compared to other European countries in the number of abortions performed.

In addition, many Protestant and Evangelical churches strongly oppose abortion. The Church of Norway declares that the unborn child is created by God and therefore has a right to live. The 1989 General Synod of the Church of Norway states that, "the number of abortions carried out since the passage of the Abortion Act 1975 is unacceptably high". However, The Church of Norway also believes that abortion is sometimes morally acceptable, such as when a baby is suffering from a serious disability. In Sweden, some 'pro-life' organizations are connected to evangelical and neo-pentecostal varieties of Christianity. However, in the public debate, such initiatives are commonly criticised, and consensus often forms around liberal abortion policies and efforts to bring abortion statistics down.

Abortion and Women's Rights in These Four European Countries

To understand the attitudes of young people towards abortion and women's rights in the four countries considered here, we require some background information about their political and judicial situations. The collapse of Communism in 1989–1990 and

[2] 'The Basis of the Social Concept of the Russian Orthodox Church. Chapter XII'. *Problems of Bioethics* (2000). Internet access: https://mospat.ru/en/documents/social-concepts/xii/. Accessed on March 21, 2017.

[3] 'Abortion. Official site of the Romanian Patriarchate'. Internet access: http://patriarhia.ro/avortul-78.html. Accessed on March 21, 2017.

the transition to democracy across almost the entire post-Communist world led to the view that democracy and political reform would rapidly become entrenched. A quarter of a century later, many of these expectations remain unfulfilled. Despite rapid progress in establishing democratic institutions during the 1990s, the transition to democracy across many of these countries is reversed a decade later. This means that our study is a comparison both of different Christian traditions and of different political regimes which produce patterns of attitudes towards abortion and women's rights.

The four countries considered in this study differ in several ways. This makes it necessary to provide an overview of their religious landscapes and legal situations with respect to abortion and women's rights. Despite all these differences, there are reasons to treat the four countries as two pairs. The Scandinavian countries in our study, Norway and Sweden, resemble each other in many respects: geographically, politically, and linguistically. They also share the same religious tradition, as both countries have adopted a Lutheran state-church system. Our two Eastern European countries, Belarus and Romania, also share the same religious tradition, namely Orthodox Christianity. However, the two countries differ when it comes to democracy and rights concerning individual freedoms. While Romania can be described as a semi-democratic country, Belarus is considered 'authoritarian' in studies of freedom and democracy (Democracy Report 2015).

Belarus

In 1991, Belarus became an independent state which declared its constitutional principles to be democracy and rule of law. Elsewhere, however, Belarus is characterised as an authoritarian regime. On *The Economist*'s Democracy Index of 2012, Belarus scored 3.04 on a scale ranging from 1 to 10; Norway, on the other hand, scored 9.93. In 2000, Belarus signed a treaty for greater cooperation with Russia. Eastern Orthodoxy (81%) is the majority religion in the country, and the Belarusian state emphasises a special role for five religions and 25 registered religious communities. Religious freedom has been declared an inalienable constitutional right, with the 2002 law regulating religious freedom defining the roles of different religions in the nation-building process as traditional and historical. The Orthodox Church was recognised as having the primary role in the historical formation and development of spiritual, cultural and state traditions of the Belarusian people; the Catholic Church was acknowledged for playing a spiritual, cultural and historical role in the territory of Belarus, while the Evangelical Lutheran Church, Judaism, and Islam were recognised for their inseparability from the common history of the Belarusian people. In 2003, a cooperation agreement was signed between the state and the Belarusian Orthodox Church. The Belarusian Orthodox Church is a canonical part of the Russian Orthodox Church. Thus, in public discourse, official documents published by the Russian Orthodox Church also define the position of the Belarusian Orthodox Church with respect to abortion and other social and ethical issues.

Gender equality has been implemented as the constitutional principle (related to the marriage, education, and employment spheres) and has become the priority of government policy in Belarus. The National Plan of Action for Gender Equality of the Republic of Belarus for 2001–2005 and the National Plan of Action to Ensure Gender Equality for 2008–2010 were adopted to "sustain the State policy against gender- based discrimination".[4] In Belarus, women are still poorly represented in political and economic decision-making processes, often earning less money than men for the same jobs.

Law on Abortion

During the 1990s, in the period of drastic socio-economic and political instability, Belarus experienced a downturn in fertility. After the independence, its public health regulation of abortions resumed the policies of the previous period, namely the 1982 decree legalising abortion for health reasons and another decree of 1987. These established a broad range of socio-economic and psychological conditions which allow abortion on request up to the 28th week of pregnancy. These conditions include the deprivation of maternity rights, divorce during pregnancy, imprisonment of the pregnant woman or her husband and many others. The new law on public health was adopted in 1993, decriminalising abortion in Belarus.[5] Article 27 of this law regulates health policies pertaining to abortion, stating that women are free to procure an abortion during the first trimester of pregnancy, that they may do so under certain conditions until the 22nd week, and that abortion may be obtained at any point during the pregnancy given certain medical conditions or when there is risk to the mother's health. In 2013, according to the Bylaw of the Council of Ministers (established by a 1987 decree), of these ten conditions only two remained which allowing an abortion to be performed after the 12th week of pregnancy. In 2014, some amendments to the law on 'public health' were adopted, which decreed that a doctor has a right to refuse to perform an abortion on grounds of conscientious objection. In 2014, the Ministry of Health Care in Belarus conducted a pro-life 'weeks-of-silence' action, under which no abortions were performed for 1 week in various cities. In the years 1994–2014, the peak abortion ratio (1922 abortions were conducted per 1000 live births) was downsized ten times and by 2014, the ratio was 210.[6]

[4] Seventh periodic report of states parties, CEDAW, Belarus, 2010.

[5] Law of the Republic of Belarus of 18 June, 1993, on public health. Internet access: http://www.pravo.by/document/?guid=3871&p0=v19302435 Accessed on March 21, 2017.

[6] Historical abortion statistics, Belarus. Internet access: http://www.johnstonsarchive.net/policy/abortion/ab-belarus.html Accessed on March 21, 2017.

Romania

Given its radical totalitarian past prior to 1989, Romania has clearly moved in the direction of becoming a full democracy. Today, it is an integrated EU member state and viewed as a respectable NATO ally. More recently, through the work of the National Anticorruption Directorate (DNA)—an independent department within the Romanian prosecutor's office designed to deal with high-level state corruption—the country is on its way to becoming a model for the wider region. According to *The Economist*, "In 2014 the DNA secured convictions of 1,138 people, including 24 mayors, five members of parliament, two ex-ministers and a former prime minister, Adrian Nastase. More than 90% of its indictments led to convictions".[7] The trend has been maintained to the present day, with the number of high-ranking officials convicted increasing every year.[8] Nevertheless, the judicial system still requires further radical reform, and civil participation in political life must increase to turn the country into a full democracy. In terms of religion and politics, several rights and privileges have nevertheless been given to the Romanian Orthodox Church (ROC)—though neither the 1992 Constitution nor the recent Law of Freedom of Religion or the General Regime of Religious Denominations afforded the Church any special status (Legea 489/2006). The historic role and clear majority represented by the Romanian Orthodox Church explain that: approximately 87% of the Romanian population have declared themselves as members of the ROC in polls from 1990 to today. Throughout the ROC's history, however, it is evident that it would almost indiscriminately offer support and legitimacy to any government which afforded the Church any special privilege under the law of the state. Today, the political-religious bond is reinforced by the provision of significant financial assistance from the government to churches and theological institutions at both central and local levels. Although financial support is legally available to all registered denominations, the ROC is one of the wealthiest institutions in the country due to the size of the benefits it receives, the priority it is given in the political sphere and its substantial real-estate holdings and investments.

Romania has in recent years made important progress in the field of gender equality, as in 2002 it amended the law concerning equal opportunities for women and men. Further efforts are, however, still necessary to increase the awareness of gender issues in all parts of Romanian society.

Law on Abortion

Due to the radical and brutal laws forbidding abortion which dominated the country's former totalitarian communist regime, one of the first laws issued after the revolution in December of 1989 legalized abortion. This law gave Romania one of the highest abortion rates in the world throughout the 1990s. Today, the New Penal Code (LEGE No. 286/2009) regulates the law concerning abortion. The issue of

[7] http://www.economist.com/news/europe/21644209-romanias-anti-corruption-agency-makes-welcome-waves-cleaning-up

[8] http://www.juridice.ro/495874/dna-sinteza-raport-de-activitate-2016.html

abortion is dealt with under articles 201–202 under the heading, 'aggressions against the human foetus'. According to this law, abortion is legal up to the 14th week (Art 201.1.c) of pregnancy and at later stages for significant, professionally determined medical reasons. The mother can get an abortion at any stage of her pregnancy without being prosecuted (Art. 201.7), and it is not considered a crime for the mother to harm the foetus throughout the whole period of the pregnancy (Art. 202.7). The current rate of abortion is half of the rate in 1990.[9]

Romanian churches and religious groups have strongly protested the changes to the legislation. They remain vocal and active in promoting the 'pro-life' perspective, both as isolated denominations and in common activities, such as the marches for life held at least annually in all major cities.

Norway

Norway, like other Nordic countries, is a welfare state. Wealth is rather evenly distributed among its citizens, social-security payments are generous and employment rates are high compared to those of other European countries. This applies to both men and women, thus, Norway scores among the highest in the world in rankings on gender equality. It was also the first country to appoint a special gender equality representative in the 1980s.

A resurgence of religion in the public sphere has occurred despite widespread secularisation. The relationship of church and state in Norway could, until recently, be said to form a state-church system. However, in 2012 this system was formally abandoned when the Norwegian Parliament voted to amend the 1814 Constitution. The state-church system favouring the national Lutheran church came under pressure because of the country's growing religious diversity. The close relationship of the Church to the state has thus been problematic *vis-à-vis* the principle of religious freedom.

A proportion comprising slightly more than 70% of the Norwegian population belongs to the national Lutheran church, a significant proportion of which attends church services such as baptism, confirmation, marriage and burial. At the same time, a growing number of people belong to other religious organisations or to no religious organisation at all. In recent years, Muslims have become the largest religious group outside the national church, and they currently account for approximately 6% of the Norwegian population overall and for some 20% of the capital of Oslo. As for the effects of ethnic and religious pluralism, the situation in large cities in the southern and eastern parts of Norway differs from that of more rural areas.

Law on Abortion

Current Norwegian legislation and public-health policy provides for abortion on demand in the first 12 weeks of pregnancy, for abortion by application up to the 18th week, and thereafter only under exceptional circumstances until the foetus is viable,

[9] http://www.johnstonsarchive.net/policy/abortion/ab-romania.html

presumably at 21 weeks. Back in the 1700s abortion was punishable by death in Norway, but after the passing of a new law in 1842 it was no longer a capital offence but could be punished by up to 6 years of imprisonment and hard labour. In 1902, new legislation allowed abortions whenever the mother's life was in danger or if the child would be stillborn.

Gradually, the law on abortion underwent liberalisation thanks to activism from pro-choice and feminist groups in society. A milestone for the issue of abortion on demand came in 1978 when the Labour Party and Socialist Left Party passed the current law with a one-vote majority. The current law provides for abortion on request for up to 12 weeks of pregnancy; after this time, abortion may be performed provided that a medical commission agreed, taking the mother's own views into consideration. The abortion rate today is 16.2 abortions per 1000 women aged 15–44.

The Lutheran majority church has protested the liberalisation of the abortion law The Church's bishops responded with a pastoral letter (hyrdebrev in Norwegian) to the Norwegian people and the government arguing against he 1978 law in the same year, the letter was read from the pulpit in all their churches. This is the first time-such a pastoral letter appeared since the Nazi occupation during World War II. When parliament voted in favour of the new liberal law, one of the bishops resigned as an act of protest, and the Christian People's Party fought for more restrictive set of abortion laws. Because of the activism of the Evangelical-Lutheran Church and Christian People's Party representatives, the political discussion on abortion has continued in recent years.

Not much has changed with respect to the laws governing abortion in recent decades. However, technology which allows pregnant women to detect abnormalities in the foetus at an early stage of pregnancy has inspired new debate on this issue. In 1994, the Christian People's Party tried to introduce a clause defining the foetus as a human being with its own rights from the moment of conception, but the other parties turned down the proposal. The main discussions have concerned so-called selective abortion, which involves choosing to abort a foetus because, for example, the foetus is likely to be born with a birth defect or impairment or the "wrong" sex. The two left-wing parties who have participated in this debate, the Labour and Socialist Left parties, have had different views on this matter. While the Labour Party has generally applied its views on abortion to selective abortion, the Socialist Left Party has expressed fears that permissive diagnostic procedures could send out the wrong signal, i.e. that the disabled are of lesser value than the able-bodied.

Sweden

Sweden can be characterised as an advanced welfare state with a high level of institutional and interpersonal trust and a great emphasis on the values of self-realisation and expression of religion and tradition (Pettersson 2006). Historically ethnically homogenous, Sweden has in recent decades become increasingly culturally and religiously diverse, however, 63% of the population still belongs to the former state church, the Church of Sweden (Lutheran). The topic of human rights has prominently appeared in public debate in Sweden since the 1970s. As in many Western countries, a search for a shared value base in Sweden, inspired by a new awareness of value pluralism, has led to an increased emphasis on human rights in public debates in general and specially in fields such as policy making and education. Since the end of the 1960s, the relative participation of women in the workforce has been rather high. Welfare services have rapidly expanded, which has both provided opportunities for female work participation and for work in the public sector, which expanded considerably. In arenas like health care, social work, education and childcare, women have been employed to perform tasks that were previously reserved for unpaid, informal workers. Today, 83% of women aged 20–64 are now employed, compared to 86% of men (2013, Statistics Sweden).

As Norway, Sweden is regarded as a leading country when it comes to equal opportunities for men and women.

Law on Abortion

Abortion rights are likely to be related to the situation of women in a country. In Sweden, abortion became legal under certain circumstances in a law introduced in 1938, and the present law, which came into force in 2015, states that abortion is legal regardless of the reasons for it and that the choice is entirely up to the mother until the end of the 18th week of pregnancy. In 2015, 38,000 abortions were performed in Sweden, which corresponds to 20.9 per 1000 women aged 15–44 years. In the same year, around 50% of the abortions were carried out before the seventh week of pregnancy, and around 90% were carried out before the 12th week. After the 18th week, abortion can be carried out only with special medical dispensation and social advice, if the pregnancy poses serious risks for the mother. In other words, it is safe to say that the right to abortion is an integral part of the gender-equal welfare society. There have been marginal debates concerning limitations on the right to abortion, with some people arguing that the present limit of 18 weeks should be lowered, as special neonatal care is sometimes able to save the lives of infants born very prematurely. Even if political debates on this issue arise from time to time, almost all political parties subscribe to the notion of abortion as a fundamental right for mothers. The only exceptions are the Christian Democrats (one of the smallest parties in Sweden, having only barely made it into parliament) and the Sweden Democrats (a right-wing populist party with racist roots).

Theoretical Perspectives

Religion's Relevance in Modern Societies

For many years, secularisation has been a hallmark of many European countries, and in the 1990s a new dynamic was introduced into the public arena. Jose Casanova (1994) was one of the first scholars to recognise the de-privatisation of religion. This recent change has influenced public debates on questions related to religion and what people generally associate with it.

According to Casanova, public forms of religion emerge because religious groups react against the marginalisation of religion that follows modernisation (Casanova 1994: 5). Because of the new visibility of religion that many European countries have recently experienced, there are heated debates in the mass media about the boundary between the religious and the secular. Thus, the de-privatisation of religion leads to religion becoming both more visible and more contested.

This means that religion and social questions have become more intertwined and that religion has gained a more prominent place in public debates. Abortion is part of a political and religious discourse and is therefore a good test case for the study of the new relevance of religion in the public sphere.

Norris and Inglehart also argue that religion continues to play a role in explaining attitudes towards social and moral questions in modern societies. According to Norris and Inglehart, it is possible even in highly modernised societies to trace value differences rooted in religious traditions. For example, the World Values surveys of 2001 suggest that the denominational aspect plays a key role in examining attitudes towards abortion (Norris and Inglehart 2004). According to the survey, one quarter of Christian Orthodox societies reckon that abortion is never justified, despite the fact that abortion had long been easily available to women as part of Soviet reproductive policy. Moreover, around one third of the population of Protestant countries who participated in the study answered that abortion can never be justified. There are, however, large differences between values found within groups of countries based on different Christian traditions. Among Christian-dominated countries, the most restrictive views are found in Catholic countries, around 45% of the population there are convinced that abortion can never be justified (Norris and Inglehart 2004: 174). Religion has, then, had an enduring effect on the moral and ethical values of European populations. Those who are brought up attending religious services as active adherents to one of the world's major faiths will be most exposed to the teachings of religious leaders and their interpretations of the moral standards found in their sacred texts. However, through a process of diffusion, everyone in religious societies might be affected by religious cultural values. According to Norris and Inglehart (2004), the major faiths of the world express divergent teachings and doctrines on many moral questions and normative beliefs, such as those surrounding the roles of women and men, the sanctity of life, and the importance of marriage and family. This means that religious traditions are still able to influence social and moral questions in society today.

Religion, Trust, and Authoritarianism

In the previous section we established grounds to think that religion is highly relevant to empirical studies of attitudes towards social and moral questions. However, we must also include theories that more directly address our research questions. Therefore, this section will discuss whether and how religion, in combination with trust in institutions and authoritarianism, represents an explanatory factor *vis-à-vis* attitudes towards human rights.

Robert Putnam (2000) finds that trust is a key factor in citizens' engagement in society, and that one can distinguish between trust in fellow citizens and trust in public institutions. Putnam and Campbell (2010) report that religiously active Americans are more trusting and more involved in voluntary work than non-religious Americans, they explain it with the fact that religious networks have a stronger moral component than other networks. Much of Putnam's research is based on data from the United States, and so it is not evident that the interplay between trust and religion is the same in the European context, with some researchers accordingly doubting whether Putnam's findings are transferable. Indeed, analysis of data from The World Values Study shows that religiosity is negatively related to measures of social trust in many European countries (Wollebæk 2013).

Religious and other social institutions contribute to social order and stability while at the same time restricting the freedom of individuals. Devos et al. (2002) argue that levels of trust in various institutions correlate positively with values connected to conservatism and correlate negatively with values which emphasise independent thought and favour change. They also argue that religious individuals and politically right-wing supporters express more trust in institutions than expressed by non-religious individuals and left-wingers. When individual autonomy becomes a priority, institutions are more likely to be regarded with suspicion as constraining forces (Morselli et al. 2012). Socio-economic development leads to change in needs and attitudes. The results are paradoxical: trust in institutions and authorities seems to decline in long-standing democratic and wealthy countries (Dalton 2004). Socio-economic and democratic developments do not erode trust *per se*; rather, they shift priorities in a direction which implies a more critical attitude towards authorities.

Staerkle et al. (1998) report that populations living in democratic countries differ from those living in authoritarian countries with respect to views on human rights. In authoritarian countries, human rights are often seen as an imposition introduced by democratic countries. On this basis, we might expect that the degree of trust in governmental institutions has a different effect on attitudes towards human rights in democratic countries than it has in semi-democratic or authoritarian countries. This possibility can be examined with our data.

According to studies of democracy and freedom, Belarus is characterised as authoritarian and Romania as a 'flawed democracy' (The Economist Intelligence Unit 2016). Norway and Sweden, on the other hand, have very high scores on the same index. Our data also allows us to study 'authoritarianism' on an individual level, since previous studies report that attitudes towards human rights are connected to a country's status (democratic or authoritarian), we might also expect authoritarianism as an individual disposition to influence attitudes towards human rights.

The measurement we use is a development of the traditional 'authoritarianism' scale introduced in the 1950s by scholars such as Theodor Adorno et al. (Adorno et al. 1950) and reworked into the 'right-wing authoritarianism' scale by Bob Altemeyer (1998). Authoritarianism and democracy are not entirely opposed to one another; it is possible that authoritarian attitudes are prevalent on an individual level even in developed democracies. Persons with authoritarian values support leaders and institutions they regard as legitimate, and they condemn those who do not follow the same ideas and leaders. Authoritarians often want to control other people's freedom and punish actions they find deviant. Even though Altemeyer talks about right-wing authoritarianism, the phenomenon also exists among people who support the political left. According to Altemeyer (1998), *authoritarianism* refers to submission to authority and a willingness to follow conventions. Authoritarianism seems to have the same (negative) effect on human rights as trust in governmental institutions—especially if the institutions in question represent a semi-democratic state. Religion may be positively or negatively correlated with trust in authorities, and in some societies, religion may even function as an alternative source of authority, while in other cases the state represents a certain religious tradition.

Authoritarianism can be both positively and negatively correlated with religiosity, as there are different ways of being religious and research has discovered a high positive correlation between authoritarianism and fundamentalist forms of religiosity. Since much of the research on authoritarianism and religion has been conducted in the United States and Canada, it is interesting to see how this measure will work in a European setting.

Research Questions

According to the considerations above, we have formulated the following research questions:

1. Does religious affiliation have any effect on attitudes towards abortion and women's rights?
2. Is religiosity a good predictor of attitudes towards abortion and women's rights?
3. Do the background variables and the independent variables have the same types of effects on attitudes to abortion and attitudes to women's rights?
4. What role does trust in institutions play *vis-à-vis* attitudes towards human rights in countries with different scores on our democracy scale?
5. Does authoritarianism correlate negatively with attitudes towards human rights when other factors are controlled?

Conceptual Elaboration of Key Terms

Dependent Variables

We propose to use attitudes towards abortion and attitudes towards women's rights as dependent variables. The Universal Declaration of Human Rights (UDHR) of 1948 went further than any national laws of its time in acknowledging equality for women, and Article 3 of the UDHR can be read as stating that birth, not conception, is the decisive moment when human rights set in. Some institutions, usually churches, argue that the right to life starts at conception. In many European countries, the political discussion on legal rights to abortion is closely related to the discussion of women's rights, though this chapter does not take part in the discussion of whether access to legal abortion is a part of women's rights. Since this is an empirical study, we want to determine whether the same factors explain attitudes towards abortion and attitudes towards women's rights and how religion relates to both.

All of the questions on abortion are concerned with determining the circumstances in which abortion can be justified.

The seven statements used are as follows:

- Abortion should be prohibited in all circumstances because it terminates a human life (reversed).
- Abortion should be permitted in cases of rape.
- Abortion should be permitted in cases of incest.
- Abortion should be permitted when there is a strong chance of serious defect in the baby.
- Abortion should be permitted when the mother's own health is seriously endangered by the pregnancy.
- Abortion should be permitted when the mother cannot economically afford to support any more children.
- Abortion should be permitted when the mother cannot psychologically cope with raising any more children.

Based on these seven statements, we make an additive index.[10] The Cronbach's alpha for the whole sample is 0.90, and the lowest alpha found is for Norway (0.871), the highest being for Belarus (0.903). The answering scheme runs from 1 (disagreement) to 5 (agreement).

The index measuring women's rights is based on the following three statements:

- The state should protect women's rights to adequate job opportunities.
- Women should have the right to be protected from sexual harassment in the workplace.
- Women should have the right to equal pay.

Based on the whole sample, the Cronbach's alpha for this index is 0.80. The empirical analysis shows how the two indexes relate to each other and what factors are best suited to explain attitudes towards abortion and women's rights. The individual alphas for the four countries are as follows:

0.729 (Norway), 0.795 (Belarus), 0.809 (Romania) and 0.831 (Sweden). The answering scheme runs from 1 (disagreement) to 5 (agreement).

[10] The scores are divided by 7, so the values will continue to be in the range of 1–5.

Independent Variables

As independent variables, we are mainly interested in three sets: affiliation with major Christian traditions (Protestantism vs. Christian Orthodoxy), religiosity, and trust in institutions. Religious affiliation is operationalised as membership to a religious group, which is measured by religious self-identification. Individual religiosity is measured by using the Centrality of Religiosity Scale (CRS) which has five dimensions: intellectual, ideological, public practice, private practice and religious experience (Huber and Huber 2012).

In addition to these variables, we introduced one more variable related to religion, namely views on church and state. This variable is intended to examine views regarding the preferred relationship between religion and politics (i.e., to what extent religious leaders should influence political decisions). Attitudes on this question are related to both, democracy and freedom of religion, and our index for this issue is based on two statements in the questionnaire. The answering scheme runs from 1 = disagreement to 5 = agreement:

- Politicians may consult religious leaders about any ethical problem in the country but should make their ultimate decisions independently.
- Parliament should decide on school laws regardless of religious leaders' opinions.

As discussed earlier, we are interested in the relationship between trust in state institutions and attitudes regarding human rights. According to previous research, this relationship depends on a country's stance on freedom and democracy, and, in our study, trust in institutions is measured by an index which consists of scores on eight questions concerning satisfaction with state institutions. The first three questions concern the three state powers (legislature, executive and judiciary), while the remaining five concern those institutions the state is responsible for, such as the parliament, the government, the economy, democracy, the educational system and the health-care system. Our reliability test shows that these variables can be used in an index. Cronbach's alpha for the whole sample is 0.84, and Cronbach's alpha in each individual country is >0.70.

Because the four countries in this study have regimes with varying scores on the democratic- authoritarian dimension, we decided to include another variable measuring degree of authoritarianism on an individual level. To operationalise Altimeter's authoritarianism index, we used four statements from the questionnaire. The students were asked if they agree or disagree with the following statements. The answering scheme runs from 1 = disagreement to 5 = agreement:

- Most of those who criticise proper authorities in government and religion merely create useless doubts in people's minds.
- What our country really needs instead of more 'civil rights' is much more law and order.

- Obedience and respect for authority are the most important values children should learn.
- The facts on crime, sexual immorality and public disorder all show that we have to crack down harder on deviant groups and troublemakers if we are going to save our moral standards and preserve law and order.[11]

As background variables, we use gender, political preference and the educational level of the father.

Conceptual Model

The conceptual model displays the following three groups of variables. The dependent variables are the students' attitudes towards abortion and women's rights (Fig. 11.1), while the independent variables are the three religious variables described earlier together with trust in institutions. The control variables are students' population characteristics (i.e., gender, political preferences, and father's education level). The conceptual model also displays the interrelationships of these groups, which are symbolised by arrows which indicate the impact of one group on the other. This study emphasises the impact of religious variables and values on attitudes towards human rights while accounting for the impact of the population's characteristics on attitudes towards human rights.

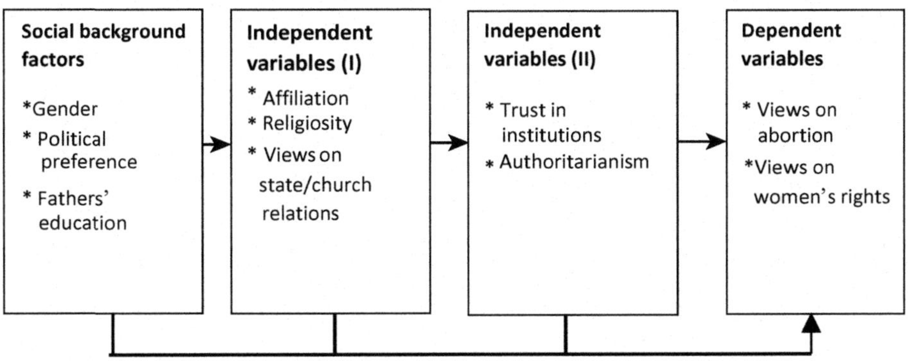

Fig. 11.1 The dependent variables are the students' attitudes towards abortion and women's rights

[11]The Cronbach's alpha based on the whole sample is 0.62. For individual countries, the scores vary from 0.55 to 0.67.

Method and Sample

This section concerns our research questions and data-collection methods, also describing our research sample, measuring instruments and the statistical methods used in our data analysis.

The selection of countries reflects two different strategies in comparative research: the most-similar systems design (MSSD) and the most-different systems design (MDSD). The MSSD is the dominating approach, intending to investigate the phenomenon in question by maximising the number of variables in which the systems differ (Anckar 2008). If one finds similar patterns in very different countries, one has good reason to believe that the findings will also apply to other countries. We have chosen to look at two pairs of countries: the Lutheran-Protestant countries of Norway and Sweden and the Christian Orthodox countries of Belarus and Romania. Norway and Sweden are similar in more respects than Belarus and Romania. Because Romania became a member of the EU in 2007 and Belarus maintains a strategic partnership with Russia (it signed a treaty for greater cooperation with Russia in 2000), it is interesting to view the position in the International Democracy Index of the compared countries. In the 2015 Democracy Index, Romania is ranked number 59 and Belarus is ranked number 127 of all the countries worldwide. Still, Romania is not regarded as a 'full democracy' but rather as a 'flawed democracy', together with other EU states such as Italy and Poland (Table 11.1).

Table 11.1 International Democracy Index 2016, excerpts (The Economist Intelligence Unit)

Country	Rank	Overall score	Electoral process and pluralism	Functioning of government	Political participation	Political culture	Civil liberties
Full democracies							
Norway	**1**	**9.93**	**10.00**	**9.64**	**10.00**	**10.00**	**10.00**
Sweden	**3**	**9.45**	**9.58**	**9.64**	**8.33**	**10.00**	**9.71**
Netherlands	10	8.92	9.58	8.57	8.89	8.13	9.41
Germany	13	8.64	9.58	8.57	7.78	8.13	9.12
Flawed democracies							
Italy	21	7.98	9.58	6.43	7.22	8.13	8.53
Lithuania	38	7.54	9.58	6.07	6.11	6.25	9.71
Poland	48	7.09	9.58	5.71	6.67	4.38	9.12
Romania	**59**	**6.68**	**9.17**	**5.71**	**5.00**	**5.00**	**8.53**
Hybrid regime							
Georgia	82	5.88	8.67	4.29	5.56	5.00	5.88
Turkey	97	5.12	6.67	5.36	5.00	5.63	2.94
Nigeria	108	4.62	6.08	4.29	3.33	5.00	4.41
Pakistan	112	4.40	6.00	5.71	2.78	2.50	5.00
Authoritarian							
Belarus	**127**	**3.62**	**1.75**	**3.57**	**3.89**	**6.25**	**2.65**
Russia	132	3.31	2.67	2.86	5.00	2.50	3.53
China	136	3.14	0.00	4.64	3.33	6.25	1.47

Legend: score 1 = low, 5 = high

Romania has a much higher score than Belarus, which is classified as an authoritarian regime. Norway and Sweden are both at the top of the list; having been assessed as ‘full democracies’ and with Norway exhibiting near-maximum scores on all criteria. Sweden’s somewhat lower position is related to several circumstances: it becomes increasingly less involved in traditional forms of party politics (membership, meeting attendance), and sometimes it keeps people in pre-trial detention for long periods, it also discriminates against minorities and deals improperly with immigration and refugee laws (Amnesty International Report 2016/17: The state of the world’s human rights, 2017).

Data Collection

This study was conducted in the period 2014–2015 in or around the largest cities of all four of the countries compared. An online survey system was created by the project coordinating team for the Belarusian respondents. 714 respondents participated in the survey, most of them were undergraduate university students. Participation in the online survey was secured with individual passwords. The age of the students in the first and second year of university education (17–19 years old) is comparable with the age of upper secondary-school students in Norway and Sweden, as Belarus has an 11-year secondary education system. Students participating in the survey were mostly from Minsk, but also from Vitebsk, Brest, Hrodna, Gomel, Mogilev and other smaller towns.

In Romania, the study was conducted in high schools in eight major cities covering the whole country: Bucuresti, Cluj-Napoca, Constanta, Craiova, Iasi, Ploiesti, Sibiu and Timisoara. These cities cover all regions of the country and reflect population sizes. The study comprised 681 high-school students studying at well-run high schools in these cities. The schools chosen qualified at the top three of their respective regions according to the 2014 National Evaluation System, which is run on a yearly basis. The participants were 16–18 years old. We used a stratified random sample of high-school classes—strata being computed for regions of Romania. We questioned all students in the participating class, and the questionnaire was filled in online, under the direct supervision of the ICT-tutors.

In Norway, the sample was collected in 20 upper secondary schools in the Oslo area— i.e., two classes from each participating school, on average. The survey was conducted in their classrooms, resulting in a response rate of around 90%. The students completed the questionnaires during the school day with pencil and paper in regular religious-education or social-study classes. The sample is regarded as representative of those attending this level of public schools in the age group 16–20. Most of the students had studied religion and ethics during the previous year, thus, they were better prepared than others to answer questions related to human rights and religion.

In Sweden, the sample was collected from 30 upper secondary schools in the Stockholm, Gothenburg and Malmö area. On average, two classes from each school participated. Because of our theoretical interest in comparing religious sub-groups, schools with a relatively large number of pupils with foreign backgrounds were particularly welcomed to participate. Thus, the Swedish data is a strategic sample directed at comparing Christian, Muslim and non-religious students. This means that the share of nominal Protestants and the education level of the parents is lower than in a general population sample. Nevertheless, it is possible to use the Swedish sample for the present analysis, as the relevant sub-groups are of adequate size.

Population Description

Norway and Sweden

Both Nordic countries have a Lutheran background and a Lutheran church as their majority religion. In our questionnaire students were asked about their affiliation with a specific church or religious community (see Table 11.2). This phrasing of the question tends to exclude those who are nominal members of the majority church and do not feel that they belong to a religious community. These nominal members go to church perhaps once or twice a year, often for special holidays or family events, which explains why fewer than one third of young people in large Scandinavian cities state that they belong to a Protestant church despite statistics which tell us that between 60% and 70% of the population belongs to the Lutheran majority church in these countries.

Table 11.2 Sample characteristics, Belarus, Norway, Romania and Sweden (in %, except age). In our questionnaire students were asked about their affiliation with a specific church or religious community

	Belarus (N = 712)	Romania (N = 621)	Norway (N = 987)	Sweden (N = 992)
Mean age	18.3	16.8	18.2	17.7
Female	66.3	51.9	49.5	55.1
Mother born on another continent	1.1	0	15.3	35.7
Father with university education	52.5	52.3	66.5	37.0
Leaning to the political left	48.6	39.0	35.9	61.1
Roman-Catholic	5.2	3.2	2.1	4.9
Protestant	1.3	1.3	32.2	13.1
Christian-Orthodox	56.3	72.1	1.3	10.7
Muslim	0.7	2.3	6.9	24.3
Religious in a general sense	8.3	4.5	3.9	3.0
Non-religious	24.7	10.0	47.8	38.6
Believe in God or higher power	47.2	65.8	36.0	48.5
Pray at least weekly	20.4	61.0	12.6	26.7
Attend religious rituals at least monthly	17.0	26.9	9.6	18.4

Due to differences in sampling methods, there are significant differences in the Norwegian and Swedish samples, which would not necessarily be the case if the samples were strictly representative of both countries. Based on the data, it appears that the Swedish group is more religious than the Norwegian cohort (Table 11.2), which is probably not the case on a general level, but due to the strategic sampling procedure applied in the Swedish case, as mentioned above. This affects the pooled data set in several ways. Because people with foreign backgrounds (i.e., Catholic, Assyrian Orthodox or Muslim backgrounds) are often more religious than ethnic Swedes (who are often nominal Lutherans), the figures measuring religiosity show higher levels in Sweden than in Norway. These differences also become manifest in factors such as their mother's background and their father's level of education.

Belarus and Romania

In Belarus and Romania, *most* young people say that they belong to the Christian Orthodox Church; however, the percentage of Orthodox youth is slightly higher in Romania (72% against 56% in Belarus). While data on belonging to majority and minority religions in the assessed samples allows us to discuss similarities, the 'religious in a general sense' and 'non-religious' identities reveal the differences in the assessed samples. The groups of 'religious in a general sense' and 'non-religious' are twice as large in the Belarusian sample as in the Romanian youth sample. Another difference between Belarusian and Romanian Orthodox youth can be seen in the level of religiosity in its ideological and private/public-practice dimensions. All religious characteristics are significantly higher in the Romanian sample, indicating that this group is the most religious of all four countries compared here. Those who believe in God comprise three quarters of Romanian youth (66%) and almost half of the Belarusian young people (47%). Weekly prayer is exercised three times more often in Romania (61%, against 21% in Belarus), and monthly church attendance is 27% in Romania against 17% in Belarus. It is important to mention, however, that the respondents in the Romanian sample are slightly younger—particularly in comparison with the Belarusian sample (cf. Table 11.2).

Statistical Methods

In our study we used variance analysis to compare the means of both dependent and independent variables and the control variables among the sub-populations, namely Christians and Muslims. We used ordinary linear regression analysis to investigate the impact of religiosity and trust in institutions on attitudes towards abortion and euthanasia. What follows is a brief description of our methods:

Anova

Young people in Belarus, Romania, Norway and Sweden were compared with each other in the course of our study, also incorporating an analysis of those who identify as Catholics, Protestants and those who are non-religious. Most measurements use a five-point Likert scale (1 for low value to 5 for high value).

Regression Analysis

A regression analysis was used to examine the impact of religious variables and other personal values on support for abortion and women's rights. For this article, a limited number of independent variables (i.e., religiosity and trust in institutions) and control variables (i.e., population characteristics) were selected.

All of the scales used in our regression analysis (except gender and religious affiliation) were at the ordinal level, but they may be analysed at the interval level. We conducted four regression analyses, examining attitudes towards abortion and women's rights in four countries.

Empirical Research

Comparisons Based on Univariate Statistics

What follows is a presentation of our empirical results based on the student data from these four countries. The countries are presented in two pairs: the Eastern European countries form one group, and the Scandinavian countries form another. We present four regression tables which focus on attitudes towards abortion and women's rights, and by including women's rights, we can determine if attitudes about abortion follow the same patterns as those towards women's rights.

We have already presented five research questions to be discussed based on the empirical data. This chapter addresses them one by one, beginning with the first question: What is the effect of religious affiliation on attitudes towards abortion?

The level of support for the statement that abortion should be prohibited in all circumstances gives us a rough picture of the differences and similarities between the four countries. The Orthodox countries are the most restrictive, and Protestant countries are the most liberal or permissive regarding abortion. In this case, the two Protestant countries resemble each other, as do the two Orthodox countries. A one-way ANOVA was conducted to analyse the variances of views about abortion and women's rights between the Orthodox and Protestant countries. Our findings suggest that there was a statistically significant effect of belonging to Orthodox or Protestant country for young people on views about abortion. However, country effect for Eastern European and Scandinavian youth had no statistically significant difference

Table 11.3 View on abortion in the four countries (in %)

Agreement with the statement:	Belarus	Romania	Norway	Sweden
Abortion should be prohibited in all circumstances because it terminates beginning life human life.	25.3	36.5	8.8	13.1
N	712	661	981	971

Table 11.4 Views on abortion by denomination (in %) while Protestants in Scandinavia comprise the least restrictive group

Agreement with the statement:	Catholics	Christian-Orthodox, Belarus	Christian-Orthodox, Romania	Protestants, Norway	Protestants, Sweden
Abortion should be prohibited in all circumstances because it terminates the beginning of human life.	21.8	29.7	38.9	8.6	5.6
N	127	401	478	312	123

Based on data from all four countries

Table 11.5 Mean scores on the dependent variables

Scores	Belarus	Romania	Norway	Sweden
Abortion index	3.4	3.3	4.2	3.9
Women's rights	4.3	4.3	4.5	4.3
N	712	661	981	971

Answer scheme: 1 = totally disagree to 5 = totally agree

for views on women's rights. The rationale for treating the countries as two pairs (Belarus/Romania versus Norway/Sweden) is thus underlined (Table 11.3).

To what extent is this difference related to religious identity? Considering abortion, the Christian Orthodox group has the most restrictive views, followed by Catholics (based on the whole sample), while Protestants in Scandinavia comprise the least restrictive group (Table 11.4). This reflects both differences in theology and differences in national legislation and political traditions.

Is the pattern the same when we introduce the women's-rights variable? Based on the whole sample (N = 3417), we noticed that attitudes towards abortion and women's rights have a moderately positive correlation (Pearson's r .30). We found the highest correlation in Sweden (r .438) and the lowest in Romania (r .095), with Norway and Belarus somewhere in between. This means that, at least in some countries, attitudes about abortion and women's rights are part of the same cluster of attitudes (Table 11.5).

The highest mean scores for the two indices are found in Norway. Romania has the lowest scores on the abortion index together with Belarus. However, when it comes to women's rights, we observe similar scores of means. This suggests that some of the attitudes may be more widely shared among the European youth, across national boundaries.

Table 11.6 Mean scores on independent variables. The level of education of the father is lowest in Sweden, probably due to the oversampling of immigrant groups

Mean scores	Belarus	Romania	Norway	Sweden
Father's education (1–4)	3.4	3.4	3.4	2.8
Left-right position (1–10)	5.3	6.0	6.1	5.3
Religiosity (1–5)	2.7	3.1	2.3	2.6
Separation of church and state (1–5)	3.6	3.2	3.8	3.4
Authoritarianism scale (1–5)	2.7	3.2	2.9	3.0
Trust in institutions (1–5)	2.6	2.3	3.5	2.9
N	712	661	981	971

Legend: Numbers between brackets indicate the scale format

When we compare the mean scores of our independent and background variables, the differences between the countries are not significant. The level of education of the father is lowest in Sweden, probably due to the oversampling of immigrant groups (Table 11.6). The political preferences of the students vary from 5.3 to 6.1, with Norway and Romania being the most right-leaning of the countries. Not surprisingly, Romania comes out as the most religious of these countries, and Norway appears to be the least religious. Support for the separation of church and state is rather high in all countries, with Norway at the top and Romania at the bottom of the scale. The prevalence of authoritarianism, as measured by the Altemeyer index, is highest in Romania and lowest in Belarus. This is somewhat surprising, as Belarus is the only country which is characterized as "authoritarian" in *The Economist*'s democracy report. However, we must also point out that the sample consists not of the general population but of students whose attitudes may be more 'radical' than that of the older citizens. It may also mean that the younger generations in Romania do not know very much about its recent totalitarian past, since the horrific dimensions of Romania's past were not fully disclosed by the state-controlled Romanian educational establishment—not at least until university study. At the same time, Belarusian students may not be so easily enchanted by the current totalitarian regime, as trust in institutions is highest in Norway and Sweden and lower in Romania and Belarus. The levels of trust are highest in the most democratic of these countries, but the trust scale does not always correspond with scores on the democracy scale. For example, the level of trust in institutions is higher in Belarus than in Romania.

Multivariate Model

In this section we discuss how we carried out our regression analyses to answer our research questions. We have already discussed the effects of religious affiliation, and based on multivariate empirical analysis, this section discusses the effects of religiosity, authoritarianism and trust in institutions in different types of countries and *vis-à-vis* different attitude scales related to abortion and women's rights.

The format of this analysis was to split these countries into two pairs: Belarus and Romania (as the Christian Orthodox samples), and Norway and Sweden (as the mainly Protestant samples). We then compared the outcomes of the analyses for the two pairs. First, we looked at regression models for attitudes towards abortion in Belarus and Romania before doing the same for Norway and Sweden. Finally, we compared regression models for attitudes towards women's rights in Orthodox countries with those for Protestant Scandinavia.

Attitudes Towards Abortion

One of the aims of our study is to determine what role the factors in the conceptual model play *vis-a-vis* attitudes towards human-rights questions, our focus being on three factors: religion, trust in institutions and authoritarianism. In this paper our main issue is on the effect each of the factors has in relation to attitudes towards human rights rather than on the possible interconnectedness of the independent factors.

According to the theoretical perspectives, these factors will likely influence attitudes towards human rights, as a country's dominant religious tradition is likely to influence attitudes among the population towards social questions—especially when these questions concern private morality (Norris and Inglehart 2004).

Trust in institutions is found to be positively related to values which stress stability and conservatism. In democratic countries, human rights are often associated with such values, while in non-democratic or newly democratic countries human rights may be associated with reform and change. The effect of trust in institutions may thus vary with the status of democracy.

Authoritarianism is measured on the micro level. Nevertheless, the factor could be related to the status of the country's democracy. Since one of the countries in our study is characterised as 'authoritarian', we might expect that this factor will have different effects depending on the type of regime.

Our model explains 23% of the variance in the dependent variable. The variables with the strongest predictive power are religiosity (negative), separation of church and state (positive), gender, and trust in institutions (negative).

One of our research questions relates to the role religiosity plays *vis-à-vis* attitudes towards human rights. Our empirical analysis shows that religiosity is a strong predictor of private morality and family matters such as abortion (cf. Norris and Inglehart 2004), which means that religious people in general are rather sceptical towards abortion and that those in favour of a clear separation of church and state are more positive about abortion than others. Identifying as Orthodox has only a small negative effect on attitudes, which is rather surprising when we think of the strong effect of religiosity. This probably reflects the fact that Orthodoxy is a majority faith in these countries and that it includes people who do not have a high score on the religiosity index. It is not possible, however, based on these results alone, to determine whether religiosity has become a more important predictor of socio-political questions, as scholars such as Jose Casanova predict. To study this would require access to longitudinal data.

Devos et al. (2002) indicate that trust in institutions tends to go together with protection of traditional practices. In countries like Belarus and Romania, this means supporting restrictive abortion laws. The empirical analysis shows that trust in institutions goes together with negative views about abortion. This result is in line with the prediction made on the basis of the former study. In Scandinavian countries which have had liberal abortion laws in recent decades, trust in institutions may have the opposite effect on attitudes.

One interesting finding is that trust in public institutions is negatively correlated with support for abortion (as a right). One interpretation of this is that public authorities (in partnership with the church) are sceptical about abortion. Here it is important to remember the meaning of 'trust in institutions', namely that one trusts public authorities to make the right decisions.

Authoritarianism has no significant effect; nor does political preference. This is somewhat surprising, and it could mean that abortion is not a politicised question in these countries, but rather a problem that has to be solved by a cooperation of state and the majority church.

Gender is another factor that has a significant effect in the analysis, as men are more hesitant than females on the subject of abortion. The same pattern is observed in all the four tables in this section. We now move on to the Scandinavian countries: Norway and Sweden.

The model explains 27% of the variance in abortion attitudes. The variables with the strongest predictive power are religiosity, separation of church/state, and gender. The effects these three variables have on attitudes resemble those found in Table 11.7, and it is interesting to find similar statistical patterns in countries with different religious and political traditions (Table 11.8).

As we found earlier, religiosity has a strongly negative effect on attitudes towards abortion, and a desire for a clear separation between church and state has a positive effect on such attitudes. Despite the negative effect of religiosity and the positive effect of a strict separation of church and state on attitudes regarding abortion, iden-

Table 11.7 Attitudes towards abortion in Christian Orthodox countries (Belarus and Romania, N = 1360). Regression analysis

	Beta	Sig.
Gender	−.10	.000
Father's education	.08	.001
Political scale	.02	Ns
Religiosity scale	−.33	.000
Christian Orthodox identity	−.06	.02
Trust in institutions/government	−.08	.001
Authoritarianism scale	−.04	Ns
Separation of church/state	.20	.000
Explained variance	23%	

Reference: Gender: female=0, male=1

Table 11.8 Attitudes towards Abortion in Lutheran countries (Norway and Sweden, N = 1930). Regression analysis

	Beta	Sig.
Gender	−.13	.000
Father's education	.05	.02
Political scale	.02	Ns
Religiosity scale	−.33	.000
Protestant identity	.05	.01
Trust in institutions	.04	.03
Authoritarianism	−.09	.000
Separation church/state	.25	.000
Explained variance	27%	

Reference: Gender: female=0, male=1

tifying with the dominating church has different meanings in the two contexts. Identifying as a Protestant, which in most cases means being a member of the Lutheran majority church, has a positive impact on attitudes. One possible interpretation of this correlation is that identifying with the majority church implies that one is identifying with the dominant political culture. In Scandinavia, this means supporting liberal abortion laws; in the two predominantly Orthodox countries, however, this means supporting more restrictive laws. This argument is supported when we consider that trust in institutions has an effect on attitudes in Protestant Scandinavia which is opposite to that which it has in Orthodox countries (from negative to positive).

Authoritarianism and acceptance of abortion are negatively correlated. This may be explained by the fact that the political struggle for liberal abortion laws was fought mainly in Protestant dominated countries during the 1970s, such that today only small religious groups are actively fighting against the liberalisation of abortion laws.

As we saw in Table 11.7, women are somewhat more permissive than men when it comes to abortion.

The education of the father has a small, albeit positive, effect on attitudes, and political preferences do not have any significant effect, which is rather surprising, since leftist parties were in the forefront when abortion rights were established.

Attitudes Towards Women's Rights

In the introductory sections of this paper the relationship between attitudes towards abortion and human rights was discussed. Many people, especially those who are religious, tend to see abortion as related to what is called 'the right to life'. Others—especially people in countries where the right to abortion was established after years of protests against restrictive laws by women's-rights groups—regard the right to secure abortion as an integrated part of women's rights. Additionally, some UN reports have discussed the possibility of including

Table 11.9 Attitudes towards women's rights in Christian Orthodox countries (Belarus and Romania, N = 1360). Regression

	Beta	Sig.
Gender	−.21	.000
Father's education	.03	Ns
Political scale	.01	Ns
Religiosity scale	.09	.002
Christian Orthodox identity	−.05	.05
Trust in institutions	−.14	.000
Authoritarianism	.06	.03
Separation church/state	.28	.000
Explained variance	14%	

Reference: Gender: female=0, male=1

legal access to abortion as falling under the umbrella of the human-rights principle of 'reproductive health'.

When analysing support for women's rights in the two predominantly Orthodox countries, we find some of the same effects we found when analysing attitudes towards abortion, for example that the separation of church and state has a strong predictive power, and the same goes for gender.

This time, however, the effect of religiosity is reversed with respect to the tables related to abortion. This means that religious people tend to support women's rights more than others, even after accounting for gender and other variables. Religion can in certain situations be a factor supporting reform (Table 11.9), as the introductory section of this paper indicates. This is underlined by the fact that separation of church and state has a strong predictive power with respect to women's rights, as those who do not want church and secular authorities to be closely related tend to be more in favour of women's rights than others.

Table 11.9 shows that trust in institutions has a negative effect on attitudes, which is parallel to the finding reported in Table 11.7. Trust in institutions goes together with low support for women's rights. According to the theory, trust in institutions goes hand in hand with conservative views and preservation of the *status quo*. This probably means that public authorities in these countries are not seen as supportive of women's rights.

Authoritarianism has a small but positive effect on women's rights. In these countries, authoritarianism may also be seen as an indicator of support for the public authorities and the current political situation. It is also striking that political preferences do not have any effect on support for women's rights. This is an indicator of the minor role that the struggle between political parties plays when it comes to attitudes towards women's rights.

In the Scandinavian countries the multivariate model outlines more of the total variance in attitudes towards women's rights. Again, separation of church and state is a strong predictor of such attitudes.

Table 11.9 shows that religiosity has a positive impact on women's rights. In all the other three tables, religiosity has a negative impact on the attitudes we are studying. In Scandinavia, the most religious people are also among those who are most

Table 11.10 Attitudes towards women's rights in Lutheran countries (Norway and Sweden, N = 1930). Regression analysis

Regression analysis	Beta	Sig.
Gender	−.30	.000
Father's education	.06	.008
Political scale	−.09	.000
Religiosity scale	−.09	.000
Protestant identity	.06	.008
Trust in institutions	.07	.002
Authoritarianism	−.04	.06
Separation church/state	.23	.000
Explained variance	19%	

Reference: Gender: female=0, male=1

negative towards women's rights, which is in line with what we found regarding attitudes towards abortion.

As before, we found that trust in public institutions has an effect in the Protestant countries in our study, which is opposite to that in our Orthodox countries. This probably indicates that women's rights are among the dominant political values in Scandinavian countries and are strongly supported by official authorities there, something which is not necessarily the case in our Orthodox countries.

Authoritarianism has no significant effect. As Table 11.10 shows, the political variable has a negative effect, which means that people on the political left tend to support women's rights more than those who lean to the right. As was the case in Belarus and Romania, women are clearly more in favour of these rights than men are, and the education of the respondent's father also has some explanatory power. The higher the level of their father's education, the more they tend to support women's rights.

Discussion and Conclusion

In this study, we found both interesting similarities and differences between the two groups of countries in our comparison. Given that we found the same statistical patterns in countries with different religious and political cultures, we may conclude that the findings are strongly supported and that they will also apply to other countries (Anckar 2008). This clearly is the case regarding the effect of religiosity on attitudes towards abortion and the effect of the separation of church and state on both abortion and women's rights. Even if Lutheranism and Christian Orthodoxy are part of the same Christian religion, scholars such as Norris & Inglehart emphasise the consequences of different denominations on social values—especially values concerning private morality. Our empirical analysis did not find that affiliation had much impact—at least, not compared to other factors, and so the theory of Norris and Inglehart is not well supported by our analysis. Religiosity also has the same effect on attitudes towards abortion in the two groups of countries, something which may be explained by the fact that Lutheranism and Christian Orthodoxy have the same origin in the Christian religion. It would be interesting to see the results of the same analysis in countries based on traditions such as Islam.

The effects of the factors are not quite the same in the tables presenting attitudes towards abortion and attitudes towards women's rights. However, in countries like the Scandinavian nations, the two attitude scales are also positively correlated. We found many of the same effects upon analysing the two scales. At least in a Scandinavian setting, it is probably right to see both abortion and women's rights as being related to sexual and reproductive health, and the consistent effect of gender supports this interpretation. In both groups of countries, women tended to be more supportive than men with respect to both abortion and women's rights.

The most interesting finding in this study relates to the role of trust in state institutions. Previous research has shown that trust in institutions relates to traditional and conservative attitudes, which probably explains the negative effects discovered in Eastern European countries between trust in institutions and support for human rights. In the Scandinavian countries, however, there is a positive relationship between trust in institutions and support for these rights.

This indicates that there is a positive relationship in full democracies between trust in institutions and the provision of individual rights to the population. In the two countries, one of which is characterised as 'authoritarian' and other as 'flawed democracy', we found that trust in institutions has the opposite (negative) effect on attitudes, something which is consistent with the assumptions based on earlier research into attitudes regarding human rights which show that trust in institutions goes together with support for the dominating views in society. Our data, however, does not support the assumption that trust in state institutions is higher in non-democratic societies than in democratic countries.

Since we discussed the differences between democratic and authoritarian countries, we also desired to see whether authoritarianism on the individual level had any impact on attitudes. The factor called authoritarianism, however, did not have any clear and consistent effect on such attitudes, and the same can be said for the effect of one's political preferences. Only regarding women's rights in Scandinavia does the political factor have any significant impact. Abortion does not seem to be a part of the current struggle between political groups in the societies we have analysed.

References

Adorno, T. W., Frenkel-Brunswik, E., Levinson, D. J., & Sanford, R. N. (1950). *The authoritarian personality*. New York: Harper and Row.

Altemeyer, B. (1998). The other "authoritarian personality". In M. Zanna (Ed.), *Advances in experimental social psychology* (Vol. 30, pp. 47–92). San Diego: Academic.

Anckar, C. (2008). On the applicability of the most similar systems design and the most different systems design in comparative research. *International Journal of Social Research Methodology, 11*, 389–401.

Casanova, J. (1994). *Public religions in the modern world.* Chicago: University of Chicago Press.

Casanova, J. (2003). What is a public religion? In H. Heclo & W. M. McClay (Eds.), *Religion returns to the public square* (pp. 111–141). Washington, DC: Woodrow Wilson Center Press.
Casanova, J. (2009, winter). The Secular and Secularisms. *Social Research, 76*(4), 1049–1066.
Dalton, R. (2004). *Democratic challenges, democratic choices: The Erosion of political support in advanced industrial democracies*. Oxford: Oxford University Press.
Democracy Index. (2015). The economist intelligence unit 2016. Democracy Index 2015.
Devos, T., Spini, D., & Schwartz, S. (2002). Conflicts among human values and trust in institutions. *British Journal of Social Psychology, 41*, 481–494.
Huber, S., & Huber, O. W. (2012). The centrality of religiosity scale (CRS). *Religions, 3*, 710–724.
Morselli, S., Morselli, D., Spini, D., & Devos, T. (2012). Hu values and trust in institutions across countries: A multilevel test of Schwartz's hypothesis of structural equivalence. *Survey Research Methods, 6*(1), 49–60.
Norris, P., & Inglehart, R. (2004). *Sacred and secular. Religion and politics worldwide*. New York: Cambridge University Press.
Pettersson, T. (2006). Religion in contemporary society: Eroded by human well-being, supported by cultural diversity. *Comparative Sociology, 5*(6), 231–257.
Putnam, R. D. (2000). *Bowling alone: The collapse and revival of the American community*. New York: Simon and Schuster.
Putnam, R. D., & Campbell, D. E. (2010). *American grace. How religion divides and unites us*. New York: Simon and Schuster.
Staerklé, C., Clémence, A., & Doise, W. (1998). Representation of human rights across different national contexts: the role of democratic and non-democratic populations and governments. *European Journal of Social Psychology, 28*, 207–226
The Basis of the Social Concept of the Russian Orthodox Church. (2000). Internet access: https://mospat.ru/en/documents/social-concepts/xii/. Accessed on March 21, 2017.
Wollebæk, D. (2013). *Religion og sosial kapital. Hva kan spørreundersøkelser fortelle oss?* (Religion and Social Capital: What do International Surveys Tell Us?) *Senter for forskning på sivilsamfunn og frivillige organisasjoner*, 4/13.

Index

H.-G. Ziebertz, F. Zaccaria (eds.), *Euthanasia, Abortion, Death Penalty and Religion – The Right to Life and its Limitations*, Religion and Human Rights 4, https://doi.org/10.1007/978-3-319-98773-6

Printed by Printforce, the Netherlands